The Life of Paper

The publisher and the University of California Press Foundation gratefully acknowledge the generous support of the Ahmanson Foundation Endowment Fund in Humanities.

The Life of Paper

LETTERS AND A POETICS OF LIVING
BEYOND CAPTIVITY

Sharon Luk

UNIVERSITY OF CALIFORNIA PRESS

University of California Press, one of the most distinguished university presses in the United States, enriches lives around the world by advancing scholarship in the humanities, social sciences, and natural sciences. Its activities are supported by the UC Press Foundation and by philanthropic contributions from individuals and institutions. For more information, visit www.ucpress.edu.

University of California Press
Oakland, California

Library of Congress Cataloging-in-Publication Data

Names: Luk, Sharon, 1979- author.
Title: The life of paper : letters and a poetics of living beyond captivity / Sharon Luk.
Description: Oakland, California : University of California Press, [2018] | Includes bibliographical references and index.
Identifiers: LCCN 2017031749| ISBN 9780520296237 (cloth : alk. paper) | ISBN 9780520296244 (pbk : alk. paper) | ISBN 9780520968820 (ebook)
Subjects: LCSH: Prisoners—California—Correspondence—20th century. | Imprisonment—California—History. | Chinese Americans—Effect of imprisonment on—California—19th century. | Chinese Americans—Effect of imprisonment on—California—20th century. | Japanese Americans—Effect of imprisonment on—California—20th century. | African Americans—Effect of imprisonment on—California—20th century. | Prisoners—California—Social conditions—20th century. | Prisoners—Civil rights—California—20th century. | United States—Emigration and immigration—History.
Classification: LCC HV9475.C2 L85 2018 | DDC 365/.450923—dc23
LC record available at https://lccn.loc.gov/2017031749

27 26 25 24 23 22 21 20 19 18
10 9 8 7 6 5 4 3 2 1

Thus, monks, this spiritual life is lived with mutual support for the purposes of crossing the flood and making a complete end of suffering.

ITIVUTTAKA III

AMERICAN CROSSROADS

Edited by Earl Lewis, George Lipsitz, George Sánchez, Dana Takagi, Laura Briggs, and Nikhil Pal Singh

CONTENTS

ILLUSTRATIONS

Introduction

THE LIFE OF PAPER

ascesis

involved in writing
my history

i've been waking in
night sweats &

it's not the sheets,
those things in-

side are
burning out

of love

17 JUNE 2009

WRITING AND REWRITING THIS BOOK has been a slow burn—as the case may be now for you, too, kindly reading it. On the one hand, to myself and to those who have shared their stories with me (and probably also to others still holding their stories close to themselves), the central argument of this study is obvious, almost *too* obvious to necessitate book-length explanation: this is, simply, that letters can mean the world to the people attached to them, and distinctively so for communities ripped apart by incarceration. In the first and final instance, this is a formulation of "the life of paper" that you must accept at face value in its plenitude, a plenitude that is all but better represented by understatement than long-winded analysis. If one does not

I

CORRECT AND
INCORRECT POSITIONS.

FIGURE 1. H. T. Loomis, *Practical Letter Writing* (Cleveland, OH: Practical Textbook Co., 1897), 6. Original caption reads, "Correct and Incorrect positions."

accept this, chances are that no amount of research could effect otherwise because the problem would not have been a matter of fact, even if it becomes so profoundly one of logic.

Yet, on the other hand, I have nevertheless felt compelled to corroborate the existence of such a phenomenon, plain as it may be. And once I committed to doing so by giving it name, the self-evidence of all meaning seemed to vanish. And so, each and every time I come to the page, my own creativity always begins at a loss.

Part of the problem I experience with narrating this life of paper is, indeed, an effect of my object of study, the letter itself; in turn, my issues become productive of the very means through which I problematize the letter for the sake of study, too. Assumptions of both the transparency and the significance of the letter have long captured civic imagination, as conveyed by H. T. Loomis in the introduction to his textbook, *Practical Letter Writing* (1897): "One's habits and abilities are judged by his letters,—and usually correctly.... The qualifications necessary to enable a person to write a good business or social letter are a fair English education, ready command of language, and good general knowledge of the affairs of life. These may all be acquired if the student does not possess them. To be a good correspondent, one must be able to think intelligently, and to display business tact."[1]

By the time of his book's publication at the close of the nineteenth century, Loomis was already lamenting the assumed obsolescence of the handwritten letter, casualty in the sweeping momentum of technological advance wherein "these busy days, the old-fashioned letter is replaced by brief notes, telegrams, or telephonic messages." Rendered defunct by the progress of human genius and invention, apparently the epistolary would have no place in ages to come. Yet, if he begins by announcing the letter's extinction, then why write the book—and moreover, why characterize its activity as practical? For Loomis, the ultimate function of this education in the "neatness, correct forms, and established customs in writing letters" seems to reside less in the use-value or objectivity of the letter as commodity than in the object the letter itself produces: Western civilization as such—its embodiment in and through "correct and incorrect positions" (figure 1), acquisition of proper habits, abilities, intelligence, and business tact, achievement of general mastery over the affairs of life.

If the epistolary thus mediates man's becoming at this most essential scale of economy, then my own questions become: what is a letter, what does it do and how does it work, on the other side of human mastery—thought and learned, written and read, sent and received from an other side of history? What vitalizes human relationships to the letter when the human embodies the crisis rather than cultivation of man and the mortal stakes of the problem of representation? In three parts, *The Life of Paper* hence deals with these questions at the interstices of aesthetic, racial, geographic, and ontological form: exploring the lifeworlds maintained through letter correspondence in particular contexts of racism and mass incarceration in California history. Tracing the contradictions of modernity that inhere in as well as mobilize around the letter itself, its mediation of social struggles to define "Western civilization" as well as its reinvention of ways of life that the latter cannot subsume, this investigation unfolds in three cycles to uncover how letters facilitate a form of communal life for groups targeted for racialized confinement in different phases of development in California, this distinctive or iconic part of the U.S. West.

Part 1, "Detained," focuses on migrants from southern China during the peak years of U.S. Chinese Exclusion (1890s–1920s). These chapters elaborate the distinct pathways that detained communities forged—in and through letters—to rearticulate emergent infrastructures defining an epoch of global imperialist expansion, capitalist industrialization, and nation-state formation predicated on exclusions understood in terms of "racial" distinction. Part 2, "Interned," focuses on families of Japanese ancestry during the World War II period (1930s–1940s) and examines processes of aesthetic production in interned communities through letters, in dialectic with global developments in systems of censorship and surveillance. Part 3, "Imprisoned," focuses on socialities of Blackness in the post–Civil Rights era (1960s–present), interrogating how the Black radical tradition has vitalized practices of reembodying the human as imprisoned communities of different ethnoracial heritage engage letter correspondence to survive collectively through dramatic restructurings of global capitalism, U.S. apartheid, and racial order that all bond societies in California and beyond to prisons as anchoring institutions of civic life.

On the one hand, this book examines the contradictions of mass incarceration as a process of systematic social dismantling, situating research on letters within global capitalist movements, multiple racial logics, and overlapping modes of social control that have taken distinctive shape in the U.S. West and conditioned the dependence on imprisonment as a way of life. On the other hand, framing letters within this political violence that qualifies them, this work explores how the mundane activities of communities to sustain themselves, as manifest in letter correspondence, emerge discernibly as constitutive of social life rather than seemingly adjunct to it. Invested with the urgency of struggles to survive, I argue, the production and circulation of letters open real and imaginative possibilities, both engrained in the letter and in excess of it. Thus, in "the life of paper," I interrogate the processes that connect paper objects to historical human identity and being. I also analyze how these forms of connection—structural, physical, ideological, and affective labor internalized in the letter—create alternative conditions that both ground and animate endeavors to reinvent people's own means of living. As such, these acts of self-making provide a glimpse into how communities under such constraint can reproduce themselves at every scale of existence, from bodily integrity to subjectivity to collective and spiritual being. I hence call the life of paper a "poetics": an art of becoming, mediated in and through the letter and the interaction of literature with history, that prioritizes the dynamics of creative essence to generate an other kind of social power bound to the unfathomable.

Certainly, no shortage of research exists to help establish how something as ordinary as the letter could be an axis around which the most consequential social, political-economic, and literary problems in the modern age have revolved. Scholars across disciplines have researched the role of letters in revolutionizing Europe during the seventeenth and eighteenth centuries, beginning with the ways that correspondence among radicals and intellectuals during the French Revolution fundamentally shaped their earliest understandings and demands for human rights to communication and press. In this historical legacy and political vision, the letter also helped to catalyze the founding of the United States of America, as opposition to imperial stamp acts and paper taxes fomented the eventual overthrow of British rule by Anglo colonial settlers in the "new world" who viewed such economic policies as politically repressive attacks—encumbering people who, in this period of colonial expansion, relied on transatlantic correspondence to coordinate the social reproduction of Western European and Euro-American communities.[2] As an abundance of scholarship has already suggested, the ascent of print capitalism in the early nineteenth century further transformed Eurocentric democratic culture through the contradictory creation of diverse literate and literary publics, on the one hand, and the mobilization and control of communication technologies by political-economic elites in the service of privatized accumulation, on the other. During this decisive period of struggle to redefine "imagined communities," English letter-writing instruction, popularly instituted in England beginning in the eighteenth century and subsequently globalized throughout its colonies, instilled the values of social order, Christian morality, and character; moreover, learning the formal aesthetics of a proper letter also structured a population's concepts of rationalism, social refinement, and upward mobility, as letters mediated—and generic convention represented—bourgeois and governmental order during this time. Training in civic practices of reading and writing, epitomized in Loomis's *Practical Letter Writing* as tedious in practice yet monumental in effect, thus helped to facilitate a secular reorganization of space-time, a shared sense of human identity tethered to official nationalisms, and new modes of governmentality in both European nation-states and their colonies.[3]

In geopolitical terms, the letter also provides a distinct lens to view the construction of modern infrastructure from both imperialist and anti-imperialist perspectives. Specific to the United States, scholars have studied the postal system as it constituted the national geography, largest federal civilian workforce, and central administrative apparatus of both government and corporate commercial enterprise in the first half of the nineteenth century.[4] This form of geopolitical organization—coordinating the development of key infrastructure such as roads, railroads, steamships, and the telegraph—achieved global hegemony in 1874 with the creation of the Universal Postal Union, establishing uniform practices and arrangements in the Western nation-states for the international exchange of mail.[5] If the letter thus served as building block of capitalist empires, it also affected their antithesis. In V.I. Lenin's 1871 call to revolution, for example, his vision of a democratic socialist state and economy was also exemplified by nothing other than the postal service: "To organize the whole economy on the lines of the postal service . . . that is our immediate aim. This is what will bring about the abolition of parliamentarianism and the preservation of representative institutions. This is what will rid the laboring classes of the bourgeoisie's prostitution of these institutions."[6] In this sense, wherein the articulation of racial capitalism and imperialism vis-à-vis the post simultaneously actuates grounds for the dictatorship of the proletariat, the letter functions as metonym for how systems of domination reproduce their own negation.

Indeed, Antonio Gramsci, revitalizing the fight against fascism with his insights into the interlockings of political economy and culture, knew intimately the significance of letters at the nexus of physical and ideological force. While his *Prison Notebooks* have most influenced contemporary thought, Gramsci's personal correspondence underlying his expository writings on techniques of war highlights the multidimensional means, terrains, and activities through which social struggles over life and death unfold, exemplified in this present book as "the life of paper." In a letter from prison addressed to his mother, dated 24 August 1931, for instance, Gramsci reproaches:

> This is what I think: people don't write to a prisoner either out of indifference or because of a lack of imagination. In your case and with everyone else at home I never even thought it could be a matter of indifference. I think rather that it is a lack of imagination: you can't picture exactly what life in prison is like and what essential importance correspondence has, how it fills the days and also gives a certain flavor to one's life. I never speak of the negative aspects of my life. . . . But this does not mean that the negative aspect of my life as a prisoner does not exist and is not very burdensome and should at least not

be rendered more onerous by those who are dear to me. In any event, this little speech is not addressed to you, but to Teresina, Grazietta, and Mea, who indeed could at least send me a postcard now and then.[7]

Gramsci's allusions here to his reliance on feminized reproductive labor, the performance of that labor in this context through the letter, the imaginative space that correspondence opens at the interstices of mind, body, and feeling, and the dialogical or intersubjective condition of existence that the letter lays bare: each of these aspects, even if left untheorized by Gramsci himself, clearly becomes a facet of war and survival that, in this case, he could no longer take for granted.

In these regards, as central as the epistolary has been to the very production of modern rationality and its myriad contradictory manifestations, questions about the "arcane of reproduction"[8] as embedded in Gramsci's missive have also compelled a turn to the letter as a means to problematize the concept of objectivity as such. Jacques Lacan, for example, transforming intellectual history with his interrogations of language and its determination of the subject, attends to the epistolary in order to elucidate the ultimate stakes of his project: "The problem, that of *man's relationship to the letter*, calls history itself into question."[9] In shifting analytical priority from "literary criticism to literary condition,"[10] Lacan investigates how the letter instantiates critical revelations or crises that destabilize at least two core suppositions of Western thought: first, that of a linear correspondence in the symbolic universe between signifier and signified; and second, that of human communication as static transfer of data between autonomous rational entities. Hence dissembling "reality" itself, these interventions rupture fundamental assumptions of modern man and the substance of being as delimited through Cartesian systems and have thus contributed to groundbreaking movements in both psychoanalysis and poststructuralism: revolutionizing the study of relational dynamics within and between dominant social institutions, language, and desire; language, desire, and the "unconscious"; and the unconscious and conscious parts of the mind, or the existence of the Other *within* the self. From this perspective, perhaps most associated with the oeuvre of Jacques Derrida,[11] the ontological indeterminacies that the letter represents, its deconstruction of transparency and thereby of the entire epistemological fabric that presumes it, animate the letter as microcosm for the problem of a most primal human alienation from the essence of knowing or of being known.

Applying these frameworks to epistolary studies in literature, then, scholars have built vibrant discourse around the letter, its dialogical and historical condition, as it unravels pretenses of authenticity or coherence of subjectivity, gender, voice, authorship, textuality, genre, consciousness, place, and space-time.[12] As Rebecca Earle points out, this basic dilemma of undecidability, in fact, manifests in and as epistolary scholars' own lack of agreement on the very definition of a letter, since it formally structures or hybridizes with so many other forms of communication such as news media, commerce, intimacy, politics, travelogues, and poetry.[13] This question of aesthetic origins—as further reflected in discussions about relationships between the letter, the novel, the dominant Anglo literary canon, and literature at large—poses an important problem. Exploring and historicizing the relationships between genres helps to explain the techniques through which literature represents historical reality and thereby helps to create those realities as such.[14] Hence scholars of literature are fascinated with the indeterminate nature of the letter, its decisive yet ambivalent relationship to all forms and extensions of literary culture: as the inability either to define what constitutes a letter or to understand with certainty its syncretic relationships with other forms, again, destabilizes the onto-epistemological assumptions attendant on European generic conventions and hierarchies of aesthetic value. In addition to forming dominant European literary genres and canons, such epistemological and aesthetic conventions operate at other registers of knowledge production such as the organization of scientific schema, academic disciplines, and race thinking; in the final analysis, generic questions and anxieties raised by the letter therefore return us to a breakdown of the boundaries of modern thought as such.

THE DIFFERENCE THAT RACISM MAKES

This book proceeds under the premise that the contradictions and ultimate emergencies, the difference, thus mediated through the letter open out to other realms of meaning when understood within studies of modernity as the movement of racism and of modern civilization as constituted in, by, and through the historicity of "race." In these latter contexts, the problem for history, that of man's relationship to the letter, redoubles in its encounter with the question of what it means to be the problem for man, as W. E. B. DuBois famously forecasted the crisis posed by the color line for the twentieth century.[15] At this crucible of multiplying negations—the problems posed to the coherence of historical reality and of the human, of their interlocking in productions of racial distinction[16]—attention to the letter hence provides unique means to study both movements of racial capitalist development, its requisites and ideals of civic life, on the one hand; and on the other, the lifeworlds created beyond, or deep within, the official limits of historical representation and through emergent representations of horizons beyond, or deep within, man.

Such perspective afforded by the problematization of the letter further contours this study's central contribution to contemporary discourse on mass incarceration: namely, the analytic it offers to understand the "prison industrial complex"[17] as foremost a problem of civilization rather than punishment and, as such, a priority of social reproduction that cannot be fully rationalized through logics of capitalist production alone. In part, this framework builds on Lisa Lowe's decisive positioning of Asian American Studies as means to interrogate the production of racial distinction within contradictions of and between racial capitalism and nation-statecraft.[18] My work extends this view to investigate social formation at the interstices of racial capitalism, racial apartheid, and their overdeterminations as they manifest historically through mass incarceration. Politically and analytically, this question of how to distinguish as well as interconnect the two—capitalism and apartheid, each system's reliance on the production of "racial" distinctions to maintain their operational capacities—has remained at the heart of twentieth-century U.S. social movements. In pursuits of social justice, for example, consider early Civil Rights struggles committed to dismantling segregation yet, at times, less clear about what positions to take on capitalism (and correlatively, intensified state violence on deepening senses of the need to abolish both), or evolving overlaps and fissures between cultural nationalism and revolutionary internationalism as ideologies of antiracism. In perhaps unexpected ways, then, *The Life of Paper* addresses such unresolved questions as they loom today in conflicting characterizations of mass incarceration as either a slave labor regime or a new caste system, both frames imbued with tremendous rhetorical and affective force and yet ultimately inconsistent or limited in their explanatory potential. In this regard, readers most compelled by contemporary problematics might start reading this book at part 3 and make their way backwards; whether read chronologically or not, the main arguments arrive at more or less the same points.

Two qualifications regarding this study's spatial assumptions help further to introduce how the problem of "race" is also situated in this work. First, this analysis develops Ruth Wilson Gilmore's formulation of carceral geographies that locates the prison's place within the broader fabric of *public* life and infrastructure; in this sense, the identified object of study, or the problem, is not restricted to prisons or the people housed there but instead stretches across scales to name and investigate the fuller articulation of social relations that drive, and are driven by, contradictions of capitalist development and racialized apartheid as they have defined modern civilization.[19] Through this lens, grappling with crises of mass incarceration entails less an exclusive emphasis on sites of incarceration than on the role these sites play in the reproduction of dominant landscapes as a whole—in other words, the ways that racialized orders of confinement anchor, even as their effects may appear isolated from, all of what we know as civilized life. It is in this respect that, parallel with the letter, the carceral emerges in this research as another site around or through which the most consequential social, political-economic, and ideological formations cohere.

Second, I hope this book will play a part in the regional historicization of mass incarceration in the U.S. West as it is inextricable yet distinguishable from histories drawn from U.S. Southern and Atlantic regions.[20] At the outset of this endeavor, I privilege activity that routes across the United States and East Asian Pacific in order to pursue questions of dominant regional articulation. This research follows from Adam McKeown's argument that the international policing of Asian migration to white settler states and its attendant forms of racialization around the turn of the twentieth century served as a primary means of consolidating nation-states, globalizing borders, standardizing transnational diplomatic and commercial interactions defining "civilization," and regulating human identities.[21] From this standpoint, and further contextualized by concurrent struggles taking shape in other political geographies, this work therefore assumes that attention to these trans-Pacific relations can enrich our thinking on conditions of possibility for more contemporary regimes of racism and mass incarceration even as, of course, it does not and cannot fully explain them. In the latter regard, I invite others also invested in such research to advance or overhaul the analyses offered here with other studies. For instance, examinations of Plains Indian ledger art (drawings done in business ledgers and notebooks by tribes that include the Arapaho, Northern and Southern Cheyenne, Kiowa, and Lakota-Sioux during their confinement to reservations),[22] or other iterations of the life of paper that center the American hemisphere or the Pacific islands in their regional scope, would certainly compel revisions of historical interpretations extended in this book and change the dimensionality of its insights. Nevertheless, I maintain some faith that the general methods, conceptual orientations, and affective gestalts shared here may prove useful to the carrying out of such important undertakings and augment the foundations on which our awareness can grow.

Within these boundaries, then, I approach the study of racism with a view that analytically suspends its hegemonic connotations as discrimination or perception—even when these understandings are framed as structural—in order first to prioritize engagement with racism as a matter of life and death within which all other social processes must be understood. Namely, in fleshing out Gilmore's definition of racism as the "state-sanctioned or extralegal production and exploitation of group-differentiated vulnerability to premature death, in distinct yet densely articulated political geographies,"[23] common concerns such as racial bias, stereotype, or parity, which naturalize or take for granted "race" as a known quantity, yield to renewed questions about the productivity and processes of racialized ascription themselves: the construction or reinvention of human categories that organize and justify differentiated exposure to killing.[24] Such a perspective thus foregrounds two essential problems for analysis in every instance of studying racism and its trajectories: first, the imperatives of human sacrifice concomitant with each particularized movement of modern progress and development; and second, the epistemological architecture necessary to build analytics that, relative to each instance, make sense of difference to rationalize and striate the devastation as well as the spoils of war. In this research, I hence exert substantial analytical energy toward clarifying how human differences are rendered though the production of racial distinction in order to facilitate social movement whose ultimate stakes drive the fate of Western civilization as such.

It is perhaps at these levels of analysis—given both the theoretical orientations and the regional scope of this study—that one can make the most generative sense of how it came to focus on historical articulations of both Asiatic and Black racial distinction and, moreover, how and why it would do so in a shared trajectory despite the more outstanding differences between the two. Beginning with the planetary domination of "white only" imperialist and Free Soil movements at the moment of California statehood, part 1 privileges the regulation of citizenship, the production of Chinese racial distinction, and the construction of the Angel Island Immigration Detention Center as critical to the history of mass incarceration in the U.S. West. Unlike struggles over nation-state reconstruction taking place in the U.S. South, where convict leasing emerged as central to reforming existing racial regimes and plantation power, ideological constructions and physical policing of immigration rather than crime in the western region most clearly articulated the correlation between dominant productions of racial distinction, on the one hand, and, on the other, the turn to systematic confinement as necessary foundation for the reproduction of capitalism, white supremacy, and dominant civic life. Specific to the Pacific Coast, then, examining movements of regional migration and localized containment, more than criminal justice policy or early construction of jails, may provide valuable insights on the relationship between mass incarceration and the institutionalization of a progressive racial grammar distinct from, even if interarticulated with, residual ideologies of race and emergent racial ideologies of crime prevalent in other nation-state struggles during this transformative period of modernity.

Part 2, "Interned," further elaborates this evolution of racialized incarceration as a measure of national civic engagement rather than a matter of crime and punishment, also highlighting progressive rather than conservative ideological tendencies in the broader development of a modern security state with intensive and extensive reach. The contemporary import of this analysis becomes more apparent in light of escalated struggles between dominant multicultural and white extremist blocs for control of national military and government forces—the most recent 2016 U.S. presidential and congressional elections a stunning example of how consequential yet thin the line between the two, their shared worldview of white supremacy despite both cosmetic and substantive differences in how the latter is configured. Epitomizing politically moderate tendencies under the Obama administration, the U.S. Department of Justice in August 2016 acknowledged the need both to decarcerate and to end prison privatization. In his analysis of those political trends, American Civil Liberties Union staff attorney, Carl Takei, projected that private corporations, which have dominated in the administration of U.S. immigrant detention centers but not of prisons, would play a leading role in the prison decarceration process: absorbing into their capacities the construction and governance of "community" facilities, supervision, and corrections that will have replaced state and federal oversight of criminal warehousing and social control.[25]

In a still more dramatic turn of events, people around the world are bracing ourselves in the aftermath, just one week ago at the time of writing, of the victory of ultra-right factions elected to power in the United States on platforms of white racial purity, unbridled police surveillance and military aggression, construction of an apartheid wall, and reconsideration of ethnoracial concentration camps as a linchpin of national security: promises to employ the deadliest uses of state capacity to privatize the means of human survival. At this conjuncture, examining the problematics of U.S. population management during World War II, correlated with contradictory productions of Japanese racial distinction at that time, provides a lens through which to engage current struggles over civic and carceral reform similarly rendered through competing ideologies of progressive transitions, optimized community development, and triumph of concerns for natural rights. That is, critical investigation of wartime precedents may help us to think through another catastrophic cycle of negotiation between, on the one hand, tendencies principally reliant on negative forms of surveillance and reactionary forms of race thinking; and, on the other, those based on formal appropriation of human rights struggles and their repositioning in new modes of apartheid as the claim and the victory of democratic movements. Shaping the evolution of both worldviews as well as their ultimate inextricability from one another, the history of Japanese internment and reconcentration reveals a process of nation-state recuperation that intensified rather than abolished racism precisely in the encounter of contending formulations of "community" as a dominant reproductive racial logic and, ultimately, the displacement of ungovernability into a renewed reliance on incarceration as part of the process of civic belonging.

It thus remains prevailing assertions of universal man and universal rights of man that keep the dynamics of killing in systematic operation today. As such, perhaps the most crucial way to understand part 3 is through its attempt to testify to the persistent challenge to dominant assumptions of human being posed by Black life: the culmination of struggles imbricated in African diasporic traditions that transform the concept of civilization and manifest the vital import of such transformation on practices of universal justice, democracy, and peace. In this sense, part 3's analysis of contemporary mass incarceration raises somewhat of a resistance or an alternative to hegemonic paradigms of critical race thinking. Logics of the latter share a common point of departure with the presumption that although socially constructed, race is still real. In general, much of critical race and ethnic theory proceeds to turn its goals toward illuminating the real *effects* of the social construction of race, in forms such as disparate rates of poverty, unemployment, home ownership, wealth accumulation, health care, access to resources, exposure to environmental toxicity, victimization by state violence, emotional trauma, and on and on and on. This kind of emphasis on effects also relates to a contemporary political economy of knowledge production in which both our methodological training and our desire for resources lend privilege to generic conventions that revolve around procedural diagnostics, deliverable interventions, and measurable impact as means of demonstrating the relevance of scholar activism. Of course, such studies fulfill themselves in their own historical effects that correlate with (even if they are not determined by) the vision and strength of their specific articulations of social life, many of which have contributed to community development with urgency and significance.

As a perhaps unintended consequence of this approach, however, race is often treated as a historically descriptive rather than creative category in order to render more immediately intelligible the "gaps" or inequalities that the research seeks to fill, whether in a specialized body of scholarship or in the lifeblood of an oppressed people. Yet, if the effects of racism are examined in ways disarticulated from actual productions of racial distinction, then in the final instance race can only be understood through the sieve of legalistic, representative, or instrumental frames that themselves circumscribe the human subjection we wish to overturn. People thus remain locked in the same positions in the ideological terrain of suffering because no intellectual means have been offered to give name to humanity beyond what is already constructed by and through the sources of our anguish. It is in this sense, then, that part 3 attempts to crystallize race as an *ontological* problematic and to examine further how Black social movements in the last half of the twentieth century revolutionized the race *concept* in order to preserve possibilities for being. This analysis spills into our current dilemma: living in a place and time in which certain preexisting modifiers to racial distinction or hierarchy have been tentatively abolished but not yet the basic function of human differentiation in the dominant grammar of a de jure post-racial apartheid society. We might conceive of this function as a conjunctive one, ironically enough, in which the simulation of ontological divisions not only rationalizes the war, exploitation, and genocide wrought by modern man, but such abstraction also enables the reproduction of Western civilization by suturing or dressing the most apparent places it bleeds, hemorrhages where its own structural contradictions and overdeterminations cannot be resolved except through mass purges that require both cause and explanation.

On the one hand, then, those today seeking to preserve their claims to world domination face the persistent problem of how to construct new ideological modifiers to define their boundaries of human achievement and degeneracy, necessary means to maintain the operational capacities of processes originally structured and understood in explicit terms of "racial" difference. (For the new dominant party, the challenge may be more precisely how to maintain the rhetorical appeal of reactionary ideologies of racial purity while responding to the progressive demands of racial capitalist reproduction.) On yet another hand, those of us seeking social justice face a different and ongoing problem, the preservation of *being* in the latter's intimacies as well as its totalities. The essentialism of such a view, as alternately simplified and grandiose as it may seem, marks a basic distinction between movements for decarceration and those for abolition, the latter of which does not stop at reforming prisons but only at abolishing racism as such—what is most succinctly communicated through the pronouncement "Black Life Matters" and wherein contestations around the terms *life* and *matters* cohere and must be enunciated as the difference connoted by the existential qualification "Black."[26] From this perspective, and through the overall paradigm of social reproduction offered in this study, I thus strive to anthropologize the contending terms through which dominant groups delimit the facts of "life": historicizing rather than idealizing these social movements or visions not only to stop their reproduction and thereby the cycles from which their suffering arises and ceases, but, more urgently, to clear contemplative space to dwell in the social reproduction of other ways of life that abide by different dynamics than those governing dominant articulations of *world*.

Therefore, while interrogating movements taking shape in and giving shape to dominant landscapes, this book's primary aspiration is to discern the more nebulous regions or social articulations formed through the life of paper and, concurrently, the epistemological shifts both necessary for and affected by such efforts toward discernment: an ultimate concern influenced by the elaboration of Black geographies as the unfinished production of space, driven by the struggles, practices, consciousness, and ontological worldviews of "people who occupy the 'nonexistent'" and put demands on spatial arrangement through new forms of life.[27] In the first and final instance, then, while attentive to contradictory movements of development and confinement in planetary realms of war, this project is essentially motivated by Clyde Woods's injunction to prioritize analytically the "presence of contending ontologies" in order to crystallize the endurance of worldviews and ways of life that have not been subsumed by racial capitalism, even as their forms of appearance may be obscured by or through structures of domination and of mediation.[28] My applications of these formulations compel at least two final clarifications. First, the methodological and epistemological approaches of Black studies of modernity, their attempts to narrativize histories of the African diaspora in modes necessarily shorn of—at least, in contradiction with—the will to knowledge or recovery, themselves entail a delimiting of the lived specificities of racism and productions of difference in each instance of their particular articulations.[29] In this sense, turning to paradigms that issue from Black radical traditions as the means for this present study is not to equate or conflate experiences of differently racialized groups but rather to socialize the former's techniques of analyzing lived conditions and to explore further the implications of preexisting analyses for extended processes of racial differentiation.

Second, just as this project does not assume equivalences, neither does it seek to draw comparisons even as my research points out certain repetitions. Instead, by concentrating on "the life of paper," I am working to problematize the production of collectivities and communal ways of existence that—on the one hand, while only recognizable as and through creations of racial distinction, constrained by history and/or conditioned by ancestors—also uncover modes of racialized, gendered, and sexualized embodiment that can be understood within or alongside dominant structurings of human being without being simply derivative of them. From this perspective, within the ultimate mystery of social reproduction as the production of difference, each case therefore represents a certain kind of singularity for which, in the final analysis, there can exist no comparison: dynamics of a basic enigma, or dialectics between ontological continuity and differentiation, between vital energy and material substance, that are detectable in mediations of the letter and which I am thus calling a "poetics," for lack of perhaps a better term.

A POETICS

In his studies of ancient Greco-Roman culture, Michel Foucault theorizes that the epistolary—alongside *hupomnemata,* or notebooks acting as memory aids—constituted "arts of oneself[,] . . . a labor of thought, a labor through writing, a labor in reality" that served an ethopoietic function: writing as agent of the transformation of truth into character.[30] Influenced by this concept of letters as mediating an "aesthetics of existence," I likewise approach the life of paper's "poetics" as an art of social reproduction, embedded in a set of individual as well as collective practices that generate life potential and give definition to, as much as they are defined by, the labor to sustain human being. However, specific to imbrications of racism and the unfolding of Western thought—the historicity of concepts of truth and character and the racialization of modern aesthetics of existence—elaborations of the care and technologies of the self in each of the cases presented here hence necessitate other epistemological resources not only to explain the negative effects of dominant ethopoietic processes but also to distinguish other modes of becoming within deepening articulations of global crisis and cultures.

In this latter regard, Sylvia Wynter interrogates the historical transformations that *poesis*, "acts of making," underwent in the age of modernity. Addressing the first international symposium on "ethnopoetics" in 1976, Wynter criticizes the contemporary invocation of the latter term itself, weary of its potential to reinscribe rather than challenge the "MUTATION" of human being that took place in the sixteenth century. That is, Wynter argues that uncritically employing *ethno* (Greek, "the people") to distinguish "*ethno*poetics" from a more universalized "poetics" subtly perpetuates the dichotomies produced during the globalization of Western civilization: the "detotalization of the world picture" and its "retotalization" through binaries such as Christian / heathen, civilized / savage, human / Other, West / rest, and eventually First / Third World vis-à-vis racism.[31] As a more precise formulation, Wynter instead suggests the pursuit of "socio poetics," cultural production that can historicize and anthropologize the West / rest relation and, ultimately, further globalize a "concretely universal *ethnos*" as already instantiated by struggles of African diasporic peoples to sustain themselves beyond movements of genocide. From this perspective of Black life, binding the production of "a WE that needed no OTHER to constitute their Being," particularity augments rather than opposes universality as meaning attached to every form of difference conserves Being rather than negates it.[32] In socializing this latter world order, then, the praxis of socio poetics entails "approaching the CULTURES OF THE OTHER in order to construct an alternative process of making ourselves human."[33] It is precisely this model of poetics that guides my own approach to the cultures of those racially and spatially segregated as modernity's Others, as much as it more essentially also characterizes the work of these epistolary cultures themselves, within their own otherness, to construct alternative processes of human being.

This framework of socio poetics syncretizes well with methods of Asian American cultural studies that further enrich the scope of historical materialist analysis and correlate with the specificities of my engagements in this project. Namely, in his consideration of Chinese poetry written from 1910 to

1940 on the walls of the Angel Island U.S. Immigration Detention Center, where part 1 of this book begins, Yunte Huang also works through the concept of poetics, its varying etymologies and epistemological interpretations, in order to illuminate differentiated historical effects and implications. Distinguishing modern mutations of the Greek *poesis* from the concept of poetry in classical Chinese literary criticism, *shi yan zhi,* Huang asserts:

> The word *poem,* with its Greek roots in *poima* and *poein* (to make), suggests an object made, an outside separated from an inside; by contrast, *shi,* the Chinese word for poetry or poem, means not an object made by the writer but actually the writer him- or herself. As Stephen Owen points out, *shi yan zhi* [variously translated as "poetry says the mind" or "poetry expresses human nature"] may well be a tautological statement. The character *shi* consists of the components *yan* and *si.* . . . Hence, we may legitimately interpret *shi yan zhi* as meaning "poetry says," with a stress on the intransitive verb. . . . This emphasis [is] not on something out there to be represented by the poem, but on the act of saying itself.[34]

From this perspective, Huang argues that we must understand poetry on the walls of Angel Island through *shi yan zhi,* "an expressive-affective conception of poetry as opposed to the mimetic-representative conception in the Western tradition,"[35] in order more seriously to appreciate the work of art as constituting lived experience more than reflecting it. Therefore, reading Angel Island poetry less as empirical documentation of immigrant detention than as instantiating acts to survive beyond it, this hermeneutic moves away from emphasis on accuracy of translation—as well as its corollary assumption that proper language could capture the transparency of meaning or experience—to focus on analytically restoring the interlocking of literary activity with the conditions of its material production and historical stakes. Huang's "poetics of error" thereby crystallizes the functions of aesthetic labor to shape social life and struggle rather than merely to describe them: an approach to literary studies that I also appropriate as means to foreground the inextricability rather than autonomy of literary, material, and epistemological concerns throughout this study and that, in turn, refines our views of the materiality of the word as well as of the ontological significance of literary enunciation. This epistemological standpoint extends into readings of Japanese poetics whose practice and innovations by Issei, or first-generation Japanese migrants, are discussed at greater length in part 2 and, finally, routes back again in part 3 to the Black radical tradition, the injunction of Wynter's socio poetics "to free the Western concept of humanism[,] . . . transforming its abstract universal premise into the concretely human global, the concretely WE."[36] As I will continue to make clear, the turns I take in these aesthetics of existence, in sum, do not abide by a mimetic-representative conception of language but rather by approaches to literary labor as acts of making or transformation—acts that preserve creative essence, as Fred Moten discloses, precisely "in the break" between the irreducibility of Being, historical movements to simulate its detotalization through racial capitalist logics and machinations of war, and its enduring self-evidence in manifold struggles to make an "art of making art" through which revelation reemerges even if, or because, it cannot be contained.[37]

In this latter sense, and thus conditioned by the premise that art and literature help to surrogate as much as they represent geopolitical and cultural formations—and do so through articulations of presence as much as of absence—scholarship instrumental in the development of Asian American Studies specifically thinks through the dilemma of *form* as the latter cuts across problems of history, geopolitics, aesthetics, and humanism. Groundbreaking work by Edward Said and Lisa Lowe, for example, articulates the role of the novel and its "highly regulated plot mechanism," the bildungsroman, to rationalize the productive erasures embedded in contradictions of racial capitalism and modern statecraft as well as to mediate imperialist subjectivities, as readers invest in dominant systems of social reference—building their consciousness around the novel's formal renderings of social-geographic space and hierarchies of family, property, and nation.[38] Amplifying these insights, and responding to an unintentional tendency of structural approaches to race studies to underestimate the complexities of ideology, Colleen Lye's paradigm of "racial form" brings into sharper relief the mutually constitutive rather than epiphenomenal relationship of language to material processes in regimes of racialization: reviving our attention to the centrality of aesthetic movements in generating racial logics that reproduce or displace political, economic, and social crisis in dominant landscapes.[39] In this current project, the concept of racial form, or the problematic posed by it, thus facilitates closer examination both of the extraordinary ideological labor required to produce and reproduce carceral geographies and their attendant methods of control and, underneath the weight of this constant duress, of how the life of paper reasserts new ways of being human toward the transformation of catastrophe. In deliberating the latter, I take particular care to consider the consistency with which the life of paper's formal subversions of the bildungsroman mediate historical ruptures in the telos of progress and open out other terrains through which to connect and struggle with what it means to be alive, to be in life, to *be.*

Insofar as the bildungsroman also structures the conventions of historiography, as Lowe convincingly argues, this book is itself conditioned by these ideological mechanics at the same time that it is not proper to them. This contradiction, which I confront through acts of research and writing but cannot claim to resolve, further bears on the historical and literary approaches required to execute this work in any degree of consonance with its aims or horizons. In these regards, the letters grounding this project are the fruit of original archival research conducted at the National Archives and Records Administration—Pacific Region, the Chinese Historical Society of Southern California, UC Berkeley's Bancroft Library, the University of Washington Library Special Collections, the Southern California Library for Social Studies and Research, Freedom Archives, and several private archives. In addition—and for part 3 in particular, which, due to its timeliness, relies exclusively on previously published or publicly circulated materials—I incorporate epistolary traces from literary, historical, and testimonial sources including poetry, memoir, and film. Whenever possible, I also opened dialogues with those to whom the letters belong and have considered their analyses as I have constructed my own. Thus grounded in these epistolary archives and research, this work aims not only to denaturalize the geographic borders, political-economic laws, and civic norms that expose people to state-sanctioned violence, but, more critically, to privilege a sense of the activities and worldviews of disenfranchised populations who struggle to transform existing conditions.

In these endeavors, modes of orientation and engagement with the archives in the framework of "a poetics" must necessarily veer from dominant historical methods that are centrally preoccupied with the legitimacy of the epistolary's status as evidence: the letter's reliability, the problem of ephemerality for data analysis, and ongoing debates among academic historians about the validity of popular texts.[40] In contrast to such questions, tethered to assumptions of the transparency of meaning and experience as well as the lifeworld of the bildungsroman that I have already disclaimed, I am not concerned with using epistolary data to construct an empirical truth about the experience of mass incarceration. Instead, I argue precisely that these letters are neither representative of nor anomalous to a generalizable experience but that they are, in the essence of the word, *original,* even if, in deep ways, not unprecedented. Therefore, what I attempt through exposition is less to reinscribe investments in static renderings of lived events than to make meaning of the past in order to live through the present and, as Aurora Levins Morales urges, "to examine carefully what aspects of our history we offer our communities as sources of pride."[41] In this sense, the circumstances under which the archives even exist—such as the contradiction of the racial state government's preservation of the very letters they intended to erase, or the inextricability of social justice archival institutions from contemporary social justice movements[42]—illustrate concretely how the historicity of archives themselves, their "illegitimacy" in terms of our lacking ability to take their truth-value for granted, indeed establishes rather than nullifies the conditions of possibility for critical inquiry here.[43] It might be most precise to say, then, that my narrativizations mark an effort to *envision* rather than record the past as means of addressing the problems of historical being now.

My methods of reading are hence not directed at restoring literal truths; instead, compelled by other studies of incarceration and inflected practices of reading, I avow the contexts of our own desires in order to interrogate literary activity as projects of self-creation and as part of meeting the need to transform governing structures and institutions.[44] This approach, pursuant to the discourse on *shi yan zhi,* indeed influences the treatment of translation: most explicitly pertaining to research in part 1, which relies on the original translations by U.S. Immigration and Naturalization Services of intercepted letters from Chinese into English; and in part 2, which relies when necessary on professional translations previously commissioned by families or anthology editors of letters from Japanese into English. In *all* cases, for letters written in or across any language, my analytical priorities center on the hyper-mediation of the letters themselves—the language as it *moves* in and through the historicity of epistolary production, reproduction, consumption, and circulation in their specific contexts—and on the effects of the letter as either narrativized or arguably manifested by those creating and created by it. This emphasis on the sociality of signification in historical motion follows from scholarship in Ethnic and Queer Studies that has provided tools to derive insights from the difference rather than verisimilitude between aesthetic representation and empirical fact. While theorized through a multitude of frames such as Blackness, queerness, mestizaje, creolization, interlanguage, or haunting, these perspectives each highlight how the impossibility rather than accuracy of translation incites meaning, particularly for people whose access to their historical, intellectual, and psychic heritage happens through incomplete or unthinkable processes of retrieval.[45]

In this light, the slippages, imprecisions, and losses in translation carry their own significance and, in this particular context, become a constitutive part of the life of paper, too.

Such precedents in Ethnic, Queer, and Performance Studies therefore variously conceptualize the ephemeral as means to disrupt hegemonic constructions both of space-time as linear and of communication as a function of knowability and capitalist productivity.[46] In this vein, this book works through the epistolary, as a category of ephemera, to build on these contributions to thought which, on the one hand, excavate understudied modes of social struggle and overlooked epistemologies of transformation, change, agency, or will; and, on the other, bring elements of social reproduction such as affect, performance, and corporeality to bear on public cultures and political life. Despite the irresolvable conflicts involved, there remain places throughout this study in which I offer substantive readings of materials based on translations whose accuracy cannot be verified; I have attempted in these instances to make assertions rooted in generalizable communications of affect and the performativity of the letter itself. These theorizations focus on discernible themes that emerge from my assumptions of connotation rather than denotation in order to link the contents of letters to their formal functions in processes of social reproduction—an orientation consistent with distinguishing the letter here as a gift rather than capitalist commodity, only coming more deeply into being the more it is consumed.[47] In doing so, my methods of close reading consider ephemerality as it draws our awareness to the continuum rather than opposition between the impermanent and the enduring, as well as the ways that our lives and their expressions, while ephemeral, sustain and give shape to the definition of "tradition" as the latter is constant but not fixed and is contingent on the past as well as what is to come.

Finally, then, much work remains to be done regarding the exploration of Marxian theories of labor power (and labor power as *wealth*) vis-à-vis ethnic epistemologies of vital energy or life force, of which this work on the life of paper as a poetics of social reproduction is but an introductory view. As a process of producing labor power, each of these cases presents conditions under which racism, war, and mass incarceration have significantly affected the ways that communities have reorganized normatively gendered reproductive labor in order to survive. Specific to the brutalities of confinement, the structuring of domination through racial and gendered segregation conditions a form of compulsory, highly regulated homosociality, which, in the contemporary period, is ultimately only intensified rather than negated by the development of segregated prisons for transgender people.[48] Moreover, this coerced form of homosociality remains in contradiction with dominant cultures of pathological heterosexuality articulated through sexualized, gendered, and racial oppression as the modalities through which class is lived.[49] Under such constraints, then, insofar as the life of paper has played a role in revising these configurations, the new or renewed intimacies produced through the totality of labors bringing letters to life help to form relationships that exceed sanctioned identities or roles understood along axes such as race, gender, and sexuality. From this perspective, the life of paper mediates the production or survival of "contraband" love,[50] a kind of vital energy or life force, that transgresses systematic violence as the latter manifests in dynamic articulations of coercive force. While this study focuses on the heteronormative, often heterosexist, reproductive unit of incarcerated communities, the family, as it exists, it also emphasizes the necessity—if not the striving—mediated through the life of paper for different ways to create and re-create oneself, one's family, community, and social world through love in myriad and dynamic forms.

In this sense, this poetics, in the circulation of creative resource that survives regimes of killing, opens out toward the vibrant relationships yet to be known or fulfilled—as well as ways to realize them—that we cannot anticipate, and yet each ensures that we move collectively toward a different horizon. In the final analysis, at last, in a world structured by domination, the existential problem and living process of becoming human thus shape the life of paper as activity that makes manifest the deepest mystery at the heart of social reproduction: a poetics that comes from, as it also enacts, dialectical movements of differentiation and multiplicity inherent in the revelation of ontological totality, the work of its preservation and representation, and the resulting production and reproduction of a concretely universal "we" that is both bound and open to life as yet unimaginable potential.

FIGURE 2. Hong Kong Post's "Four Great Inventions of Ancient China" Special Stamp, issued on 18 August 2005 (clockwise: compass, printing, paper, gunpowder). Photograph by the author.

PART ONE

Detained

BY 1915, THE SCANDAL HAD just grown too out of control. After more than thirty years of U.S. government involvement in illegal "Chinese smuggling plots," someone had to clean out the system once and for all—and the secretary of labor put his best investigator, John B. Densmore, on the job. Initiated at the federal level in 1915, the Densmore Investigation was going to be different from all the other investigations since 1882: all the ones that reformed U.S. immigration law enforcement with administrations that "soon became worse than those removed," as a Treasury Department official put it in 1899.[1] The Densmore Investigation was committed to serving both the American and the Chinese people by weeding out government "fraud" at the Angel Island port of immigrant entry and thus restore proper enforcement of the class-stratified 1882 U.S. Chinese Exclusion Act. This internal shakedown attempted to control, though not necessarily to resolve, rampant corruption that supported the growth of illegal working-class Chinese communities in the United States.[2] Specifically, the unsanctioned networks facilitating the proliferation of Chinese "paper families" had to be discovered and destroyed.

These were no simple cases of mistaken identity, or of cat and mouse. The production of social relationships at this time involved processes counterintuitive to how they appeared. In other words, things were not what they looked like—and all parties faced the problem of accounting for the difference. No easy task, especially when the evidence resided in "difficult personalities."

San Francisco, Cal.
October 30th 1917.

Hon. J.B. Densmore,
Department of Labor,
Angel Island, Cal.

I have read in the daily presses, and found you have done a great Justice to our Chinese peoples. (That is you have made a clean sweep oust all the crooks, and grafters, which is in Angel Island.) Of course, There are some our peoples is not appreciate what you have done, those who he is belongs to Stidger and Kennah's Gang. But the majority is very thankful of your gratitutes.

There is a chinese, who's name was Quan Shown Tuey, alias S.T. Quan. also called himself a native son, He and another who's name is Lem War Yew, alias Walter Lem, they both have been framed up fake sons of natives affidavits, landed more sons of natives into this port than any of those that you had already have them in custody. Quan is not only importing coolies into this country, but girls for peostitite, and opiums too.

Lem War Yew, just returned from China short times ago, he went back there to open up a headquarter to do importing collies in Hong Kong, and Canton, he will return to china to act as a school teacher to teach the coolies, about the different street in San Francisco, etc. why these two mens not to be punish? Is they any better crooks than those you have already caught?

Yours Respectfully,
afraid to show his right name.

The contradictions that punctuate this letter raise both questions and clues about why its writer would be "afraid to show his right name" (and also point to the anxiety embedded in what his "right name" would be), as the letter indicates most basically the problem that Densmore sought to contain: that is, how Chinese migrants were mobilizing paper, information, and transportation technologies to produce legal status under Chinese Exclusion laws. Namely, Chinese migrant communities were creating "paper families" by means of the paper-generated invention of new identities and kinship ties to facilitate legal migration. Such labor involved activities such as stealing

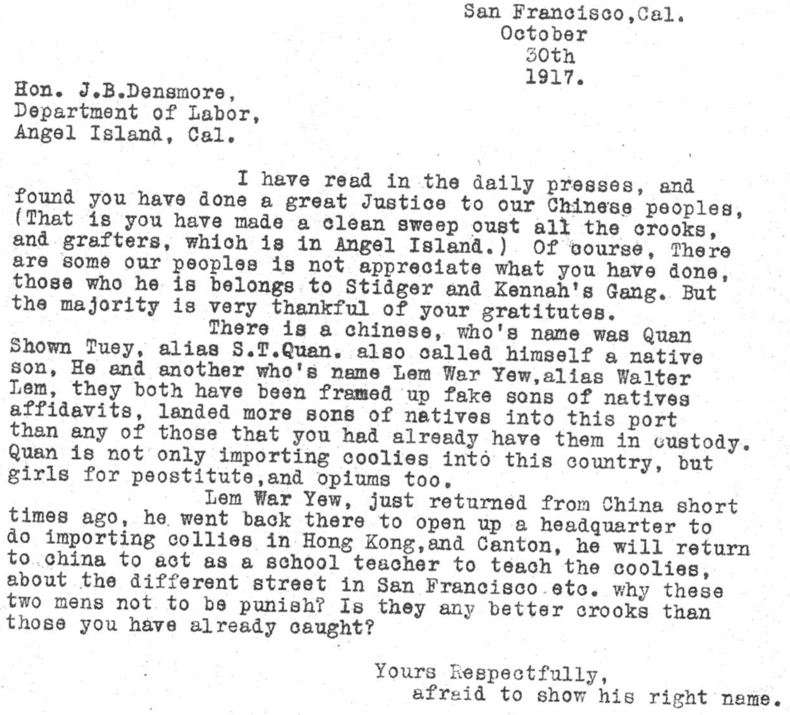

Hon. J.B.Densmore,
Department of Labor,
Angel Island, Cal.

I have read in the daily presses, and
found you have done a great Justice to our Chinese peoples,
(That is you have made a clean sweep oust all the crooks,
and grafters, which is in Angel Island.) Of course, There
are some our peoples is not appreciate what you have done,
those who he is belongs to Stidger and Kennah's Gang. But
the majority is very thankful of your gratitutes.
There is a chinese, who's name was Quan
Shown Tuey, alias S.T.Quan. also called himself a native
son, He and another who's name Lem War Yew,alias Walter
Lem, they both have been framed up fake sons of natives
affidavits, landed more sons of natives into this port
than any of those that you had already have them in custody.
Quan is not only importing coolies into this country, but
girls for peostitute,and opiums too.
Lem War Yew, just returned from China short
times ago, he went back there to open up a headquarter to
do importing collies in Hong Kong,and Canton, he will return
to china to act as a school teacher to teach the coolies,
about the different street in San Francisco.etc. why these
two mens not to be punish? Is they any better crooks than
those you have already caught?

Yours Respectfully,
afraid to show his right name.

FIGURE 3. Anonymous to Hon. J.B. Densmore, 30 October 1917; Folder 3 of Box 4, Entry 232; Densmore Investigation Files, Record Group 85; National Archives and Records Administration–Pacific Region (NARA) (San Francisco).

and doctoring official immigration documents as well as exchanging "coaching letters" that instructed migrants on how to pass rigorous physical and oral examinations at California ports of entry. Legal entry depended upon successfully fabricating family ties with Chinese merchant or educated classes—an endeavor that, as the contents of this letter further suggest, also hailed the production of qualitatively distinct social and economic networks simultaneously at the center and at the margins of dominant world systems emerging during this period.

Yet, as the very conditions of both this anonymous letter and the Densmore Investigation itself illustrate, these social and economic networks revolving around paper families were anything but clear-cut. Other details contained in the letter break down binary assumptions about both racial and state formation and instantiate how the seeming coherence of both must

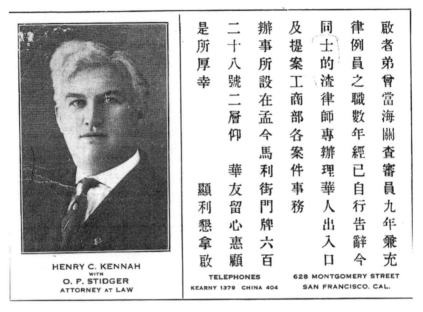

敢者弟曾當海關查審員九年兼充
律例員之職數年經已自行告辭今
同士的渣律師專辦理華人出入口
及提案工商部各案件事務
辦事所設在孟今馬利街門牌六百
二十八號二層仰　華友留心惠顧
是所厚幸　　顯利懇拿啟

HENRY C. KENNAH
WITH
O. P. STIDGER
ATTORNEY AT LAW

TELEPHONES
KEARNY 1379　CHINA 404

628 MONTGOMERY STREET
SAN FRANCISCO. CAL.

FIGURE 4. Newspaper advertisement for Kennah and Stidger, Attorneys at Law; Folder 5 of Box 3, Entry 232; Densmore Investigation Files, RG 85; NARA–Pacific Region (SF).

be historically investigated rather than presumed. For instance, reference to the leadership of immigration attorneys O. P. Stidger and Henry C. Kennah (figure 4) points to the bonds of cooperation, consent, exchange, and reform—not just those of coercion and antagonism—that animated relationships between Chinese migrant communities and American law officials throughout the Exclusion period.

Moreover, regarding the instabilities of progressivism, the "crooks and grafters" under investigation refers not to Chinese detainees but to the government officials in charge of them. Conversely, the writer's support of the Densmore Investigation (whether or not we can confirm that the writer was indeed a Chinese migrant) exemplifies how immigration officials actively encouraged and recruited Chinese migrant participation in efforts to enforce Chinese Exclusion. Yet the specificity of the author's purpose for writing, as when his closing objective clearly singles out his targets ("Why these two mens not to be punish?"), suggests preexisting ulterior motives and histories: it indicates that the informant's investments in the investigation have more to do with how Densmore's project coalesces with, rather than defines, a prior web of social relations already in motion.

Finally, then, this letter gives us glimpses into the expansive implications of paper families as they materialized through dense global structures of racialized-gendered labor differentiation, economic and geographic organization, and knowledge production. Specifically, "afraid to show his right name" points toward the reconfiguration of sexual divisions of labor that reproduced paper families: distinguishing the "import" business along the categories "fake sons of natives," "girls for peostitute [sic]," and "coolies," or male contract laborers. Moreover, at the interstices of legality and illegality, this articulation of immigration through commodity relations, profit, and exchange interlocks with the rise of qualitatively new educational institutions and epistemological encounters, indicated by reference to emergent networks "to teach the coolies, about the different street in San Francisco etc." Last, these three short paragraphs allude to the multiple geographic paradigms that ordered the realm of diasporic social life—trans-Pacific networks with "headquarters" at emerging nodal points such as Hong Kong and Canton—as the letter links racialized carceral space (people "in custody" at Angel Island) to globalized discursive, administrative, maritime, and urban development.

This part explores such intrigues in deeper detail, interrogating the structural foundations both conditioning and created by the social reproduction of Chinese paper families coming into being deep inside the heat of global imperialist warfare and capitalist movements to "modernize" the world market in the mid-nineteenth century. Inseparable from the infrastructural importance of the epistolary form itself during this period, part 1 traces appositional investments in letters as both medium and commodity, wherein letters were both organizing and generating capital as well as labor power, in addition to architecting—as letters cohered—global infrastructures for their production. As such, epistolary content and form, in their totality, staged a literal battleground through which modernity itself was unfolding. In this context, then, chapters 1 and 2 focus on asymmetrically interlocked struggles to develop infrastructural matrices that both mediate and are mediated by the letter. In particular, I focus on distinct forms of globalization occurring through interarticulated transformations in technology, epistemology, and human kinship. I study these transformations from around 1854, when the Free Soil Movement won hegemony in the United States and Western Allied Forces officially declared the sovereign International Settlement of Shanghai, to around 1924, when the United States passed the Johnson-Reed Immigration Act to normalize further the globality of racial humanism, borders as understood by the dominant economic and political blocs, and comprehensive regimes of regulation and policing. To undertake this investigation, I look primarily at structural transformations occurring within and across three distinct yet densely articulated, or stretched, places: Guangdong, China, where migrants originally started; California, U.S.A., where they arrive; and the place made through and *as* the life of paper—an ineffable region comprising a mix of places, renovating the "familiar" and the "foreign" into new combinations or mixes of relationships, aspiration, knowledge, and being.[3]

Following the paper trail, I argue that the life of paper generates a particular social form that manifests across, as it sutures, different historical articulations of geography, aesthetics, and race at the heart of struggles to define modernity. To demonstrate this, chapter 1 first elaborates the significance of letters to constitute racial capitalism and dominant forms of nation, state, and empire across the East Asian and U.S. Pacific. As battles over international infrastructures of letter conveyance and circulation mediated global wars to secure territorial domination, the practice of letter writing itself played a central role in these struggles, serving as the standard medium of both government and business administration throughout the modernizing world and as the primary mode of training modern subjectivity and proper citizenship. In this context, and amidst the globalization of colonial and civil warfare, engagements with paper, print, and postal technologies thus significantly shaped forms of both U.S. white supremacist and incipient Chinese nationalisms as well as evolving forms of Chinese and U.S. imperialisms in this period.

Precisely because of the contradictions facing Chinese migrants—differently marginalized from dominant movements in both the United States and China, entangled in both yet represented in neither—their full engagement with the epistolary therefore mediated original kinds of regional administration and culture, distinct from either those of U.S. or emergent Chinese nation-state formations and identities. Caught between competing political and economic imperatives, the "material archaeology" of Chinese paper families carried explosive meanings in such a world in which language, print, and knowledge production shaped and regulated historical being under conditions of domination and its exceeding calculations.[4]

Chapter 2 explores how the life of paper for Chinese migrants produced alternative articulations of space, sociality, and subjectivity that diverged from more readily apparent forms. It begins by examining how letter correspondence in and among the diaspora was a highly coordinated—even if, or perhaps because, improvised—activity that necessitated an infrastructure underlying the production of paper families so that disparate people stretched across space could do the work of social reproduction more effectively and, in a modernizing sense, efficiently. The chapter continues with close readings of letters composing paper families, pursuing how migrants' epistolary productivity, navigating through shifting terms of truth and "fraud" inside the excesses of exclusion, responded to yet differed from dominant uses of communication and transportation technologies to facilitate conditions of possibility for other forms of social life.

ONE

The Inventions of China

THIS CHAPTER EXAMINES MODERNITY FROM a trans-Pacific perspective, with a focus on the interdependent formations of China and the West vis-à-vis the development and control of infrastructures cohering around and through letters. Starting in Guangdong, struggles over technological change at this time mediated, as they were mediated by, imperialist and civil wars happening in China to control land and resources and to define national identities in an era of intensified global colonial and anticolonial ambitions in East Asia. As battles to develop and mobilize communication and transportation infrastructures in China operated as the literal form of modern statecraft and empire, these battles were inseparable from, and made fully manifest by, transformations in knowledge production—the latter also revolving around discourses of paper and print technologies. Such epistemological movements sought to invest or reorganize human meaning in competing articulations of space and thereby normalize changing operations of power in and through the architecture of social life. As the specificities of these productions of constraint and opportunity thrust migrants from Guangdong to the Anglo settler state of California, conflicting ideological imperatives of nascent nationalisms and regional capitalisms, also mediated through infrastructures of the epistolary, exacerbated global crisis and its particular manifestation in California. These contradictions culminated in the emergence of structured exclusions in order to reform rather than resolve the crisis, producing a paradigm of human detention and Angel Island as a spatial suture for differentiated processes of homogenization and unreconciled systems of global exploitation.

This journey begins in the 1870s in Guangdong, a southern province in China, during a period of transforming social investments in paper, print, and postal technologies. At the emergent nation-state scale, these transformations both reflected and facilitated the mass displacements and reorganization of land occurring as a result of wars between and among Chinese, Japanese, U.S., and European imperialists, in addition to competing Chinese nationalist parties and, most relevant at the rural and local levels, an array of patrilineal clan groups.[1] The standing Qing empire, led by descendants of the Jin dynasty (ca. 265–420 C.E.) identified ethnically as Manchu, rose to power in 1644 as an inclusive empire formally recognizing the Han majority as well as ethnic minority populations. Of primary concern for the purposes of this analysis are the circumstances surrounding late Qing reforms: from the 1850s to 1911, political struggles included escalating civil war with regional ethnic uprisings, warlordism, and the Taiping Rebellions targeting both European missionary and Qing government authorities; military conflict with Britain, Japan, and France; lower intensity warfare with the United States, Russia, Austria, Portugal, and Germany; and attempts to secure the Qing government's own imperial assets in Korea, Vietnam, Burma, and Taiwan. With such pressures thus bringing the Qing dynasty beyond the brink of crisis, imperial reformers launched the Self-Strengthening Movement (1860–95), instituting sweeping structural adjustments based on deliberations of how best to appropriate Western technologies to promote Chinese imperialism. It is in this context that design and control over print and postal infrastructures in China marked a primary arena through which imperialist and anti-imperialist struggles were unfolding.

This investigatation of such sweeping changes thus starts with situating them within everyday traditions and practices indigenous to villages in Guangdong at this time, where paper already possessed long-standing social meaning and sacred value. In her studies of Han Chinese folk tradition, Janet Lee Scott argues that paper *itself,* distinct from Holy Scripture such as the Bible or the Qu'ran, acted as "the material aspect, the physical representation of worship and belief."[2] In such social and spiritual practices, paper and its making, offering, and burning serve as means to communicate and maintain relationships with gods, ghosts, ancestors, and the natural world. Moreover, respect for the *paper,* hierarchized by perceived quality and inclusive of specific categories for paper bearing characters or print, mediates and coheres particularized worldviews of an ontological totality. As Roderick Cave further contextualizes, "The value of paper bearing written or printed characters is recognized in the pious Confucian motto, 'Respect scrap paper bearing characters' (*jingxi zizhi*), the Buddhist tradition that special rewards will be earned by those who respect and preserve paper bearing sacred messages, and the Daoists' plentiful use of paper charms."[3] These values assigned to paper by Guangdong communities corresponded with the venerated craft of papermaking, the latter involving intricate rituals of collective labor, cooperative living during the papermaking season, and production synchronized with the vaster ecology to ensure optimal climactic conditions and access to water and fibers.[4]

By the 1870s, however, the importation of the mechanical printing press to the colonized territories of Shanghai introduced commercial modes of both print and papermaking that expanded alongside preexisting methods and began exerting uneven pressures for government control, deskilling, and transformation of production processes.[5] Prior to this time, Qing rulers resisted the importation of Western printing technology for cultural, financial, and aesthetic reasons. Market-oriented industrialization did not begin in Shanghai until 1876–77, after Chinese entrepreneurs experimented with Western-style lithography first imported by Catholic missionaries to print religious imagery. By 1895, this mechanization of print media, alongside the prototype for the organization of production that commercial industrialization introduced, created a mass culture connected to Shanghai's publishing industry and spreading through print news and modern periodicals. Such changes occurred through a distinct "Chinese" nationalist print capitalism that syncretized Western techniques of production and "progress" with imperialist Chinese print and political culture, the latter rooted in existing social hierarchies and values of public service embodied by the government scholar and literati elites.[6]

Rather than exemplify a democratic encounter between systems in a globalizing world, this hybridity took shape as Western Allied Forces colonized China by means of occupying the Qing government itself—prompting the historian John L. Fairbank, for instance, to reflect that the real curiosity of modern infrastructure in China is that "there is no way to say whether it is 'foreign' or 'Chinese.'"[7] In these regards, perhaps geographic detail most succinctly illustrates the tense, unequal interdependence of U.S., European, and late-Qing Chinese imperialisms at this time, in this industry, and through this medium, as Shanghai's Wenhuajie district (culture and education streets), housing China's major trade and journalistic publishers and associated retailers, was located just behind the financial arsenals of the Bund and in the heart of the International Settlement of Shanghai.[8] The International Settlement, officially dated 1854–1943, formed a unique sovereign territory negotiated mainly among British, French, and U.S. officials. These governments intentionally designed the settlement to prevent the colonization of Shanghai, China's largest city and one of the world's largest ports, by a single Western imperialist force—also creating their own multinational settler government, the Shanghai Municipal Council (SMC), which formally excluded Chinese membership until 1928.[9] In this context, perhaps the bankrolls most succinctly illustrate further the material conditions of dependency of Qing rule on Western imperialists: the historian Christopher A. Reed finds that "between 1862 and 1905, seven foreign firms invested 3.9 million yuan in Shanghai's nascent machinery industry; in the same period, ninety-one Chinese firms invested no more than 87,000 yuan." Existing figures on printing machinery in Shanghai before 1930 reveal that an average of 76 percent was imported.[10]

As the modern Chinese print industry in the late nineteenth century thus effected, as it was effected by, processes of colonial settlement, land enclosure, privatization of the means of production, and competitive capitalist domination, efforts led by the British to build a modern postal system in China further concretized these developments. Prior to modernization, the postal system in China began with the establishment of government courier services dating to the Zhao dynasty (1122–255 B.C.E.). Originally called Yu or Youyi, this imperial postal system was reorganized during the Han dynasty (206 B.C.E.–23 C.E.) and renamed Yi Zhan. Yi Zhan integrated money courier services during the Tang dynasty (618–905 C.E.) and served as the government postal service in China until about 1914—delivering primarily government documents, letters, and military information. During a period of the Ming dynasty, sometime between 1402 and 1424, commercial need led to the emergence of private or unofficial postal institutions called *minchu*. For the next five hundred years, *minchu* served merchants, businessmen, and segments of the general population requiring postal services.[11]

Thus plans for a new postal system in China had far-reaching significance, operating as the means for massive physical, epistemological, and political alienation and conversion. That is, this comprehensive restructuring of land marked the very institutionalization of modern nation-state borders and colonial governmentality, as implementation mediated the dismantling of existing infrastructure and its replacement with a new state apparatus that would systematically reorganize and fix both space, through the creation of addresses, and time, through the standardization of scheduled delivery.[12] Qing government officials resisted the introduction of both modern postal and telegraphic technologies for as long as possible, since such technologies constituted the concrete *form* of colonialism and marked the ultimate political and economic demise of the dynasty. Specifically, representatives of the failing empire foresaw the perilous effects of Western control of modern technology within China, the flood of further concessions that would follow initial treaty negotiations for its development and use, and the amplification of precedents by which colonial forces demanded reparations from the Qing government for property damages exacted by anticolonial popular movements. For these same reasons, Robert Hart—a British official working in the Qing government as inspector general of imperial maritime customs— prioritized the modernization of the Chinese national post in 1861, contemporaneous with his role in establishing an illegal telegraph line operated from Shanghai to Wusong by the Great Northern Telegraph Company.[13] Hart's plans for the Chinese Maritime Customs Post, facing tremendous resistance, did not come to full fruition until its official opening on 20 March 1896; eventually evolving into the Chinese National Post based in Shanghai, the latter did not achieve full command until 1926, making the post office the last institution in China to become modernized.[14]

In this context, burgeoning scholarship to facilitate and rationalize such multinational colonial projects in East Asia precipitated an encounter between British and U.S. Orientalist formations and their historical suturing at this conjuncture. This shared ideological undertaking occurred precisely through narrative constructions of the Chinese "invention" of both paper and print, under the framework of "the four great inventions of ancient China," to socialize movements of enclosure and economic dependency. Beginning in 1859, foundations for this discourse were laid with the work of the British scholar and missionary Joseph Edkins, who sought to convince his readers that the opening of China would be "highly promising to western enterprise." Arguing that "in the practical qualities that constitute the greatness of a nation the Chinese are superior [to the Japanese and Hindoos]," Edkins's evidence for such an assertion includes the comparative claim that

Japan, unlike China, "can boast of no remarkable inventions and discoveries, such as printing, paper-making, the mariner's compass, and the composition of gunpowder."[15] Edkins's thesis was discovered and popularized in 1925 by Thomas Francis Carter, an American professor at Columbia University who served as a school superintendent in China from 1910 to 1925. Generating a universalized origin story about paper and print as articulated with technologies of navigation and warfare, Carter thus fully elaborates the discourse of "the four great inventions":

> Four great inventions that spread through Europe at the beginning of the Renaissance had a large share in creating the modern world. Paper and printing paved the way for the religious reformation and made possible popular education. Gunpowder leveled the feudal system and created citizen armies. The compass discovered America and made the world instead of Europe the theater for history. In these inventions and others as well, China claims to have had a conspicuous part. . . .
>
> The restlessness of the tribes of Central Asia during the early centuries of our era brought several hundred years of anarchy in China, corresponding to the Dark Ages in Europe; but as these barbarian migrations did not cause quite such a complete rooting up of classic civilization in Eastern Asia as they did in the West, China quickly recovered and was earlier ready for those inventions which came into Christendom with the beginning of the Renaissance. Marco Polo's record shows us a China whose civilization already in the thirteenth century had come to full bloom and had advanced very much further than that of contemporary Europe.[16]

Through a story of shared technology, this mythologizing narrative dispossesses "classic civilization in Eastern Asia" of historicity in order assimilate a fetishized Chinese past into the trajectory of Western imperialist conquest in the region. The discourse thus mediated, as it sanitized, the brutality characterizing contact between "East" and "West" in the Asian Pacific as it was in the context of coercion, warfare, and occupation that Carter concluded his 1925 study, *The Invention of Printing in China and Its Spread Westward,* "Ts'ai Lun [Chinese diety/mythic inventor of paper] and Gutenberg, spiritual father and spiritual son."[17] Such a formulation of civilized affinities, while erasing movements of colonial violence from public memory, also furnished justification for warfare against an ostensibly shared enemy of man—the latter constructed in negative contradiction through the ideology of "barbarian migrations." Ironically then, we shall soon see that the spiritual brethren that Anglos wanted to make in China are the very same as the barbarian migrations that Anglos wanted to destroy in California!

Ancient Chinese had an advanced understanding of the sciences of physics, engineering, chemistry and astronomy. Their numerous discoveries and inventions have shaped the development of science and impacted on human civilisations around the world. In this new series of stamps, "Four Great Inventions of Ancient China," Hong Kong Post showcases four revolutionary Chinese technologies—the compass, printing, gunpowder and papermaking. . . . These ancient inventions have profoundly changed the world since they emerged many centuries ago. The compass ushered in a brave new world of exploration and trade; the invention of gunpowder changed warfare tactics through the development of weaponry; and printing and papermaking facilitated the spreading of knowledge to lay the cornerstone for universal education.

HONG KONG POST, *18 August 2005*

Concurrent with this density of colonial pressures, the Qing government collapsed in the midst of widespread social movements—articulated along a variety of axes including economic, ethnic, and religious differences—that culminated in the Revolution of 1911.[18] Throughout the country, struggles for political dominance that characterized and followed the revolution forced the Imperialist Chinese bloc to restructure and, in efforts to retain state power and legitimacy under an unstable republican government, redraft a collective self in modern nationalist terms: more precisely, reimagining a popular supremacist identity through deployments of technological innovation. The latter refers both to the physical means of print production that the defunct Qing government still controlled relative to competing Chinese nationalist blocs and to the ideological content produced by the dominant intelligentsia.[19] That is, revised by nothing other than the intervention of Thomas Francis Carter, the release in China of *The Invention of Printing in China and Its Spread Westward* immediately moved Chinese imperialist discourse from a defensive to an agreeable position vis-à-vis competing ideologies with the West of world technological history; as Reed argues, "Convinced, even inspired, by Carter's argument that the source of one of the distinguishing technologies of Europe's modern period lay in China, the Chinese now began to lay emphasis on their country's central place in the world technological history in general and, more specifically, in printing history."[20] Hence, with the official Chinese appropriation of Carter's work, the banner "The Four Great Inventions of Ancient China" (*Zhong Guo si da fa ming*) became so pivotal to solidifying modern Chinese nationhood that it eventually formed part of the compulsory Chinese elementary school curriculum and as recently as 2008 provided a theme for the Beijing Summer Olympics.[21] In what might be considered more precisely here as "strategic Orientalism,"[22] the Imperialist Chinese bloc's authentication of Carter's claims thereby served to reassert the former's political viability in a mode that could appear consistent with the imperial tradition and referential universe and yet, mediated through an emergent discourse of the West, could also place imperial China in a modern planetary context that was becoming "global" through processes of racial capitalist domination. So animates a genealogy of quasi-antagonistic yet deeply cooperative multicultural histories of science and technology, wrapping around paper and print and ultimately interweaving to fortify both Western and Chinese imperialisms during a period of dramatic world-making and epic battles over the definitions of civilization.

Further changes in the ritualization of regional material cultures also significantly mediated this nationalist transformation, a perspective that somewhat inflects Benedict Anderson's well-received argument regarding the displacement of sacred value assigned to the word into the secularization of popular literacy in Europe.[23] That is, given, first, that *form* and proper performance of rites in China took precedent over their literal or written contents and, second, that rites created order in the world of men understood to correspond to the order of heaven, the historian Adam McKeown asserts that control over ritual practice mediated the articulation of imperial authority and/or local autonomy in rural Guangdong. This perspective on reforms to the proper performance of rites as helping to "bridge the gap between imperial ideology and local practices, creating a field within which differing interests could be articulated,"[24] provides additional context to understand the significance of legal prohibitions instituted against the selling and burning of incense, candles, and paper for god and ancestor worship at the turn of the twentieth century.[25] In this light, regulatory changes to ritual practice, as they reconfigure the formal aspects of both human and cosmological order, hence stand out as a primary mode of ideological conversion attendant on geopolitical struggles taking place in the broader landscape. As such, these struggles ultimately crystallize the social, material, and ontological significance invested in the meaning and uses of paper at this time.

At the national scale, then, other historical formations—namely, the Nationalist Party and emergent Communist blocs—also struggled through nascent print culture to organize political identities. First, between 1900 and the late 1920s, the Nationalist Party under Sun Yatsen, as well as student movements both aligned and not aligned with the Nationalist Party, actively sought to unify the peoples of China by adapting forms of modern nationalism and nation-statecraft to which they had become exposed in the university and through international student exchange. Democratic experiments within the print industry and transformations in aesthetic practices and values—as instantiated by the 1915–21 New Culture Movement, its response to the Treaty of Versailles and revolutionizing of conservative literary conventions with vernacular styles—played a central role in these efforts to produce a contending Chinese nationalism and to socialize it as a democratic Chinese nationality. Likewise, an emergent Communist bloc began to organize at the level of the "print proletarians," launching revolutionary print worker strikes starting in the 1910s.[26]

Regionally, migrant communities from the southern province of Guangdong found themselves at the intersections and margins and in the heart of this varied Imperialist, Nationalist Party, and Communist organizing, and the particular articulation of political power and identity in this region wove together aspects of disparate elements. Geopolitically, local organizations in Guangdong were uniquely positioned to incorporate aspects of Western capitalism into their national capitalist practices, aspects of Nationalist Party nationalism into their ideological practices, and aspects of Qing order into their political practices.[27] Situated away from the concentration of political organizing happening farther north—in the biggest cities, dominant industries, and major universities—Guangdong also served as a primary nodal point for colonial activities, located adjacent to British-occupied Hong Kong and Portuguese-occupied Macao and harboring four coveted port cities—Canton, Swatow, Hoihow, and Pakhoi (pinyin: Guangzhou, Shantou, Haikou, and Behai)—that were settled by capitalists, bureaucrats, and Christian missionaries primarily from Britain, France, Germany, and the United States. Guangdong also served as an early hub of Sun Yatsen's Nationalist Party activities and was the site of China's first labor union, the Society for the Study of Machines, organized by engineering mechanics in 1909.[28]

The articulation of opportunity, rather than of disorder or poverty, thus better explains the concentration of people migrating specifically from this region: that is, from areas surrounding Hong Kong and in close proximity to Anglo settler states, including Australia, Canada, and California.[29] On the one hand, as long-standing host to global commercial maritime activity, Guangdong served as a prime marketplace for the mid-nineteenth-century British "coolie trade," further developing into more complex systems of international labor brokerage by the turn of the century.[30] On the other hand, the proliferation of modern print culture placed Guangdong in the center of new and dynamic flows of both people and information, facilitated predominantly by a globalized postal system. Specifically, in the context of Anglo domination in the U.S. West by the mid-nineteenth century, representatives of western U.S. railroad companies and western state immigration commissions—those whom Oscar O. Winther calls the "agents of the West"—began distributing literatures throughout the Anglo diaspora promoting migration and settlement. These promotional materials included "correspondence, special crop exhibits, newspaper advertisements, small circulars, large posters, two-color handbills, photographs, maps, brochures, and various combinations of the same,"[31] and arose alongside the establishment of three major daily English-language newspapers serving the Anglo population in Hong Kong.[32] In addition to the labor recruitment circulars distributed by the same "agents of the West" to communities in southern China and the growing networks of personal letters and word of mouth among Chinese migrant communities, an abundance of information thus circulated through globalized infrastructures to create a communication bridge between Guangdong and the American West.[33] These circumstances would further stimulate migration between these regions and fundamentally transform the organization of social life throughout the Pacific.

RACE; OR, THE AMERICAN DREAM

In the U.S. western settler colonial context, concurrent expansions of modern technological and epistemological infrastructures laid the foundations for integrating California into the struggling U.S. nation-state following the 1848 Treaty of Guadalupe-Hidalgo.[34] These developments illustrate adjoining methods of U.S. empire building across the Pacific, as well as the interarticulation of regional racial capitalist regimes and, finally, the contradictory role of Chinese labor at the conflicted interstices of these processes. The conquest of California, formalized in 1848 and followed by statehood in 1850, occurred as dominant historical blocs in the United States struggled to resolve internal ideological and logistical crises regarding organizations of land, labor, capital, and state capacity.[35] In these years preceding the Civil War, antagonistic Democratic and Republican blocs nevertheless shared one commonality across otherwise growing irreconcilable differences: the will to occupy California and the West based on an epistemological fabrication of whiteness as divine right underlying Manifest Destiny.[36] In particular, the Union-Republican Party advanced the Free Soil Movement, arguing for the abolition of slavery as a means to secure the full emancipation of workers—the latter class articulated through whiteness as the universalized measure of humanity and social purity. Under this worldview, Anglos imagined California as a "white-only" Eden for an ascendant Euro-American middle class.[37]

As the Free Soil Movement seized control of the U.S. government in 1854, the same year that the United States co-pioneered the International Settlement of Shanghai, concurrent development of transportation and communication systems in the American West demonstrates the interconnectedness of international and domestic constructions of U.S. imperialist infrastructure and overlapping techniques of domination and settlement.[38] That is, just as Western Allied Forces wrestled for control over modern statecraft in China, development of the transcontinental railroad, telegraph, and postal systems—forming as well as formed by the bond between capital and state interests—also articulated the United States following the occupation of the American West and reconstituted the Union following the U.S. Civil War. A 1904 retrospective in *Harper's Monthly Magazine,* for instance, reported on construction of the first U.S. transcontinental railroad:

> The building of a Pacific road had every war argument in its favor. Such a line, it was urged, would bind California more closely to the Northern interest, and would enable the United States more promptly to repel any attack on the coast ports. Moreover, it would enable the government easily to control Indian outbreaks. . . .
>
> The very name used by Congress in creating the corporation, "The Union Pacific Railroad Company," implies a reflection of the Union sentiment of the civil-war period. The use of the word has been ascribed to the "union" of various corporations and plans in the project. But there is undoubtedly more than this to it. By far the most powerful arguments in favor of the road were the war needs of the government.[39]

Critical scholarship on this topic of U.S. railroad history has demonstrated how struggles to build the first transcontinental railroad mediated negotiations of the role that technology and industrial capitalism would play in the development of the West, both regionally and in global context.[40] Solidifying the enmeshment of corporate and government corruption in the forging of U.S. monopoly capitalism, construction of the railroad also facilitated regional American Indian removal and Anglo settlement while establishing national ties between otherwise competing capitalist interests across commerce, industry, and agriculture. Hence building and bonding different movements of racialized settlement and capital accumulation in the U.S. North, South, and emergent West, the first transcontinental railroad was finished in 1869 by joining the Union Pacific and Central Pacific Railroad lines, the latter half built by Chinese labor.

In these regards, as technological infrastructure networked regional political economies, attendant developments in epistemological infrastructure elaborated their respective racial regimes as the modality of organizing economic and civic life and, specific to the American West, outlined the role that Chinese labor would fill in the expansion of racial capitalism. While logics of white supremacy rationalized U.S. wars of occupation across all scales, processes of U.S. labor differentiation along the axis of ethnoracial distinction varied by region, structured by specificities of ideological articulation at particular historical and geographic conjunctures. Namely, in the decades following the Civil War, the imperatives of colonial settlement, capital accumulation, and racial ideological production differed in the U.S. South and West even as they shared key general tendencies.[41] On the one hand, reconsolidation of planter power in the South depended on movements to restructure the systematic dismantling of African American communities through economic and political disfranchisement alongside rampant state and civil violence.[42] These activities aimed to solve the problem, as the planter William M. Burwell stated it in 1869, of how "to retain in the hands of whites the control and direction of social and political action, without impairing the content of the labor capacity of the colored race."[43] As the triumph of the Free Soil Movement also functioned to exclude African Americans from westward migration, the overthrow of radical Reconstruction hence pummeled African Americans "back toward slavery"[44] vis-à-vis structural apartheid and death-inducing exploitation within reconstructed plantation regimes.[45]

As Clyde Woods argues, the "representational grid" facilitating these movements at the turn of the twentieth century was largely innovated by the rise of the social science disciplines and the national prominence of plantation bloc scholars such as the sociologists Alfred Holt Stone and Howard Odum. For example, Odum, the "father of regionalism" and a founding scholar of Blues criticism, investigated African American musical forms as "the superlative of the repulsive" epitomizing African Americans "as the embodiment of fiendish filth incarnated in the tabernacle of the soul."[46] Such developments in scholarship and cultural production socialized theories of African American barbarism and inferiority, "white" unity and supremacy, and mythic paternalism aimed at convincing audiences that any form of African American autonomy would end in tragedy or disaster without close supervision by white supremacist blocs. This ideological exertion straddled theological, scientific, and cultural race concepts and solidified intellectual foundations for the complex evolution of academic discourses of Blackness as "social death."[47]

On the other hand, if the dominance of Jim Crow ended the question of Chinese labor recruitment in the South, it conversely amplified the question of Chinese recruitment in the West.[48] That is, the isolation of African American working classes—forced into sharecropping as the primary mode of capital accumulation in the South—marked one of many factors contextualizing the social positioning of Chinese migrants in the West as a labor force both structuring and disciplining the region's Euro-American class stratifications, the latter ideologically arranged through "whiteness" as a category of existence. Chinese labor recruitment also unfolded during transformations in race-class structures in the American West as occupying forces in the territory shifted from Mexican to U.S. state control following the 1848 Treaty of Guadalupe-Hidalgo. In this context, U.S. developers worked to neutralize American Indian populations through death, dispossession, and/or forced assimilation while more ambiguously repositioning Mexican nationals through the terms of the treaty. Landholding elites who claimed European ancestry and human reason (*gente de razón*) were legally recognized as "white," a tentative albeit privileged racial ascription that nevertheless occurred alongside massive land dispossession and ownership transfers. Working-class populations, despite formal entitlement to U.S. citizenship, remained racially and economically alienated as Anglo settlers strategized to keep territorially colonized populations small in number and isolated in the most subordinate economic and geographic sectors.[49] In sum, these circumstances thus created openings in the regional capitalist labor market that, through the 1910s and 1920s, found its complement in trans-Pacific migrations.

Under these conditions, capitalist recruitment of Chinese labor in the new West only deepened contradictions between the U.S. Constitution, colonial genocide, and slavery in the mid- and late nineteenth century as the incorporation of Chinese labor intensified rather than resolved racialized crisis.[50] Existing research has well established how ideological productions of Chinese working classes as this time and place's racial Other mobilized and disciplined Euro-American working classes as "white" through popular anti-Chinese sentiment and violence. The hegemony of negative racial ascriptions of Chinese barbarism and criminality along the U.S. Pacific Coast, contemporaneous with positive racial ascriptions of Chinese cultivation and reason in the East Asian Pacific, thus illuminates the inconsistencies embedded in negotiating the often conflicting ideological demands of U.S. Pacific expansion and domestic containment.[51] In the latter regard, and in the context of Chinese migrants' marginal economic enfranchisement as labor source for racial capitalist development, anti-Chinese ideological production also rationalized official movements to subordinate Chinese in racial terms through political exclusion. Logics of exclusion displaced the irreconcilability of democracy and capitalism—as well as conflicting processes of national homogenization and capitalist labor differentiation—through the legislation of a structuring erasure.[52]

As Mark V. Cushman has demonstrated, emergent measures targeting Chinese were grounded in legal, administrative, and discursive precedents established through the legislation of fugitive slave laws, as the latter instituted legal doctrine for the formal demarcation of excludable persons and the jurisdiction of the federal government over state governments to administer migration policy and control. In this context, congressional debates over the citizenship status of freed African Americans vis à vis ratification of the Civil Rights Act of 1866 and the Fourteenth Amendment were directly triangulated with pending decisions about the ambiguous naturalization rights of Chinese and Native Americans in the new West. Ultimately pivoting around an interpretation of the Fourteenth Amendment's definition of a citizen as one who is "subject to the jurisdiction thereof," the prevailing logic regarding both Chinese and Native Americans posited that each group's ties to an asserted sovereign nation, to whose jurisdiction they could also be subject, rendered them excludable from citizenship.[53] Hence formalizing this constitutional resolution to the Chinese problem, the Page Act of 1875 banned working-class Chinese women from entry into the United States, paving the way for the Chinese Exclusion Act of 1882.

Given different techniques to administer exclusion again developed from slavery and colonialism, by the Chinese Exclusion era, dominant U.S. blocs drew from multiple methods to subordinate Chinese migrants vis-à-vis racialized political disfranchisement, with a primary set of tools relying precisely on the uses and power of the literary. During and after slavery in the South, for instance, these precedents included legal prohibitions on African American literacy and, in the postbellum period, the subsequent institution of literacy tests as a requirement to vote.[54] The latter form of political disfranchisement functioned alongside the persistent and active underdevelopment and racial segregation of postbellum educational institutions to resecure planter hegemony.[55] Precedents established by colonial practices under Manifest Destiny, on the other hand, involved the use of *positive* coercive force as Anglo American missionaries taught English literacy skills to American Indians on reservations beginning in 1869 and in off-reservation schools beginning in 1879.[56] Such training involved the coordinated kidnapping of Indian children for forced attendance at boarding schools and aimed to dismantle indigenous knowledge systems and social cohesion. By the 1880s, Euro-American groups such as Friends of the Indians worked contemporaneously with the U.S. Bureau of Indian Affairs reform programs, structured after the British colonial model of indirect rule, to bring "savage-born" American Indians "under the civilizing influence of the law."[57]

Entangled with these histories, the placement of Chinese laborers in the Union's expanding racial-ideological milieu, correlated with the specific imperatives of U.S. capitalist expansion in the West, thus created both the urgency and the opportunity to refine existing techniques of control in the application of positive and negative methods simultaneously. Namely, by the early twentieth century, the regulation of Chinese migrants included both English literacy tests as a requirement to enter the United States starting in 1917[58] and the presence of civilizing activity in California Chinatowns and ports of entry, the latter primarily targeting Chinese women.[59] In these ways, the deepening institutionalization of literacy socialized as well as enforced an epistemology of whiteness in the language of humanism. Moreover, such cultural activity formed part of more comprehensive systems of administration, expanded both to legitimate and to document the boundaries of Western imperialist civilization and its eligible members as citizen-subjects.[60] As such, global developments in immigration as a bureaucratic state apparatus thus solidified a worldwide infrastructure for the production and regulation of the "free" self-determining individual: a regime of "universal rights" and human identification scaffolding and scaffolded by ongoing forms of social dismantling and erasure.

DETAINED

As Chinese working classes embodied the necessary difference that had to be erased in order to reproduce the nation, physical methods to enforce exclusion also drew from precedents in U.S. spatial organization that marshaled regional technology and planning to control dynamics of racialized movement and confinement. In this regard, I have already alluded to a core contradiction of racialized movement at this time and place as developers of the West recruited Chinese labor precisely to help build the central communication and transportation infrastructure comprising the nation-state. Such a cruel irony of racial capitalism, wherein subordinated groups labor to build the mechanisms mobilized for their own exploitation, also carried over to the relationship specifically between Chinese people and U.S. postal technologies during this period. That is, in addition to transporting the letters of the diaspora, the primary role of U.S. postal cargo ships was to carry Chinese migrants themselves to the United States. Travel arrangements were made by what were called "steering companies," or *jinshanzhuang* (Gold Mountain firms), operated on both formal and informal bases by Chinese merchants.[61] The use of U.S. and British cargo ships reflected the dominance of Western capital over a nascent Chinese national proto-capitalism that could not yet accumulate enough wealth to finance its own national steamship company.[62] Furthermore, leading to the passage of the Page Act, the California state commissioner of immigration held the Pacific Mail Steamship Company responsible either to deport or to post the $500 bond per woman for Chinese women, classified as prostitutes by statute, arriving at the San Francisco port of entry.[63] For the majority of Chinese migrants who disembarked between 1875 and 1910, the converted two-story shed at the Pacific Mail Steamship Company wharf served as detention cells under the Exclusion Acts until the opening of Angel Island.[64]

This history thus illuminates new aspects of how, quite literally, the productive apparatuses defining nation-state boundaries, government, and civility are the very same as those orchestrating racialized exclusion and confinement, making the latter not accidental but innate to U.S. democracy and capitalism and constitutive of their modes of global development. From this perspective, the ascent and global hegemony of the U.S. carceral system must be understood in the context of U.S. imperialist expansion alongside the domestic reforms of and following Reconstruction. In this light, while inseparable from historical precedents, the structural foundations for mass incarceration were deeply connected to yet *distinct* from the economic order that organized—and the political, social, and spatial orders that rationalized—pre–Civil War genocides of U.S. plantation slavery and settler colonialism. That is, rather than to restore and reproduce previous orders exactly, the burgeoning "prison industrial complex" emerged to address and control qualitatively new social conditions and to meet qualitatively new social demands. Hence, as Ruth Wilson Gilmore argues, under the extremities of crisis and the necessary reconfiguration of defunct U.S. regimes of apartheid and accumulation,

> Jim Crow, then, did not only work to suppress Black people; it was both template and caution for all who were not members of the sovereign race. [The nineteenth] century's globalizing contradictions, characterized by indigenous exterminations, wars of territorial expansion, socio-spatial segregation, racist science and eugenics, the redrawing of the world's imperial contours, and the spread of democratized blood-and-soil nationalism, coalesced at the time of the 1898 Spanish-American war, and these forces in sum gave both political and theoretical shape to the twentieth century's continuing human-sacrifice rampage.[65]

Such an explanation of mass incarceration in the United States, as a mode of organizing all of civic life, stretches across regional and global scales of analysis and locates its emergence in the context of progressive racial capitalist movement as much as in the tendencies of reactionary conservatism. Moreover, through this lens, the conditions of carceral state development specific to the American West come into clearer view as the long-wave conjoining of multiple paradigms of racialized confinement: the globalization of borders—historically innovated through plantation and reservation regimes—that in the *particular* social and geographic articulations of the Western region further developed primarily in and through the form of Immigration rather than the strictest sense of "crime" control.[66]

In the specific context of trans-Pacific migrations and U.S. law enforcement, then, the construction of Angel Island served as a geographic resolution to neutralize the perpetual problems of social and political-economic crisis at this time and place, initiating the physical isolation of people whose presence would otherwise rupture fantasies of both capitalism and whiteness as humanly sustainable. Furthermore, Angel Island's opening in 1910 signaled the intensification of a new regime of policing and detention that harnessed the potential and use of new fingerprinting and photographic technologies, as well as extensive medical exams and subjective interrogations, to build the regulatory force of racial state bureaucracy.[67] Immigration officials held Chinese migrants at Angel Island while administering the process of entry or denial precisely because of its isolated island location—modeled after the Alcatraz Island prison—that enforced the terms of the nation while suppressing the communication and sociality of those detained. Writing on the walls of Angel Island through the 1910s thus posed the existential dilemma of whether the wars migrants had just left in Guangdong were preferable to the ones they found in California. Stripped of their belongings, anonymous migrants collectively wrote poetry on the walls of their detention units, one of which Him Mark Lai and Genny Lim have translated as follows:

> I am distressed that we Chinese are detained in this wooden building.
> It is actually racial barriers which cause difficulties on Yingtai Island.
> Even when they are tyrannical, they still claim to be humanitarian.
> I should regret my taking the risks of coming in the first place.[68]

Indeed, "racial barriers"—physical and epistemological, local and global, "tyrannical" and "humanitarian"—significantly structured migrants' life possibilities at this time. These barriers, whose fuller trans-Pacific architecture and articulations I have traced in this chapter, established the boundaries both constraining and conditioning the diaspora's own literary production at this time. Finally, then, inside the heat of such dense global struggles to direct the course of human civilization as such, it is this latter life of paper to which we will now turn.

TWO

———

*Imagined Genealogies (for All Who
Cannot Arrive)*

THE CHINESE EXCLUSION ACT, in place from 1882 to 1943, barred all
working-class people from China from legal U.S. immigration; further legislation established exceptions and specific regulations for the legal entry of
Chinese merchant and educated classes and allowed those legal migrants to
petition for the entry of certain members of their families. These limits and
the historical matrix grounding them thus contextualized the conditions of
possibility for the phenomenon of "paper sons" or "paper families": the elaborate systems that Chinese diasporic communities designed to facilitate legal
migration by inventing kinship "slots" in the families of legal categories of
migrants. Essentially, making paper families entailed selling or fabricating
identification and bureaucratic paperwork to pass an illegal migrant off as the
kin, usually a son, of a legal migrant, and then to secure his legal entry. While
the social and economic networks forming paper families began to evolve by
the 1880s and 1890s, the networks proliferated after the 1906 San Francisco
earthquake, when fires destroyed most Pacific Coast immigration archives
and thus created opportunities, literally, to make people up.

This chapter, then, focuses on the production of paper families as they
were mediated through letters of the detained. I explore how the life of paper
emerged within, while it also enacted, structural transformations across
space. The chapter begins with a reexamination of technological changes to
illustrate how the life of paper articulated a distinctive regional geography
that diverged from the Eurocentric telos of modern development. Next, it
investigates the ways that the production of "coaching letters," or documents
educating people on how to "pass" Immigration interrogations, elaborated
new epistemological terrains. That is, this section interrogates how the act of
ordering and representing knowledge on paper forced a confrontation

between different systems of thought that transformed what, and how, people thought of themselves and the world. Last, a series of close readings demonstrates transformations in social structures occurring through the life of paper and returns to the essential point: such movements, articulated through epistolarity, constitute a creative reinvention of human connectivity under the constraints of racialized alienation and confinement—a poetics, or process of collective self-making, producing an unapparent place *inside* and *between* material realities to sustain possibilities for social life in the midst of crisis.

POST(AL) WARS

A closer look at the postal infrastructure connecting the Chinese diaspora reveals the technological idiosyncrasies of this life of paper, conditioned by the development of modern postal infrastructures in both China and the United States that, as argued in chapter 1, solidified military conquests in respective nation-state formations. Caught in this global milieu, diasporic postal networks based in Hong Kong proliferated by uniquely mobilizing the technological resources from *multiple* places, making the surrounding context crucial to understanding how these businesses grew. I follow Chi-Ming Hou's argument:

> It would be interesting and useful to study, perhaps through the channels of transportation and communication, the steps in which modern economic activity impinged upon the life of various zones of [China] from the middle of the nineteenth century. The indigenous response to modern development might be better understood by examining the changes, if any, in attitudes and institutions in areas where foreign and Chinese merchants tried to secure their desired raw materials, such as cotton.[1]

Particular to this case, in which foreign and Chinese merchants dealt in the business of human immigration, associated "attitudes" and "desired raw materials" take on particularly significant meanings at the boundaries of commodity production as the production of history. At this impasse, as working-class Chinese communities were differently marginalized from dominant movements and institutions in both China and the United States, the trans-Pacific postal systems and businesses developed by Chinese merchants capitalized on the burdens of modern technology that migrants faced.

FIGURE 5. Envelope processed through *minchu;* Folder 4 of Box 1, Entry 232; Densmore Investigation Files, RG 85; NARA–Pacific Region (SF).

Recall from chapter 1 that Robert Hart's plan to implement a modern postal infrastructure in China, initiated in 1861, required dismantling both the long-standing I Chan system serving the imperialist Chinese government and the unofficial *minchu* institutions serving commercial and civic sectors. According to C. W. Dougan, the three dominant sources of opposition to Hart's Imperial Customs Post were high officials against the suppression of the I Chan; commercial and letter-writing Chinese nationalists loyal to the *minchu;* and foreign post offices, which paid for overseas transport of mails and did not trust Chinese governmental postal services for local turnover.[2] John L. Fairbank notes that as these struggles unfolded, starting in the late nineteenth century and at the height of postal modernization efforts, there also occurred a seemingly counterintuitive proliferation of the traditional *minchu.*[3] While he and Dougan both argue that this proliferation constituted an oppositional movement against the colonial forces infiltrating the Chinese government, I attribute this too to the vexed interdependence between Chinese merchant and migrant working-classes emerging in this context: the former finding lucrative business opportunities facilitating the mobility and communication of the latter. In this sense, migrant mail businesses, evolving out of the *minchu* and serving the Chinese diaspora during the Exclusion period, functioned as a response and an alternative to the postal wars—as migrant communities belonged to both and neither and were literally caught between struggles in the dominant landscapes.

Discernible details about this diasporic postal system suggest an organizational and economic structure drawing, yet distinct, from dominant forms emerging in both the United States and China at the national scales. The envelope shown in figure 5, for example, with the merchant's stamp in the upper left-hand side, illustrates the *minchu*'s specialized capacity at this time to mitigate the substantive difference between Chinese and U.S. postal/address systems in order to facilitate delivery. Furthermore, an excerpt from the translation of "Letter #18" (figure 6) alludes to at least three key points about postal operations.

San Kai Kak, Lungdo, Hongshang,
Canton, China, C.R. 6–9–6 (new cal.)

Letter #18.
(September 6, 1917).

Mr. Lau Pock Toon (L.D. Sing),
1631 Fillmore Street,
San Francisco, Cal.

Dear eldest Brother:
Your letters #21 and #22 have been received and contents noted. I have shown your letters to Mr. -?- Chee Chew and talked with him personally on the matter. But he said the time was too short, as the steamer Shinyo Maru sailed only 5 or 6 days after your letter #21 was received. In view of the fact that there was danger to travel on such steamers (probably referring to danger of being attacked by enemy raider), Mr. Chee Chew said that he had to consult with his family again. Then I went to see the old customers who had wanted to come to the United States, but they also said that the time was rather short and they had to have some time to raise the money. These people, however, said that they would see me again later.

As your instruction cannot be carried out on this steamer and since Mr. Liu —————— is soon to proceed to the United States, I have put off my other duties and have come to Hong Kong to see him personally about the matter, so that the scheme may be carried out by the next steamer. Mr. Liu and I have talked over and agreed on the different points you wrote about in your letters. But he requires $300 (Hongkong) in advance (in each case) and a responsible merchant to guarantee (the payment of the balance); and these conditions must be agreed upon by both parties (the steering party and the steered party).

First, methods of payment, both for migration services in general and for postal services in particular, were flexible and varied. Consistent with this merchant's attention to the specific financial situation of his customer, other methods of payment for *minchu* services included split payments by multiple parties, payments upon delivery, advanced payments with fee waivers, account passbooks, and fixed sum per annum. In addition, Ying-Wan Cheng has found that "it was not unusual that the relationship between the [*minchu*] and their clients rested more or less on a personal basis. . . . [A]gencies tried their best to meet the requirements of their clients and, in the face of keen competition, offered all kinds of inducements to retain their patronage."[4]

Second, the multiple channels of information indicated in Letter #18, both personal and business, also allude to the social "mix" that the *minchu* helped network. In fact, the *minchu* coordinated a variety of institutions and parties across land and sea. A generalizable pattern of organization that Cheng found, for instance, starts with a clan leader or "headman" who collected and bundled all the letters of a migrant group and sent them through the post office of the "host" country to a letter merchant or *minchu* in southern China—usually eventually transferred either to Amoy in Fujian province or Swatow in Guangdong province. Individuals or *minchu* agents then hand-delivered the letters, many including money remittances, to recipients in the surrounding villages. In these regards, despite general reliability of the *minchu* to secure delivery, such routines could create consequential temporal lags in letter sending and receiving. For example, details in Letter #18 point out the challenges of planning around unpredictable delivery times as the latter also needed to be coordinated with steamship schedules in order to secure migration.

The diasporic postal network thus gave shape to an emergent geography as well as a distinct political economy of migration based on the reinvention of existing postal forms. In this light, the persistence rather than assumed obsolescence of older technologies illustrates how the homogenizing tendencies of Western capitalism must be understood alongside processes of differentiation and uneven development, which, as many scholars of have already argued, can create unpredicted and underrecognized sites of social formation.[5] Moreover, this postal history provides glimpses into how an emergent diasporic Chinese merchant-capitalist class articulated itself within a superstructure of global crisis and opportunity, as dominant modes of capital accumulation shifted during this period from labor extraction to what Adam

Letter #18.

San Kai Kak, Lungdo, Hongshang,
Canton, China, C.R.6-9-6(new cal.)
(September 6, 1917).

Mr. Lau Pock Toon (L. D. Sing),
    1631 Fillmore Street,
        San Francisco, Cal.

Dear eldest Brother:

Your letters #21 and #22 have been received and contents noted. I have shown your letters to Mr. -?- Chee Chew and talked with him personally on the matter. But he said the time was too short, as the steamer Shinyo Maru sailed only 5 or 6 days after your letter #21 was received. In view of the fact that there was danger to travel on such steamers (probably referring to danger of being attacked by enemy raider), Mr. Chee Chew said that he had to consult with his family again. Then I went to see the old customers who had wanted to come to the United States, but they also said that the time was rather short and they had to have some time to raise the money. These people, however, said that they would see me again later.

As your instruction cannot be carried out on this steamer and since Mr. Liu ---- ---- is soon to proceed to the United States, I have put off my other duties and have come to Hong Kong to see him personally about the matter, so that the scheme may be carried out by the next steamer. Mr. Liu and I have talked over and agreed on the different points you wrote about in your letters. But he requires $300 (Hongkong) in advance (in each case) and a responsible merchant to guarantee (the payment of the balance); and these conditions must be agreed upon by both parties (the steering party and the steered party).

FIGURES 6 and 7. Excerpt from Lau Sai Jan to Lau Pock Toon, ca. 6 September 1917 (translation by Immigration interpreter H. K. Tang and original letter); Folder 7 of Box 1, Entry 232; Densmore Investigation Files, RG 85; NARA–Pacific Region (SF).

收安復扶動念、李風階寄回滙單說陸帝一百員另文定等回訓神

及蒙資共其區單一托仲港帝陸扥費均經代寄收回照信委交矣人

收入矣統扥金便呈持致李風階君知之事盼惟近二月內陸帝每

竹之補水四元成妃左右火鑒每元找有臺十三元真有天壤之別仍此情形、

陸帝每手補水百餘元每舍伯找有臺十三元真有天壤之別仍此情形、

省臺回興港帝平換前用銀帝交易貿誠不值笑、

廣東省長李雅漢已於本月五陸接即視事惟省中駐軍隊松乏餉難、

滇軍久欲出菨援湘兩陸鷾廷絢械又菨之製时故滇軍收士有牌肉之

漢理軍政存山擊援中山為大元帥陸榮廷完先為元帥舟瑞狼把桅

有人或云困見沉沒也、

袁喪復任為香山統汝寺於省城興我都地方此連之虞成兵築壘防禦

我都一若此臨大廠左乃政村陸人民又興風鶴之漢、庸人自援地菨一

嘘、

昨聞廣華之狂棣等、因病身故深為惋惜、但現在扑妲如何、便祈

為我道信子廣華之三兄四足接的、森葉振告棣等身故情狀祖為領

McKeown has characterized as control over networks.[6] In other words, we might view hegemonic tendencies of accumulation in the mid- and late nineteenth century as transitioning from capital generated through the control and exploitation of labor needed to build capitalist infrastructure to capital harnessed from the infrastructural organization and control of production and social reproduction. In this context, the case of diasporic postal networks presents a cogent example of how Chinese merchants participated in capitalist expansion in the region through articulations that were neither merely mimetic or epiphenomenal to Western capitalism nor shaped only in accordance with the latter's needs.

MAKING (FAMILY) TREES FROM PAPER

Indeed, the diasporic postal system cohered an extended infrastructure necessary for the production of paper families, the latter mediated through vast networks that included systematized citizenship brokerage operations called *jinshanzhuang* (*gam saan jong,* or Gold Mountain firms, in Cantonese). Mostly centered in Hong Kong, such firms managed the major steps in forming paper families, from matching suppliers and buyers of kinship slots to securing successful entry through the rigors of U.S. Immigration enforcement.[7] Precisely because the growth of this enterprise correlated directly with the elaboration of U.S. state bureaucracy vis-à-vis Immigration policy and practice, the "migration business" thus also coordinated a widening variety of other physical and intellectual activities in dialectic with the system it aimed to navigate and, in a complex antagonism, also helped to create.[8]

For instance, the anonymous letter by "afraid to show his right name" at the start of part 1 (see figure 2) mentions schools that opened in Hong Kong to train its students for immigration. The Densmore Investigation, commissioned by the U.S. government in 1915 to control the production of paper families, uncovered other components of the operation such as the recruitment of Chinese translators who, in their official employment as interpreters for U.S. Immigration, accepted bribes to communicate scripted answers in English during oral interrogation or in written transcription. The Investigation also documented other related roles, including people paid to play the parts of witnesses or substitute translators in the theater of interrogation, as well as those working in other capacities within the U.S. government itself—in positions ranging from stenographers to investigators in the upper echelons of administration—who exchanged with Chinese migration businesses. In order to access further the various types of paperwork on which successful legal entry depended, migration businesses also worked with janitors, electricians, plumbers, and night watchmen who helped steal and/or doctor necessary documents, in addition to prison guards who accepted payments to deliver goods and coaching letters to the Detained.[9]

The composition of coaching letters themselves further involved intricate processes of knowledge production constitutive of community development, race, space, and subjectivity, as successful legal entry required "passing" *through* the technologies that Immigration inspectors used to test the integrity of asserted identities.[10] The collective labor of writing coaching letters thus entailed the study of methods and practices of U.S. interrogation in order to deduce probable questions and script acceptable responses. This information was produced and delivered in the form of coaching letters to detained migrants, who memorized the letters and then destroyed them. As the scrutiny of questions comprising interrogation grew more intense, precisely in reaction to the activities of this life of paper, the need for research also grew. Merchants, migrants, and their families trained themselves in basic methods of the modern social sciences in order to meet the demands of "study" for the high-stakes test.

In these ways, coaching letters evidence how Chinese migrant communities' shifting worldviews were shaped by the exigencies of the U.S. Immigration process—the latter not only a practice of material and physical constraint, but one that enforced a particular epistemology. Yet dramatic changes in diasporic knowledge production—manifest in and through coaching letters—were not merely wholesale conscriptions to dominant understandings of subjectivity, identity, history, or geography but rather delimitations of the struggles and negotiations that Chinese migrants had to perform in order to fit their lives into national epistemic demands.[11] Through this lens, further insights into the production of coaching letters can thus illuminate how, even as migrants faced interrogation alone, they articulated themselves through a collective labor in which the effects of a "self" can only be understood in and as a set of relations among others.

A closer reading of coaching letters illustrates these points and crystallizes how the immigration "fraud" produced new meanings and realities, born on paper. The coaching letter shown in figures 8 and 9 represents a standard communication. On the one hand, it conveys the objective information that a paper son needed to learn in order to become his new self, under circumstances in which the form of the interrogation significantly conditioned and structured the possibilities of the response and thus bore urgently on how and whom people trained themselves to become. The imperative to know documentary family narratives, as well as seemingly inane details such as "the location of toilet houses," disciplined and forced people to live under extreme duress, needing to account for every fact of their (paper) lives.

[*Handwriting:* "L" Exhibit 10]

Find out the name and age of the maternal grandfather, and also the name of his village.

Find out the name and age of the maternal grandmother, and whether she has natural feet.

Find out how far is the maternal grandparents' village form our village, and whether my brothers and I have ever been there.

Find out the location of the village alter in the (or our) village.

Find out the style of building of the Ngee Ging ancestral hall,— whether it has a front entrance.

Find out: location of toilet houses in the (or our) village; location of cemetery and how far it is from the (or our) village.

Make out a check in favor of Hang On Hai for the steamer passage.

Write a letter to Yip Chuck and send it back together with his address.

Please take this matter up with my brother at once and send it (probably referring to coaching paper and affidavit) back to me. In doing things we should be on the safe side so as to avoid trouble.

Tell Sing (probably referring to Yip Sing) to come over to my place tomorrow night and go over the testimony together and see if it is all right and then send it back right away.

(Translated by H. K. Tang, 12/8/24.)

Yet under this pressure, what Lisa Lowe calls "sedimented sites of collective memory" also emerged.[12] For example, the conclusion reads, "Tell Sing to come to my place tomorrow night and go over the testimony together and see if it is all right and then send it back right away." This instruction gestures to sustained socialities that developed as part of the process of making paper families, fomented by new human information circuits and shared time and energy rehearsing and revising scripts. In this latter regard, such letters—in ways perhaps comparable to yet distinct from the epistolary novel—also give us a different lens with which to approach broader questions central to the study of *all* literatures, such as authorship, authenticity, voice, plot structure, and the role of literature to give shape to history.[13] That is, coaching letters instantiated acts of *collective* writing: the social negotiation of imagination, consent, and performance to produce as well as to embody a text whose coherence is both fabricated and real, singular and many, composed yet unfinished. Moreover, coaching letters evidence how naturalized ideologies of liberal individualism stemmed from movements of "racial" alienation that made possible a particular definition of human being. Yet the deliberate appropriation of the latter through coaching letters does not effect the actual atomization of a modern citizen-subject so much as constitute a testament to the vigor of social practice and collective labor to produce its form of appearance.

Figure 10 takes a step further, *visually* representing both family/village genealogies and their physical geography.[14] This diagram of a Chinese village, conventionally organized by kinship clans, exteriorizes changes happening in migrants' "cognitive maps."[15] That is, the epistemological constraints of Western history and geography that discursively structured the questions asked during interrogation, coupled with the physical constraints of the actual paper of the coaching letter as the material boundaries of the drafted response, compelled the researcher to produce a schematic map of a flattened village and to standardize family histories with a given descriptive formula. Generic conventions of the latter, as instantiated here, include name, age, kinship tie, marital status, and number and age of children, with emphasis on the detail of women's "bound feet" reflecting U.S. inspectors' assumption that this practice evidenced a desirable class background.[16] In the fullest sense, then, the order assigned to village life in coaching letters such as these illustrate a process of people grappling with modern Eurocentric epistemology, heteronormativity, and aesthetic representation in order to communicate their own humanity and material condition in a way that could be both memorized by the migrants and recognized by the interrogators.

Finally, the letter translated in figure 11 and shown in figure 12 indicates ways that the socialization of paper families produced new human realities. The letter writer coaches, "Because it is feared they will ask who live next or back of Ngee Ging Ancestral Hall, these few people or houses are added. Be sure that all agree in their testimony." This instruction illustrates at least two

Find out the name and age of the maternal grandfather, and also the name of his village.

Find out the name and age of the maternal grandmother, and whether she had natural feet.

Find out how far is the maternal grandparents' village from our village, and whether my brothers and I have ever been there.

Find out the location of the village altar in the (or our) village.

Find out the style of building of the Ngee Ging ancestral hall,- whether it has a front entrance.

Find out: location of toilet houses in the (or our) village; location of cemetery and how far is it from the (or our) village.

Make out a check in favor of Hang On Hai for the steamer passage.

Write a letter to Yip Chuck and send it back together with his address.

Please take this matter up with my brother at once and send it (probably referring to coaching paper and affidavit) back to me. In doing things we should be on the safe side so as to avoid trouble.

Tell Sing (probably referring to Yip Sing) to come over to my place tomorrow night and go over the testimony together and see if it is all right and then send it back right away.

(Translated by H. K. Tang, 12/8/24.)

FIGURES 8 and 9. Coaching letter #1, ca. 1924 (translation by Immigration interpreter H. K. Tang and original letter); Folder 6 of Box 1, Entry 232; Densmore Investigation Files, RG 85; NARA–Pacific Region (SF).

things. First, the village histories produced in coaching letters, in asymmetrical correspondence with U.S. interrogation methods and approaches, mark brand-new ways that diasporic subjects were learning to *see* their home communities. That is, people involved in making paper families were learning a particular system of thought in order to train an ability to anticipate forms of the question that would confront migrants. Only in response to these conditions did the few people or houses added to the village—whether or not they actually existed—appear as parts that needed to be articulated in the

San Francisco

Gold
Silver
Currency
Checks

DOLLARS   CENTS

同外祖公卅卅人又以姓人矣年歲外祖婆又公年歲

大腳各壽我村有鬱遠我鄰兄弟全枚去違差

本村社在于卅卅

義敬祠堂武卅卅或正面門二座

自然屋鄰有墙碑歪

又進則卅在于卅嶺本村幾遠

又入本村卅在于卅嶺本村腳遠

又弟名封信交葉卓及往址一合村返号候

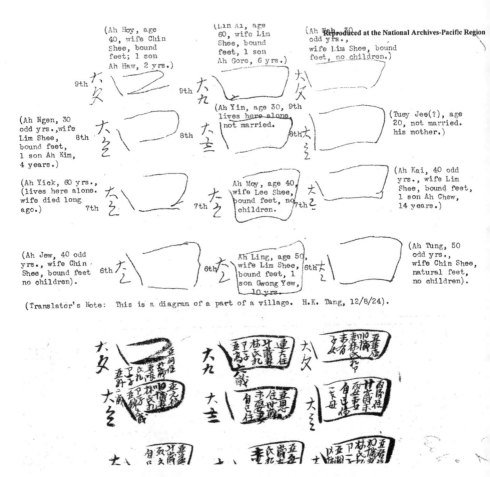

(Ah Hoy, age 40, wife Chin Shee, bound feet; 1 son Ah Haw, 2 yrs.)

(Lin Ai, age 60, wife Lim Shee, bound feet, 1 son Ah Gore, 6 yrs.)

(Ah Yon, 30 odd yrs., wife Lim Shee, bound feet, no children.)

(Ah Ngen, 30 odd yrs.,wife Lim Shee, bound feet, 1 son Ah Kim, 4 years.)

(Ah Yin, age 30, lives here alone, not married.)

(Tuey Jee(?), age 20, not married. his mother.)

(Ah Yick, 60 yrs., (lives here alone. wife died long ago.)

Ah May, age 40, wife Lee Shee, bound feet, no children.

(Ah Kai, 40 odd yrs., wife Lim Shee, bound feet, 1 son Ah Chew, 14 years.)

(Ah Jew, 40 odd yrs., wife Chin Shee, bound feet no children).

Ah Ling, age 50, wife Lim Shee, bound feet, 1 son Gwong Yew, 10 yrs.

(Ah Tung, 50 odd yrs., wife Chin Shee, natural feet, no children).

9th 8th 7th 6th

(Translator's Note: This is a diagram of a part of a village. H.K. Tang, 12/8/24).

FIGURE 10. Coaching letter #2, ca. 1924 (translation by Immigration interpreter H.K. Tang and original letter); Folder 6 of Box 1, Entry 232; Densmore Investigation Files, RG 85; NARA–Pacific Region (SF).

narrative of a place. Second, and especially as paper families became hyper-extended over the years, the absolute necessity of *shared* testimonies or understandings of village histories and geographies produced real social dependencies. As Estelle T. Lau argues, the stability of Chinese diasporic communities hinged not only on memorizing the fictions of paper families, but *living* them. New kinships were realized due to immigration policing as well as social need. Thus living the new intimacies produced through paper families, as well as figuring out how to articulate preexisting familial bonds with the new, became the heart of Chinese diasporic life under crisis.[17]

Densmore called this process "immigration fraud." Yet for Chinese migrant communities the life of paper was in fact where—and how—social authenticity and fraud converged, both preserving and transforming existing social life in ways that people in the diaspora themselves could not fully account for or predict. A closer examination of these transformations in infrastructures of kinship, then, begins with changes happening in the social structure in Guangdong, discussed in chapter 1 as shaped by institutionalized ideologies of Taoist, Buddhist, and Confucian traditions. While I have been using the term *paper families,* the migratory networks that frame this chapter are more commonly referred to by researchers as the system of *paper sons.* This diasporic movement's emphasis on male reproduction and kinship further alludes to ideologies of male supremacy and gendered norms of labor in both dominant Confucian and U.S. cultures of the era. Their historical conjoining privileged Chinese men for migration and made them significant and highly visible actors in the development of the Chinese diaspora. Indeed, the structure of paper families grew out of the hegemonic mode of social organization and identification in Guangdong at the turn of the twentieth century: localized patriarchal clans signified by surname, in institutionalized interpretations of the Confucian morals of filial piety and ontological obligations to family. The ancestral halls that these groups built (referenced, for instance, in figure 11) represented their status and wealth in a village and served as the village's schools, family or clan meeting grounds, and houses of worship. The strength of social kinship and organization based on an imagination of shared patrilineal ancestry, specific to rural Guangdong, marked a "truth" that even U.S. agents recognized. As the historian Haiming Liu argues:

> Ancestral halls became far more numerous than in many other regions, because of intense competition over land, widespread clan organizations, and epidemic social instability. Many immigration officers noticed this cultural feature of rural Guangdong through their conversations with Chinese immigrants, and therefore questions on ancestral halls became an important component of admission interrogations. Immigration officers routinely asked Chinese immigrants about the number of ancestral halls in their villages as a way to verify if a person was really from a given village.[18]

In this context, letters from male migrants in California to their families in Guangdong expressed contradictory aspects of this social structure under

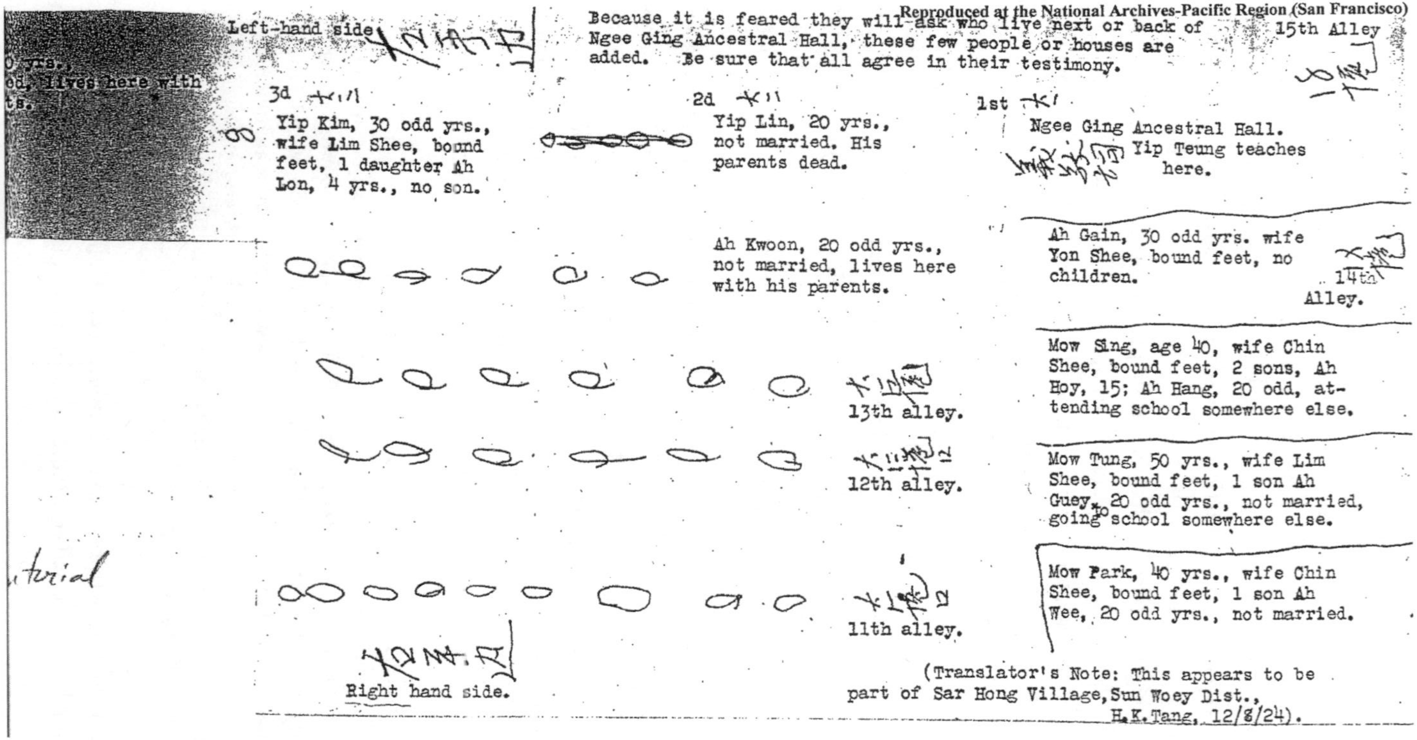

Left-hand side

o.yrs.,
od. lives here with
s.

Because it is feared they will
Ngee Ging Ancestral Hall, these few people or houses are
added. Be sure that all agree in their testimony.

Reproduced at the National Archives-Pacific Region (San Francisco)
also who live next or back of 15th Alley

3d

Yip Kim, 30 odd yrs.,
wife Lim Shee, bound
feet, 1 daughter Ah
Lon, 4 yrs., no son.

2d

Yip Lim, 20 yrs.,
not married. His
parents dead.

1st

Ngee Ging Ancestral Hall.
Yip Teung teaches
here.

Ah Gain, 30 odd yrs. wife
Yon Shee, bound feet, no
children.

14th
Alley.

Mow Sing, age 40, wife Chin
Shee, bound feet, 2 sons, Ah
Hoy, 15; Ah Hang, 20 odd, at-
tending school somewhere else.

Mow Tung, 50 yrs., wife Lim
Shee, bound feet, 1 son Ah
Guey, 20 odd yrs., not married,
going to school somewhere else.

Mow Park, 40 yrs., wife Chin
Shee, bound feet, 1 son Ah
Wee, 20 odd yrs., not married.

Ah Kwoon, 20 odd yrs.,
not married, lives here
with his parents.

13th alley.

12th alley.

11th alley.

Right hand side.

(Translator's Note: This appears to be
part of Sar Hong Village, Sun Woey Dist.,
H.K.Tang, 12/8/24)

FIGURES 11 and 12. Coaching letter #3, ca. 1924 (translation by Immigration interpreter H.K. Tang and original letter); Folder 6 of Box 1, Entry 232; Densmore Investigation Files, RG 85; NARA–Pacific Region (SF).

年廿歲未娶妻

全父母住

葉錦□□ 妻林氏扎□ 妯亞開□歲

大二

二□子

左手边

因慈善諸善初做隐典何人便恩□加□此歎

人□手册大家變□□□

葉連□歲未娶妻

全父母未在

大二

大二

義毅詞葉偉先生立此歎識

亞懷 全父母住

未娶妻

亞近□歲未有妻

大三懷口

大三懷口

茂松廿歲 妻院氏扎□□有□

别迁

茂成廿歲 妻亞開□歲未娶妻

妻林氏扎□□有二□

妻陳氏扎□□有子

亞香□歲讀書

讀書

茂相廿歲 妻亞惟□歲未署

右手边

○○○○○○○ ○ ○

大懷口

transformative crisis. For example, on the one hand, excerpts from the epistolary archive compiled and translated by Liu communicate experiences of rampant social disorder and disintegration.[19]

Sam Chang to female cousin, 5 January 1922:

I have read Brother Zhongping's [Weizong's] letter about the bandits and seen how thin and exhausted he looks in the photo. After guiding the [local government] army to fight the bandits, my brother's hair all turned white. He also coughed blood. I could not fall asleep and have composed the following poems.

Tough is your double responsibility
Suppressing the bandits and protecting the kin.
In five years of fighting,
My brother has gone through fire and water.

Sam Chang to Weizong, 9 March 1922:

You must always keep in mind that we are a weak family branch. Stay away from the lineage affairs a much as possible. Keep a low profile. It is a tragedy that strong sibling families bully the weak sibling families within the wufu [five mourning grades in a lineage] . . . Remember how Dapei was killed, how a servant girl was kidnapped, how our property was looted, how a hundred clan members had to flee before that criminal was sentenced to death . . . In my observation, the decline and the final dissolve of our family cannot be helped. The longer you stay in the home village and Guangdong, the more deeply you will get yourself involved in family affairs. . . . That is not good.

As Liu suggests in his reading of these archives, however, even as Chang's letters document widespread social crises, these very threats of dissolution also compelled and were compelled by contradictory reconsolidations of lineage organizations. More specifically, the latters' shifting dynamics mediated regional political-economic struggles and realignments in the context of industrial transformation in the southern China Pearl River Delta region during the mid-nineteenth and early twentieth century. Studies of the silk industry, for example, one of the Pearl Delta's most significant and comprehensive economic sectors, have illustrated how local Pearl Delta elites, unlike their counterparts in the northern Yangtze region, succeeded in marginally fending off foreign capitalist encroachment in their struggles both to maintain sericulture as village or town based and to gain power as an emergent entrepreneurial class. To do so, local elites negotiated with Qing and other imperialist groups as well as the peasantry, who generally reacted to social crises by strengthening their local affiliations through lineage organizations. It was precisely this adherence to collective organization based on patriarchal lineage, set apart from ethnoracial nationalisms articulating at broader scales, that local gentries exploited in their rise as a landowning class. That is, in order to win the support and cooperation of anticapitalist subsistence communities, gentry elites negotiated schemes to purchase memberships into lineage organizations and then used their positions within them to monopolize local political-economic power. By 1920, this corporatization of lineage in Guangdong manifested as filatures built by lineage gentry, organized as joint-stock companies, and rented out to lineage members responsible to pay both regular rents and supplements to the lineage treasury.[20]

Such manifold upheaval and change, then, particularly as it was articulated alongside migrant sojourning, rearranged the intertwining organization and practices of both commodity production and social reproduction as family-based labor regimes and, moreover, shaped the life of paper as a mode of paradoxical preservation and transformation of gendered roles and expectations. Illustrating these points, the set of letters presented in figures 13 through 16 provides articulations of the structural dynamics of the dominant Confucian family as a (re)productive unit and, furthermore, highlight how the life of paper enacted a distinctive performance and transformation of the normative patriarchy. First, in Yee Fon to his sons, dated 13 March 1918 (figures 13 and 14), the letter communicates shame on Yee Fon's sons for their failure to exercise proper authority and to regulate gendered relations.

Stockton, Cal., C.R. 7–2(?)-1.

(March 13, 1918).

Louie Kim Sin & Louie Kim Min,
Dear Sons:
Your letter, saying that Sere Huey is not to be married for the present, was received. The money I sent home for his marriage was

borrowed from the clansmen; and if he is not to be married yet, I could harly have the nerve to face the clansmen here. I would rather have him married and buy him a cow or water-buffalo, so that he may become a rice farmer in order to make his own livelihood.

I have heard that your mother often goes to the market, exhibiting more showiness than other people. I ask you whether you are ashamed of yourself to do that. If you do not feel the shame, I would feel it myself when I heard of such a thing. The clansmen say that since I cannot control my own family, I shouldn't be a man. If you don't feel the disgrace, you should consider my name,—whose wife is that that gives such exhibition? To me such remark is bad; it hurts my name or reputation, and I can have no hope for a day of success. Hereafter, if you put away your bad conduct and aim to do that which is good, you may hope to have your children succeed some day. If you will not change your conduct, you may not expect me to send any more money home hereafter.

If a man marries a bad wife, he cannot have a single hope for success. If you do not trust Sere Huey to buy anything for you, there are many other clansmen in the village whom you can trust to buy for you. If you do not trust any of them, I have my mother at home whom you can trust. Why don't you trust her? Then, you have children, though young, but you can give them the money to go with the clansmen of the village who would buy for them. Why don't you consider these ways good? When I heard of these things about you, I would feel ashamed of myself to face the clansmen. I hope you will change for the better at once. I am well here, and I suppose my sons are also well.

I am sending you one $5.00 gold piece by Fon Ging of Haw Mook Village. Receive it for the household expenses.

(Signed): Yee Fon.
(or Louie Yee Fon).
To the one that reads this letter: Please read the whole letter; do not keep anything back.

Translated by Interpreter H.K. Tang, June 11, 1918.
[In handwriting: See list of Foo Lung Co, Stockton, Cal. look up villages. case (illegible) before this office]

Through this letter, Yee Fon attempts to teach his sons several interconnected lessons about the norms of patriarchal respectability. Most essentially, regarding ideal organization of village life, the letter speaks to the centrality of women's and children's reproductive labor to men's lives and livelihoods and the duty of the patriarch to control it. Within this framework, Yee shames his sons for their failure to exercise proper authority, a problem that implies shortcomings of character as well as dire social consequences. Namely, the letter alludes to the indignities of marital disappointments, the conceits that the sons also allow women in the family to exhibit, and, as final result, an emasculated family identity and dishonored reputation in the village.

Yet contradiction animates the letter's attempts to preserve Yee's vision of proper order through the act of letter correspondence, particularly as migration contributed to local economic change and the latter's relation to productions of both individual and collective identities. Specifically, Yee's frustrations demonstrate that what burdened the migrant as debt could simultaneously function as an experience of wealth for his family. As implied by his dissatisfaction in this letter, such multidimensional changes in day-to-day economic life produced new social dynamics, which Yee addresses from an asserted position of patriarchal authority. Through this letter, such as in the thought, "If you don't feel the disgrace, you should consider my name," Yee emphasizes how his own sacrifices for the family should compel others to abide reciprocally by his expectations of appropriate gender, class, and filial performance. In this sense, vis-à-vis a contradictory appeal to *affective* debt, Yee attempts to mitigate the ways that the introduction of new forms of wealth were transforming gendered and generational roles as well as ideals of respectability. This communication thus emerges from the tension between, on the one hand, changes in both feminized and filial behaviors, correlated with transformations in the local political economy and social fabric;[21] and, on the other hand, Yee's reaction to it—his conservative, almost nostalgic, attempt to recuperate an idealized family life through the instantiation of this letter.

In some contrast to Yee Fon's assertions of dominance, the following excerpt of another letter, Guey Hock to his nephews, dated 4 March 1918 (figures 15 and 16), conveys a sense of the multiplicity of perspectives and responses to Confucian structure in crisis, as Guey Hock shares an acknowledgment and affective expression of patriarchal *failure*.

7th year 1st month 22nd day.
(March 4, 1918).

Louie Suey Sang & Louie Suey Wing,
Dear nephews:
When I take up the pen, my tears run down like rain. Ever since your 2nd older brother died several months ago, I have not had any peace of mind and my eyes are still wet with tears. Since his death I have not been feeling well, so I cannot do any work yet. There are many things which make me feel sad, and I feel worse day after day.

Seeing such condition we descendants of our Tong ancestor will have such a hard time to succeed. Besides, we have but little wealth and little blessing. We are always in financial difficulty and can have but little hope to attain success, so we shall have to let people look down on us. But, what can we do? The old saying goes: An insult coming from a man means nothing; but when it comes from Heaven, it gives a man no place to stand. This is a true saying.

I am now old and cannot work. I have so much sorrow in my heart, so I would rather die soon, so that I may end my sorrow on earth.

Concerning the share your 2nd older brother had in the business he bought his share with the money that he had borrowed from people and from mutual loan societies; so, when he died, the people took over his share in order to get their money back. The money from his share in the business was not enough to pay back what he owed. I could say nothing in the matter; the people had accounts to prove their claims. The matter was thoroughly and justly discussed by the clansmen in So Yuen Tong (a society), and I have to wait to see what will come out of it later.

Your 2nd older brother's conduct was changed last year; he spent a lot of money on friends, so that is why he did not send any money home the whole year last year. I think this is due to "foong-sui," so it is needless for us to worry over anything.

You need not ask about the accounts between uncle and nephews. I cannot say anything about the nephews going abroad to make money. I am feeling very bad, very sad.

I am sending you $2.00 Mex. Do not let people read (?) this letter, but you may let people read (?) the other.

(Signed): Guey Hock.
(or Louie Guey Hock).

Translated by Interpreter H. K. Tang, June 11, 1918.
Note: The Chinese letter is very poorly written.

Reading Yee Fon's and Guey Hock's seemingly disparate letters alongside each other yields at least two significant insights. First, although the messages of each letter present opposing perspectives, both men use correspondence as a means to assume their responsibilities as patriarchs—something that the *letter* gives them the capacity to do. Furthermore, both measure their own manhood through terms of both ancestral honor and material success. Thus Yee Fon writes with ambition and pride, "Please read the whole letter, do no keep anything back," while with shame and grief Guey Hock ultimately instructs at the conclusion of his letter, "Do not let people read this letter." This contrast highlights how Confucian order has subtly transformed through the life of paper, as fulfilling patriarchal duties relies on the letter's circulation: the latter mediated both through the letter's receiver and/or reader and through the socialized act of reading. Second, the rhetoric of both letters noticeably relies on their *emotional* force, a deviation from what David A. Gerber generalizes as the norm of immigrant letters to exaggerate their senders' comfort, tranquility, and wealth in order to shield the letters' receivers from shame or worry.[22] The stark contrast between these structures of feeling—such emotionally heightened rather than subdued or generic forms of expression—calls attention to the self-conscious performativity of moral affect in Yee Fon and Guey Hock's letters. In this sense, this mobilization of sentiment through the life of paper could function to attenuate the alienating effects of physical distance, as to simulate or augment the patriarch's ability to exercise authority despite his absence.

THE SOCIALITY OF THE HER

In the context of this life of paper in the California diaspora, then, within circumstances of protracted patriarchal war in China and racialized labor struggles in the United States, the existing common sense of filial duty privileged Chinese male workers for migration in service of the family. This group thus formed the most apparent focus of containment efforts in California as U.S. Immigration officials grew increasingly frustrated with the cumulating problem of paper families and the channels the latter opened to legal rights. The detention cells of Angel Island, built specifically for Chinese male migrants to stop the flow of paper, attest to the earliest American wrath against same-sex families, these formed through letters exchanged among men.

Stockton, Cal., C.R. 7-2(?)-1.
(March 13, 1918).

Louie Kim Sin & Louie Kim Min,

Dear sons:

Your letter, saying that Sere Huey is not to be married
for the present, was received. The money I sent home for his
marriage was borrowed from the clansmen; and if he is not to be
married yet, I could harly have the nerve to face the clansmen here.
I would rather have him married and buy him a cow or water-buffalo,
so that he may become a rice farmer in order to make his own livelihood.

I have heard that your mother often goes to the market, exhibiting more showiness than other people. I ask you whether you are
ashamed of yourself to do that. If you do not feel the shame, I
would feel it myself when I heard of such thing. The clansmen say
that since I cannot control my own family, I shouldn't be a man.
If you don't feel the disgrace, you should consider my name,--
whose wife is that that gives such exhibition? To me such remark
is bad; it hurts my name or reputation, and I can have no hope for
a day of success. Hereafter, if you put away your bad conduct and
aim to do that which is good, you may hope to have your children
succeed some day. If you will not change your conduct, you may
not expect me to send any more money home hereafter.

If a man marries a bad wife, he cannot have a single hope for
success. If you do not trust Sere Huey to buy anything for you,
there are many other clansmen in the village whom you can trust to
buy for you. If you do not trust any of them, I have my mother at
home whom you can trust. Why don't you trust her? Then, you have
children, though young, but you can give them the money to go with
the clansmen of the village who would buy for them. Why don't you
consider these ways good? When I heard of these things about you,
I would feel ashamed of myself to face the clansmen. I hope you
will change for the better at once. I am well here, and I XXXXXXXX
suppose my sons are also well.

I am sending you one $5.00 gold piece by Fon Ging of Haw Mook
Village. Receive it for the household expenses.

(Signed): Yee Fon.
(or Louie Yee Fon).

To the one that reads this letter: Please read the whole letter;
do not keep anything back.

Translated by Interpreter H. K. Tang, June 11, 1918.

FIGURES 13 and 14. Yee Fon to sons Louie Kim Sin and Louie Kim Min, ca. 13 March 1918
(translation by Immigration interpreter H. K. Tang and original letter); Folder 4 of Box 1,
Entry 232; Densmore Investigation Files, RG 85; NARA–Pacific Region (SF).

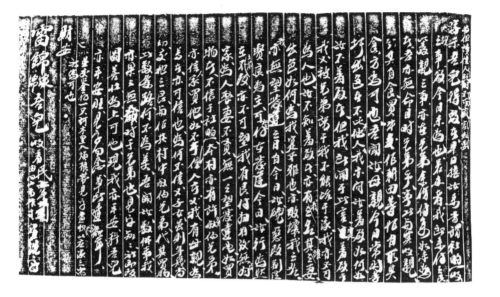

Facing circumstances of forced confinement in dehumanizing conditions, the socialization of reproductive labor among male detainees at Angel Island culminated in 1922 with the formation of Zizhihui (Self-Governing Association, also anglicized as the Angel Island Liberty Association). Zizhihui had a formal political structure wherein its leadership was elected primarily from among those who had been detained the longest; its expressed purpose was to provide mutual aid and to maintain order. Official activities included protesting to secure adequate quality of food on the island as well as organizing social practices to maintain paper lifelines through the collectivized work of reading, writing, delivering, and receiving letters.[23] Such socialization at Angel Island also prepared migrants for the predominantly homosocial societies they would have to build in the United States during the earlier period of Chinese Exclusion, distinct from the family structures they knew before.[24]

As Lai, Lim, and Yung note, no corresponding organization developed among women on the island.[25] Indeed, gender segregation at Angel Island both reflected and reproduced the gendered differentiation co-constituting the production of racial distinction in California. During this period, migrant Chinese women negotiated their often vulnerable positions in the Confucian social hierarchy as well as the particularly sexualized form of their criminalization in U.S. law and popular racial ideology. For example, an

Louie Suey Sang & Louie Suey Wing,

Dear nephews:

When I take up the pen, my tears run down like rain.
Ever since your 2nd older brother died several months ago, I have
not had any peace of mind and my eyes are still wet with tears.
Since his death I have not been feeling well, so I cannot do any
work yet. There are many things which make me feel sad, and I
feel worse day after day.

Seeing such condition we descendants of our Tong ancestor will
have a hard time to succeed. Besides, we have but little wealth
and little blessing. We are always in financial difficulty and
can have but little hope to attain success, so we shall have to let
people look down on us. But, what can we do? The old saying
goes: An insult coming from a man means nothing; but when it comes
from Heaven, it gives a man no place to stand. This is a true
saying.

I am now old and cannot work. I have so much sorrow in my
heart, so I would rather die soon, so that I may end my sorrow on
earth.
Concerning the share your 2nd older brother had in the business he bought his share with the money that he had borrowed from
people and from mutual loan societies; so, when he died, the people
took over his share in order to get their money back. The money
from his share in the business was not enough to pay back what he
owed. I could say nothing in the matter; the people had accounts
to prove their claims. The matter was thoroughly and justly discussed by the clansmen in So Yuen Tong (a society), and I have to
wait to see what will come out of it later.
Your 2nd older brother's conduct was changed last year; he
spent a lot of money on friends, so that is why he did not send any
money home the whole year last year. I think this is due to
"foong-sui," so it is needless for us to worry over anything.
You need not ask about the accounts between uncle and nephews.
I cannot say anything about the nephews going abroad to make money.
I am feeling very bad, very sad.
I am sending you $2.00 Mex. Do not let people read(?) this
letter, but you may let people read(?) the other.

(Signed): Guey Hock.
(or Louie Guey Hock).

Translated by Interpreter H. K. Tang, June 11, 1918.

Note: The Chinese letter is very poorly written.

FIGURES 15 and 16. Guey Hock to nephews Louie Suey Sang and Louie Suey Wing, ca. 4
March 1918 (translation by Immigration interpreter H. K. Tang and original letter); Folder
7 of Box 1, Entry 232; Densmore Investigation Files, RG 85; NARA–Pacific Region (SF).

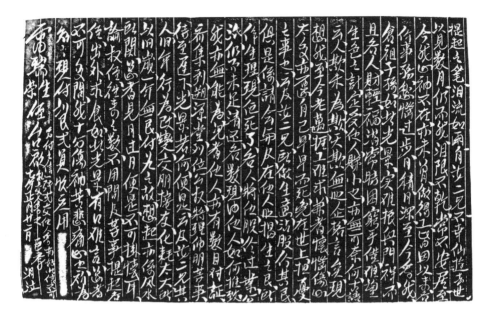

excerpt from the translation of Wong Som Gar's letter to his father (figure 17), the original letter (figure 18) dated 18 December 1916 and sent from a *minchu* in Hong Kong to San Francisco, indicates the dangers that working-class Chinese women faced at this time and place.

I have a friend who is of the Lee family, and he has two native daughters' papers—one for 20 years old and one for 18 years old. These native daughters left San Francisco for China when 1 or 2 years old. Now, this friend wants me to be a party in the scheme to send two girls to the United States for the purpose of prostitution. I don't know whether you can look after this matter. *Confidentially:* The papers belong to Lee Ham Doo's daughters. He has a midwife as a witness and all other necessary evidence in the two cases, so I think as soon as they arrive, they will be landed. In Hong Kong it costs about $1200.00 (probably H.K. currency) to buy a girl, her paper (i.e., the affidavit showing a girl to be a native daughter), and her steamer ticket. I don't know how much a girl could be sold for in San Francisco. Please investigate the market condition (for slave girls) and let me know about it, so that I may talk it over with my friends, and if we find that there is profit in the business, we will at once carry out the enterprice.

- - - - - - - - - - - - -
- - - - - - - - - - - - -

Everybody at home, both young and old, is well, so please don't be anxious about us.

Your son,
(Wong) Bing Foon, (Wong Doon Ngip).

Translated by Interpreter H. K. Tang, October 26, 1917.

This letter highlights the contradictions of both U.S. and Chinese capitalist cultures that shaped the diaspora throughout this time, as Chinese American economies underwent significant shifts in their racial as well as gender regimes. That is, as certain forms of reproductive labor, such as food and clothing provisions, became industrialized and commercialized as businesses in homosocial U.S. Chinatowns, members of the diasporic community ideologically assimilated such labor in this context as appropriate forms of work for men.[26] On the other hand, sexual reproductive labor, as mediated through capitalist market relations scaffolding the "immigration business," remained women's work, in a structure of opportunity and constraint wherein for paper daughters, as opposed to paper sons, prostitution served as a main avenue through which women paid off their debt.[27] These developments thus rearticulated feminized exploitation and intensified sexual and gendered, as they mediated emergent class, domination. In this sense, prevailing institutionalized notions of shared ethical community obligation—the well-being of "everyone at home"—apparently did not extend to women who performed reproductive labor outside the boundaries of respectable matriarchal roles and service. Yet feminized labor "outside" the norms of respectability, as it intersected with the commercial sector, nonetheless played a notable role in both economically organizing and socially reproducing paper families in the diaspora.[28]

Under these conditions during this period, Chinese women became the object of much ideological investment and social activism among citizens in

California. On the one hand, the 1875 Page Act evidences the popularity of early Progressive discourses about Chinese women as sexual deviants who would bring disease to the racial purity of white supremacy; on the other hand, such ideologies were tempered by those of Christian missionaries, who were committed to rescuing and reforming the lives of Chinese women. In the language of popular public health discourse emerging by the turn of the century, religious and increasing numbers of civic reformers sought to train Chinese women for physical and moral fitness to undertake the demands of democratic citizenship, arguing that such activity could eventually sanitize and uplift the whole Chinese community.[29] In these regards, the following entry in the U.S. Customs letter log, dated 15 December 1887 and written by San Francisco customs surveyor, W. J. Simmins, speaks indirectly to the methods of moral reform that Christian missionaries used at this time.[30]

Hon John S Hager,
Collector,
Sir,
I respectfully report, that on receipt of your letter of the 12th inst, I served on the following day, the notice attached hereto, on Capt E. C. Reed the Master of the Steamship San Pablo, by delivering said notice to the Steamship Officer in command of the San Pablo, and Capt Reed was afterwards found on the wharf, and was informed of the contents of the same, and that it had been delivered to his officer then in charge of said vessel.

There was at that time fifty-five Chinese females on board the San Pablo, some of them having arrived here on that vessel and more being held for examination as to their right to land here, and there were twenty-six who had been put on board by the United States Marshal.

It is impossible for me to notify the females as to their status, or right to land, for the reasons,
First,—that they do not speak the English language,
Second—I can not distinguish or identify those put on board by the United States Marshal from those who come here on the vessel.

Respectfully submitted
W J Simmins
Surveyor

I have a friend who is of the Lee family, and he has two native
daughters' papers --one for 20 years old and one for 18 years old.
These native daughters left San Francisco for China when 1 or 2
years old.   Now, this friend wants me to be a party in the scheme
to send two girls to the United States for the purpose of prostitution.   I don't know whether you can look after this matter.
Confidentially: The papers belong to Lee Ham Doo's daughters.   He
has a midwife as a witness and all other necessary evidence in the
two cases, so I think as soon as they arrive, they will be landed.
In Hong Kong it costs about $1200.00 (probably H.K. currency) to
buy a girl, her paper (i.e., the affidavit showing a girl to be a
native daughter), and her steamer ticket.   I don't know how much
a girl could be sold for in San Francisco.   Please investigate the
market condition (for slave girls) and let me know about it, so that

WSG.--(12/18/16)--2.

I may talk it over with my friends, and if we find that there is
profit in the business, we will at once carry out the enterprice.
- - - -- - - - - - - - - - - - -- - - - - - - - - - - - - - - -
- -
        Everybody at home, both young and old, *are* well, so please
don't be anxious about us.

                    Your son,

                        (Wong) Bing Foon, (Wong Doon Ngip).

                    ─────────────────

Translated by Interpreter H. K. Tang, October 26, 1917.

FIGURES 17 and 18. Excerpt from Wong Sor Gam to Father, ca. 18 December 1916 (translation by Immigration interpreter H. K. Tang and original letter); Folder 7 of Box 1, Entry 232;
Densmore Investigation Files, RG 85; NARA–Pacific Region (SF).

父親大人膝下　敬稟者　昨廿日已上　料叢青反美玉云俊業

這次高業款取作懺之出世仔前來一件沿用談牢仍來

要妻況何艮太高是以而曾的取号候作別臨此祖告俊業

祖就是現有李姓友有出世女仔帝二姓（一）妹廿歲（一）姓信懺此

係由大坪二歲回唐今談友歡何办女子二姓來義以當妓此

來祖　大人可得当妾呈乃李添祖之女他有証人执生

媽者遷搜料一步即可登岸此兩在港買帝及賣人艇信每

口付用艮贖稅之向但此大坪未祖每口法艮若干其

救們在幾何干祉查實示發容呈與各友商量必有判可圖

定即蒙此順祖現在家老少們皆要好旹寫掛心前來兵仔

今將沽清仍有賓此向此生嘉诉勝于別物此因易收藏

況承幸你輕囬必有口之咳祉寒、己丁付未便是仵好音波

告此佈

金安

Here, Simmins evokes Chinese women's *linguistic* difference, privileged before physical or visual racial ascriptions, to rationalize the impossibility of determining the status of Chinese women and to demarcate their absolute alienation from whiteness as the latter defines the "right to land." This inclusion of language as an essential—material yet not always visible— part of racist aesthetic judgment speaks to the urgency of battles waged through the life of paper at this time, as Christian missionaries in Chinatown engaged in *epistolary* training to discipline and assimilate Chinese women through forced literacy practice, the latter simultaneously furnishing material records that could affect a sense of regulating and knowing the Other with greater documentary transparency.[31] The formal specificities that distinguish Chinese from English and nearly all other writing systems further heighten the epistemological stakes of such a mode of conversion. That is, the remarkable feature of Chinese script, its endurance as a nonalphabetic, nonphonetic system based instead on visual symbols, corresponds with a social and philosophical reality in which, unlike other contexts of modern language and literacy, the written system's evolution does not necessarily demand the homogenization or destruction of localized language traditions and vernacular cultures.[32] This conceivable coexistence of unity and heterogeneity, perhaps amplifying anxieties about Chinese populations during the Exclusion era as unrepresentable people whose "mystery always points to the presence of something not shown,"[33] ultimately points to the essential worldview or "ethnic ontology" that reformers sought to dismantle in the institutionalization of standard English language literacy and learning.[34]

Thus, in this context, with organizational structures of colonial epistolary training already in place, reformers' adaptation of such means of racial disciplining for Chinese women included Immigration officials' recruitment of Christian "matrons" to do this work at Angel Island. In 1912, Deaconess Katharine Maurer, known as the "Angel of Angel Island," was officially appointed to administer women's civilizing activities with funding and gifts from the Daughters of the American Revolution, an organization that also ardently lobbied for the Page and Chinese Exclusion Acts.[35] Reformers taught Chinese female migrants how to speak English, write letters, and perform other services in order to effectuate their conversion to civilized feminine life. Such work on Angel Island and in Chinatowns produced letters such as this "Letter by a Chinese Girl," reprinted in the Rev. Otis Gibson's *The Chinese in America* (1877):

> LETTER BY A CHINESE GIRL
>
> Miss B,—You ask me to write about my life. I can not write very well, but will do the best I can.
> I was born in Sin Lam, China, seventeen years ago. My father was a weaver and my mother had small feet. I had a sister and brother

younger than myself. My father was an industrious man, but we were very poor. My feet were never bound; I am thankful they were not. My father sold me when I was about seven years old; my mother cried. I was afraid, and ran under the bed to hide. My father came to see me once and brought me some fruit; but my mistress told me to say that he was not my father. I did so, but afterward I felt very sorry. He seemed very sad, and when he went away he gave me a few cash, and wished me prosperity. That was the last time I saw him. I was sold four times. I came to California about five years ago. My mistress was very cruel to me; she used to whip me, pull my hair, and pinch the inside of my cheeks. A friend of mine told me of this place, and at night I ran away. My friend pointed out the house. I was very much afraid while I was coming up the street; the dogs barked, and I was afraid my mistress was coming after me. I rang the bell twice, and when the door was opened I ran in quickly. I thank God that he led me to this place. I have now been here nearly three years. I am very happy, for I do not have those troubles which I had before. I have kind friends, but most of all, I am thankful that Jesus died to save me. God has given me the Bible to read, which teaches me that 'Straight is the gate and narrow is the way that leadeth unto life.' I was very bad before I came here. I used to gamble, lie, and steal. Now I love Jesus, and by God's help I will try to be obedient, and do those things which will please him.

Yours, truly,   SING KUM
SAN FRANCISCO, January 4, 1876.

Finally, then, deep in the heart of this life of paper, I conclude this chapter by interrogating the social transformations that occurred through the introduction of English literacy to migrant Chinese women's lives. Whatever may or may not be "fraudulent" about how Sing Kum speaks of her life, the significance of her narrative resides in the process and act of remembering that produce and are produced by the letter. In essence, Sing Kum uses Miss B's assignment, in whatever interrogative form it may have come, to imagine and write her own paper family: a meaningful gesture in view of how she remembers alienation from her natal community, a remembering through which she otherwise still defines herself here. It is in this context of how she knows her own sorrow and gratitude—elements that are vitally absent in the letter—that her claims matter.

In these chapters, I have provided a fuller view of the physical and discursive constraints that condition the writing of this letter in order to create a window now to see Sing Kum invoking her ancestors using a foreign language: an act of subjectivization that syncretizes her preexisting ethnic ontology with the ideological material of an imposed Christianity. In this letter, Sing Kum dutifully abides by the norms of her racial humanist training through literary self-representation; yet, parallel to the ways that the slave narrative simultaneously enacts and subverts the conventions of the colonial Christian narrative, plotting the movement from abjection to redemption,[36] Sing Kum also simultaneously enacts the form's undoing—in her case, as she writes in a cyclical rather than linear rhetorical structure. That is, rather than reproduce perfectly the linear plot structure of the Christian bildungsroman to represent a singular and coherent journey into humanity, this letter evolves through three distinct cycles of transformative catharsis or conversion.

In the first cycle, from the introduction roughly through when she writes, "I did so, but afterward I felt very sorry," she defines her abjection more through the conditions of alienation than poverty or backwardness. In this sense, her expression of atonement affects a contradictory redemption in which recollection of a transformative incident conjures both confession of sin and its transcendence and narratively transitions into another life cycle, as she is "sold four times." In this second phase of Sing Kum's journey, she comes to California and travails through a different experience of crisis until "I thank God that he led me to this place." Even as she arrives at and is rescued by an Anglo God, however, the ideological training instantiated by the letter undergoes another kind of reversal, as the root of abjection in this narrative resides not in the sins of Sing Kum herself but in the cruelty of her mistress—and thus, the proper object of what will have had to be redeemed appears not to be in Sing Kum's uncivilized ways but in the very relations of coloniality. In the final cycle, then, from when she writes, "I have now been here nearly three years," to the conclusion, Sing Kum achieves the most correct, even if still imperfect, performance of the narrative convention. Yet judgment of the ways "I was very bad before I came here" loses its intended narrative power and is thereby unraveled, as it follows from, and is contextualized by, the information contained in the prior two cycles. In these ways, Sing Kum's inverted biblical recitation of the verse, "Straight is the gate and narrow is the way that leadeth unto life," perhaps indicates a more fundamental slippage in appropriation, leading unto its own other kind of passage.

These instabilities of meaning thus brought to the fore, it becomes more thinkable that as she strives toward "God" in her letter, both the act of writing and the materiality of the medium *matter,* bearing in mind the sacred value assigned to printed paper raised at the start of this analysis. To this point, summarizing the common sense about women and writing in this context, the paper son Tung Pok Chin reflects in his memoir, "My mother . . . could also barely read or write. It didn't matter much for an old-fashioned girl anyway, because Confucius said: 'For a girl, having no education is a virtue.'"[37] By learning how to read and write, then, women like Sing Kum were in their own ways socially repositioning themselves as they accessed the privileges and responsibilities reserved for the highest literati, government officials, and religious clergy in dominant Confucian society. From this perspective, articulated through her deference to Jesus and God—a compulsion embedded in the training of the form itself—Sing Kum's letter hence also falls within indigenous traditions of using paper "to give thanks; beg for assistance; express love and devotion; ease the suffering of the unknown and neglected dead."[38] This particularly resonates in the context of Sing Kum's expressed remorse for her verbal disavowal of her father, a disgrace to the ancestors and violation of Chinese religious and social tradition. Moreover, situated in the profound rupture of ritual practice vis-à-vis its alienation from the land of ancestral origin, Sing Kum's letter also reproduces, through difference, the life of paper as a space of communal worship, stripped or in excess of its territorial moorings. She says, "I can not write very well, but will do the best I can." Thus struggling to figure her place between languages, between ontologies, between living histories and their recounting, perhaps, as Hortense Spillers says of Toni Morrison's illegible character *Sula,* "The importance of this text is that she speaks at all."[39]

CONCLUSION: PAPER BEFORE PAPERS

Throughout part 1, I have covered different structural aspects of the life of paper for the Detained during the Chinese Exclusion era at multiple geographic sites and scales, changing world communities in ways that people in the diaspora themselves could neither fully account for nor predict. In these regards, this analysis has also shed some light on the decisions people made to use their tools—technological, epistemological, social, aesthetic—to mediate the radical openness of "freedom" as potential. On the one hand, in this case, certain legacies reflect how the Chinese diaspora used potential to reproduce forms of racism, racial capitalism, and gendered exploitation: for instance, in the rampant debt bondage, intraethnic class bifurcations, and racial and gendered labor regimes that came to structure U.S. Chinatowns.[40] Yet, on the other hand, I have also examined how the life of paper created real opportunities for what Nayan Shah calls "queer domesticities,"[41] qualitatively new intimacies and unique configurations of reproductive labor that subverted dominant race-gender paradigms on both sides of the Chinese and North American Pacific. Finally, through rigorous readings of letters such as Sing Kum's, we also glimpsed traces of the ultimate *Mystery* in how different ethnic traditions and worldviews of the "sacred" are simultaneously preserved, challenged, and radically transformed as they are displaced into other forms of appearance.

In conclusion, then, part 1 ends at the beginning, back to the worldviews of the sacred in Guangdong where this journey began. In the sacred paper rituals practiced by cultures there, people do not keep paper offerings to hoard or display. Instead, the nature of the offerings transforms as they are sent to the ancestors, gods, or ghosts through the papers' burning, an act of sending into *absence* that accomplishes the vital transformation connecting the secular with the sacred.[42] This chapter has explored how the Detained, in new relations of presence and absence, transformed the infrastructures of making and circulating their paper offerings. In doing so, it has offered a view of transformations in the technological, epistemological, and social practices that gave paper its life: a "poetics" bonding the seen and the unseen to preserve detained communities' potential for collective survival and vitality at this time.

We tagged our baggage with the family number, 13660, and
pinned the personal tags on ourselves; we were ready at last.

FIGURE 19. From Miné Okubo's *Citizen 13660* (1946, 22).

PART TWO

Interned

IN HER PREFACE TO THE 1983 edition of *Citizen 13660* (originally published in 1946), the artist Miné Okubo explains the genesis of her graphic novel:

> In the camps, first at Tanforan [California] and then at Topaz in Utah, I had the opportunity to study the human race from the cradle to the grave, and to see what happens to people when reduced to one status and condition. Cameras and photographs were not permitted in the camps, so I recorded everything in sketches, drawings, and paintings. *Citizen 13660* began as a special group of drawings made to tell the story of camp life for my many friends who faithfully sent letters and packages to let us know we were not forgotten.[1]

Indeed, the very name of Okubo's work alludes to the productive process of reducing people "to one status and condition": the quantification of social order and identity, ironically juxtaposed with the positive ideal and human concept represented by the figure of the "citizen." In this sense, Okubo's titular self-identification as *Citizen* troubles the latter's own fabrication as a universal status, laying bare its contradictory formulation through the modern reduction of human life to a number. Moreover, the paradox of "Citizen 13360" as a name of distinction, as what can only be ascribed to Okubo specifically and yet signifies the status and condition of an objectified collective (or twinned yet opposing collectives, an us and a them, embodied by Okubo at their crossroad), alludes to an essential problematic embedded in the very organization of Western civilization itself—that is, its binarized forms of positivity (citizenship) and negativity (alienation), their historical interlocking, the dissimulation of their interlocking, and finally, deep within the architecture of social control, the dynamics of the life force still moving inside it. It is in this context that Okubo situates her recordings of mass incarceration as a meditation on existence as such, the study of human life "from the cradle to the grave," both enacted as and mediated by an aesthetic sociality at the limits of constraint. Interweaving visual and written correspondence to crisscross civilian landscapes of war as well as its regime of censors, Okubo's graphic assertion of her family name "Okubu," amidst numerical ascriptions tagging both luggage and people rounded for mass incarceration (figure 19), thus splices the page as simplest affirmation of historical being, written to be seen.

Part 2, "Interned," takes place against the evolving backdrop of global productions of Asiatic racial distinction whose dominant forms in Anglo settler states, as elaborated in part 1, mystified violent contradictions between and within the development of modern world empires and discrete capitalist nation-states. As demonstrated in the discussion offered under the heading "Detained," infrastructural regulation of Chinese diasporic reproduction and movement undergirded a dominating view of the world as comprising inherently separate nations whose sovereignty and integrity depended on the fortification of state borders. Throughout the first half of the twentieth century, struggles to maintain this hegemonic world order intensified through the creation of a modern security state and international systems to control and protect borders across the world.[2] The discussion at hand in part 2, then, details an understanding of the evolution of modernity as a global project of scientific management and apartheid, engineering imperialist space through dynamic forms of militarization and uneven development alongside attendant racial regimes calculated as "population management." In this regard, following from historical precedents introduced in part 1, the era of the "Interned" also marked the progression of an epistemological architecture of "civilization" tethered to movements for geopolitical domination: a "fatal coupling"[3] that deepened the core contradiction of the modern world—that is, social order wrought through the chaos of permanent war.

In this context, the shifting position of Japan in the global imperialist terrain through the end of World War II dramatically altered the development of forms of Asiatic racial distinction as well as modern civilization and, moreover, illustrates the dynamic historical contingencies of their mutual reproduction. The imperialist Japanese bloc's expanding military power, alongside their diplomatic acumen in the arena of international law, formalized tentative mutual—albeit unequal—cooperations among Japanese,

European, and U.S. imperialist ventures in the Pacific at the turn of the twentieth century. After Japan's military victory over Russia in the 1904–5 war, European diplomats and lawyers marginally enfranchised Japan in the European imperialist "family of nations," accommodated by the hegemonic displacement of the language of Christendom into that of "civilization." This movement, to codify standards and conditions for incorporation into the civilized world by secular terms of international law, formally rearticulated the ideological terrain on which a global minority could universalize their world designs.[4]

The negotiation of Japan's ambivalent position in this evolving world system exacerbated preexisting contradictions, specifically at the triangulated impasse of Chinese, Japanese, and U.S. imperialist relations. In particular, tensions mounted as Japan's elevating imperialist status emboldened more relaxed policing of migration to the American West, which Japan had previously agreed to restrict in diplomatic and commercial treaties with Western nations. Consistent with the Orientalist conundrum that complicated Anglo imperialist ambitions in China, U.S. diplomats faced conflicting political-economic imperatives at the international and nation-state scales: on the one hand, they desired cooperative relations with Japan to secure extraterritorial treaties favorable to U.S. imperialist projects in the Pacific; and on the other, following precedents established by the Chinese Exclusion acts, they pursued exclusionary stances on migration from Japan to the U.S. Pacific Coast. These developments framed how Japanese imperialists would navigate their tenuous alliances in the East Asian Pacific and U.S. imperialists their tenuous alliances with Japan.[5]

These contradictions also conditioned the twinned problem of rendering a coherent Japanese racial form under these circumstances of limited enfranchisement in the world imperialist context and, yet, of Asiatic disfranchisement from Anglo settler states in the context of nation-state border control. This ideological crisis further manifested in uneven transitions between the universal language of modern civilization and positive rights in international law, on the one hand, and on the other, negative restrictions on international migration written into U.S. nation-state law in the explicit language of racial distinction. As a temporary resolution to this crisis, U.S. officials defined the Japanese problem as one of diplomacy rather than exclusion—that is, as engagement with a civilized nation capable of self-regulation and international cooperation. The 1907 Gentleman's Agreement, in which the Japanese government resumed responsibility to restrict emigration, hence formally differentiated Japan from China and Asia while withholding privileges of "civilized" status by informally extending terms of U.S. immigrant exclusions. This strategy thereby also rearticulated, through calculated *omission* of language, the discursive boundaries of Asiatic racial status as an arbiter of political rights, including those to movement, in the global context of U.S. empire.[6]

Despite subsequent commercial treaties and pledges of support for respective imperialist interests in Korea and the Philippines, tentative agreements between Japan and the United States fell apart again following World War I. Well-established historiographical explanations locate at least three key events ultimately leading to the formal declaration of war between the two countries. First, in the wake of World War I, the League of Nations refused Japan's attempt to insert a racial equality clause in its 1919 charter—thus signifying, again through calculated omission of language, Japan's subordination in the "family" vis-à-vis the League's commitment to white supremacy as natural law. Second, the U.S. Immigration Act of 1924 officially legislated Japanese exclusion, ideologically adjusting terms of racial distinction by instituting a quota system formalized through universal measures and modern social scientific principle. Fixed quotas, based on proportions of current U.S. residents of a specific "national stock," biologized nationalism by transposing racial category with the language of inborn national and/or geographic essence while a legal tautology prohibiting immigration of "aliens ineligible for naturalization" reenacted Asian exclusion. Together, both discursive maneuvers reproduced the political conditions of U.S. anti-Asian racism without repeating its original racial lexicon. Last, then, Japanese imperialists shifted from diplomatic compliance to overt threats against Allied imperialist interests and assets in Asia, marked by Japanese colonial invasions of Manchuria and the rest of China throughout the 1930s and occupation of Indochina in 1940. Conflicts swelled in July 1941 as U.S. President Franklin D. Roosevelt, along with the governments of Australia, Britain, and the Dutch East Indies, initiated trade embargoes to isolate Japan.[7]

Thus when Japan dropped bombs on Pearl Harbor and the United States declared war on a new foreign enemy on 8 December 1941, it meant something very different in the United States to say, "I am Chinese." The Chinese American poet Nellie Wong writes:

When World War II was declared
on the morning radio,

we glued our ears, widened our eyes.
Our bodies shivered...
Shortly our Japanese neighbors vanished
and my parents continued to whisper:
We are Chinese, we are Chinese.
We wore black arm bands,
put up a sign
in bold letters.[8]

As people around the world, indeed, glued their ears to the morning radio, Japanese war propagandists in Tokyo—pointing specifically to the social positioning of Chinese people in the United States—also saturated their airwaves with the news that "far from waging this war to liberate the oppressed people of the world, the Anglo-American leaders are trying to restore the obsolete system of imperialism."[9] Ironically yet logically enough, then, right in the middle of the Second Sino-Japanese War, the Japanese imperialist force exacting World War II's "forgotten holocaust" in China was the very same one defending the rights of Chinese people in the United States![10] Hence compelled to change the terms of contradiction, FDR issued a statement on 11 October 1943: "China is our ally.... By the repeal of the Chinese exclusion law, we can correct a historic mistake and silence the distorted Japanese propaganda."[11] The Magnuson Act, passed by Congress two months later, provided for an annual quota of 105 Chinese immigrants and extended naturalized citizenship rights to an Asian group for the first time since the Naturalization Act of 1790. However, repeating rather than correcting the "historic mistake," by this time the U.S. government had also declared the entire Pacific Coast a military zone and orchestrated the mass incarceration of all people of Japanese ancestry living within it.

Part 2 examines in detail this next phase of "civilization" in California and the U.S. West as evolving regimes of race and incarceration formed the backdrop for another generation of the life of paper. Specifically, I situate this life of paper within the development of state "intelligence"—new apparatuses of knowledge production and information control—that anchored, as they remained anchored by, dominant struggles to regulate sociospatial order and identities. Furthermore, as letter correspondence remained a primary medium of social cohesion for the Interned, I argue that the epistolary again provides a unique and distinctly illuminating lens to view modernity's evolving contradictions: the letter, as object of racial state management around which enormous physical and epistemological infrastructures of censorship revolved; and as the object, in its subtleties and its brokenness, facilitating social life that "constantly escapes."[12]

In chapter 3, I investigate systematic efforts to dismantle Japanese diasporic communities living on the U.S. West Coast alongside the broader emergence of a U.S. wartime security or surveillance state. I explore the expansion of infrastructures to control the limits of human knowledge and information as it occurred through two interlocked and evolving movements: first, intensified experiments with mass incarceration as a dominant mode of organizing public life and culture; and second, the transforming production of racial distinction through conflated languages of geopolitics and nation-state citizenship, culture or ethnicity, and moral affect. In particular, chapter 3 elaborates these movements as they unfolded within a longer history of U.S. warfare in the Asian Pacific and as they established the physical, administrative, discursive, and subjective forms of censorship conditioning the life of paper for the Interned.

In chapter 4, I examine the life of paper as part of an intensive aesthetic process, mediating a particular mode of sociality that survives, as it must reckon with, regimes of alienation, incarceration, and censorship. As such social (dis)order barred access to normative channels of communication and self-representation for interned communities, the life of paper facilitated distinctive forms of both individual and collective being, in their essential dialectic. In this sense, I analyze how this dialectic operates through the letter's dialogical form in ways that necessarily exceed dominant Anglophonic literary assumptions and practices. With attention to how interned communities thus turned to aesthetic production to exist through and beyond the terms of "population management," I place the life of paper broadly within preexisting Japanese aesthetic traditions and corresponding onto-epistemologies of presence, absence, and the work of art. In this context, I read letters of the Interned with a focus on how they communicate affect to produce alternate forms of knowledge and truth value under historical constraint, ultimately creating an archive of material for the reassertion of social bonds, sutured through difference and across generations.

THREE

"Detained Alien Enemy Mail:
Examined"

THIS CHAPTER ELABORATES THE RACIAL state project of mass incarceration during World War II, with a focus on systematic developments in knowledge production and information control and with the aim of outlining broadly the conditions of aesthetic production and written correspondence that must shape our understanding of what acts of correspondence *do,* what their forms and contents may mean and how they may operate, in such a context. I argue that massively reorganizing the regional carceral geography necessitated, as it also hailed, expanding infrastructures to control the limits of knowledge and information, and I interrogate these limits as they established both formal and informal constraints on the life of paper. I thus begin with an overview of the U.S. government's production of categorical boundaries necessary to enact the racial and spatial project of forced removal and internment during World War II. I look closely at the production and exploitation of axes of difference—namely, immigration status, gender, and age—to effect the social dismantling of Japanese American (or U.S. Nikkei) ethnic communities,[1] and also at the discursive and physical redefinition of space in order to reform competing or previously localized processes of racial articulation along the U.S. West Coast. This analysis highlights the place of the East Asian Pacific in dramatic expansions of U.S. nation-state surveillance systems, situating the latter both as a goal of public policy and as part of redoubled U.S. movements for economic and geopolitical domination in the regional sphere.[2]

In this context, as exacerbated spatial and epistemological contradictions heightened the need for censorship as a process of dissimulating war,[3] I further examine the subjective and dialogical, inextricable from physical, constraints imposed on those who were incarcerated. I illustrate how, at the crossroads of dominant constructions of national security and national identity, regulation of Nikkei social order and racialized identities—particularly through control over human communications—played a key role in U.S. movements for "ethnic cleansing"[4] vis-à-vis the logic, status, and militarization of nation-state citizenship. In conclusion, I focus on the contradictory military and civil administration of racialized incarceration as the swelling of crisis, manifest most starkly in the ensuing creation of the "Loyalty Questionnaire" and intensified criminalization as constitutive of the structure of democratic consent. Thus further inducing Nikkei alienation and community dissolution, these circumstances would, in turn, also deepen the significance of the life of paper to preserve existing structures of kinship and to reinvent a terrain of social articulation.

THE WIDELY LESSER-KNOWN TRUTH

> But out there is in here too, related—
> it's a matter of perspective, like lines . . .
> Yes, if I had a big enough piece
> of paper, I'd draw the line
> tracing the way we came, smooth
> as tracks clear back to California . . .
>
> LAWSON FUSAO INADA,
> *Drawing the Line*

For Lawson Fusao Inada, the creative act is one in present progressive tense: drawing, a single line . . . a tear opening out to all lines of space and time, reckoning memory with futurity in the essence of *now* and thus retroactively granting the wish to trace the way they came, the imaginative elaboration of paper from which the line follows, back. Similarly, historiographical perspectives on World War II Nikkei incarceration have also engaged in the act of disrupting spatial binaries of "out there" and "*in here*," as well as temporal and subjective assumptions associated with this differentiation. Namely, a synthesis of historical research about these events illustrates how, seemingly counterintuitively, Japanese internment happened *before* what we know now as the internment. That is, by the time FDR called for the mass removal of Japanese Americans from the U.S. West Coast with Executive Order 9066 on 19 February 1942, Japanese internment was, in fact, already done.

The project of internment traces back, at least, to the 1924 Johnson-Reed Immigration Act, or the Japanese Exclusion Act, followed by Japan's military occupation of Manchuria in September 1931. In his pathbreaking research, Bob Kumamoto documents that by the time Japan defied U.S. imperialist dreams of an "open door" in the Pacific, hardly any person of Japanese ancestry in the entire Western Hemisphere was formally exempt from U.S. surveillance.[5] In an undated report traceable to the early years of information gathering, U.S. Naval Intelligence asserted:

> The racial and patriotic characteristics of the Japanese are so strong that it can be assumed that *every* adult Japanese resident, alien or U.S. citizen, will furnish information if requested to do so[;] ... that a *large number* of Japanese civilians aid the Japanese Intelligence is beyond doubt[;] ... that *certain* Japanese civilians are closely connected with the Japanese Intelligence Service is absolutely positive.[6]

By 1932, the U.S. State Department, the Office of Naval Intelligence (ONI), the Commerce and Justice Departments, and Army Intelligence (G-2) began coordinating secret surveillance of the entire Japanese community within the U.S. as well as in trade zones in Central and South America and the Caribbean. This added to preexisting Military Intelligence activities around "the Japanese problem" in Hawaii that began as early as World War I.[7] In 1939, the Federal Bureau of Investigation (FBI), with the cooperation of the U.S. Post Office, initiated mail surveillance of select "resident aliens" to build the dossiers on such potential threats to national security—mostly people of Japanese, and to a lesser extent of German and Italian, ancestry.[8] To augment information gathering, FDR also set up a secret White House intelligence unit, establishing the basis for the wartime Office of Strategic Services (OSS) that eventually became the Central Intelligence Agency (CIA).[9]

By the start of 1941, then, almost a year before the United States declared war on Japan, the FBI had already whittled its focus and completed data collection and analysis on just over two thousand people of Japanese ancestry living in the United States. During the course of this research, the FBI had concluded that not "*every* adult Japanese resident" was a spy, as the ONI report cited above had suggested, since the FBI surmised that Japan would not rely on people born and raised in the United States (Nisei and Sansei, second- and third-generation U.S. citizens, respectively) for purposes of espionage. Under this premise, the U.S. government built dossier files mostly on male community leaders who were either born in Japan (Issei) or born in the United States but educated in Japan (Kibei). Conversely, at this time the

FBI also initiated recruitment of male Nisei to serve as FBI informants, with particular interest in the Japanese American Citizen's League (JACL).[10]

These developments reveal aspects of how, alongside efforts to destroy longer-standing social movements within U.S. borders,[11] U.S. surveillance infrastructures expanded in direct response to imperialist ambitions and movements for domination abroad; moreover, this history illuminates how U.S. agencies within this infrastructure fabricated, defined, and ascribed Japanese generational difference in the context of war.[12] This enormous work of "intelligence" exploited the categorical production of legal recognition that granted Nisei and Kibei citizenship through birthright while simultaneously disfranchising Issei through naturalization and land laws.[13] In this context, the development of U.S. capital and its regulation, vis-à-vis the uneven distribution of political and economic rights, directly mediated people's embodied experiences as kin. FBI activities further intensified this process of alienation as the reproduction of familial intimacies necessarily took place in and through dominant nationalist ideologies rationalizing war.

Building the groundwork for such profound undermining of Nikkei social life and relationships, FBI methodology and data analysis created three categories into which the government placed those targeted as public enemies, hierarchically reorganizing individuals and communities according to levels of perceived threat to national security. Group A, the "known dangerous," included people assumed to promote Japanese commercial or government interests, namely, fisherman, produce distributors, Shinto and Buddhist priests, farmers, influential businessmen, and members of the Japanese consulate. Group B consisted of the "potentially dangerous" and Group C of peripheral figures scrutinized for their "pro-Japanese" inclinations or propagandist activities. Specifically, Groups B and C targeted Japanese language teachers, Kibei, martial arts instructors, community servants, travel agents, social directors, and editors of the vernacular presses.[14]

This discursive infrastructure, creating systematic boundaries for the naming and understanding of social identity in this context, manifested its most fulsome force with the conjoined production of its physical carceral geography. In his extensive research on World War II incarceration and censorship, Louis Fiset documents that in 1941 the U.S. Immigration and Naturalization Service (INS) already had in custody nearly 1,700 "enemy noncombatants," German and Italian commercial seamen captured in international waters since 1939. When Ellis Island, New York, reached maximum overcrowding, the INS created detention centers out of military installations at Fort Stanton, New Mexico; Fort Lincoln, North Dakota; and Fort Missoula, Montana. Hence, when Japanese planes dropped bombs on Pearl Harbor on 7 December 1941, ideological and physical architectures were already in place for activities to unfold very quickly thereafter. FBI emergency arrests began before sundown under a blanket presidential warrant signed by Attorney General Francis Biddle. Congress declared war on Japan the next day, and within the hour, FDR signed three restraint-and-removal proclamations against Japanese, German, and Italian nationals residing in the continental United States. By his signature, the 314,105 German, 690,551 Italian, and 47,305 Japanese residents of the U.S. mainland who had registered with the state, in accordance with the 1940 Alien Registration Act, became "enemy aliens."[15] Under the first Alien Enemy Act of 1798, as amended in 1918, the president legally possessed absolute power over enemy aliens in time of war, including the right to subject them to internment.[16] The very next day, then, the INS had 1,792 enemy aliens in custody, among them 1,212 resident Japanese nationals. And so explains how a story about "the detained" has become one about "the interned." By the time FDR called for the mass removal of Japanese Americans from the West Coast through EO 9066, 3,021 Japanese people in the United States had already been apprehended by the FBI and/or interned as enemy aliens by the INS.[17] In fact, these are the specific and only people to whom "internment" technically refers, all rounded up *before* EO 9066.[18]

SCORCHING THE EARTH

Bob Kumamoto thus notes the paradox of EO 9066, that it ordered "the mass evacuation of the entire Japanese community—but it also thereby undermined any legitimate justification for the initial ABC roundup and called into question the efficiency of the ten-year counter-intelligence surveillance. Hoover recognized this nuance and declared his steadfast objections to 9066 on the contention that the roundup had encompassed all potential saboteurs."[19] Historically speaking, then, the persistent and politicized confusion about what to call the camps created by EO 9066 reflects the most basic ambiguities about what they, in fact, were. Regarding the contemporary problem of language, Toru Saito, a camp survivor, remarks on his use of the increasingly common term, *prison camp:*

And I hate this damn word, internment camp, relocation camp, those are just words that people use. . . . Uh, I always use the word *prison*. We were put into a *prison* camp, we were *imprisoned*. I don't say this bullshit, "We were interned; we were relocated"! I worked in the jails! I never had one guy tell me, "Hey uh, I've been relocated into this jail cell." Fuck! You're in prison! You're in jail man![20]

Various historiographers note that FDR himself, on at least two occasions, used the term *concentration camp,* another name favored by many camp survivors despite qualitative differences between European and American concentration camps during World War II.[21] While dominant historical representations have diminished the malnutrition, disease, and brute force prevalent in specific areas among all U.S. camps,[22] it may be valuable to call attention to how it was precisely the more quotidian qualities of U.S. World War II prison or concentration camps that enabled and normalized more complexly articulated experiments with genocide in the Asian Pacific.[23] Such an inquiry does not negate crucial scholarly insights relating Japanese American internment to capitalist agribusiness, settler colonialism, and political-economic exigencies specific to the U.S. western states;[24] rather, investigating the camps in relation to U.S. global pursuits complement these historical materialist studies with elaboration at concurrent scales of analysis.

A brief interlude through the background of key U.S. imperialist practices in the Asian Pacific opens up an understanding of U.S. camps during the war as part of a tradition of strategic killing in the region—consistent with, rather than outside of, developing the U.S. nation-state itself. That is, if the camps assembled under EO 9066 were indeed "concentration camps" for 120,000 Japanese Americans on the West Coast, they were not formally the first in U.S. history. During global imperialist wars at the turn of the twentieth century, both European and U.S. colonial regimes systematically instituted concentration camps as part of "scorched earth" war tactics to liquidate guerrilla resistance: first isolating guerrilla armies by capturing their communities of origin, then corralling families into camps before annihilating everything in the surrounding landscape. Earliest documentation of such campaigns includes Britain's use of concentration camps from 1899 to 1902 against their colonial antagonist in South Africa—Dutch Boers—as well as displaced native peoples,[25] preceded in 1895 by Spain's "reconcentrado" program to destroy anticolonial guerrilla armies in rural Cuba.[26] Regarding the latter project of forced resettlement and internment that killed an estimated 200,000 to 500,000 people, President William McKinley asserted in his first message to Congress in 1897, "This cruel policy of concentration . . . was not civilized warfare. It was extermination."[27] The public denunciation of such atrocities helped change the form of U.S. intervention in the region from diplomacy toward Spain to declaration of war in 1898. After a quick U.S. military victory, Spain ceded the Philippines, Guam, and Puerto Rico and transferred occupation of Cuba to the United States in the Treaty of Paris, approved on 17 March 1899.

Yet, in midst of the treaty, when Filipino nationalists declared war against the United States on 16 March 1899 and adapted guerrilla tactics drawn from both Cuba and South Africa, concentration camps deemed atrocious in Cuba did not prove as objectionable in the Philippines. Starting in December 1900, the United States implemented its own policy of reconcentration that lasted through 1902. According to Paul A. Kramer:

> The policy aimed at the isolation and starvation of guerillas through the deliberate annihilation of the rural economy: peasants in resistant areas were ordered to relocate to garrisoned towns by a given date, leaving behind all but the most basic provisions. Outside the policed, fenced-in perimeters of these "reconcentration camps," troops would then undertake a scorched-earth policy, burning residences and rice stores, destroying or capturing livestock, and killing every person they encountered.[28]

As E. San Juan argues, the slaughter of 1.4 million Filipinos from 1899 to 1905 by the U.S. military constitutes genocide, a "by-product" of imperial expansion.[29]

This context provides an expanded framework with which we may further reflect on the significance of EO 9066 and the camps it produced, situated in another global restructuring of Western civilization and the intensified contradiction between the development of modern nation-states, on the one hand, and the production of colonial space as concentrated sites of war and killing, on the other.[30] Through this lens, we can view the global reconcentration of Nikkei communities not only as a problem of domestic policy and citizenship contained within U.S. borders but also as an extension of the history of U.S. genocide and conquest across the Pacific. That is, we may understand World World II U.S. concentration camps, building on prior colonial articulations, as nodal points in an organized imperialist campaign for military and political-economic domination at any cost. Contextualized as such, within evolving U.S. and European military practices and the modern rationality of genocide, these concentration camps come more specifically into focus in their direct correlation with the pogrom war strategy deployed by Allied forces distinctively in the Japanese Pacific. As the poet and retired U.S. Air Force B-29 gunner John Ciardi described the latter, "We were in the terrible business of burning Japanese towns. That meant women and old people, children. One part of me—a surviving savage voice—says, I'm sorry we left any of them living. I wish we'd finished killing them all. . . . I did want every Japanese dead. . . . We were there to eliminate them."[31]

Thus consistent with historical precedent and responsive to more developed contradictions of globalization at the height of World War II, the geographic diffusion of U.S. concentration camps throughout the Americas during this period, as part of an international campaign to dismantle an "enemy" force,[32] corresponded with amplified scorched earth war tactics that ultimately culminated in unparalleled holocausts at Hiroshima and Nagasaki. Moreover, Nikkei incarceration further enforced a process of systematic dehumanization necessary to reproduce consent for wars of elimination and, particularly in the context of the nascent Cold War and nuclear arms race, the mass annihilation of people who lived in a convenient site for atomic experiment.[33]

In this light, the enduring legacy of EO 9066 may reside not necessarily in its form of racial targeting or ascription, as is more commonly pointed out, but more crucially in its innovation of *geopolitical* ascription to rationalize ruptures in the imagined integrity of nation-state borders and in the ideological coherence of nation-state citizenship. That is, EO 9066 rearticulated space through the comprehensive rezoning of Washington, Oregon, California, and Arizona as "Military Areas" No. 1 and No. 2, in addition to ancillary military rezonings of Idaho, Montana, Nevada, and Utah, in the first weeks of March 1942. Using U.S. Census data and social science research on the locations and characteristics of U.S. Nikkei communities, the U.S. Army Western Defense Command meticulously mapped these "exclusion areas" for the coordinated reconcentration of approximately 120,000 Nikkei, the vast majority of the nearly 127,000 people of Japanese ancestry living in the continental United States during this period.[34] This act, the systematic renaming of space in order to reterritorialize the civilian landscape, had at least three productive effects vis-à-vis the ways Nikkei incarceration mediated or interarticulated U.S. terror in the East Asian Pacific and U.S. Pacific regional development.

First, it reproduced conditions of possibility for racialized disfranchisement. That is, the rearticulation of space temporarily mitigated irreconcilable fractures in dominant productions of "race" as ideology, the latter necessary to legitimate acts of killing, exploitation, and war as functions of U.S. democracy[35] and contextualized specifically at this time by the U.S. military's ostensible objections to racial fascism. In these regards, FBI Director J. Edgar Hoover himself opposed civilian reconcentration on the grounds of its logical inconsistency,[36] an allusion to how U.S. enemy alien internment took place through an ideological process of Nikkei differentiation that itself destabilized notions of "racial" uniformity reascribed under EO 9066. In this immediate sense, the formulation of EO 9066 tentatively circumvented the racial ideological impasse, or conflicts embedded in competing historical exigencies and productions of dominant Japanese racial form, by displacing the latter in objectified geographic terms that thereby also rendered space inert. By homogenizing space through blanket militarization and government redesignation of targeted areas as exclusion zones, EO 9066 thus established new formal conditions and a new lexicon to reconsolidate competing and/or previously localized processes of racial differentiation.

Second, then, in the process of militarizing public space, EO 9066 also intensified the deputization of whiteness as the form and practice of citizenship, discernible in the creation of fenced camp perimeters to map racial difference,[37] as well as the formulation of camp "common sense" to rationalize this arrangement. Exemplifying the latter, Reverend Daisuke Kitagawa, reflecting on his incarceration and ministry at Pinedale Assembly Center and Tule Lake Relocation Center in California, documents that camp terminology named camp inmates as "colonists" and camp administrators as "Caucasians"; he further notes that "the official policy was to discourage fraternization between colonists and appointed personnel[;] ... for administrative purposes even Negro [personnel] were classified as Caucasians."[38] This language signifies the ambivalent positioning both of Nikkei as colonized people and of state workers and civilians as representatives of a militarized and culturally reformed whiteness. Indeed, the instability of racial terms at this time correlates with historical movements that forced ruptures in and between colonial subjection articulated through legal status, on the one hand, and whiteness articulated through preexisting color lines, on the other. Ironically, the boundary drawn between Japanese "colonists" and Negro "Caucasians" in Kitagawa's example illustrates the full circle of racial contradiction and alienation, as both groups were charged in opposite ways with defending capitalist nation-state integrity as whiteness precisely within the process of racialized political differentiation in relation to its rights.

Third, geopolitical rearticulation under EO 9066 helped normalize domestic militarization as a function of U.S. public policy and mass incarceration as a perceived necessity for public safety, specifically within the vision of liberal progressivism. In this regard, I again consider the point of historical distinction not necessarily in the Executive Order's formalized racial targeting, as is more commonly claimed and held today as a national shame—since this aspect of EO 9066 remained consistent with, not anomalous to, the living legacies of racialized genocide and contemporaneous hegemony of Jim Crow. Rather, EO 9066 made a more substantial mark through the mode of its implementation: the process of institutional transformation not only to renovate the U.S. Pacific Coast as stage for imperialist consolidation but also to expand and retrofit a democratically rationalized system of apartheid within an emerging new world order. In this sense, the creation of concentration camps, coordinating sweeping regional, national, and international changes, formally integrated military surveillance and civil service. That is, initiated as a military operation, the creation of World War II U.S. concentration camps—from the formal disassembly of existing social networks to the practical assembly of prisons—materialized wholly as a public community enterprise that amalgamated warcraft, criminal justice, and immigration control under the official auspices of civil administration.

Logistically, with regard to land conversion, Fiset notes that "existing public spaces such as fairgrounds, racetracks, and livestock pavilions provided acreage and infrastructure needed to quickly assemble centers" where civilian officers prepared people for camp and temporarily detained them until the completion of prison camp construction.[39] Characterizing the latter as the production of "new colonial cities," Lynne Horiuchi argues that planning and developing camps, which required "new infrastructure—roads, sewer lines, utilities, connections to regional transportation—with planned areas for housing, military police, government, industry," literally built on preexisting colonial regimes and modeled progressive ideological values of neatness, efficiency, and scientific management.[40] In this vein, several U.S. social welfare agencies took administrative charge of processing U.S. Nikkei for incarceration. Under the umbrella Federal Security Organization, the U.S. Employment Service established and provided oversight of Civilian Control stations; the U.S. Social Security Board registered evacuees; the U.S. Public Health Service administered medical exams; and the U.S. Work Progress Administration served as personnel. Public entities, such as the Federal Reserve Bank of San Francisco and the Farm Security Administration, also facilitated economic dispossession through the management of property transfers and sales.[41] From these foundations, the War Relocation Authority (WRA), established on 18 March 1942 and drawing employees from those with managerial experience in the Office of Indian Affairs and California's migrant worker programs, oversaw the administration of concentration camps under formal civic principles of state paternalism and social rehabilitation: that is, state protection from nonsanctioned racial violence and community development of American principles and practices.[42]

EO 9066 and its corollary policies thus functioned significantly to solidify a new hegemony, as it socialized a "common sense" of race and incarceration whose core ideological tendencies and organizational structure were not toward (anti)social conservatism but rather Western democratic change aligned with FDR's New Deal legacy.[43] In this sense, and despite concurrent policy and social movements to maximize the redistributive aspects of state-organized political-economic reform at this time,[44] the full articulation of EO 9066 hence crystallized the contradictions of a progressive racial state in which human entitlements and public culture depend on the normalization of war, apartheid, and ethnic cleansing. Moreover, state administration of law and order collapsed any real or ascribed distinctions between repressive and civic institutions in the U.S. West and innovated the framework of consent for systematic confinement as a permanent feature of U.S. racial democracy. Yet such methods of reform would only manifest as crisis again in the amplified contradictions and disasters of camp management—particularly as maintaining the boundaries of World War II U.S. Nikkei incarceration, beyond initial project execution, demanded even further control over knowledge and information.

DRAWING THE LINES

Alongside its use of scorched earth tactics in South Africa, the British military organized the first systematic program to develop existing censorship technologies, producing the template for both British and American censorship regimes during World War I.[45] Still, U.S. censorship practices directly tied to international war efforts remained relatively unofficial until 4 June 1941, when FDR approved a plan that involved the U.S. Army, the U.S. Navy, the FBI, and the Office of the Postmaster General in establishing a modern censorship program to anchor a wartime security state. The approved plan, set in motion with Japanese internment immediately following the bombing of Pearl Harbor, sought to routinize communications surveillance of international post, cable, radiotelegraph, and radiotelephone circuits. On 19 December 1941, FDR signed EO 8985, authorizing the creation of the Office of Censorship (OOC) under the War Department and catalyzing the production of the world's largest censorship operation to date.[46] Formally commingling media expertise and military interest, FDR appointed Associated Press news veteran Byron Price OOC director, with authority to censor at his absolute discretion international communications including cable traffic, mail, broadcasting, and the press.[47] Within the week, a virtually nonexistent army postal censorship staff grew to 349 people, employed in field stations from New York City to Honolulu; the number climbed to 3,547 postal censors by March 1942 and to more than 10,000 at the program's peak in September 1942.[48]

As Fiset documents, rules defining objectionable mail included a government ban on

> information relating directly to camps, [for example]: physical layouts, internee arrival and departure dates, population size, location, strength of guards, and transfers from one camp to another. Complaints about mail restrictions or personal treatment, governmental agencies, or the Red Cross were also prohibited. . . . In an ironic twist, inmates were advised to avoid exaggerating any favorable conditions of detention that might lead the U.S. citizenry to conclude that enemy aliens were being coddled and treated better than American soldiers.[49]

Mobilizing linguistic difference as a tool of racialized repression, INS camp administrators also initially required that Japanese internees write outgoing letters in English only, further isolating Issei who could only communicate in Japanese or who could not find an English scribe. Then, in 1942, with an increasing number of U.S. citizens also held in detention or internment in Asia and Europe, the governments of Germany, Italy, Japan, and the United States agreed that they would each treat captured civilian detainees and internees in their jurisdiction under the 1929 Geneva Convention's guidelines for the treatment of POWs. Under these conventions, people held in captivity must be allowed to send and receive letters and postcards in their native language, and censorship of their outgoing mail should be carried out "expeditiously." To meet these guidelines, the INS censorship division, the OOC, and the Provost Marshal General's Office of the U.S. Army recruited

Japanese-language censors from resident aliens of Korean ancestry who knew Japanese as a colonial language.[50]

A striking contradiction developed out of this systematic effort to censor U.S. "enemy alien" correspondence. On the one hand, it highlights the positive recognition of letter correspondence as part of modern statecraft, as letter-writing conventions became formally encoded in the terms and definition of "civilized" warfare under the Geneva guidelines adopted by U.S. policy. On the other hand, however, international formalization of letter correspondence as a human right reproduced the negative exercise of law enforcement insofar as regulation at times intensified the state-sanctioned brutalities of war. In the latter regard, rule violation could result in psychological torture of U.S. internees through restrictions or loss of mail privileges, thereby nullifying the concept of communications as a "human right," and could also lead to internees' physical torture and abuse.[51] For example, Fiset documents a case in which a Japanese "enemy alien" under INS custody in Santa Fe, New Mexico, received twenty days in solitary confinement for statements made in a postcard, dated 10 August 1945:

> Rights and freedom are restricted so I am having an awful time. All the Caucasian officials in here are big and seem strong, but they are good for nothing. They are useless. Also the censors in here are damn fools. Our desire is to see those damn fool censors be destroyed.[52]

Interestingly, the internee uses the postcard to stage a confrontation with camp officials, an encounter otherwise largely preempted by conditions of physical repression. I interrogate precisely these dynamics of creative agency, or what I am calling the "life of paper" in this context, after the systematic constraints obscuring this vitality are cleared away analytically in the remainder of this chapter.

Pursuing such inquiry, then, formal expansion of U.S. surveillance bureaucracies involved binary yet conjoined censorship paradigms for U.S. Nikkei held under terms of enemy alien internment, on the one hand, and U.S. Nikkei held under terms of civilian reconcentration, on the other. That is, dynamics of civilian camp censorship operated in productive contrast with the structure of prohibition facing enemy aliens, as FDR and the OOC intentionally designed the "domestic" censorship program to rely primarily on voluntary compliance by civilians and the press.[53] Thus, while U.S. officials engaged in a degree of unsanctioned punitive censorship in civilian camps,[54] domestic censorship—in line with the official mission of the

WRA—operated principally as a positive engagement with the populace and through a progressive disciplinary ethos in which, as Fiset observes, "every letter is an exercise in good citizenship, and acquiescence to its regulations represents a contribution to the war effort."[55] Analogous to the effects of EO 9066, then, this domestic censorship regime also officially integrated military surveillance and civic participation—in this context, at the scale of heightened formal training of processes of human cognition and representation.

The specificities of epistemological conditioning for those in U.S. civilian camps during World War II, as discernible in the regulation of letter correspondence for those incarcerated and/or separated by global war, must also be understood in the context of at least two critical developments. First, the proliferation of capitalist mass media and popular culture comprehensively transformed the production of human subjectivity and history as such, a phenomenon that centrally preoccupied contemporaneous European intellectuals also displaced by the rise of fascism around this time.[56] Second, the vexed structure of "voluntary" participation for Japanese American civilians evolved specifically out of longer-standing techniques of conquest deployed by the United States in Japan.[57] As Emily Roxworthy has argued, the structure of U.S. white supremacy in Japan—beginning with U.S. military and diplomatic intervention under Commodore Perry during the Meiji period of Westernization (1868–1912)—occurred less through negative and objectifying terms of Japanese racial ascription than through a coercive racial gaze that policed the performance of Westernized Japanese self-assertion. These complex dynamics of positive and negative force, coercion and consent, thus established precedent for conditions of Japanese American incarceration. That is, U.S. government and mass media officials' public acknowledgment and open broadcast of the injustices of Nikkei internment paradoxically constrained the expression of U.S. Nikkei resistance; moreover, media spectacle conditioned Japanese American performances of good citizenship, or their show of cooperation and sacrifice, as a contradictory sign of their racial abjection. Together with the material conditions of unfreedom that grounded "free speech," an entire industrialized military and ideological machinery thus scaffolded, as much as it was scaffolded by, the training of epistolary practice for the Interned. Moreover, this intelligence infrastructure intensified the torture of confinement by monopolizing control over the experience and reproduction of historical reality itself vis-à-vis the forms and processes of its mediation.

Dear Miss Breed,
 . . . I may have complained about my new environment but I know
it will be difficult to adapt myself to the new surroundings right away.
I am sure everything will brighten up soon and in a few more weeks I
will begin to love this place almost as much as my home in San Diego.
When I stop to think how the Pilgrims started their life, similar to ours,
it makes me feel grand for it gives me the feeling of being a pure full-
blooded American.

Most Sincerely,
Louise Ogawa [age seventeen]

Deepened perspective on the historical development and formal operations
of censorship can change our ways of reading recently published epistolary
archives documenting camp life, such as the *Dear Miss Breed* letters, anthologized by Joanne Oppenheim.[58] This collection provides a record of the wartime correspondence between Nisei youth and Miss Breed, their home district librarian in San Diego, California.[59] As the subtitle, "True Stories of the
Japanese American Incarceration during World War II and a Librarian Who
Made a Difference," suggests, Oppenheim's editorial interventions situate
the archive within a contemporary ideological framework of national recovery and reconciliation, as the letters provide evidence for the innocence and
resilience of Nisei as well as the early sympathies and exemplary friendship
offered by their interlocutor from the other side of camp. Yet if we understand dominant practices of letter correspondence as constitutive of—rather
than autonomous from—processes of war, then investigating the *Miss Breed*
anthology can also offer insights into the formal interlocking of the two in
mediations of the letter itself. Situating Louise Ogawa's letter here within the
historical limits of its production, for example, can restore otherwise
obscured terrains of meaning as they relate specifically to problematics posed
by the pedagogical and dialogical structure enforcing U.S. concentration
camps.

Pedagogically, the *Miss Breed* correspondences archive the ideological
program of Americanization taking place in civilian reconcentration camps

under the progressivism of the WRA administration. Critical historiographical approaches have developed a view of camp practices of Americanization as a process of ethnic cleansing.[60] This perspective resonates particularly in light of progressive health and hygiene campaigns that dovetailed with camp management, evolving from racial eugenics movements to reorganize urban apartheid through positive constructions of human and reproductive fitness, civic order, and modern aesthetics.[61] As Gary Okihiro's pathbreaking work has argued, the ethnic cleansing project specifically for Issei unfolded through extreme modes of alienation, as the ritualization of habits in conformity with dominant Anglo culture and values involved actively dismantling family, language, and religious affiliations. Many Issei, in turn, intensified the contradiction by redoubling their investments in the very practices Americanization efforts sought to erase.[62]

For over half of the population in camp who were Nisei youth, however, the *Miss Breed* letters mark, and are marked by, the excruciating contradictions of Americanization for those rendered vulnerable along axes of both race and age, particularly as these categories of human differentiation shaped the rights and conventions of U.S. citizenship. That is, inseparable yet distinct from the moral conversion of "alien" immigrants, aesthetic disciplining of Nisei youth mediated the embodiment and performance of their status as citizens, bound by the cruel limits of self-assertion within U.S. surveillance and censorship regimes. Epistolary training for Nisei youth thus distinctively combined the civilizing mission intended for "illegal aliens," as in the previous case of the Detained or the present case of the Issei Interned, with the interpellative function intended for children of the national body. In this sense, the pedagogical project facilitated through correspondence played a pivotal role in broader movements of literary and aesthetic assimilation that occurred in the process of Japanese American internment, as in Colleen Lye's analysis of how popular naturalist representations of the event ultimately articulated the regional incorporation of Japanese Americans into the U.S. body politic.[63] Correlated with this macro process, in this case, epistolary practice functioned conversely to assimilate Americanization efforts into the micro processes of Nisei cognitive development and subject formation as U.S. citizens and as youth.

From this perspective, Louise Ogawa's letter exemplifies a struggle to apply the ideology of American exceptionalism and its universalized model of humanity to the circumstances of Ogawa's own life, as she expresses a desire to outgrow the abjection of her "complaining" and mature into acceptance of confinement as her civic obligation. In this context, Ogawa's bildungs-roman also illustrates a secularization of Anglo Christian approaches to epistolary training discussed in part 1, wherein ontological assumptions previously organized through the letter in religious terms have been transubstantiated into the omnipotence and grammar of capitalist nation-state development and identification. She thus concludes, "When I stop to think how the Pilgrims started their life, similar to ours, it makes me feel grand for it gives me the feeling of being a pure full-blooded American." In this gesture, proximity to "the Pilgrims" replaces proximity to Jesus or God as the promise of catharsis or moral perfectability. Moreover, in her fantasy of purity—drawn from both ethical and biological imaginaries, or in hyper-abstracted terms of both grandeur and blood—Ogawa communicates the end of her coming-of-age as the human achievement connoted by the term *American.*

Yet, in a contrapuntal sense, elaboration of the fuller limits of the letter's dialogical condition also highlights further the impossibility of literalist readings proposed by dominant hermeneutics, calling attention instead to the coercive racial gaze policing the performance of Nisei self-assertion.[64] In this regard, the *Miss Breed* letters illuminate the complex processes of deputizing the "Caucasian" civilian populace as part of the project of World War II incarceration. For Nisei youth writing from concentration camps, individuals like Miss Breed embodied the larger structure of political authority dictating the terms of unfreedom, a lived form of synecdoche. Bessie Masuda recalls letter writing to U.S. government officials and civilians during her incarceration as a teenager—creating an extensive personal archive that informs much of chapter 4:

MASUDA: . . . Ya know, at that age, we just thought we were writing to
    someone that would help us bring my dad back [from DOJ internment].
Q: Did you think that if you did it that he might come back?
MASUDA: *Yeees,* yeah.
Q: That you were talking to someone that was going to help you?
MASUDA: Uh-huh, uh-huh, uh-huh, yeah.[65]

Under such dynamics of alienation, power, and powerlessness, wartime correspondence between those who were subjected to Americanization and the "Caucasians" who defined its terms could reinforce as much as relieve conditions of confinement, regardless of the kind intentions often motivating communications. This applies particularly in cases such as the *Miss Breed* letters, in which youth entered into dialogical relations with an adult in an immediate and concrete authority role as their educator. Crucially, Miss Breed's benevolence—rather than any negative expression of violence—animates the force of coercion,[66] a contradiction that undergirds the *Miss Breed* letters in at least two discernible ways.

First, in the many letters like Ogawa's that rehearse ethical discourses of U.S. citizenship, communication of positive sentiment served as a practical response to material and economic conditions of incarceration. That is, cultivating affective bonds through appeals to shared national origins, while demonstrating proper fulfillment of pedagogical expectations in the program of Americanization, also governed access to mundane material necessities and goods otherwise withheld from those who were interned. Formal sentimental connections made through letters were at times inseparable from lists of itemized economic needs that an outside party could help to meet. For example, eighteen-year-old Fusa Tsumagari wrote to Miss Breed on 28 May 1942, from an assembly camp in Santa Anita, California:[67]

> I wonder if you come up on the 14th if you wouldn't be too inconvenienced by getting me a few things. I have enclosed a money order for the sum of $5.00. If you cannot bring them would you please send them. If you come, please bring them because that is the best excuse I have for seeing you—I hope you know what I mean. I would like the following items: [List of eight line items, including price by piece, subtotals, and grand total].

In this context, the point is neither to question the integrity of such letters' sentiments nor to read into them any plots of manipulation on the part of Nisei. Rather, such communications indicate how performances of Nisei self-assertion, mediated through letters predominantly as a wholehearted appropriation of national affinities, were bound under coercive terms to the humiliations of paternalistic dependency and the prospect of material deprivation or reward, in outcomes wholly dictated by the benevolence of the "Caucasian" subject position in the correspondence.

Correlatively, epistolary performances of Nisei self-assertion also governed access to channels of public support vis-à-vis the mass media, in a field of articulation again wholly controlled by the "Caucasian" subject position in the correspondence. In this specific case, Clara Breed's prolific correspondence with Nisei occurred alongside her wartime activism and political advocacy on their behalf; yet the terms of Breed's will to help—albeit perhaps admirable in the context of her own historical limits—ultimately reproduced the underlying conditions of subjection. For instance, in the June 1942 *Library Journal* symposium article, "War Children on the Pacific," Clara Breed writes, "They believe in America, and they believe in democracy, and they intend to prove their loyalty to the doubters."[68] Such a political framework limited Breed's efforts to address injustice, as her position perpetuated progressive ideologies of U.S. imperialist domination and racial democracy that articulated rather than challenged the very creation of camps.

More critically, in her journal and magazine publications, with titles such as "Americans with the Wrong Ancestors," Breed publicly cites Nisei letters as proof of loyalty, in one example, publicizing Ogawa's letter as "evidence that some at least of the young American-born evacuees hold fast to their faith in America."[69] These discursive conditions imposed constraints, however unspoken, on Nisei youth engaged in acts of correspondence with desires for relief. Namely, Breed's activism created circumstances under which Miss Breed, the historical agent and explicit dialogical participant in the letter, simultaneously represented in real terms a popular "Caucasian" audience of doubters to whom incarcerated youth were enjoined to prove their loyalty with active instruction from their educator and benefactor. In this context, the positive terms through which Nisei substantiated their "faith in America," in bitter contradiction, mark a learned expression of the indignities of mass incarceration and public spectacle. Such complexities thus animate epistolary performances in which the medium of relief itself, the contents and form of the letter, exists in tension with the forces of coercion compelling the very act of writing under these circumstances. Ultimately, this antidialogical system—mystifying precisely because it took the form of letters, understood as dialogical language—amplified the hurt of historical trauma inherently defined by the impossibility of articulation. As Amy Iwasaki Mass, six years old when the government issued EO 9066, testified before the Commission of Wartime Relocation and Internment of Civilians (CWRIC) on 6 August 1981:

> [Years later] I have come to the realization that we lulled ourselves into believing the propaganda of the 1940s so that we could maintain our idealized image of a benevolent protective Uncle Sam. We were told that this was a patriotic sacrifice necessary for national security. The pain, trauma, stress of

the incarceration experience was so overwhelming. . . . On the surface we do not look like former concentration camp victims, but we are still vulnerable. Our scars are permanent and deep.[70]

"JUST LIKE BEING PREGNANT"

The hyper-positive forms of censorship confronting Nisei not only harmed youth themselves but also deepened the structural rifts created between generations in the organized effort to dismantle U.S. Nikkei social life. Clara Breed's position on internment, for instance, crystallizes the systematic divisions drawn between Issei and Nisei in formal processes of Americanization, as Breed wrote in 1942, "Although [FBI arrests following Pearl Harbor] were swift, they were also just."[71] By counterposing the legitimacy of Issei internment against the travesty of Nisei reconcentration in this way, advocates like Breed actively reinforced the production of generational estrangement as part of the process of proper Nisei subject formation. These conditions thus instantiate, at an intimate scale, how dominant nation-state affiliation depends on a fundamental destruction as, in this context, American assimilation for Nisei demanded a prerequisite disarticulation of natal identifications and kinships. The deliberate structure of camp administration further affected this program of ethnic and social dismantling, the disclaiming of "wrong ancestors." That is, U.S. officials intentionally undermined generational relations by exclusively promoting Nisei leadership, thereby humiliating Issei authority and instigating intracommunal social disorder through the manipulation of existing hierarchies.[72] At the same time, however, such efforts only made camp management more unsustainable, since inducing communal breakdown compounded the very crises that the camps themselves had to contain.

This chapter concludes, then, with an outline of the ever-intensifying contradictions that forged an impossible existence of binary oppositions. Throughout 1942, these contradictions manifested most starkly in bifurcated measures of population management: on the one hand, establishing a process of work, school, and/or military release for those deemed fit; and on the other, escalating measures of state repression for those deemed noncooperative. These polarizing tactics included the creation of a segregated Nisei U.S. Army infantry regiment, the 100th/442nd Regimental Combat Team,[73] alongside the use of military force against those involved in camp uprisings—

most notably in Poston, Arizona, and Manzanar, California, where popula-tions organized protests against conditions of camp labor, surveillance, and violence.[74] In Manzanar, where U.S. military police imposed martial law at the peak of the crisis, the use of tear gas and machine guns on 6 December 1942 killed two and injured at least nine protesters, and another sixteen "troublemakers" were arrested, transferred, and jailed. Such resistance led to the first WRA penal colonies, established in December 1942 in Moab, Utah, and Death Valley, California, followed by a third in April 1943 in Leupp, Arizona.[75]

Compounding layers of both ideological and operational instability thus forced the U.S. War Department and the WRA to shift their positions by the close of 1942, revising their mission from administering concentration camps to overseeing U.S. Nikkei relocation to areas east of declared military zones.[76] The instrument created to assess individual suitability for release, or to differentiate between the Americanized and the enemy, took the form of a camp questionnaire—a nearly identical document alternately called "Statement of United States Citizenship of Japanese Ancestry" (Selective Service Form 304A) for draft-age Nisei males and "Application for Leave Clearance" (WRA Form 126 Rev) for male and female Issei and Nisei females over the age of seventeen. Administered in February 1943, infamous ques-tions #27 and #28 required, respectively, that U.S. Nikkei consent to serve in the U.S. Armed Forces and pledge unqualified allegiance to the United States while disavowing any form of allegiance to Japan. Popularly referred to by those in government and camps alike as the "Loyalty Questionnaire," the form placed Issei in an impossible position, prompted to claim U.S. citi-zenship rights by the same government that prohibited them from doing so. Moreover, many—both Issei and Kibei—trapped inside that moment of war with no foreseeable end, deliberated over nonmilitary allegiance to their other "home" country as perhaps the only viable possibility to escape U.S. prison camps.[77]

While questions #27 and #28 have hence emerged as a common historio-graphical index of crises embedded in the Loyalty Questionnaire, the latter's overall formal composition perhaps characterizes its most enduring, though less emphasized, historical legacy. Chizo Omori documents the question-naire's comprehensive schema to quantify U.S. Nikkei social life, a research design starting with optimized data collection on each individual's family, social activity, language, literacy, education, religion, travel, finance, and employment history, followed by assessment using a rigid point system purported to measure fitness for release.[78] Exemplifying how the project of World War II racial internment and reconcentration coalesced with expanded uses and techniques of social science,[79] the questionnaire's violence resides precisely in its objective form, the subtleties of assumed legitimacy and naturalized claims on both ethics and rationality. While elaboration of this profound problem lies beyond the scope of this analysis, the broad context raises two basic points relevant for discussion here. First, these circumstances illustrate how censorship and surveillance operate through dialectics that include systematic restriction as well as claims to knowledge as functions of social control. More particularly, then, the Loyalty Questionnaire marks the progression of an enormous intellectual exertion to reduce the significance and depth of human life to a standardized metric intended to signify the universal measure of man.[80]

Ultimately, these dimensions of the Loyalty Questionnaire highlight its place in the broader transformation of dominant racial grammar at this time—the formal template it issued for what many scholars have noted as the "morphing of race into ethnicity" during this period.[81] In this sense, the questionnaire instantiates how dominant processes of racialization, as a mode of organizing human genocides, occurred at this time through hegemonic sublimation of the language of "race" into a dynamic mix of nationalist, capitalist, geopolitical, sentimental, scientific, and cultural discourse—in many ways, inverting previous tautological logics through which ideologies named explicitly as "race" mediated the articulative boundaries of the latter formations. The questionnaire thus archives as much as it enacted a formal proclamation of U.S. whiteness and global white supremacy vis-à-vis its contouring of preexisting racial forms with objectified measures of normative behavior, imagined and ritualized affiliations, moral training, and active investment in social positioning through regimes of racial capitalism and the priorities of killing. On the one hand, this evolution in dominant racial logic mystified relations of war largely through signifiers of sentimental attachment, moral character, and ethical value judgment;[82] on the other hand, such an "infrastructure of feeling"[83] redoubled the historical significance of other forms of affect and aesthetics that would reemerge through the life of paper.

In the final instance, the limits produced in and through discourse remained inseparable from the physical constraints of racial incarceration, which the Loyalty Questionnaire—reproducing the essential structure of contradiction—also heightened as much as relieved. That is, although the WRA's plan to verify "loyalty" provided a channel for camp release, it also deepened the structure and chaos of binary oppositions that expanded classifications of "enemy" and attendant apparatuses for their subjection. The latter category included about 9,000 new people—namely, "no-no boys," or Nisei who answered negatively to both question #27 and question #28; war resisters or conscientious objectors; and renunciants of U.S. citizenship or residency.[84] To deal with these "disloyals," the WRA converted the camp at Tule Lake, already known for its particularly defiant population, into the official Segregation Center on 15 July 1943.[85] That year saw the transfer of more than 15,000 people both in and out of Tule Lake, alongside mounting camp strikes, uprisings, and demonstrations. In response to persistent unrest, the WRA constructed yet another inner ring of confinement called the Military Stockade or Area Three. Stockade prisoners, many of them between the ages of fifteen and seventeen, were quarantined under twenty-four-hour surveillance by floodlight and submachine gun, without visitors or outside communication.[86] Persistent prisoner strikes compelled camp administrators to declare martial law on 13 November 1943; by the year's end, the U.S. Army replaced the WRA as primary authority over Tule Lake, committing 1,200 men and eight tanks to join 300 camp guards and six radio patrol vehicles monitoring twenty-four hours a day. The last large contingent of U.S. Nikkei, about 2,000 men, was transferred for segregation at Tule Lake in February 1944.[87]

As with the FBI's initial ABC roundup, then, the U.S. Loyalty Questionnaire again forced separations, violations that manifested most apparently along axes of generation and gender. The questionnaire intentionally reduced the different times, places, and historical conditions of Nikkei communities to a series of right/wrong answers on one or another side of a gun, a guard tower, a wall, a war, and an ocean. Distorting the heritage of difference, WRA director, Milton Eisenhower, in helping to prepare the questionnaire, projected that 50 percent of Issei would not pass as "loyal," compared to the predicted 15 to 20 percent of Nisei, and urged FDR to make a strong public statement on behalf of "loyal Nisei."[88] This fatal ascription of generational difference, formalized by prewar secret intelligence reports and more deeply exploited by the ABC roundup, changed in dimension when people of Japanese ancestry were forced to assert themselves using terms not of their own making or choosing. Militarized action enabled by and directly following the questionnaire again systematically removed remaining males from their communities, as thousands more Issei, Kibei, and Nisei men joined those on original ABC lists in criminal segregation or DOJ internment camps and thousands more were drafted for war.

In sum, both intensive and extensive systems of surveillance and social control thus fixated on the foundations of U.S. Nikkei communal life. This agonizing process integrated global and intimate dimensions of war as practices of state patriarchy—exercised through internment, reconcentration, and "relocation"—and dramatically altered preexisting forms of patriarchy articulated at the family scale. In the latter regard, the systematic removal of Issei males from their communities produced the conditions under which single motherhood competed with the two-parent patriarchal household as the normative reproductive unit in civilian camps. Yet the militarized violence that caused this to be so also worked against women's capacity to perform as heads of households, or perhaps more urgently, to generate new configurations for social reproduction under the duress of camp life. This duress was manifested most immediately in tolls on physical, mental, and emotional health that, in turn, augmented subtler yet equally visceral registers of censorship. For instance, Hanaye Matsushita, at the camp in Minidoka, Idaho, writes to her husband, Iwao, who is interned at Fort Missoula, on 15 July 1942:[89]

I want to write more often but my eyesight seems to be going. It's probably my age. My nerves are also on edge, and when I take up a pen my heart leaps into my throat and I can't write. Forgive me . . . Every day keeps me busy, with little free time to do what I want . . . Please know that I'm working as hard as I can. I continue to pray to God that we will see each other as soon as possible. I'm overwhelmed with thoughts of how you spend each day. While I realize that I need to stay level-headed, it's depressing to feel as though I have to take care of everything myself.

Such depression, moreover, devastates the entire chain of social reproduction as the pain and atrophy caused by systematic violence passes down. For example, Toru Saito, four years old when he went through the concentration camp in Topaz, Utah, recalls:

Certainly, my formative years have been, you know, moulded around my mother's feelings, I mean, what I perceived my mother's experience being because my mother didn't speak English. . . . She went through *hell*, and I remember that hell through my mother's eyes. From her inability to explain or to understand. So it was, I think it magnified things for me, you know. When you see your mother suffering, you suffer.[90]

Saito makes sense of his family's suffering by contextualizing their "hell" in the political situation that produced it:

I can't even say those goddamn words, "with liberty and justice for all," you know. If you look up the word "liberty" in the dictionary, it says, "the legal right to freedom from restriction and control." That's what liberty means. "With liberty and justice for all?" Is there justice for all in this country? . . . [People say,] shut up Toru, everything is equal, you gotta, just don't go into these areas. Well, either you have freedom or you don't, you know. It's just like being pregnant. You can't be part pregnant! You're either pregnant or you're not pregnant, you know? You have freedom or you don't.[91]

In his comments here, Saito does not clearly distinguish between individual and collective subjects of freedom, as he organically interchanges cases of the plural ("justice for all") and the singular ("You have freedom or you don't"). In this sense, I interpret Saito's stream of consciousness to suggest not so much that freedom is all or nothing, but perhaps more that it is all or none. Equally profound, Saito's metaphor of pregnancy speaks to the gendered and reproductive aspects of racial violence that resonates across scales, from threats at the immediate level against feminized bodily integrity and reproductive rights to more abstracted levels of politics as the administration of life and premature death. Finally, then, in such a context of war, Saito's sustained identification with his mother—withstanding the immensity of forces examined in this chapter—animates his refusal to disclaim the historical experience of injustice despite every systematic effort harnessed against him. It is precisely this enduring sense of social connectivity, bound to Saito's search for freedom and expressed as a condition of birthing or creativity, that calls attention to what may remain in the life of paper and the universes of meaning still palpable within it.

FOUR

Censorship and the
Work of Art (Where They Barbed the
Fourth Corner Open

An artist is a person who lives in the triangle which remains after
the angle which we may call common sense has been removed
from this four-cornered world.

NATSUME SOSEKI (1867–1916), quoted in James
Masao Mitsui, *From a Three-Cornered World*

CRITICAL APPRECIATION OF THE LETTER has hardly been understated. It is an esteem succinctly conveyed, for example, by Jacques Derrida's
assertion, "Mixture is the letter, the epistle, which is not a genre but all genres,
literature itself."[1] Of the letter's inherent sociality, Terry Eagleton writes:

> In the very heart of anguish or confession, the letter can never forget that it
> is turned outwards to another, that its discourse is ineradicably social. Such
> sociality is not just contingent, a mere matter of its destination; it is the very
> material condition of its existence. The other to whom the letter is addressed
> is included within it, an absent recipient present within each phrase. As
> speech-for-another, the letter must reckon that recipient's likely response into
> its every gesture.[2]

Of the letter's role in knowledge production, Carolyn Steedman notes that
popular epistolary fiction disappeared into the form of the novel in the nineteenth century, when literary publics ceased to read in the role of voyeur and
"became the intended readers of the book in their hands." This shift represented changes in the functions of, and relationships between, literature and
history. Tongue in cheek, Steedman describes historical research as something like a meta-dramatic labor, wherein one finds oneself back inside an
epistolary fiction: "But the Historian who goes into the Archive must always
be an unintended reader, will always read that which was never intended
for his or her eyes. . . . The Historian always reads an unintended, purloined

letter."[3] Perhaps further evidence for Eagleton's argument, "Nothing could be at once more intimate and more alienable [than the letter]. . . . The letter comes to signify . . . that folded secret place which is always open to violent intrusion."[4] Yet so much talk of "always" assumes an ability to indulge in fantasies of the timelessness of history. When serving time cannot afford such luxuries, always either falls apart or becomes never again. In the latter contexts, most letters are addressed to a purloined other and written for an unintended reader; they must reckon multiple and contradictory (non)recipients' responses into their every gesture. And the letter sees the Historian although the Historian may not see the letter back.

So it is that detained enemy alien Iwao Matsushita, interned at Fort Missoula, Montana, starts a letter to Hanaye Matsushita, incarcerated in Minidoka, Idaho, "My dear wife, As the Japanese censor is away again, I write this in English."[5]

This chapter interrogates the social processes and productivity of letter correspondence for the Interned, as such activity routes through the densities of war, censorship, and limits placed on media. I approach the life of paper in this context as the work of art—a mix of embodied and affective labor, political intervention, and discernible literary and aesthetic practices—wherein the object created is not only the letter itself, but the heart of collective being that the letter mediates. I hence investigate these dynamics, on the one hand, with concern for material form and the significance of details such as handwriting, paper, and physical practices of letter writing and circulation under constraint. On the other hand, I argue, the contents embedded in the letter form also instantiate the production of a different historical and onto-epistemological fabric coming into being in dialectic with the boundaries of camp existence. In this regard, I pay critical attention to three primary points: first, the creative mediation of a collective subject that does not evade but primarily works *through* the censor, as evinced above by the paradoxical rather than absolute transparency of Iwao Matsushita's text; second, the mobilization of affect as mode of historical intervention, contextualized both by prohibitions on formal self-representation and by dominant reproductions of selfhood as an autonomous rational subject; and third, alternative formulations of spatial-temporal consciousness and historical being that are not simply subsumed by the reterritorialization and ideological assumptions of U.S. racial state democracy. In ways such as these, the "life of paper" sustained or created possibilities for communal life surviving forced separation, movement, and confinement.

Indeed, the uncertainties and liabilities of living under surveillance, in prison camps, during a war of elimination waged at a planetary scale, placed unique significance on letter correspondence. These urgencies are captured in letters between Iwao and Hanaye Matsushita that have been painstakingly anthologized by Louis Fiset and, as needed, translated from Japanese to English by Akimichi Kimura, Megumi Inoue, Christine Marran, and Takehiko Abe for the volume *Imprisoned Apart*. In one such letter, for instance, in which the couple contemplates the stakes and effects of forced separation, Hanaye writes to Iwao on 30 December 1942 (translated from Japanese):[6]

> I've been inquiring around about your internment camp. I worry that impediments will arise in trying to correspond with the outside if I move to your camp and am given the same treatment you receive. I want to consider this a bit longer. After a request for a transfer, decisions take two to three months, but I don't want to ask for a transfer until after the hearing decision [to reverse Iwao's "enemy alien" status, allowing him to join her at a civilian camp in Minidoka]. There is nothing I can do about the fact that I may have to continue living alone . . . I must also consider the possibility of your coming here or our being forced to repatriate to Japan together. If I'm outside at that time, I can take care of things and we can return to Japan. It's important to consider the various possibilities. I want to see you as soon as possible, but I also want to go on to a new camp only after investigating its regulations regarding family.
>
> Just as it was when you were at the Seattle Immigration Station, where you could see a visitor for only five to ten minutes once a week and had to speak in English, there are times now when it's easier to communicate by letter, although in New Mexico or Louisiana, English letters take five or six weeks to arrive. Important news is apparently sent by telegram. At night, unable to sleep, I lie in bed thinking about what to do but am still at a loss. Let me know how you feel about the situation.

This example illustrates how dialectics of confinement and forced movement prompted people to prioritize the ability to communicate through letters over being together in person. Such existential triage points to the necessity of strategic planning for long-term collective survival, taking into meticulous consideration the various uncertainties of historical circumstance and their unfolding. In this context, as Hanaye argues, letter correspondence could serve as a better form of communication and means of social relation than even physical contact or proximity—a productivity that parallels the ways coaching letters rearticulated rather than merely reflected or described village life, as I sought to show in part 1. In this situation, Hanaye thus measures their survival options against the conditions regulating letter correspondence at different camps, including varied treatment by letter censors, language policies, and estimated correspondence time lags.

Moreover, these latter deliberations indicate, again consistent across contexts, that the dynamics of the life of paper do not transcend limits so much as move *through* them. That is, the potential of letter correspondence is qualified by rather than "free" from constraint; as such, the form of appearance of the letter's social possibilities contains, even when it transgresses or exceeds, the disciplining that circumscribes its existence. In this sense, physical structures of presence and absence wrought through internment and reconcentration—as when Hanaye makes explicit her condition of isolation by noting that "there is nothing I can do about the fact that I may have to continue living alone"—correlate with representational boundaries imposed by censorship that determine the form of the letter itself. These interlockings and contradictions manifest, for example, in the following letter from Isohei Hatashita, written in the process of his internment and anthologized by Lawson Fusao Inada.[7]

Fort Missoula, Montana
Feb 9, 1942

Dear Wife Kazue Hatashita and family,
... This place is nice, not as cold as I imagined even snow falled about eight inches deep last night. How are all the family at home after I left? I am all right, don't worry. All officers are understanding our position, very kind, treating us with sympathy.
It was wholesale eviction of alien Japanese fisherman in Terminal Island, far inland.
When we arrived Missoula, our group separated in three part, our group [censored] persons encamped at Missoula, last of other part of

group gone for North Dakota. In the camp at Missoula are about [censored] Japanese. In one house forty persons are living and sleeping side by side. My bed, mattress, and blankets are all new, so it's better than my twenty-years-old bed at home. [censored] I received my suits case. I want some more shirts my black shirts which I weared when I was fishing, jacket, safety razor, heavy kubimaki [scarf], looking glass, etc. [conclusion lost]

In this letter, the vulnerabilities of those who are interned channel through the obvious impositions of the censor, signs of repression that appear unambiguously in the form of exclusions and leave their trace in the form of positive statements. In this regard, editorial inclusion of this letter itself in contemporary efforts of historical preservation, replete with annotations of the letter's redactions and permanently irretrievable parts, also extends meaning. That is, its inclusion suggests that for the purposes of archivization, the letter remains meaningful precisely *because* of, not despite, the explicitness with which censorship delineates its contents—both what is sayable and what is not.

If the letter can carry this retroactive significance for those seeking to historicize the internment, however, the process of making meaning seems more vexed for those whose recollections of the historical moment themselves defy closure. As Bessie Masuda recalls the experience of letter correspondence within and among camps:

I remember receiving letters [from Dad] and it's all censored. You can't even read it because it's all cut out. The letters are censored. Ya know, so why they, why they even *delivered,* I don't know. . . . But we were forever writing, [though] maybe we didn't send. . . . And I was always keeping in touch with [friends who were not in camp] . . . you know I was writing to friends. And they would write too but it's always censored so, what's the point? . . . My sister, she was writing to a service man, ya know, in the 442 [U.S. Army Infantry Regiment]? And his letters were always censored, cut out, too.[8]

In contrast to a provisional sense of resolution that accompanies exposure of censorship practices and their documentation in the historical record, Masuda's memories reflect a deeper-seated, if passive, refusal to render the past coherent in any easy or foregone way. Unlike the assured readings scholars are enjoined to perform on texts by definition of our task, Masuda remains profoundly ambivalent about what anything *means,* a lack of reconciliation that comes through and peaks in her question, "so, what's the point?" Furthermore, this seeming dispassion frames Masuda's other comments that imply the futility not only of having delivered letters, but of sending them at all. Nevertheless, within this negativity, Masuda's remarks intimate that this reticence was not at odds but actually coterminous with a compulsion to keep corresponding, as she notes that "we were forever writing. . . . And I was always keeping in touch. . . . And they would write too." This persistence, while perhaps inassimilable to any definitive explanatory framework to make sense of the matter, gestures to an unspoken, perhaps unspeakable, role of letter correspondence as a life-preserving activity in camp whose fullest productivity exceeds attachment to fixed outcomes.

As a problem for thought, then, the life of paper foregrounds the layers of uncertainty underlying every form of appearance of order and provides alternative grounds to interrogate processes of literary, social, and political signification in this light. For instance, considering the dynamics of the life of paper across each of these examples already offers another way to interpret the popular phrase commonly attributed to Issei and their response to wartime internment and reconcentration: *Shikata ga nai,* "It cannot be helped." This phrase is ritually cited as evidence for Issei passivity or unmitigated tolerance for subjection.[9] Yet, as letters or comments by Mastushita, Hatashita, and Masuda demonstrate, radical acceptance of separation and isolation did not necessarily actualize consent for confinement so much as establish conditions of possibility to move through the event in ways that do not easily register in binary terms of oppression and resistance. While this perspective begs related questions regarding onto-epistemological orientation, which I return to later in this chapter, it also has immediate implications for how we might approach the life of paper as a mundane practice triggered by internment and inextricable from social and material reorganizations of daily life. In this regard, reading through a final series of letters from Hanaye to Iwao Mastushita offers insights into quotidian processes of community struggle and creative adaptation that transpire through letter correspondence, dynamics between limitation and movement, and mediations of social reproduction despite the instability of relationships and their daily articulations in this context.

An early letter, written after Iwao's internment as Hanaye awaited her own removal from their home in Seattle, details preexisting family conflicts that would only heighten with the stress of reconcentration and systematic exacerbation of intimate crises. Hanaye writes on 6 August 1942 (translated from Japanese, figure 20):[10]

> Every day has been busy. I just finished cleaning the bathroom and now hastily pick up my pen to write. I'm behind in responding to you because my left eye has worsened and it makes it hard to write. It's probably just age, so don't worry. I told Uncle about it, but he ignores my complaints, so I cling to God. Most days we don't see each other all day long. I look forward to living by myself after the move . . . [Uncle] continues to demonstrate the usual disregard for anything and everything. I've finally gotten it through my head that he's a completely unreliable person . . . Writing a letter in English is difficult and it frustrates me that Uncle won't help me.

In this passage, Hanaye expresses anger and frustration directed at Uncle, alluding to the gendered division of labor in the Matsushita household after Iwao's internment and reaching the perhaps hyperbolic point, "I look forward to living by myself after the move." This mention of "the move," the looming specter of forced removal and incarceration, also insinuates a broader structure of anxiety contextualizing the immediate antagonism as well as the emotional and physical degeneration Hanaye describes in the letter. Interestingly, her antipathy culminates in the identification of letter correspondence as a form of reproductive labor: a domestic duty as habitual as "cleaning the bathrooms" and a social or collectivized undertaking in which Hanaye resents Uncle for not accepting his responsibilities in this process.

After "the move" from their home to the Puyallup Relocation Center in Washington and final arrival at the camp in Idaho, Hanaye's correspondence suggests her adaptation to the gendered reorganization of the reproductive sphere and rearticulation of her own social position under the constraints of this new setting. She writes to Iwao on 20 August 1942 (translated from Japanese):[11]

> I'm resigned to trying to live a bachelor's life. Aunt Kaneko and I are doing well living together. I owe a lot to her. Two or three single women will move in nearby since here are not enough living quarters to go around.

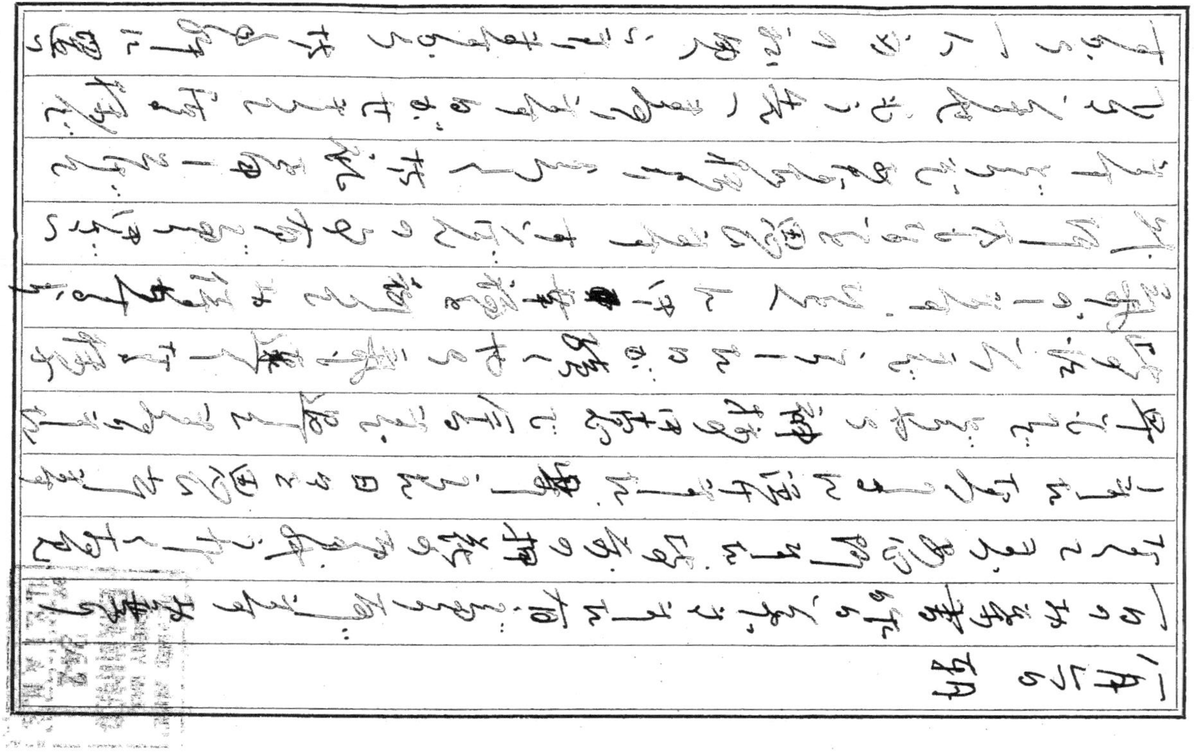

I. MATSUSHITA

FIGURE 20. Excerpt from Hanaye to Iwao Matsushita, 6 August 1942; University of Washington Libraries, Special Collections, Iwao Matsushita Papers, Acc. 2718–001, Box 9, Folder 9.

As she describes her new living arrangements in this letter, Hanaye notes her resignation to gender segregation—or the gendered processes of racial differentiation in this context—wherein acceptance of imposed limitations regenerates other social possibilities. That is, Hanaye's attempt "to live a bachelor's life," a perhaps subtle claim to her female masculinity, anchors the cultivation of same-sex communities as a mode of collective survival,[12] discernible in this passage not only through the mention of single women living together but also in the social implications of the assertion that "I owe a lot to her." In this sense, Hanaye documents how communities in camp responded to constraint by transforming gendered agency and sexual divisions of reproductive labor.[13] Fiset has found that this reinvention included the socialization of the process of letter correspondence as more educated or physically able women served others as scribes.[14]

These arrangements, while on the one hand a show of acceptance as the precondition for adaptation and resilience, on the other hand, did not cancel out preoccupations with misery and dying that also remain palpable in the shared psychic space afforded by the letter. As Hanaye continues in the next paragraph of this 20 August letter:[15]

> It's unendurably hot and dusty, though eventually I'll get used to it. My body is weak and can only stand so much. I pray to God for strength and tolerance. At times like this I wish day and night for your quick return. . . .
> I have many things to tell you, but in the afternoons I am worthless because of the horrible heat. When I dwell on this situation, I have suicidal feelings, but I've got to keep myself together until your return. I imagine you're also experiencing rough times. I have come to understand what it's like to live alone in this world. People tease me, calling me the Montana widow.

In this mediation of bodily and psychic experience, the letter represents both Hanaye's turn to imagination as a means of transgressing embodied constraint and, conversely, physical and emotional strain as an absolute limit on the dialogical space of the letter. Similar contradictions bear on the innermost edges of imagination as the letter at once facilitates Hanaye's ability to connect with Iwao and enunciates the breaking points of that connection. In this sense, perhaps we may understand these internal dynamics as constitutive of the life of paper's very center of gravity, the uneven movement rather than patent resolution of irreconcilable animating energies. This ontological instability finally manifests in the deep irony embedded in the term *Montana widow,* which simultaneously reinscribes the sinister simulation of Iwao's death, connotes Hanaye's struggle to live through the peculiarities of her own experience of dying, and, in the act of reaching for him through the letter, marks a lived attempt to raise the "dead."

"WE"; OR, MAKING THE CASE

The bitter contradictions were certainly not lost on Iwao. Taken from his home by the FBI on 7 December 1941, Iwao, in his letters from internment, plainly spells out the urgency of the life of paper in the context of existential deprivations. Iwao implores Hanaye in a letter dated 2 June 1942 (translated from Japanese):[16]

> Dear Hanaye,
> I've been waiting anxiously to hear from you, but I haven't received any word, not even acknowledgement that you received my "song" or the stones I sent you. Mr. Fukano and others have received their letters a week ago. According to a letter from your camp, my stones apparently reached you, but since I don't have direct word from you I'm worried.
> I hear that many in your camp have become ill, and I'm concerned that you are busy at the hospital or that you yourself have gotten sick.
> Letters are the sole comfort and assurance when we are far apart like we are. I realize that you aren't an ardent letter writer, but please write at least once a week.

If examples taken from Hanaye's letters illustrate the (albeit ambivalent) positivity of letter correspondence—acts of writing that mediate Hanaye's own subjective and social experience—this excerpt from Iwao's letter, on the other hand, calls attention to negative aspects of the life of paper's constitutive contradictions. That is, whereas Hanaye's letters locate her tentative sense of presence in the wake of Iwao's absence, Iwao's letter outlines a lapse in correspondence that, in marking the breakdown of communication, reinscribes

Hanaye's absence in Iwao's life and, in turn, Iwao's own sense of disappearance writ large. Interestingly, in this case, the articulation of Iwao's subjectivity remains relatively arcane, as the letter communicates Iwao's anxiety and worry; his expressed anxiety and worry mediate his desire to reestablish connection with Hanaye; and questions about Hanaye's condition replace further information about Iwao's own physical and emotional state. In this sense, Iwao indeed appears in this letter primarily through a modality of negation.

While moving in this negative trajectory, however, the excerpt from Iwao's letter, like previous discussion of those from Hanaye, also provides insights into elements of the communal process through which letters mediated collectivity in the interned context. Two points stand out in this regard. First, this passage introduces dialectics of passive and active positions, both as Iwao documents "waiting"—the seeming absence of motion—as a kind of social activity and as Iwao emphasizes *receiving* letters even more than writing them as crucial to the life of paper's metabolic functioning. Notably, when he implores that "letters are the sole comfort and assurance when we are far apart like we are," Iwao does not make himself the subject of the need for comfort and assurance; instead, the agent, and hence agency, becomes the letter. Second, then, the amount of social activity that coheres around letter correspondence, as described by Iwao, situates his final use of the subjective case "we" in a polyvocal discursive context that can lend elasticity to the referent. On the one hand, at the most immediate level, "we" represents Iwao and Hanaye specifically and their particular circumstances of distance. Yet, on the other hand, Iwao's comment emerges out of the context of "Mr. Fukano and others" who have received their letters, alongside Iwao's remarks about "your camp" and its associated voices as implicitly distinguished from "mine" or "ours." At a more generalizable level, then, "we" can also represent the collective condition of Issei internees of war, all of whom depended on receiving letters "as the sole comfort and assurance" or literal social tie to the rest of the world that internees experience as "far apart."

From this latter perspective, further consideration of the positionality of internees or "enemy aliens"—specifically vis-à-vis interlocked economies of their representation, social reproduction, and camp administration—may uncover deeper aspects of a multivalent collectivity mediated by letters, as well as the life of paper's responsiveness to multiple levels of constraint facing them. On the one hand, another early letter by Iwao to Hanaye Matsushita highlights the particularities of isolation and its subjective impact for those interned by the Department of Justice. From Fort Missoula on 15 July 1942, Iwao writes (translated from Japanese):[17]

> I was very glad to receive your four-page letter dated the 26th. When-
> ever I see your letter, I can't help feeling hopelessly inadequate
> for not being able to be there to see you through all the anxieties.
> Although there are people to whom I owe my thanks for looking after
> your welfare, I've not written because I sense many are wary of hav-
> ing any correspondence from this camp. Can you please give them
> my regards and thanks?

In this passage, beginning with the interchangeability of Hanaye's letter and Hanaye herself, Iwao expresses feelings of inadequacy in relation to Hanaye and reticence in relation to their broader community that, in turn, compel self-censorship in excess of any specific state policy or practice. Iwao moves on to characterize his alienation in spatial and epistolary rather than subjective terms. That is, Iwao does not articulate otherness through an expressed split between "you" and "me/us" but rather one between "there" and "this camp." Embedded in this understanding, when Iwao explains his sense that "many are wary of having any correspondence from this camp," the posi-tioning of internees is again folded into an agency attributed to "correspon-dence." Such entanglements of meaning thus confer on letters the capacity to mediate not only subjectivity but also place, as Iwao interprets civilian desires as a triangulated and simultaneous dissociation from correspondence, the camp itself, and the people interned there under explicit ascriptions of enmity.

On the other hand, parallel to Hanaye's circumstances in reconcentration, internees under their specific conditions of isolation reinvented means of collective life and new patterns of socializing reproductive labor vis-à-vis the life of paper. In a letter dated 23 March 1943, Iwao documents the leadership position he assumed in these regards (translated from Japanese):[18]

> Dear Hanaye,
>   I'm thankful I can write again in Japanese now that the Japanese
> censor is finally back.
>   It was quite a sudden decision, but Hayasaka-san will be moving to
> your center. Although I personally don't relish taking over his duties
> as the group leader, I'll do my best if it'll help others.

Springlike weather suddenly came upon us last night, and the snow has begun to melt, making large pools we have to detour around.

I received a letter from Kanazawa-san, whom I haven't heard from in several months. He said he saw you at church and that you looked fine. I was relieved to hear that. Please take good care of your health and try to enjoy each day.

Well, I'll stop here for today. When you're feeling well, please write me even if it's only a short note.

Please give my regards to Tsune-san and his family, and to Doc too.

Sayonara, Iwao

At least two contradictions active in this letter give context to the "group" formations both producing and produced by it. First, the letter begins with a seemingly banal acknowledgment of the censor's presence that infiltrates but cannot fully preempt the letter's vitality. Such a juxtaposition of intimacy and intrusion brings out the paradox of the life of paper as an "open secret" whose workings cannot be entirely accounted for even as its very existence hails containment.[19] Second, Iwao's poetic interlude about the change of seasons subverts the alienation negatively associated with the letter's mediation of place, instead subtly turning or returning to the vaster ecology whose ontological impositions lend perspective to—without minimizing—the historical circumstances of internment (figure 21).

This latter conjuring of an irreducible totality rather fittingly bridges two different instantiations of the life of paper's communal culture. In the first case, Iwao mentions his new "duties as the group leader," or spokesperson for the Japanese contingent at Fort Missoula. While this refers most formally to his representative role in the camp's administration and functioning, in other letters to Hanaye, Iwao also documents ongoing unofficial intellectual duties such as teaching English class.[20] In fact, Iwao speaks more to the burdens of serving in this capacity when he writes to Hanaye on 3 April 1943 (translated from Japanese), "I haven't been able to do any studying on my own or write letters when I want to because of the extra duties I've assumed. I want to write to Doc and Tsune-san, but please tell them what I've said."[21] This sentence underscores the second aspect of communal culture that also arises in Iwao's 23 March 1943 as well as earlier 15 July 1942 letters: that is, explicit reference

FIGURE 21. Leaves enclosed with a letter from Iwao to Hanaye Matsushita, August 1942; University of Washington Libraries, Special Collections, Iwao Matsushita Papers, Acc. 2718–001, Box 9, Folder 9.

to the collective context in which interned and reconcentrated communities wrote, shared, and circulated letters.

Considered alongside each other, these group formations call attention to letter correspondence as a multilayered activity with potential to reproduce an appositional communal autonomy, dispersed yet shared within and across camps through the life of paper. When understood in isolation and in dominant contexts and frameworks of representation, the various political and pedagogical duties of the group leader, as exemplified by Iwao, could be understood as functioning in the final instance merely to assimilate other internees or bring them into the folds of hegemonic racial state representability.[22] However, the life of paper—insofar as it takes place within and yet exceeds political and educational forms officially sanctioned by camp administration—opens another dimension of insight. From this perspective, letter correspondence harnesses and socializes "group" intellectual activity in excess of what the disciplinary regimes of camp management intended to produce. We may discern this distinct social commons or "undercommons,"[23] for instance, in the extensive networks of correspondence and circulation at work in Iwao's letters, which consistently mediate concerns for caregiving, holistic health, and pleasure. Such mediation carries the potential, in turn, to generate forms of representation beyond (though not necessarily "outside") the purview of the state: that is, to facilitate not only a sense of social recognition in relation to camp officials and other prisoner of war contingents but also new ways of understanding each other, as both were necessary conditions for sustaining collective life and identification.

In this latter sense, aspects of communal imagination developing in dialectic with communal activity also come to the fore. We have already seen how senders constructed letters with a collective audience in mind, social vision that both includes and extends beyond a discrete dialogical encounter between writer and recipient. In another example excerpted from a different archive, this communal imagination also manifests conversely in the way letters were received. On 18 April 1942, Sonoko Iwata, awaiting evacuation in Thermal, California, writes to her husband, Shigezo Iwata, taken for internment to Santa Fe, New Mexico:[24]

> When I receive words from you, I let [our friends and family] know. At other times, I do not speak of you unless they mention you first because I don't want them to know how I feel.

In the practices described in this passage, Sonoko makes explicit the sharing of Shigezo's letters while also noting moments of restraint. In the latter case, instead of signaling a rejection of collectivity, Sonoku's diffidence instantiates a way that the communal sensibility unfolds intensively as well as extensively. Namely, Sonoku's explanation, "I don't want them to know how I feel," suggests that mediating information about Shigezo exposes as much about Sonoko's own vulnerabilities as it does about his, an intersubjectivity calling attention to the porosity of personal boundaries normally perceived as separating rather than connecting people.

Such intimacies and subtleties of collectivity thus nuance our view of the reproduction of this plural subject in the dominant field of representation and the basis this subject provides for political agency and intervention. Ultimately, greater attention to these interchanges, taking shape through the life of paper in asymmetrical relation to induced estrangements, opens an avenue further to interrogate productions of collective form emerging underneath or beyond the boundaries of systematized binaries, nationalisms, and political dogmas of this time. Entangled in the latter, this communal imperative is conditioned in significant ways by the very terms of enemy alien ascription and arrest that occluded Issei from rights of citizenship or recognition as rational subjects capable of U.S. civic participation. The representative democratic process of internment following initial FBI roundup, in fact, decisively magnified rather than mitigated these contradictions through the creation of "loyalty hearing boards." Composed of three civilians and chaired by an attorney, these volunteer boards sorted Issei into "loyals" and "disloyals" and made recommendations to the attorney general for a person's release, parole, or internment.[25] As the imposed enemy alien identification itself restricted self-representation, recommendations largely hinged on evidence provided by character witnesses who could testify on behalf of those who had been arrested.

Caught in this matrix of social alienation and dependence, those subject to internment thus relied on the intercession of third parties—frequently in the form of letters—to "prove" their loyalty and fitness for release. For example, recalling her father Taro George Masuda's "enemy alien" conviction and their attempts to overturn it, Bessie Masuda notes that her family placed hope in the support they could marshal from respectable members of their pre–World War II community in Lodi, California, activity that generated an archive of letters and notarized statements from neighbors and people such as the local fruit shipping manager, bank cashier, and auto dealer.[26] The following letter, handwritten by a Lodi ranch owner, Charles Beckman, on 18 April 1942 (figure 22), illustrates the provocative narrative qualities of this form of testimony.

Director of Dentention [*sic*] Center
Area 2, Box 300
Bismark, North Dakota

Dear Sir:

I have been asked to write to the Dentention Center on behalf of Taro George Masuda of Lodi, California who is interned at the Dentention Center as an enemy alien.

As an American I feel if there are any facts which indicate Mr. Masuda is guilty of any wrongful activity. He then should be treated as an enemy saboteur.

But as an American and in fairness to Mr. Masuda and his children, I think it my duty to present a few facts which I have observed in dealing with Mr. Masuda.

Mr. Masuda has been my employee continually for a period of seven years. His duties consisted of general vineyard work, foreman of the ranch in case of my absence. In the harvest season Mr. Masuda acted as foreman over approximately seventy-five Japanese workers. In handling these workers Mr. Masuda was trusted with large amounts of money. Over a harvest season Mr. Masuda had excess to about 17,000 dollars. This man had every opportunity in the world to be dishonest. But I personally left the opportunity open for him in order to find out what type of man he was. In all my financial dealings with this man never did I find a trace of dishonesty. And the performance of his work and duties on my ranch were always excellent. I think anybody whom he has served as an employee in the last twenty years will draw the same conclusion.

In observing Mr. Masuda I have always noticed that this man would never send his children to the Japanese school. His answer was "my children are Americans and should be taught American ideals and customs."

Mr. Masuda always took an active part as a leader among the local Japanese people, but his attitude was always one of definite cooperation with the American citizens of this community. In my opinion Mr. Masuda has done more than any other local Japanese person to promote a feeling of cooperation and understanding between the American and Japanese people.

Mr. Masuda came to this country in 1920 at the age of 16. During that time he has made two trips to Japan once in 1924 for a period of 3 months to get married, and in 1927 to go back and get his younger brothers who were left homeless by the death of their parents. Mr. Masuda was 18 years old when both his father and mother died and upon their death took complete custody of his 3 sisters and 2 brothers all of whom were born in this country except one sister. Mr. Masuda reared his two brothers and sent financial support to Japan to his 3 sisters.

I understand up until 2 years ago he sent approximately 200 dollars a year for the support of his sisters. In his talkings with me he after complained of this fact because he said they depended on him too much for financial support. One can readily see that during Mr. Masudas life he has reared two families his fathers, and his own.

Except for his two trips to Japan Mr. Masuda very seldom leaves his home, and his work. Probably during his life in this country he has made a half dozen trips to San Francisco which is about 100 miles away from this community. Other than to San Francisco I know of no other points of interest he has traveled too [sic] in the United States. While serving me as an employee he has been continually on the job ten hours a day, six days a week.

Mr. Masuda is highly respected by local bankers and his former employees. If Mr. Masuda has any enemies in this community, it is because of his fellow workers jealously [sic] of his high efficiency and productivity, and the man being Japanese it made it easy for some of them to take advantage of the man.

In conclusion I have always thought of Mr. Masuda even though a Japanese citizen as a true American believing and practicing our American traditions. He is a man of fine character, a student deeply interested in anything that would increase his knowledge, and a man highly respected in this community.

Yours very truly,
Charles Beckman Sr.

In the introductory paragraphs of his letter, Beckman begins by authenticating his own position as a representative American, properly trained to identify—and identify with—the will to destroy enemies of the state as well as to preserve U.S. democratic ideals, the ideological justifications for that will to destroy. Upon verifying the reliability of his narrative voice, Beckman then presents primary evidence for Mr. Masuda's fitness for

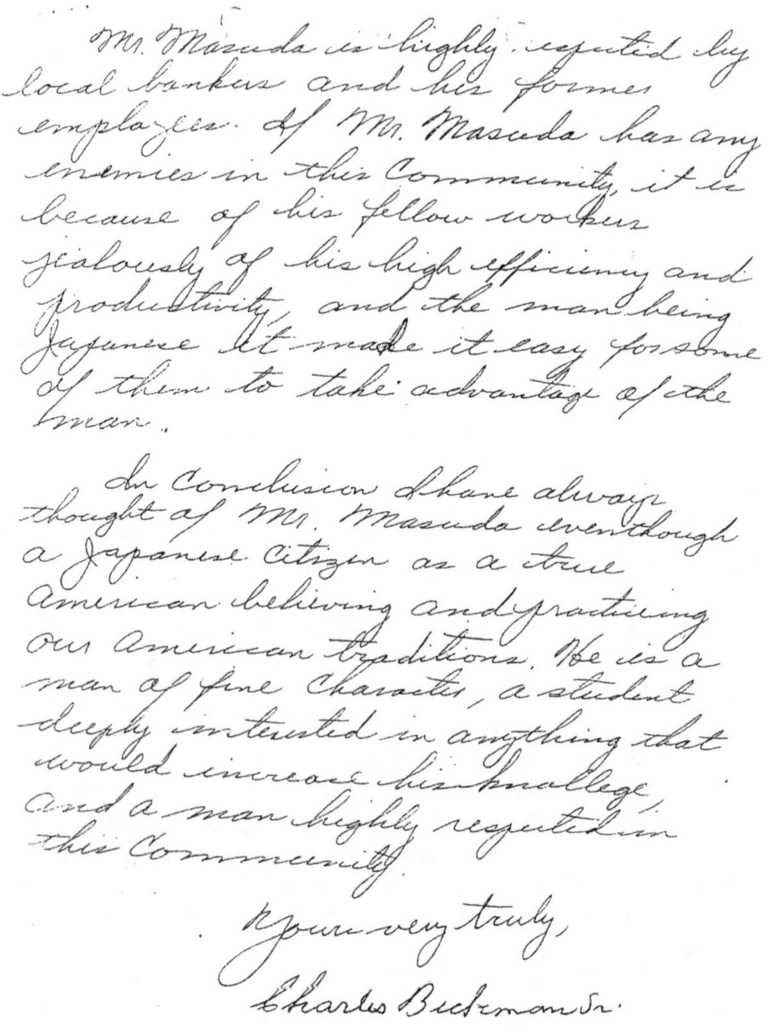

Mr. Masuda is highly reputed by local bankers and his former employees. If Mr. Masuda has any enemies in this community, it is because of his fellow workers jealously of his high efficiency and productivity, and the man being Japanese It made it easy for some of them to take advantage of the man.

In Conclusion I have always thought of Mr. Masuda even though a Japanese Citizen as a true American believing and practicing our American traditions. He is a man of fine Character, a student deeply interested in anything that would increase his knowledge, and a man highly respected in this Community.

Your very truly,

Charles Beckman Sr.

FIGURE 22. Excerpt from Charles Beckman Sr. to Director of Alien Detention, 18 April 1942; from the family archive of Bessie Masuda. Reprinted with permission.

release—that is, Masuda's integrity as an economic subject with impeccable managerial ethos, financial trustworthiness, and work ethic. The subsequent two paragraphs attempt to compensate for Masuda's illegibility as a *political* subject, providing evidence for his rectification through active attempts to convert or assimilate himself and his people to "American ideals and customs."

138 · INTERNED

In these ways, the first half of Beckman's letter enacts multiple displacements of Mr. Masuda's historical and cultural subjectivity: first, through legitimizing the terms of racial ascription and arrest; second, through reproducing a system of literary authorization that positions Mr. Masuda as object divorced from subject of knowledge; and third, through replacing Mr. Masuda's historical being with its representation in a universalized ideological framework that, in its correlation with the terms of racial ascription and arrest, comes back to binary formulations in which Mr. Masuda literally cannot be a citizen and, therefore, in the final analysis can only be an alien.

This web of contradictions, themes of sameness and their underlying attention to difference, thus leads to an increasingly unstable discursive terrain as Beckman transitions to biographical narrative: the substance of Mr. Masuda's life that, on the one hand, functions in the letter as rationalization and, on the other, must itself also be rationalized. In the former operation, Beckman's narration of Mr. Masuda's transnational affiliations—with its undertones of tragedy—seeks to account for Masuda's unequivocal social difference, neutralizing its signification as threat and investing in it instead a relation of sympathy. Beckman hence concludes by reasserting his thesis regarding Mr. Masuda's capacity to believe and practice "as a true American" despite the misfortune of his Japanese heritage. If these rhetorical maneuvers serve to counteract negative ascription or suspicion, however, they also inevitably refocus the gaps between "true Americanism" and the sociality that must be divested of its own ethnic meanings, contexts, and worldviews in order to effect positive ideological conformity. The irreducibility of that sociality, the lifeworld Beckman recounts but cannot fully explain or "know" in its difference, returns to the impossibility of total assimilation that delimits the "enemy alien" problem as such. It is, then, precisely this inability either to be captured or to be erased in the official record that ironically reinforces instead of reverses Masuda's positioning as a threat.

Under these circumstances, the terrain that letters afford for the reassertion of a collective subject becomes crucial rather than seemingly ancillary to social life and reproduction. In the following "Petition for the Reunion of Our Family Member" (figure 23), for example, the life of paper again emerges as a field of representation distinguishable from—even if caught within—the dominant, allowing the Masuda family to strip down the layers of ideological excess to reanimate meanings and contents specific to their own lives.[27]

[typed] *Answered:* 12/2/42
2 enclosures

Honorable Edward J. Ennis, Director,
Alien Enemy Control Unit,
U.S. Department of Justice,
Washington D.C.
146–13–2–11–968
Petition For Reunion of Our Family Member

Honorable Sir:

We, who sign this petition are the wives and children of those Japanese who are now detained for the duration of this war in internment camps. We are the innocent victims of circumstances for which we are not responsible and over which we have no control. Many of us now have been separated from our fathers and husbands for nearly eleven months. And when, as today, all indications point to a long war whose end we cannot as yet foresee the thought of being separated from our loved ones for an indefinite length of time fills us with inexpressible heart-ache and loneliness.

We, who are the children of these men, are American citizens brought up with a firm belief in American democracy and a strong trust in the traditions of tolerance and humanity for which it stands. Many of our brothers are now giving concrete proof of their belief by their service in the armed forces of our country.

We, who are the wives of these men, are also the mothers of American citizens and American soldiers. We have been lived in America the g[reater] part of our lives and would now be American citizens if we had been allowed to do so.

A large number of the men now interned are old and are not in the best of health. For some of them the end of their life span is not far distant. We, their children and wives are anxiously hoping that by some way we will be permitted to go and live with them. In so doing we are ready and willing to submit to such regulations and restrictions as the authorities may see fit to impose to safeguard the interests of this country.

For our sake and for the sake of the tradition of humanity for which American [*sic*] stands, we ask that the competent authorities exert their efforts toward enabling us to realize our hope.

Respectfully yours,
[Illegible] [strikethrough] 11–968 Taro Geo [strikethrough] ⇓ Mrs. Chiyomi Masuda
Amy Masuda
Bessie Masuda
Susie Masuda
Lucy Masuda
Richard Masuda

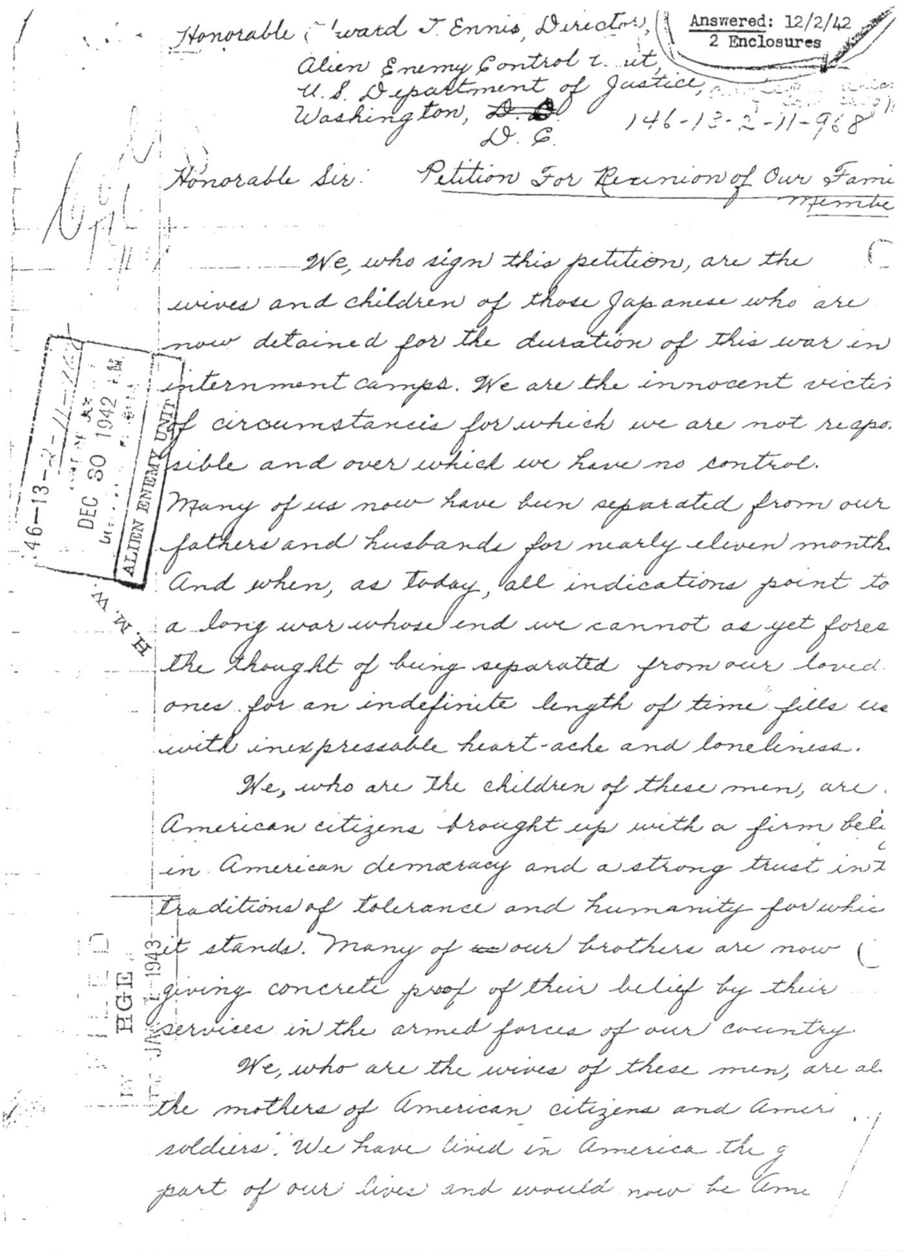

Answered: 12/2/42
2 Enclosures

Honorable Edward J. Ennis, Director,
Alien Enemy Control Unit,
U.S. Department of Justice,
Washington, ~~D.C.~~
D.C.

146-13-2-11-968

DEC 30 1942
ALIEN ENEMY UNIT
146-13-2-11-

Honorable Sir: Petition For Reunion of Our Family Member

We, who sign this petition, are the wives and children of those Japanese who are now detained for the duration of this war in internment camps. We are the innocent victi[ms] of circumstancis for which we are not respo[n]sible and over which we have no control. Many of us now have been separated from our fathers and husbands for nearly eleven month[s]. And when, as today, all indications point to a long war whose end we cannot as yet fores[ee], the thought of being separated from our loved ones for an indefinite length of time fills us with inexpressable heart-ache and loneliness.

We, who are the children of these men, are American citizens brought up with a firm beli[ef] in American democracy and a strong trust in t[he] traditions of tolerance and humanity for whic[h] it stands. Many of ~~we~~ our brothers are now giving concrete proof of their belief by their services in the armed forces of our country.

We, who are the wives of these men, are al[so] the mothers of American citizens and Ameri[can] soldiers. We have lived in America the g[reater] part of our lives and would now be Ame[ricans]

H. W. W.

FILED
JAN 1 1943
HGE

FIGURE 23. "Petition for Reunion of Our Family Member," Chiyomi, Amy, Bessie, Susie, Lucy, and Richard Masuda to Edward J. Ennis, ca. October 1942; from the family archive of Bessie Masuda. Reprinted with permission.

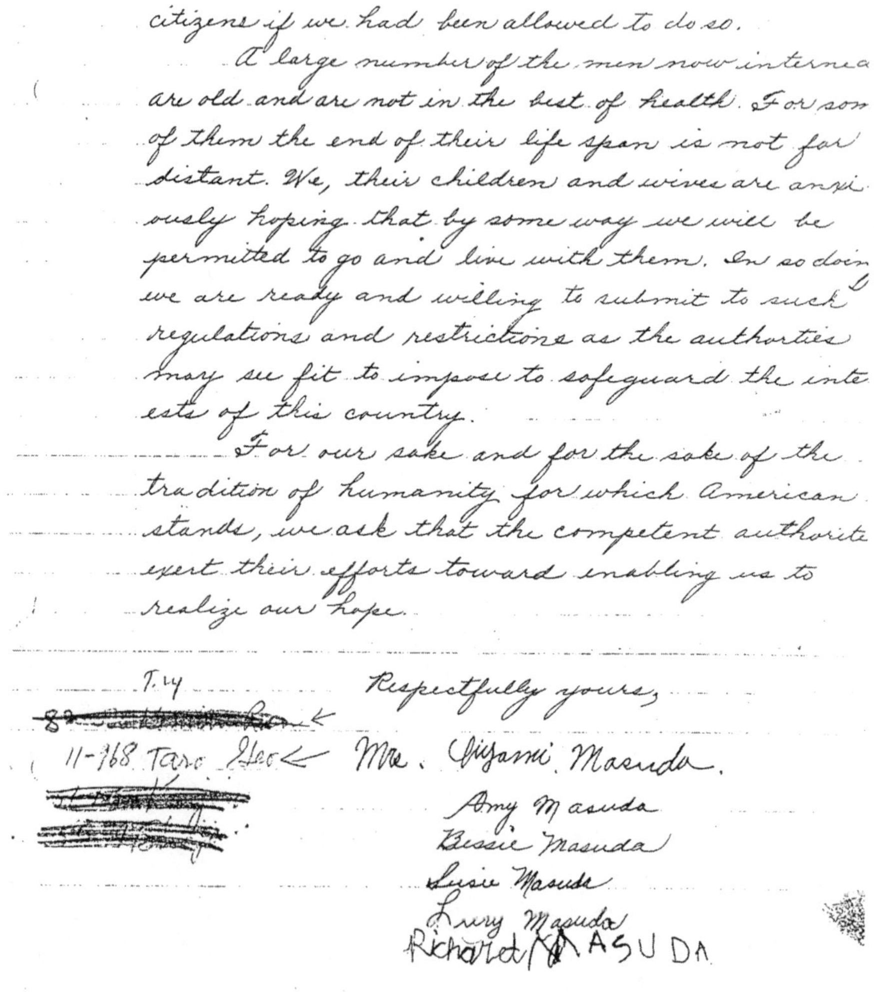

citizens if we had been allowed to do so.

A large number of the men now interned are old and are not in the best of health. For some of them the end of their life span is not far distant. We, their children and wives are anxiously hoping that by some way we will be permitted to go and live with them. In so doing we are ready and willing to submit to such regulations and restrictions as the authorities may see fit to impose to safeguard the interests of this country.

For our sake and for the sake of the tradition of humanity for which America stands, we ask that the competent authorities exert their efforts toward enabling us to realize our hope.

Respectfully yours,

T. y

11-168 Taro Heo

Mrs. Oyami Masuda.
Amy Masuda
Bessie Masuda
Susie Masuda
Lucy Masuda
Richard MASUDA

FIGURE 23. *(Continued)*

This petition letter unfolds through a series of repetitions, gradually disclosing a dynamic and multivalent "we" in which every self-assertion simultaneously differentiates itself from and augments its previous form. Such revelation begins with the "We, who sign this petition," who can serve as metonymy for *all* "wives and children of those Japanese . . . in internment camps." In the next iteration of "we" as "the innocent victims of circumstances," the self-conscious positioning of this collective subject—instead of connoting facile passivity—correlates with its assertion of a distinct collective agency that neither accepts responsibility for war nor resists it. This appositional stance enables an engagement with the dominant field that is not bound by or bound to dynamics of incorporation and erasure; neither seeking these ends, this discursive positioning instead institutes conditions for the expansion of its own onto-epistemological terrain that opens to but cannot be subsumed by the ideologies exercised by the letter's respondents. The letter thus proceeds through the claims of a collective subject who self-identifies and speaks polyvocally, in the ensemble callings of children, wives, and mothers, moving toward a horizon of consciousness not delimited only by historical or political recognitions but by the very problem of being as such, that is, the inevitable "end of their life span."

Rhetorically, this collective case explicitly ruptures dominant binary systems at multiple scales of the latter's articulation. Namely, the "we," defined as (would-be) "American citizens" and as siblings and "mothers of American citizens and American soldiers," exerts pressure on the contradictions of U.S. citizenship—denaturalizing the dichotomies structuring, and structured by, racist nationalism and disordering its epistemological grid. Disruption peaks as the Masuda family concludes by requesting to resign the privileges of their status as U.S. civilians, to be counted instead with "enemy aliens" in order to reconstruct the lived conditions of their collectivity. In these simultaneous claims to both citizen and alien subject positions, the collective case embodied by this "we" thus presents itself to the U.S. government openly as both its product and its problem, disturbing categories of propriety and enmity and seeking to inhabit their breach. This worldview clears space for Taro George finally to appear on the literal scene of the page as an ambiguous signatory at the margins of representation: the collective author, with the stroke of arrows, committed to reclaiming him as one of "we" and "we" as one of him.

THE WORK OF ART

In significant ways, dominant U.S. literary engagements with Japanese aesthetics prior to World War II established an ideological pathway for displacements of Nikkei historical and cultural subjectivity that would intensify as and through the internment process. That is, as Karen Jackson Ford has pointed out, Western modernist appropriation of the haiku form in the first half of the twentieth century—popularly credited as the beginnings of haiku in the West—assumed an aesthetic theory of impersonality inseparable from theories of Japanese racial difference.[28] Such work evolved in the period after World War II to fashion erasures of Euro-American identity that, while ultimately reaffirming rather than transcending whiteness, also obscured epistemological perspectives and interventions made by other ethnic American artists concurrently writing in the haiku form.[29] Specific to Nikkei, Ford locates the beginnings of haiku in the U.S. to Japanese immigrants in the early 1900s and traces Issei's turn to poetry during internment as a means to contest, survive, and put the experience in perspective, thus mediating, distinct from Anglo American appropriations, a mode of historical consciousness and being rather than a mode of their deferral. I am interested here in the unfolding of this aesthetic and onto-epistemological terrain, specifically in syncretic relation to the life of paper and the ways that their interarticulation across media and generational positions facilitates a different order of historical space-time.

Vibrant Issei literary culture in the preinternment period shaped as much as it was reshaped by the life of paper during the internment years. Violet Kazue de Cristoforo documents pre–World War II poetry societies, or regional *kai,* that grew in cities and towns such as San Francisco, Los Angeles, Stockton, and Fresno and focused specifically on haiku, tanka, and an avante-garde form called kaiko.[30] Translated by Kazue de Cristoforo as "crimson sea," kaiko deviated somewhat from classical haiku's concentration on scenery and objective subtleties, stressing instead "the importance of fulfilling human nature through direct expression of the poet's emotions and giving circumstances enthusiastic expression in order to satisfy the creative drive."[31] Far from Orientalist perceptions of haiku as a sign of Eastern "impersonality" and art for art's sake, poetry in these collectives mediated a flourishing Issei sociality that created rather than eviscerated emergent forms of modern subjectivity.[32]

As these movements evolved during World War II, Issei poets strayed from dominant sublimations of race into culture, instead repositioning culture in dialectic with racism. Foreseeing the imminent danger of war by mid-1941, Neiji Ozawa—founder of the Valley Ginsha Haiku Kai in Fresno and cofounder of the Delta Ginsha Haiku Kai in Stockton—presciently instructed poets to use haiku to communicate their experiences to future historians.[33] Hence, in contrast to dominant Anglo approaches, Issei turned to haiku to engage rather than negate or avoid the mundane world and, further, to stretch the horizons of the latter's limits. Moreover, Issei poetry composed during internment emphasized claims to Japanese identity much more than prewar literary production did,[34] a shift in self-assertions of ethnoracial difference that perhaps informed Rev. Daisuke Kitagawa's observation as chaplain at the Pinedale Assembly Center and the Tule Lake camp, "In fact Western civilization had penetrated into Japan much more thoroughly than into the Japanese community in America."[35] In view of such localized contradictions of global imperialist struggle and the foreclosed spaces of social imagination, camp haiku could therefore articulate unstable mixtures of progressive and reactionary racial ideologies that highlighted rather than "transcended" the production of a modern self as a racial one.

As processes of internment and reconcentration thus upended prewar Nikkei communities, preexisting intellectual formations were reconstituted through—as they also helped constitute—the life of paper as both literary and paraliterary praxis. For example, Kazue de Cristoforo alludes to these dialectics when she notes that, in the case of California's Central Valley poets, letter correspondence facilitated the preservation and continuity of their collective creative work.[36] Issei creative training in poetry could also explicitly shape their epistolary aesthetic. Iwao Matsushita, for instance, turned to haiku on many occasions to express the sentiment that perhaps prose could not channel, particularly given the formal restrictions imposed by U.S. censors—some of which, incidentally, the asceticism of haiku could well accommodate. For example, he writes to Hanaye on 5 March 1942, in both Japanese and in English (figure 24):[37]

> I regret I can't celebrate with you, but please remember that my heart is always with you. I like to dedicate the following poem which I composed for your birthday:
>
> [line in Japanese characters]
>
> (*Translation*—700 miles away amidst snow in Missoula, I alone celebrate beautiful flower's day of birth)

Ultimately, epistemological standpoints mediated through haiku add dimension to the meaning of letter correspondence itself. Kazue de Cristoforo, citing an anonymous haiku poet, notes that "haiku is only one-half of a circle; it invites each reader to join the poet."[38] This perspective raises at least two points. First, it situates Nikkei reproductions of a collective subject in the context of a long-established worldview of dynamic communalism that exceeds the

Mrs. Hanaye Matsushita
905 - 24th ave So.
Seattle, Wash.

March 5th, 1942
90 Dormitory # 24
Fort Missoula, Montana.

My dear wife,

I'm worrying about you, for I haven't heard from you for a long time. I'm always very healthy - not a single day have I been in sick bed. It's a pity that I have to let you burden yourself alone with hard problems like evacuation, tax return, property report, etc. Let's be brave + take everything as God's trial to make ourselves worthy of God's children.

If you can send me without much trouble my copy of the world almanac + my medium sized "Standard Dictionary" - black cover with my name printed on it - I'll appreciate your kindness very much, for I am one of the teachers for the English class for the whole detainees. To my surprise I found my former pupil in Fukuyama + he gave me a dozen fresh eggs, which came from California.

I believe March 9th is your birthday + I regret that I can't celebrate with you, but please remember that my heart is always with you. I like to dedicate the following poem which I composed for your birthday :-

七百哩 隔つ美空の雪の中に 独り祝はん花の生れ日
(Translation - 700 miles away amidst snow in Missoula, I alone celebrate beautiful flower's day of birth)

It is allowed now to write letters in Japanese, so you may do so, if it is more convenient for you. Take good care of yourself +write please.

Your loving husband

Iwao Matsushita

(Letter #18)

FIGURE 24. Iwao to Hanaye Matsushita, 5 March 1942; University of Washington Libraries, Special Collections, Iwao Matsushita Papers, Acc. 2718–001, Box 14, Folder 16.

sign and opens both inward and outward. Second, this ontology is further manifested in hermeneutics of haiku that rely on the intimate dialectic between poet, reader, and an aspect of Creation that the poem appreciates. Haiku's formal austerity mediates this dialectic and paradoxically structures a wealth of meaning, organized through subtle relationships between the simplicity of the words and the abundance of their surrounding silence. In this sense, silence actively both communicates and amplifies knowledge: that is, in its own way, silence also speaks. The essentialism of haiku thus reveals a different epistemology of negativity that somewhat inflects common narratives of silence as the mark of oppressive burden.[39] As such, recognizing the interplays of speech and silence, presence and absence, in this poetics can inform our view of the life of paper for the Interned—how this epistemological perspective contributed to the conditions of possibility for letter correspondence to affect social reproduction as powerfully as it did, even in the face of extreme censorship.

Likewise, these facets of Nikkei literary aesthetics also influence what we may discern of the life of paper as itself an art form, in which material culture and productions of beauty do not reflect human subjectivity and social relations so much as invent and reinvent them. In this creative process, taking place under conditions of both deprivation and surveillance, the qualities of handwriting and paper carried immediate practical significance. For example, Jiro Nakano and Kay Nakano, editors of a collection of tanka written from camp, qualify the poet Sojin Takei's prolific work by explaining that he "managed to write approximately 200 poems per sheet in minute handwriting on thin rice paper stationery which could be easily carried around without official notice."[40] In addition to pragmatic concerns, the particular aesthetic significance of both paper and handwriting befit them as media for social life and reproduction. Paper as both medium and object has long enjoyed a central place in Japanese aesthetics, in popular forms such as origami and ikebana, or paper flower arranging—each with its own attendant dynamics of austerity and embellishment, positive and negative space.[41] Prolific experiments in such arts during internment and reconcentration by individuals with little or no formal training further contextualize the life of paper and the world of beauty to which it belongs: an aesthetic sociality in which communities handcrafted or adorned mailboxes as a means to mark and inhabit place, as they also mailed small handmade gifts and paper arts along with letters as a means to maintain intimate connections.[42]

The aesthetics of handwriting, along with the contradictions it mediates, also helped reconstruct Nikkei sociality that remains beyond either capture

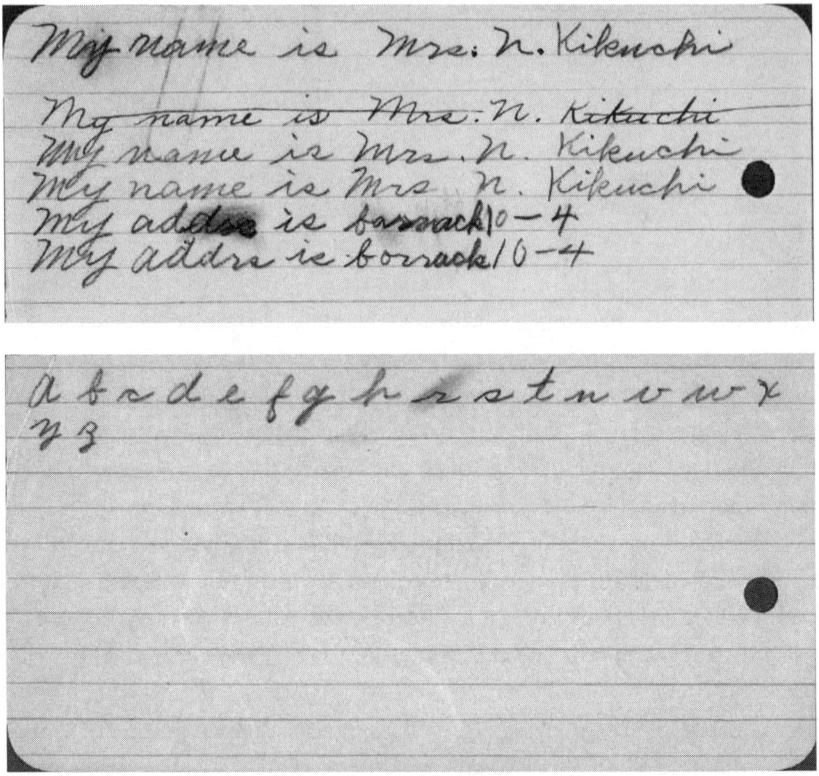

FIGURE 25. [Handwriting practice on lined paper], Japanese American Evacuation and Resettlement Records, BANC MSS 67/14 c, Box 25, Folder B12.50 (2/2). Courtesy of The Bancroft Library, University of California, Berkeley.

or erasure. On the one hand, as illustrated in ephemera from the archives of the 1942 Japanese American Evacuation and Resettlement Study (figure 25),[43] the practice of proper handwriting alludes to the significance of form as a sign of respectability, particularly in high-stakes correspondences with government officials and influential civilians.

On the other hand, beyond this disciplinary training and need for legibility in the dominant field of representation, aesthetics of handwriting could also, like haiku, mediate other forms of subjectivity, connections, and intimacy to keep Nikkei communal recognitions and aspirations alive. As Marion Kanemoto, from the camp at Minidoka, Idaho, remembers of her correspondence with her father at Fort Missoula, Montana, "Well, we corresponded, but I remember all our letters were censored with the holes either cut out or blacked out. You could hardly make heads or tails out of the message, but nevertheless, *it was his handwriting.*"[44] Kanemoto's attention to handwriting in this instance, far from corroborating an argument for the significance of "pure" form evacuated or detached from historical content, instead alludes to the way that the idiosyncrasies of a loved one's handwriting could mediate an experiential or affective sense of social connection that exceeds literal representability, their writing the very sign of living historical presence in an other world that is surrogated or affirmed by these subtler claims of recognition.

Indeed, as the poignance of Kanemoto's comment also indicates, such dynamics of human mediation affected Nisei youth in distinctive ways, given the specificity of their conditions of dependency and their particular vulnerabilities to family separation as well as systematic Americanization efforts. John Tateishi, recollecting his experiences in Manzanar, remarks of these circumstances of his childhood, "We imported so much of America into the camps because, after all, we were Americans. I was learning, as best one could learn in Manzanar, what it meant to live in America. But I was also learning the sometimes bitter price one has to pay for it."[45] Perhaps even more ironically than he intended, Tateishi articulates the ultimate contradiction of U.S. racial democracy when he connects living in camps with "what it meant to live in America," a conundrum surfacing the embedded structures of violence and elimination that give rise to American "freedoms." Yet, by distinguishing the two in his own words, between learning "what it meant to live in America" and "the sometimes bitter price one has to pay for it," Tateishi subtly also differentiates between the intended pedagogical program of Americanization and the fuller contents of his actual learning. This difference—the discrepancy between the dynamics of nation-state pedagogy and its unpredicted surplus—further manifests in and through Nisei investments in the life of paper, as the latter mediated a process of socialization in contradistinction to dominant disciplines.

Deviations can be traced most immediately within the mundane space of the classroom and the rote forms of aesthetic training in camps. For example, Raymond Muraoka, age six when he arrived at camp in Manzanar, recalls:

> I remember a beautiful girl in our class. . . . I sat next to her in class. She was pretty in face but what impressed me most was her beautiful handwriting. She wrote as if her hand was moved by mysterious influences. The time I remember most was when I tried to write like her. I had a thick black art pencil and sharpened it to a needle point. When I wrote, it looked as if I used a crayon. This beautiful girl took my pencil and showed me she could write as well with any implement.[46]

Muraoka's memories gesture to learning contents, outcomes, and imagination that depart from the standard script. Parallel to Kanemoto's evocations of filial intimacy, the art of handwriting in this instance mediates emerging experiences of desire, social connection through shared aesthetics, and inspiration by "mysterious influences" that cannot be rendered meaningful in or to the official transcript and its attendant regimens of training and representation. Perhaps not coincidentally, Lawson Fusao Inada's "Poems from Amache Camp" also conjures this sense of aesthetic play (see chapter 5), mediated through the epistolary form to re-create a sociality self-organized among Nisei in excess of state pedagogy:[47]

I.

"Dear Lawson,
    2 Ys U R,
    2 Ys U B,
    I C U R
    2 Ys 4 Me!
                Your friend,
                    Bobby"

II.

"Dear Lawson,
    I meet you early,
    I meet you late,
    I meet you at
    Amache Gate!
                Always,
                    Naomi"

While these examples harken to the unfolding of creative youth cultures in the camps, for others like Bessie Masuda such moments of wonder were precluded by a more explicit understanding of camp classrooms and schooling as part of Americanization's "bitter price" rather than its remedy. Masuda, fourteen years old at the time, reflects:

My experience in Rohwer, Arkansas, was very very unhappy. I remember very little about it. I *hated* going to school. I just didn't like going to school at all . . . It wasn't school for me, you know? It was like [pause], I don't know, my heart wasn't in it. I was always worried, having to leave my mom home knowing she was unhappy, and then going to school, and I would worry, what is mom going to do when we're away, you know? She was protective of us, but I was trying to be protective of her, you know? Um, 'cause I wanted her to be happy.[48]

In Masuda's case, Americanization efforts more conspicuously failed to neutralize an affinity to self-identify through a communal worldview at odds with dominant U.S. movements and ideologies. That is, in affective terms, Masuda recalls rejecting the processes of social alienation and isolation that preconditioned schooling and, by thus refusing to disclaim her social dependence, also derailed the process of becoming representative of the rationality or individualism that defines good citizenship. Qualified by this implicit dissent, letters written by the Masuda children also correlatively deviate from the disciplinary norms of English language learning and aesthetics, revealing instead techniques of self-assertion that abide by a divergent set of values to exert pressure on dominant boundaries of recognizability. For example, Bessie and Lucy Masuda each write to the U.S. Department of Justice (figures 26 and 27):

Block 19 Barrack 9 Apartment F
Relocation Branch
McGehee, Arkansas
February 15, 1944

Dear sir,
   We want to know when our father may come back to us. It has been so long since was away. Our father was taken on the night of Washingtons birthday and that was February 22nd, 1942. Oh please, will you release him and have him join us? We've been praying that he would come back to us soon and we hope that will be true. He does not want to stay there, but I know he wants to join us. Why can't he be released?
   We do not want to go to Tule Lake if we have to go. It's awful there and I know he won't like it their [sic] either. I am writing this letter for the sake of my mother. She always worries a lot and I don't want her to worry because she has been ill so many times. I am asking you again

to please release my father. He hasn't done any harm to this country and I know that he will not do such a thing as harming this country.

Yours very truly,
Bessie Masuda,
daughter of Mr. Taro Geo. Masuda

February 15, 1944
W.R.A.
McGehee Ark.

Dear Honorable Sir,
When will you let my father come back? We have been waiting for so long. It is nearly two years now. He didn't do any thing bad. Why don't you let him come back. We do not want to go to Tule Lake. We do not want to go to some other place too. We want to stay in Arkansas with my father. Won't you please let him come back? You know how it feels?

Yours very truly,
Lucy Masuda

Denied political rights, Bessie and Lucy Masuda turn to the letter to stage confrontations with U.S. government authorities, relying on distinct rhetorical logics to expand the ideological terrain. First, in contrast to normative frameworks in which the ostensible loyalty or disloyalty of those interned delineates the central problem, the Masudas name the grievances caused by U.S. government actions, seeking accountability and redress as they repeatedly demand explanation and even insist on their father's release. Second, thus relieved of the need to "prove" their family's loyalty or fitness for citizenship, the Masuda letters instead proceed by elaborating a structure of desire that articulates interwoven needs, longings, and aspirations at both the individual and collective scales. Like Issei haiku, this perspective emphasizes feeling as a form of knowing constitutive rather than devoid of objectivity and physical embodiment. The poignance of such a worldview peaks with Lucy Masuda's penetrating question that hails acknowledgment, "You know how

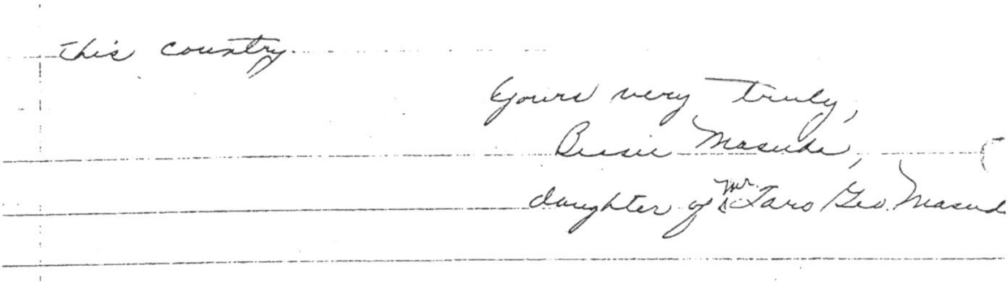
this country.

Yours very truly,
Bessie Masuda,
daughter of Mr. Taro Geo. Masud

FIGURE 26. Signature of Bessie Masuda to the U.S. Department of Justice, 15 February 1944; from the family archive of Bessie Masuda. Reprinted with permission.

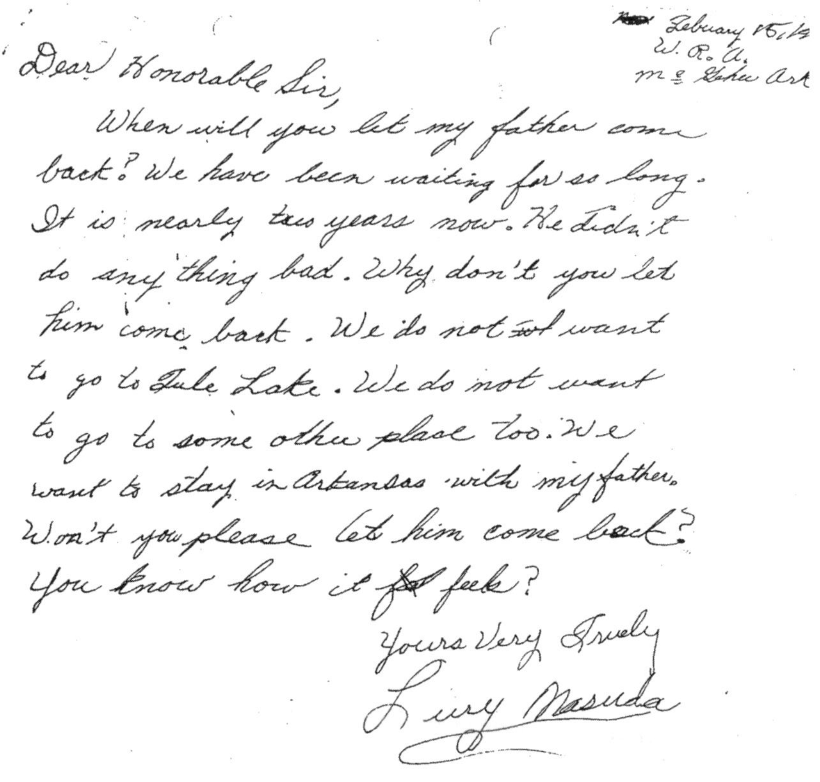
February 15, 44
W. R. A.
McGehee Ark

Dear Honorable Sir,

When will you let my father come back? We have been waiting for so long. It is nearly two years now. He didn't do any thing bad. Why don't you let him come back. We do not ~~not~~ want to go to Tule Lake. We do not want to go to some other plase too. We want to stay in Arkansas with my father. Won't you please let him come back? You know how it ~~f~~ feels?

Yours Very Truely
Lucy Masuda

FIGURE 27. Lucy Masuda to Edward J. Ennis, 15 February 1944; from the family archive of Bessie Masuda. Reprinted with permission.

it feels?" Finally, then, in both of their letters, the Masuda sisters ground selfhood in collective experience, preempting the latter's further displacement by resisting the mandate to articulate their positions as separate from those of their mother or father. Bessie's letter hence ends with a signature that simultaneously connotes singularity and plurality—the autonomous individual "Bessie Masuda" also claiming her belonging to "Mr. Taro Geo. Masuda" in a multilayered form of self-identification.

The multigenerational consistency of these positionings demonstrates that such orientations to consciousness and to embodied historical being cannot be simply incorporated into a developmental logic in which the Masuda children would, in the final instance, "outgrow" their state of dependency in order to become proper and mature citizens. In fact, the representational qualities of Lucy and Bessie Masuda's letters intensify rather than wane in the following final example from Taro George Masuda's younger brother, a letter by draft-age Kibei Mikio Masuda (figure 28), written from the camp in McGehee, Arkansas. In the wake of the Loyalty Questionnaire, Mikio addresses the Department of Justice:

February 2, 1944
Blk. 19–7-F
Relocation Branch
McGhee [*sic*], Arkansas

Hon. Edward J. Ennis
Director of Alien Enemy Control Unit
Department of Justice
Washington, D.C.
[3 ink stamps from Alien Enemy Unit, dated Feb 5 1944]

Dear Sir:
I hereby requesting a release of my brother, Taro George Masuda, who is now interned in Santa Fe, New Mexico. My reason for his release as follows. If the Army is taking loyal Japanese American under draft age like me for instance, then why should my brother be interned and classify as disloyal person for which he is not.
I am not saying this because I don't want to be in the Army. I'm only saying that before I'm draft for which I will be for sure, is that I like to see that my brother is given a square deal and to see that he

> will be able to unite with his family. I like to see both his wife and kids happy together before I leave for the Army. If this is not granted I rather be in jail I don't care how long. This may sound kind of a craze to you, for me it isn't. I really love this country it's a swell place, but I love my brother even more. He's only person I got left in this world. This may mean another letter to you, but to me it isn't, and I mean every word of it. So please think it over. Please answer.
>
> Yours truly,
> Mikio Masuda

Far from repudiating the rhetorical qualities of the other Masuda letters and their underlying epistemological foundations, Mikio Masuda's letter sustains the preferential option to self-identify as a collective subject and also builds on the use of affect as a mode of historical intervention and way of knowing. Through the letter and its form of self-assertion, Mikio creates an opportunity to speak for himself while simultaneously situating his position in an ensemble of social relations and maintaining the dialectic between individual and collective desires. At once operating within and transcending the terms assigned to him and his brother, Mikio neither consents nor reacts to the meanings imposed on him; rather, he references dominant identification categories such as Issei, Kibei, loyal, and disloyal in order to assign them his own meanings, ones that refuse reduction to the yes/no answers required by the U.S. government. In this sense, Mikio also explicitly redirects the boundaries of his own letter's reception when he emphasizes, "This may mean another letter to you, but to me it isn't, and I mean every word of it." By subtly differentiating his letter from the formal genre of letters as such, he deliberately locates himself in a position that veers from the rules of representation in order to invest new life in mediations of the word.

This transgression of alienating logics and aesthetics allows Mikio to identify himself in terms beyond patriotic nationalism and racism, as he simultaneously avows his own sense of love and duty to the United States while asserting himself through a love for people and a principle of justice that take priority over the formation of nation-states. Mikio Masuda thereby deconstructs prevailing notions of U.S. "democracy" that, in its contradictions, both rationalized the draft and defined the jail. Moreover, Mikio alludes to the implications

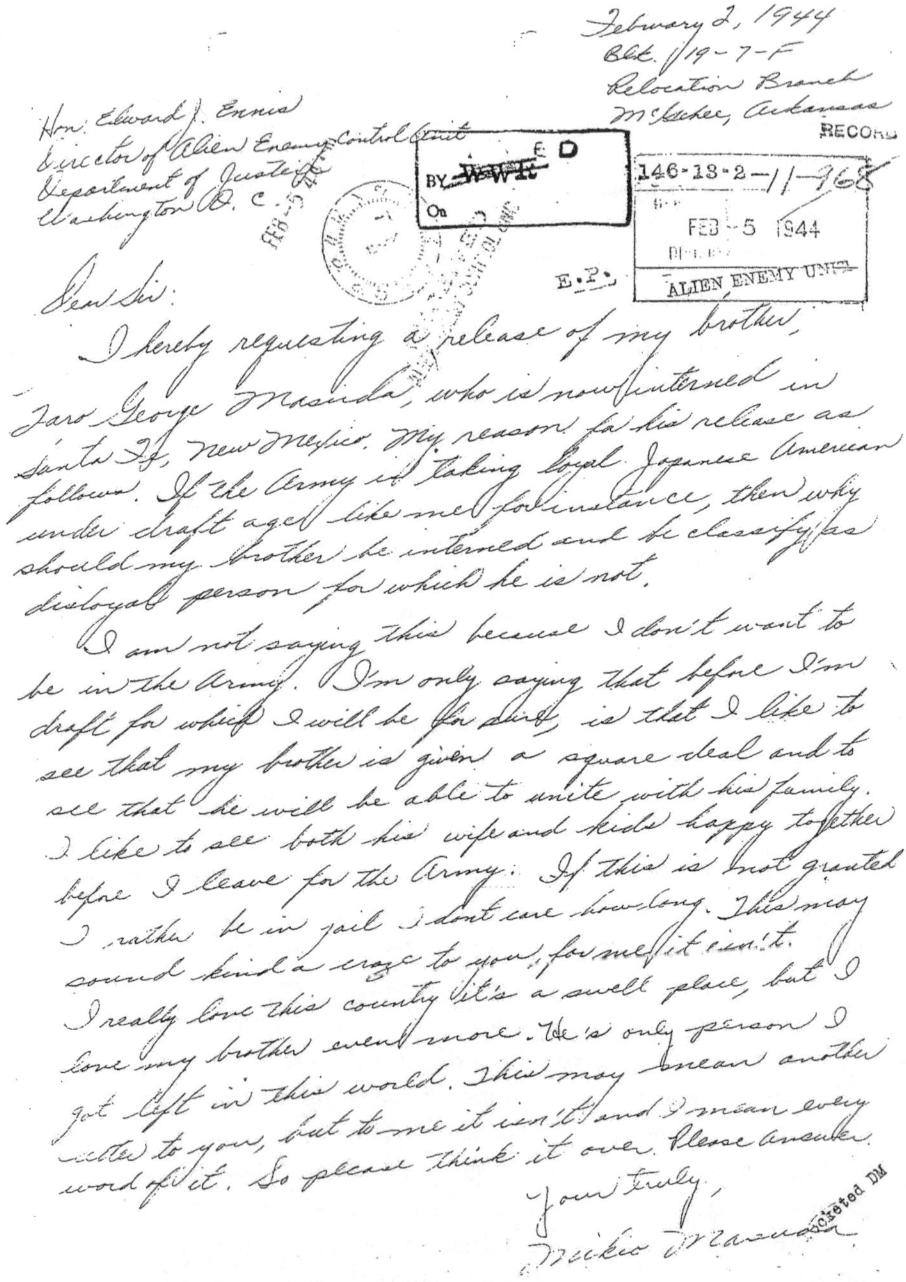

February 2, 1944
Blk. //9-7-F
Relocation Branch
McGehee, Arkansas

Hon. Edward J. Ennis
Director of Alien Enemy Control Unit
Department of Justice
Washington D. C.

Dear Sir:

I hereby requesting a release of my brother, Taro George Masuda, who is now interned in Santa Fe, New Mexico. My reason for his release as follows. If the Army is taking loyal Japanese American under draft age like me for instance, then why should my brother be interned and be classify as disloyal person for which he is not.

I am not saying this because I don't want to be in the Army. I'm only saying that before I'm draft for which I will be for sure, is that I like to see that my brother is given a square deal and to see that he will be able to unite with his family. I like to see both his wife and kids happy together before I leave for the Army. If this is not granted I rather be in jail I don't care how long. This may sound kind a craze to you, for me it isn't. I really love this country it's a swell place, but I love my brother even more. He's only person I got left in this world. This may mean another letter to you, but to me it isn't and I mean every word of it. So please think it over. Please answer.

Your truly,
Mikio Masuda

FIGURE 28. Mikio Masuda to Edward J. Ennis, 2 February 1944; from the family archive of Bessie Masuda. Reprinted with permission.

of his challenge to the U.S. military government—that is, the transformative consciousness required to register it—when he acknowledges, "This may sound kind of a craze to you, for me it isn't . . . So please think it over. Please answer." In these ways, Mikio's letter reproduces forms of meaning, thinking, and being at the outermost edges of hegemonic representability and, like haiku, invites the reader to join in the becoming of a different kind of place.

CONCLUSION: THE PURLOINED PURLOINED LETTER

In the final analysis, and consistent with the hermeneutics of haiku, the enduring aspects of this life of paper cannot be understood outside of its ephemerality: all that we can discern conditioned by all that escapes.[49] Louis Fiset manages to uncover traces of the secret worlds improvised by the Interned, such as hidden messages sent in cigarette packages that only appeared to be sealed, letters smuggled out of camps by visitors and delivered from distant post offices, and invisible writing concealed in pieces of outgoing mail.[50] In another remarkable story, documented by Satsuki Ina her 2006 film, *From a Silk Cocoon,* Kibei renunciant Itaru Ina,[51] interned at Fort Lincoln, North Dakota, and his wife, Shizuko Mitsui Ina, in the Tule Lake prison camp with their two children, Kiyoshi and Satsuki, devised alternative measures to send and receive letters in order to circumvent restrictions governing letter content and form. As Itaru describes the latter to Shizuko, in a letter dated 23 July 1945, "As far as correspondence is concerned, there is a rule that we can send two letters (each letter within 25 lines) and one post card a week."[52] According to Satsuki Ina, who was born at Tule Lake and inherited the archive of her parents' letters, Itaru Ina worked around these constraints by stripping his bedding, writing letters on the cloth, rolling them up, and hiding them inside the unstitched and resewn waistbands of pants that he sent to Tule Lake for mending.[53] As he instructs Shizuko around September or October 1945, "When I send you a package with Satsuki's name, I may enclose a letter so be watchful. Please send me another pair of thick wool pants. If you sew it well in the same place, it may not be found. I already received your letter inside the belt."[54]

For her part, Shizuko mitigated censorship not only through acts of evasion but also through direct engagement, transforming the dialogical limits of the letter itself and drawing more people into its circle. Describing the extremities of censorship at Tule Lake, Satsuki Ina recalls, "All the other [letters, besides the secret ones] are cut up and you know, you open them up and some of them are just flaps of paper." In this context, Satsuki Ina continues:

> There's one (slight laugh) of my favorite letters my mother wrote, before and after this one letter they're all cut. Some of them, for long periods of time they didn't cut anything, and then, when the idea [occurred] that my father may be deported ... the intensity really heightens because she's in the other camp with the two children and my father's over here, being threatened to be deported back to Japan after the war was over. And so she writes to my father and says, you know, let's give up our plans to return to Japan. This will be suicide for the children, blah blah blah blah, and at the bottom she says, "Dear Censor, For the sake of my children please do not cut this letter up." And it's one of the few letters that's not chopped up (laughs).[55]

In light of widespread shaming in the postwar years of those who were named "disloyal"—particularly draft resisters, no-no boys, and renunciants such as her father—Satsuki Ina shares her family's life of paper to vindicate the dead, translating her parents' archive to lend different meanings to the historical record and what people understand of it. Her work articulates across language and aesthetic genre, as she collaborates with other artists to cross-translate her parents' archive from Japanese to English back to Japanese back to English again, using the materials to make films, write books, and host events on the legacies of camp. About the process of working on her family's book (forthcoming), she explains:

> So, what I had access to is, these, my parents writing letters to each other. [But because of third-party and self-censorship], the letters exchanged actually, um, they're so restrained; it's almost stunning how restrained they are. Then I have, on my mother's side, her diaries, . . . she's writing much more about what her personal private struggles are. . . . And then, my father had a haiku journal. . . . So I have all these notebooks because he wrote "Notebook 1," "Notebook 2," and there's hundreds. That's going to be a second book. . . . So I'm trying to weave all those together in my book . . . I'm actually going to include in the book all of her diary entries woven in with the letters . . . Some of his haiku I will, but there's *so* much in his haiku.[56]

In dialectic with such literary abundance, however, perhaps even more meaning remains in the ether: the silence, disappeared ink, missing flaps, lost poems, more silence. Brian Komei Dempster, a contemporary Sansei poet who works with camp survivors to heal from trauma through writing, acknowledges the depth of this absence in the dedication of their 2001 collection of stories, *From Our Side of the Fence: Growing Up in America's Concentration Camps:*

> This book is dedicated to those, like my uncle and countless others, who passed away rarely or never speaking about their experiences. It bears witness to those who weren't able to readjust or forget; indeed, certain characters and scenes remind us that the consequences of imprisonment can be devastating, sometimes leading to mental illness and even suicide. This volume can also shed light for those too young to remember . . . who nevertheless bear the scars of the experience.[57]

Attuned to the negativity that gives shape to life stories, Dempster and the collective of Nisei writers link their work to the failures of speech and to ancestors whose presence can only be known affectively. As I have tried to show through this life of paper, such dynamics of presence and absence, seen and unseen, do not signify the difference between being and nonbeing so much as illuminate fuller dimensions of the struggle to make and manifest social life at the brink of history and all the varieties of its undoing. At its best, then, the cultural labor "to remember" not only marks survival but also persistently elaborates that communal terrain that clarifies, as Cedric Robinson defines the most capacious ends of multicultural formation, that "we are not the subjects or the subject formations of the capitalist world-system. It is merely one condition of our being."[58] The case of the Interned demonstrates that in the enmeshment of one set of conditions with the other, the ultimate concern may not be solely in loss but also in how "we" come to matter again to each other.

FIGURE 29. David Thorne and the Resistant Strains Collective, "Too Soon for Sorry," 1998, poster. Reprinted with permission from David Thorne and courtesy of the Center for the Study of Political Graphics.

PART THREE

Imprisoned

PART 3 TAKES PLACE IN A SINKING MOMENT, the way Walter Benjamin contemplates storytelling as communication that "does not aim to convey the pure essence of the thing, like information or a report," but rather "sinks the thing" into our lives in order to bring it out of us again.[1] This is the final part in my attempt to tell a story in which we are presently held in order to remind you that it is also held in us. In this creative dilemma, locating the "thing," the life of paper, in current space-time brings us to intersections that simultaneously play out as disjunctures—for instance, in the temporal scission between the campaign slogan "Never Again," used to win symbolic and financial reparations from the U.S. government for World War II internment, and the pronouncement "Too Soon for Sorry," a statement on the contemporary problem of racialized mass incarceration (figure 29). Considering the difference between these orientations to historical time, in fact, helps to unpack significant breaks as well as continuities in the transition between "then" and "now."

In an immediate sense, mainstream interpretations of World War II internment as an episodic mistake in the functioning of U.S. democracy stand in stark contrast to the long wave history conjured by the "Too Soon for Sorry" image, part of the 1998 *Maximum Security Democracy* series by the artists' collective Resistant Strains. Indeed, it is rather astonishing, given the amount of activity involved in World War II incarceration and the scope of its impact, that camps were built, filled, operated, emptied, and closed in less than five years. This ability to define seemingly clear temporal and spatial boundaries of the wartime regime, coupled with its documentation in explicit policies furnishing "facts" on specific dates, places, populations, and practices, lends the event to more digestible forms of national remembering:

empirical cause-and-effect analyses that, in the procedures of scientific method and management, frame the problem as one of data collection to be studied, evaluated, rationalized, and then solved. It is precisely this ritualized approach to U.S. policy, legal justice, and reconciliation that Resistant Strains challenges with its statement, conjuring visually a historical continuity of genocidal practices that undergird the world as we know it and, as these practices constitute the very protocols of modernity, defy clear spatial and temporal limits and are only sustained rather than resolved by measures of reform. In this sense, Resistant Strains depicts contemporary mass incarceration as the evolution of systematic killing that cannot be absorbed into movements of racial capitalist-state progress. This position antagonizes consideration of government redress for World War II internment as a social justice "victory" on the basis of recognition and reintegration of aggrieved individuals into U.S. civic life.

And yet, within this fundamental antagonism, movements for World War II camp redress and for contemporary prison abolition each have their own layers of internal differentiation, such that the temporally articulated positions associated with each also contain as they oppose the other. In the first case, the Nikkei redress movement encompassed tremendous ideological diversity and substantial opposition to dominant JACL claims and leadership. The JACL forged a settlement with the U.S. government in 1988, when President Ronald Reagan signed the Civil Liberties Act and apologized for racism by declaring that "blood that has soaked into the sands of a beach is all of one color." This act awarded up to $20,000 compensation to eligible camp survivors; the historian Alice Yang notes that limiting eligibility to living individuals avoided legitimizing claims to reparations long demanded by African Americans for slavery, American Indians for the atrocities of settler colonialism, Mexican Americans for land theft following the 1848 Treaty of Guadalupe-Hidalgo, and other groups systematically terrorized by U.S. racism and capitalist state development.[2]

While thus disarticulated from other struggles, such limited terms of restitution also obscure further claims made from within the Nikkei redress movement itself. For example, the National Council for Japanese American Redress (NCJAR) pursued a separate class action lawsuit for monetary compensation that was ultimately dismissed by the U.S. Supreme Court in 1988. The National Coalition for Redress/Reparations (NCRR), for their part, challenged the JACL to include the testimonies of working-class and non-English-speaking survivors in their campaigns and also focused on circulating at local levels to build community education and support. In this latter regard, many NCRR activists, led by Sansei, or third-generation Japanese Americans, pursued their goals for redress while denouncing U.S. imperialism in Vietnam, protesting urban redevelopment as another "forced relocation," and support-ing contiguous multiethnic and multiracial campaigns against racism. These more radical tendencies have remained integral to Nikkei political life despite prevailing JACL and U.S. nationalist ideologies of redress as a reward for patriotic individualism, closure to the perils of New Deal public welfare, and triumph of colorblindness as the end to U.S. racism.

In the contemporary case of U.S. prison abolition, on the other hand, efforts to grapple with mass incarceration as metaphor, extension, relation, or form of slavery also present their own ideological differences and need for historical specificity. Namely, the parallelism depicted in "Too Soon for Sorry" between slave ships and prison blocks, the visual rendering of their social science and economies of human accounting, locate the "prison indus-trial complex" squarely within the legacy of anti-Black racism at the heart of capital accumulation and the making of modern civilization. Due in part to the lasting impact of abolitionist rhetoric from the U.S. antebellum era, the now common view of slavery as foremost a moral abomination infuses today's prison abolitionist movements, by general association, with powerful ideo-logical appeal. Yet growing scholarship in contemporary prison studies has begun to point out the need both to historicize and to regionalize the study of mass incarceration in the late twentieth century, focusing on slavery as a mode of accumulation; uneven articulations of racism, capitalism, and social struggle; and the particular background of California as a global prison epi-center.[3] Such analytical exertion is informed, on the one hand, by investiga-tions of the uniqueness of Black California as it diverges from racial forma-tion at the national scale and, on the other hand, by the past several decades of work on the North American West in general, and California more spe-cifically, at the distinctive crucible of Pacific, U.S. continental, and American hemispheric social and political-economic development (see chapter 1).

In the context of World War II and this transition into part 3, then, his-torians of the Great Migration have noted that, while far from idyllic, California during this period offered African Americans unprecedented opportunity and prosperity relative to conditions in the rest of the country.[4] From 1940 to 1950, the Black population in the U.S. West grew by 33 percent; in California specifically, close to 300 percent—the majority of westward migrants moving to Los Angeles, San Francisco, and Oakland for defense industry jobs.[5] The postwar period, however, marked the beginning of dramatic shifts in the state's racial and spatial organization of wealth and the degeneration of multiethnic communities that had surfaced in the first half of the century. In Los Angeles, deindustrialization, suburbanization and "white flight," freeway construction, corporate agribusiness, and changes in immigration dynamics and practices all intensified rather than diminished the system of racial apartheid through the 1970s and destroyed previous conditions for African American mobility.[6] Analogous restructuring in the San Francisco Bay Area prompted James Baldwin in 1963 famously to insist that "there is no moral distance, which is to say, no distance, between the facts of life in San Francisco and the facts of life in Birmingham." Documented in the KQED National Education Television film *Take This Hammer*,[7] dialogue between Baldwin, from the front seat of his car tour through the city, and his host, Youth for Service executive director, Orville Luster, poetically captures the sense of being at a loss.

> LUSTER: I think this is one of the real troubles is, the Negro in San Francisco, he doesn't really know his place. He's trying to find his place. So, this is one of the problems, you know. I mean, what place is there for me, you know? He came out to escape.
>
> BALDWIN: Yeah, and he found another prison.
>
> LUSTER: And you find yourself facing the Pacific Ocean, you know?
>
> BALDWIN: (laughs slightly): Yes, yes, yes.

Such exchanges in the film take place against the backdrop of dramatic contractions in the city's wartime manufacturing economy and the San Francisco Redevelopment Agency's implementation of a new city plan in 1961 that displaced African Americans from the Western Addition, resegregating them to public housing projects originally built as "temporary war housing" tracts at Hunter's Point.[8] Baldwin's goal for the film, to expose the daily experiences and worldviews of Black communities in this context, ultimately put him at odds with the film's director and producers, Richard O. Moore and the board of directors of local public television station KQED. Reflecting on disagreements with Baldwin over the original cut, Moore recalls deleting significant footage of conversations with Hunter's Point residents because of the board's discomfort with "the preponderance of Black rage being expressed."[9] The 2013 release of an updated *Director's Cut* reincorporates fifteen minutes of previously censored material in which a gathering of African

American young adult males explicitly reject the mainstream Civil Rights Movement, posit the impossibility of a "truce" or effective national political-economic reform, call for revolutionary violence, and propose unification of the Black community through the Nation of Islam: expressions of rage or outrage at being trapped in an ontological worldview and historical resolution of white supremacy that render even the vastness of the Pacific Ocean part of another prison.

If such resistance remained sequestered at Hunter's Point in 1963, it exploded out of Watts by 1965. Highlighting the seemingly overnight transformation in quality of life for the largest African American population on the West Coast, Josh Sides notes that as late as 1964, an Urban League research study of sixty-eight U.S. cities still identified Los Angeles as the most desirable city for African Americans to live. While this assessment may reflect the magnitude of repression gripping African American communities in other major U.S. cities with longer histories of disfranchisement, settlement, and struggle, it also indicates the increasing political-economic polarization conditioning the Black community by the early 1960s. Overall, prominent middle-class African American leadership and civil rights agendas, exemplified by organizations such as the Urban League or the NAACP, increasingly lost appeal among those for whom the "California Dream" was no longer a conceivable reality or aspiration. In Los Angeles specifically, dominant race leadership did not or could not effectively represent the needs of working-class communities facing the most brutal effects of systematic economic disfranchisement, racial apartheid, and police violence under the regime of Police Chief William Parker. Appointed in 1950, Parker upheld a reign of white supremacy in alliance with a transplanted Southern bloc—plantation elites who had also migrated and appropriated a new place for themselves in the postwar U.S. West.[10]

The 1965 Watts uprising solidified these tendencies and crises taking shape in California cities, as the last half of the decade saw widening class bifurcation among African American urban populations, growth of ultra-right-wing political and economic power to remake whiteness and white supremacy, and deeper ideological breaks within African American communities from a politics of respectability and inclusion. Alongside these shifts, Gerald Horne has argued that the uprising, both its preconditions and its resonance, must be understood in the broader context of U.S. capitalist and government struggles against Communism, labor movements, and leftist insurgencies at the local, national, and global scales. In fact, police and military authorities in the moment explicitly made these connections as Police Chief Parker announced that "this situation is very much like fighting the Viet Cong" and the Los Angeles Police Department (LAPD) and National Guard viewed their roles as crushing a guerrilla war. Such convergences thus situate the uprising as a critical event through which to "to chart the impact of the world on Afro-America and vice versa."[11]

Through this lens, two key assessments stand out regarding the wide-reaching stakes and scope of the event, pivoting us into part 3, "Imprisoned." First, the uprising cemented the decoherence of earlier possibilities for greater social justice in the region, bringing racial articulation in the U.S. West into closer parity with the system and dynamics of anti-Blackness prevalent in the rest of the nation. Second, the event catalyzed refortifications of the infra-structure to uphold the latter and respond more effectively to popular insur-rections. Specifically, LAPD Deputy Chief Roger Murdock argued during the event that armed forces in Watts should "put as many people as we can in jail.... That's certainly no secret."[12] Lamenting the lack of preparedness to do so, LAPD leadership identified the need for expanded resources such as more manpower, better weaponry and surveillance technology, mobile jail capac-ity, and the ability to make mass bookings—changes that would come to fruition in the aftermath of Watts. Both state and national authorities praised the mix of conservative and liberal reforms to law and order in Los Angeles after 1965, which included unprecedented militarization of the LAPD alongside increased affirmative action and diversity training specifi-cally to manage Black populations.[13] Commemorating the fiftieth anniver-sary of the uprising in August 2015, a retrospective offered by the *Los Angeles Times* positioned the event as ushering in a new wave of right-wing govern-ment whose view and preservation of the "sanctity" of private property would dominate the state for the next thirty years and transform administration at the national level.[14]

Part 3 begins with the premise that such restructuring necessitated as much as it was compelled by ideological transformations to facilitate the reconsolidation of capitalist racial apartheid in the U.S. West and articulate the regional regime with those taking shape at other (regional, national, and global) scales. Dominant movements both to reconcile the dysfunctions of World War II regional development and to usher in a new era of nation-state reform hinged on inverse theses ultimately relating racialized incarceration and family structure. Among the best-known examples are, on the one hand, Daniel Moynihan's infamous 1965 report, "The Negro Family: A Case for

National Action," in which he theorizes failed Black masculinity and pathological Black matriarchy as primary causes of "delinquency and crime"; the latter, in turn, justifies state violence despite its discernible excesses. On the other hand, concurrent popular media accounts—beginning with the 9 January 1966 *New York Times* feature "Success Story: Japanese American Style"—apologize for World War II internment and reconcentration by creating a narrative of Japanese American triumph over racism through an ability to learn and balance the "transcendental values of middle-class American life" with the maintenance of "meaningful links to an alien culture." In this formulation, Japanese American family values resolve rather than cause state violence. As analyses of these two discourses have already suggested, such ideologies functioned on a practical basis to establish conditions of possibility for reconstructions of both U.S. nativism and anti-Blackness given the collapse of the dominant social order after 1965.[15]

Notably, this reconstruction revolves around exerting control over social reproduction and racial being vis-à-vis knowledge production to arrange and make sense of differentiated experiences of mass imprisonment. That is, discourses of family pathology and exceptionalism correlate with dichotomized explanations of African American and Japanese American responses to the negative excesses of national security, the former culture uncivilized and the latter meritorious. These universalized ascriptions of static ethnic traits and orientations, in turn, established ideological foundations for dominant rearticulations of Black and Asian racial distinction in order to reorganize regional systems of civic life and social dismantling. Such positionings thinly reconciled the contradictions of racism and, ultimately, shaped the contemporary hegemony of "colorblindness" by facilitating what Susan Koshy points out as the "morphing [of] race into ethnicity."[16] This logic understands anti-racism as recognition and respect for different individuals to the extent that their "cultural" expressions rooted at the household level remain compatible with a system still driven by delimitations of human being that enforce entrance to or elimination from modern civilization. As many critical race scholars of this period have already argued, movements to reconfigure axes of both racial and gendered differentiation, at their interlocking, thus function to rationalize war as a way of life and naturalize the dramatic reorganization of segregated landscapes across geographic scales.[17]

In this light, part 3 elaborates this problem of human being at the crossroads of knowledge production and social reproduction, specifically as these processes remain grounded in systematic forms of captivity and in struggles to restructure relations of race, capital, and culture after 1965. Chapter 5 clarifies theoretically the overlaps and distinctions between problematizing contemporary mass incarceration in terms of capitalist production, on the one hand, and in terms of social reproduction, on the other. I argue for the urgency of precision in this regard in order to open out the question rather than assumption of "racial" significance and signification today, specifically with reference to the "prison industrial complex" as a process of genocide, as systematic extermination by means of isolating and arresting contending forms of existence. Chapter 5 concludes by examining the manipulation of prison mail in acts of retaliation, punishment, and torture, wherein repression does not operate primarily to discipline a labor force but to deaden those who refuse to be neutralized. Considering the letter as a material sign of living potential in this context, I ultimately view the violence it magnetizes not as the negation but as the most apparent "evidence" of the letter's social force.

Chapter 6 takes up these issues of knowledge production, social reproduction, and ethnic ontologies as they come into being in and through the life of paper for the Imprisoned. In asymmetrical dialectic with the mobilization of "ethnic" narrative in techniques of social control, I explore letter correspondence across prison walls as an underrecognized site of movement and as a mode of communal preservation in the face of publicly administered torture and genocide. Paying critical attention to ruptures in modern racial epistemology realized by the insurgent socialities of twentieth-century liberation struggles, as well as to interventions of the epistolary form in this context, I ask how these legacies can shift our perspectives on communal sustainability even as current circumstances compel despair. In the final analysis, I argue that the life of paper constitutes a contradictory kind of creative shelter: a sacred place to foster social being, provide for its study, and generate a mode of its inhabitation. Reading archival materials for traces of the intellectual and affective labor they both congeal and augment, I view letter correspondence as reproductive activity that instantiates life-sustaining claims of belonging to one another and enunciates the experience and significance of being human. In these ways, the life of paper thereby nurtures forms of connection and conditions of existence that generatively stress the limits of what is currently knowable.

———

FIVE

Ephemeral Value and Disused Commodities

THIS CHAPTER OPENS BY CLARIFYING a framework for the study of contemporary mass incarceration that privileges a lens of social reproduction, which I approach in the broadest sense as the practices through which people or processes stay alive. I argue that shifting our perspective from profit to population management can lend greater precision to analyses that frame the problem in direct or exclusive relation to capital production and accumulation—opening a path to explain, in a way the latter paradigm cannot, how incarceration operates today as a process of industrialized genocide. Problematizing how racial ideologies thus function to help constitute this reality rather than merely to describe it, I apply such an understanding of race to question how the post-1965 ideological ambivalence of Asian America can help us unpack what is "new" about the "new Jim Crow." In doing so, I examine changes in processes of racial differentiation that mediate the contemporary administration of civic life and social dismantling, as the latter correlate with positive and negative polarities of enclosure in a (de jure) post-racial (apartheid) carceral regime. Last, then, I interrogate the use of letters in practices of torture within this system, as these tactics make discernible the contradictions of punishment: on the one hand, the mediation of killing through violations simultaneously isolating and diffuse and, on the other, the letter's mediation of insurgent potential that can live without the discipline it hails.

PROCESS OF ELIMINATION

In recent decades, urgent research on the emergence of "mass incarceration" in the United States focuses predominantly on histories drawn from the

Southern and Atlantic regions, tracing anti-Black racism through trajectories of slavery, Civil War and Reconstruction, convict leasing, Jim Crow, industrialization, and the unfinished project of Civil Rights. These scholarly and activist literatures have changed the world by teaching us to view mass incarceration through the lens of structural violence and to understand every instance of this violence as systematic rather than solely individuated or episodic. On the whole, such analyses define mass incarceration as itself a crime against humanity—organized dispossession that destroys communities and individuals—as opposed to the fluctuating hegemonic view of incarceration as a viable structural solution to individuated or concentrated cases of crime. In doing so, progressive arguments for decarceration often necessitate or emphasize top-down perspectives to gain insight into ways that the dominant social order operates and to theorize the most effective ways to break cycles of violence.

The ideological terrains established or fortified through these positions, as crucial as they have been, have also produced new issues to confront analytically. Troublesome side effects of the prevailing slavery-to-prison narrative include its construction or repetition as a linear story in which each successive regime follows logically and inevitably from the previous one. While social movement historians and intellectuals have already developed comprehensive critiques and alternatives to these conventions of "objectivity,"[1] I seek here to address how, correlated with the extent of their fixed tendencies, such accounts also assume static definitions of capitalism, prisons, and race and easily correspondent relationships between them. Namely, common explanations have posited that capitalists profit from prisons in one or both of two main ways: either people warehoused as wards of the state provide slave labor for corporations or corporations run privatized prisons and/or contract with the state to administer prison goods and services at exorbitant rates. In both scenarios, corporations make direct profits by exploiting a labor force in a consumer-based market—a presumably African American labor force directly correspondent with that of slavery and Jim Crow. Finally, then, these formulations thus approach "race" as an objective if not biological fact that, even if implied as "socially constructed," can be taken for granted rather than explained. This racial assumption, in turn, insinuates a definition of rac*ism* as the subjugation and/or hatred of people based on their race, a tautology in the sense that race is presumed to catalyze racism while no logical mechanism exists to define or interpret "racial" difference as the causal factor.[2]

Given the framework I have just generalized, I propose now to extend arguments attending to its limitations in order to strengthen existing modes of understanding and intervention. This attempt for greater clarity began with, and still privileges, the desire to create discursive space to contextualize the life of paper as itself a site of knowledge and activity; however, such an investigation also dovetails with urgent endeavors to comprehend mass incarceration and the "inside" of prisons in tandem with "outside" state violence that has polarized the country and world at the time of writing. The heightened visibility of murders by police or deputized civilians of young Black men and boys such as Oscar Grant, Trayvon Martin, Eric Garner, Michael Brown, Ezell Ford, Tamir Rice, Walter Scott, and Freddie Gray, and to a less focused extent, the visibility of police murders of young Black women such as Rekia Boyd, Renisha McBride, and Sandra Bland, have forced communities across the country to grapple with how Black Life Matters (also catalyzing deeper activist dialogues about gendered and transgendered differentiation of racial subjects and connections between systematic versus "isolated" homicides). Popular movements have surfaced antagonisms of life-and-death proportions that cannot be confined (even if defined) spatially or reduced strictly to a function of labor exploitation or even of moral failure. I thus initiate my inquiry by engaging debates about the relationship between capitalism and mass incarceration, aiming to refine our insights with a framework focused on crises of social reproduction before proceeding with the implications of this theorization for concepts and relations of race, civilization, and genocide.

Ruth Wilson Gilmore's approach to carceral geographies has provided a theoretical pathway to objectify social processes for the purpose of examination while attuned to their dynamic rather than static forms.[3] Her perspective identifies the place of prisons in public—distinguishable from privatized—life and infrastructure, thus making visible the specificities that define the rule of law while also demystifying the density of ideological work that affects the apparent disarticulation of what happens "inside" from civic life "outside." This lens makes possible a concept of carceral space that does not refer inanimately to prisons but rather to the multitude of differentiated yet deeply connected social geographies that necessitate, create, and maintain prison institutions. In other words, thinking through carceral space in this paradigm entails a view of the *relationships* between different places organized through and sutured by a system of racial apartheid, such that we cannot conceive of the prison, its relegated negativity and abjection (or its abolition, for that matter), without considering its definitive place in the arrangement and maintenance of positive space and value. The stratification of carceral space, therefore, does not denote the formal or operational autonomy of segregated places so much as represent normative (not absolute or necessarily real) boundaries of state and social violence, differentiated in magnitudes of its intensity and degrees of its exercise with impunity.

To unpack further these dialectics, I turn to two early works on the prison industrial complex (PIC) to build on their key interventions, perhaps neglected in more recent studies, regarding the interlocked rather than discrete processes of producing prison, public, private, and privatized spaces. First, Mike Davis's *City of Quartz* centers on the contradictions of hyperpolicing and hyper-accumulation as they shape the social geography of post-1965 Los Angeles.[4] Distinct from Southern- and Atlantic-based analyses that link the PIC to regressive or conservative regimes carried over from the past, Davis's regional focus emphasizes how mass incarceration can be driven simultaneously by progressive movements ideologically tied to notions of futurity: that is, intensified militarization as a mode of innovation in the shambles of deindustrialization and at the cutting edge of greater global efficiency, security, and peace. From this perspective, the social and spatial logics that architect ghettoes and prisons also characterize redevelopment plans for late capitalist bourgeois or settler homesteads, together re-forming the negative and positive polarities of enclosure. Their attendant regulatory imperatives—in which the conceived criminality of the former necessitates repression and the conceived sanctity of the latter, protection—in turn, restore the "public" realm's raison d'être and reinstitute its mandate to provide or define order. In this triangulation, then, vectors of collectivized dispossession and of individualized accumulation both hold the capitalist public sphere steady and, as I elaborate in sections to follow, refashion ideological foundations for dominant processes of racial differentiation in the wake of global antiracist revolutions.

In this context, Christian Parenti's *Lockdown America*[5] helps clarify the process of privatization vis-à-vis the import of mass incarceration to capitalism, bearing in mind my consideration of privatization as it relates to both the "private" and "public" spheres: that is, the former as the site of expropriation and individualization of social (and feminized) wealth and the latter in terms of the state's role in organizing social relations to facilitate processes of alienation and capital accumulation. Parenti's approach to the PIC as a problem of social control distinguishes itself from interpretations of the PIC as a problem of prison labor itself, most significantly in terms of identifying the ultimate concern or stake. In the framework of social control, prisons aid capitalism despite their high social costs and questionable profit margins for more essential reasons. That is, very basically, the inherent contradiction of capital and labor power means that capital growth occurs alongside the creation of surplus labor pools, permanently unemployed or underemployed populations whose existence also disciplines working classes with the threat of their own expendability under capitalism. Historically and in structural terms, African Americans in the aftermath slavery have constituted an unparalleled surplus; differentiated processes of capitalist economic expansion, colonial exploitation and genocide, and humanistic ideological production have also shaped simultaneous social struggles and other historically specific articulations of surplus labor under capitalist relations.[6] Prisons, then, literally contain aggregated populations who have become too much of a surplus for capitalism actually to contain, given the magnitude of contradictions that have reached a global apex at this conjuncture. In this sense, primarily U.S. prisons do not create direct profits so much as re-create conditions of possibility for the reproduction of the capitalist order itself through methods of comprehensive social control: in the final instance, arrested life as a mode of extermination, administered predominantly through state capacities in a time of worldwide catastrophe.

Refining our insights about the PIC as industrialized genocide rather than as a site of genocidal exploitation of labor resituates contemporary incarceration as foremost an ontological rather than political and/or economic dilemma. The broad details and significance of these distinctions bear repeating. As Gilmore notes of California prisons, and James Kilgore of prisons nationwide,[7] mass incarceration is a public enterprise with few, even if remarkable, exceptions—the latter of which the federal government itself had deemed wise to phase out at the twilight of the Obama administration. While, of course, this makes more apparent the centrality of prison building to dominant political life, the key operation is not in generating state profits (or even "social" capital through the arbitration of citizenship rights) but in mobilizing state capacities as means of reestablishing the legitimacy of failing capitalist state power as such. Moreover, Kilgore indicates that, as of September 2012, approximately only 8 percent of work-eligible inmates held by the Federal Bureau of Prisons were employed, in a context wherein work eligibility is itself a restricted privilege, and only 0.25 percent of all U.S. prisoners were employed by the private sector. If such numbers hardly conjure the quantitative picture of a hyper-productive commodity capitalist labor regime, then prisons instead serve capital by eliminating or neutralizing populations who have no place in, and thus threaten, the preservation of privatized wealth. In the final instance, then, the characterization of prisons as warehouses, as opposed to sweatshops or factories, is apt in the sense that people do not suffer and die in prison from overwork but from the complete lack of stimulation and activity.

Finally, the expansion of social and service industries within the PIC, in sectors such as food, lodging, transportation, and, in particular, communication, poses a slightly different problem to address theoretically. The obscene financial burdens of living through incarceration seem clear evidence of corporations making money by preying on prisoners and their communities who struggle to mitigate the deprivations forced on them. Yet we must grapple more precisely with the very notion of wealth in this context. Such forms of economic exploitation and wealth extraction, in which predatory corporations drain the most vulnerable of their material resources, are not new or unique to the PIC but a basic and universal principle of capitalist consumerism; with this in mind, it becomes clearer that imprisoned communities today live in the legacy of centuries of normalized parasitic practices. Quite simply, then, stealing from historically dispossessed communities—those who, by definition, have already been stripped of material assets—cannot generate corporate wealth, particularly of a magnitude we could consider exorbitant at this current stage of capitalist development. Instead, I propose that the most crucial function of extracting financial resources from communities targeted for incarceration resides *not* in making corporations rich from the direct transfer of funds from consumers to owners. Rather, the most crucial function resides in taking away the little means people have left to live, resources that, even in aggregated amounts, mean little to those who claim to own everything and much to those who have access to very little. In this light, the wealth that corporations generate through the expropriation of resources comes not from accumulating financial assets based on commercial operations of the PIC but from monopolizing the wealth inherent in our life force by controlling the means to our social reproduction.

Scholars and activists working toward decarceration can continue to develop the impact of these analyses by allowing questions of social reproduction to supersede limited views of capitalist production as the marrow of what we find relevant and consequential to the project of abolition. As Marxian feminists have long argued, studying the realm of social reproduction—a task definitive of further fleshing out a labor power theory of value—

remains a challenge for even the most inspired work in pursuit of social justice. For example, in a recent study of the political economy of punishment, James A. Manos offers rigorous readings of Karl Marx and the Frankfurt theorists Georg Rusche and Otto Kirchheimer to make a clarification, somewhat similar to the one presented here, that "incarceration is an organizing metaphysical principle of capitalism more broadly." He continues, "While punishment is bound to the modes of production, its function does not merely respond to and reflect the modes of production, [but] law and punishment produce and manage dispossession inherent in capitalism's primitive accumulation."[8] Manos's central assertion thus positions prisons and punishment within the structural matrix of capitalist ontology that both includes and exceeds the political-economic structure of capitalist production. That is, Manos situates modes of social control as key to the creation of the total conditions of possibility for the very existence of capitalism and for all subsequent reproductions of capitalist relations as they mediate life itself. Yet, even in the context of these urgent insights, realms of social reproduction remain so taken for granted that even an analysis explicitly debunking facile equivalences drawn between modes of punishment and modes of production turns immediately back to a paradigm of market relations, as Manos concludes that "convicts have become commodities who are exchanged among various corporations and what remains of state institutions."[9]

This argument, that convicts constitute objects in corporate commodity exchange "to be rented and reproduced," fundamentally controverts Manos's core intervention that identifies the dispossessed as those who problematize or antagonize capitalism at the metaphysical rather than solely instrumental level. As a result of this inconsistency, the stakes of dispossession in Manos's conclusion ultimately remain confined to modes and means of production, or struggles over commodities, rather than the modes and means of social reproduction, struggles mediating the historical contours of life and death as such. This distinction remains consequential even and especially in reference to the historical legacy of slavery, wherein Black life troubles the distinction between humans and commodities. It follows from the changing political-economic conditions of dispossession from the eras of slavery to mass incarceration that (Black) convicts today, even if we were to accept the supposition that they are commodities, no longer move as *capitalist* commodities, since as units of abstracted labor they are not expendable but actually obsolete or redundant under late capitalism. In the prison-as-warehouse metaphor, in other words, think of overstock items that remain after the very last clearance sale, at that final moment before store shelves are to be filled with the next phase of retail. From this corporate standpoint, the rental and reproduction of convicts carrying no recognizable use- or exchange-value would simply waste capital, whereas, in the final instance, only the capture and elimination of the convicted can conserve it.

Finally, then, if we are still to consider convicts as commodities, it must be in Zora Neale Hurston's sense of being "a brown bag of miscellany propped against a wall . . . in the company of other bags, white, red and yellow"— things filled with other things by "the Great Stuffer of Bags."[10] The life of paper, as it were, grows out of this aeconomic commodity chain.

OF COLOR

If I am lingering on seemingly slight imprecisions, it is only because I share these common confusions, and even subtle theoretical readjustments can open up different directions for our understanding. In Manos's reading, for example, "punishment creates a disposable population whose dispossession is racially distributed."[11] It may be more precise to say that capitalism is conditioned on the production and reproduction of disposable populations whose dispossession is racially distributed. Punishment, then, acts today as a primary mode of disposal. If we pursue this latter formulation, then at least two new problems present themselves for further consideration. First, we return to the original point that the core logic and function of the PIC may not refer back as much to money management and accumulation as to population management and extermination. It is likely at this register that slavery, Jim Crow, and mass incarceration most strongly cohere: that is, not as homologous racialized labor regimes but as the historical continuity of anti-Black genocide enacted through processes of systematic social dismantling. This perspective recognizes the political-economic specificities of slavery, Jim Crow, and mass incarceration as *different* rather than the same, meaning that the evolution of human disposal represented by the latter correlates with changing rather than stagnant capitalist imperatives. New dimensions hence become available to account for how and why a system that specifically and disproportionately targets African Americans for policing and punishment can simultaneously incorporate other forms of racism and capitalist exploitation that helped articulate and maintain, and were or are also articulated and maintained alongside, anti-Blackness as a racial logic and slavery as a mode of production. Thus operating in a negative mode of hegemonic "colorblind" ideology attendant to late capitalism, the PIC can aggregate multiple racial logics and multiple expendable or redundant populations into an increasingly flexible and consolidated process of disposal, preserving U.S. imperialism, nativism, and anti-Blackness at its core even when—and precisely because—the racial logics or exigencies of these ideological systems come into conflict with each other.[12]

This raises the second problem, that of "race." By pointing out the existence of multiple racial logics that mediate different historical articulations of dispossession throughout Western civilization, as well as their reconsolidations in a colorblind era, I do not mean that anti-Blackness is just one racism among the many that can all be somehow compared or rationalized through relations of equivalence.[13] I mean that in a world structured by processes of racialized differentiation that both alienate and interconnect us in their contradictions, the urgency to understand the singularity of anti-Blackness (or any other racial regime, for that matter) cannot be thwarted by analytically misconstruing singularity for formal autonomy, which as Colleen Lye has argued,[14] would only reproduce reification in the final instance. In the current moment, then, and in the context of mass incarceration, the assertion that dispossession is "racially" distributed hides deeper questions about the specificities of reproducing "race" as such, in each case of its instantiation. In this most basic sense, the question rather than assumption of what race *is* takes on particular import precisely because it allows us to interrogate instead of take for granted the processes through which productions of race—which is to say, struggles to define and live through the very *concept* of race, including its ostensible nonexistence—historically mediate matters of life and death and operate in a dominant sense to normalize genocide.

Contemporary debates addressing the dynamics of "colorblind" oppression, in which prevailing discourses alternate on either side of the contradiction of the "postracial" and the "new Jim Crow," generally continue to defer this ultimate concern. On the one hand, critical perspectives in the postracial paradigm respond urgently to changes in the historical specificities of racial articulation. For example, in asking *What Was African American Literature?*, Kenneth Warren theorizes the demise of this form of ethnoracial assertion based on the idea that today's modes of racism do not correspond with the Jim Crow formulations against which such a literary formation supposedly arose and cohered in response.[15] While his critical attention to African American bourgeois alienation may indicate that Warren's work could contribute more to historicizing an African American literary canon than to constructing a definitive genealogy of African American literatures, he raises key problems for us to reconsider, specifically regarding the contemporary production of ethnoracial subjectivities and the internal differentiation of racial identities vis-à-vis other categories of existence, such as class. Ultimately, these ever-escalating problems indicate that, rather than characterizing the United States as a postracial society, it may be said more precisely that the United States currently exists as a de jure (though not de facto) post–racial *apartheid* society, wherein legally mandated "racial integration" or tolerance in the post–Civil Rights era has reformed but does not redress the systematic human exploitation and genocide that organizes the dominant landscape.

From this perspective, the notion of a "new Jim Crow" sets out to elaborate dominant rearticulations of race, racism, and apartheid in such a (de jure) post–racial (apartheid) society. In this regard, Michelle Alexander's analysis of felon disfranchisement under the regime of "mass incarceration in the age of colorblindness" has greatly influenced popular discourses and understandings about the emergence of prisons, human categories such as "criminal," and their evolving significance to effect a "rebirth of racial caste."[16] Yet, as incisive as her general arguments are, her formulations of race remain both inconsistent (alternating between race as legal status and as biology) and tautological (racist laws help determine race while race helps determines racist law), thus mystifying the most significant questions about what is "new" about the "new Jim Crow" precisely by adhering to the very logics of race produced by and constitutive of the "old." Even at their sharpest, then, hegemonic progressive critiques of contemporary racism generally continue to reproduce class and race analyses that, on the one hand, can explain capitalism in terms of social inequality but not in terms of genocide and, on the other, can explain human differentiation as an effect of institutional power but not as productive of power or power relations as such, our abilities to catalyze and sustain activity.

As preface to the next chapter, then, in which I investigate these problematics by prioritizing perspectives of the Imprisoned, I synthesize here a general context for approaching race as an epistemological undertaking, one that articulates at the interstices of ideological and ontological formulation to mediate access to the very means of social reproduction. In fact, the Black radical tradition and its pursuit through the practices of Black study have set enduring historical precedents for interrogating rather than renaturalizing global processes of race-*making:* clarifying how the multiplicity of social movements in any given time and place dynamically reconstruct different race concepts, produced and embodied to set in motion competing methods and visions of organizing social life itself.[17] In these regards, Clyde Woods's paradigm of "Blues epistemology" presents us with a conceptual apparatus to grapple with the formative influence of African diasporic cultural and intellectual traditions on modernity as such.[18] As Woods locates the Blues in his article "Katrina's World":

> Although the evolution of the Blues paralleled Bourbonism, this Southern, now global, knowledge system, epistemology, and development agenda absorbs everything it encounters in nature and humanity. Its principle [sic] concern is not the creation of a new hierarchy, but working class leadership, social vision, sustainable communities, social justice, and the construction of a new commons. Many of the fundamental principles of the Blues tradition of social investigation and development are often derided, censored, and consequently hidden in daily life until they reemerge during times like the present.[19]

Woods's perspective on Afro-modernity and its manifestations in global development hence articulates through the historically particular in order to formulate a universalizing worldview, one bound to Blackness and produced in contradistinction to racial capitalist ontology mediated through whiteness. It merits distinguishing this perspective on appositional formations from discursive productions in earlier Ethnic Studies scholarship of a "black-white binary." In general, the latter ideological orientation revolves around three key theoretical maneuvers: first, defining *black* and *white* as binary terms that refer to objective races and historical relations between them; second, abstracting from this binary a definition of racism as the effect of structural inequality or conflict between black and white races at a representative level; and third, subsequently criticizing this formulation for excluding the presence, experiences, or interests of other objective races, namely (using here the salient racial signifiers of that ideological moment) Asian Americans and Latinos. As generative as elements of this discursive formation have been, in its opposite focus, the "black-white binary" and its critique thus move tautologically in the sense that it discursively produces the reading of race and racism that it comes forward to denounce. Moreover, if the critique itself generates the reading, then it also reproduces the core misreading through an additive model of correction that relies on repetition of the original assumptions of racial objectivity.[20]

If reifying race in these ways thus leads to a closed circuit, the apposition of "black" and "white" in the formulation I outline here opens other conduits for thought by referring not to relations between objective races of people but, instead, to ontological positionings. Second, then, these positionings are not necessarily configured as binary so much as historically coeval and, hence embedded as they both are in modern trajectories of racism, materialized and embodied through distinctions understood as "racial." Considering racism as the total set of processes that organize populations for the spectrum of civilized life and industrialized genocide, the dialectics embedded in the socialities of each respective pole—those marked for civilization and those for disposal—move differently. That is, while the world mediated through whiteness depends on fabrications of an Other that needs to be destroyed, from the ontological positioning of Blackness in the modern world emerged a mode of "*being human* as praxis," an "auto-poesis" or improvisational self- and world-making that ultimately sustains itself through generative tensions rather than binary antagonisms between difference and solidarity, singularity and interdependence.[21] Finally, in contemplating the historical dynamics within and between these two essential orientations to being, limited "black-white binary" frameworks, inadvertently reproducing the epistemology of whiteness inherent in the method of thought itself, examine forms of appearance but not their inner socialities, and thus the latter read as static, fixed, and absolute in both their internal compositions and outward exclusions. In contrast, a perspective of racialized ontologies can conceive of relationships that breathe, so to speak, and consist of patterns beyond domination, subsumption, transaction, or elimination. Through this lens, then, it becomes possible to view changing anxieties over Asiatic racial distinction and Asian American racialization in the late twentieth century as pivotal to, not erased by, the investigation of transforming historical struggles understood hegemonically in terms of black and white.

In fact, urgent work in Asian American Studies has begun to theorize this density, situating studies of race and racism within the unfolding of modernity as a global project, at the latter's intersecting matrices of empire, war, and genocide.[22] Focusing specifically on post-1965 ideological reconfigurations of Asian America, Colleen Lye argues for the need to problematize Asian American racialization beyond its theoretical positioning as either derivative of or a substitute for anti-Black racism.[23] Suggesting that the incoherence of Asian American racial formation illustrates less of a third term to racial binaries than "the genuine multiplicity of racial logics and racisms," Lye's opening premise may imply two further points. First, studying the more obvious instabilities and contingencies inherent in the production of "Asian" as a race concept can also help unlock the instabilities and contingencies inherent in the production of all race concepts, particularly those most easily naturalized and understood in their certainties. Second, by thus helping to reveal volatility in social phenomena that, at the immediate level, may appear unchanging, new dimensions become available to interrogate the paradoxical expansion of racial logics alongside the apparent contraction of social wealth: dynamics that animate contemporary movements to reconstruct conditions of possibility for racial capitalism and reconstitute the machinery of genocide.

Through this lens, dominant struggles to define Asian racial distinction are not epiphenomenal to anti-Black racism so much as vital to the social reproduction of white supremacy, wherein absolute commitment of the latter to anti-Blackness does not limit historical articulations of whiteness to only one racial logic or killing regime. By provoking us to consider how post-1965 Asian American racialization may indicate new breaks between and subsequent reforms of the symbolic and the material power of whiteness, Lye seems to point precisely to the need to examine refashioned racial logics in the symbolic realm in order to sustain white supremacy's ultimate material power: monopoly not only over the means to life but also the means to kill. In this crisis of human being, as Lye gestures to in her conclusions, investigating the role of aesthetics in historical—indeed, ontological—struggle can thus help clarify competing movements in the late twentieth century to resuture joints between the objective and subjective organization of existence.

For the sake of consistency rather than metonymy, and as a specific rather than necessarily generalizable example, ideological struggles to position the Nisei generation after World War II illustrate, first, how evolutions in the production of Asian American racial distinction can mediate changes in ontologies or lifeworlds that nevertheless remain legible through Black and white lenses; and second, how interarticulations with Asian American racial forms confirm rather than negate the latter's own ontological distinctions. On the one hand, in her study of Miné Okubo's recruitment as an ideological worker in the transwar years, Christine Hong analyzes the deployment of Okubo's work in the interests of U.S. state and international diplomacy at the end of the war.[24] Elaborating both the ideological elasticity and historical productivity of *Citizen 13660*, Hong first argues that the ambivalence represented by the figure of Okubo herself, at the crossroads of textuality and embodiment, provided grounds for U.S. nationalist reconciliation vis-à-vis contradictory processes of her ethnic authentication, cross-racial identification, and recuperation as a Nisei citizen-subject. These dynamics also reverberated at an international scale as agents of corporate and state media mobilized Okubo's art to mediate postwar U.S. occupation of Japan. In this sense, renderings of Okubo's illustrations launched ideological assertions of Nikkei rehabilitation through the democratizing influence of U.S. militarization. Such ideological production, in turn, served as a prescription for postwar U.S. governmentality in occupied Japan and its legitimation within a liberal democratic framework. In this example, adaptations to the Asian race concept vis-à-vis ideological productions of a distinctive Nisei citizen-subjectivity prove necessary to secure the postwar social reproduction of white ontology—or the universalizing reach of racial capitalism, its structure of existence and notion of human being—as articulated through U.S. empire.

Under such circumstances, in which changes in the material power of whiteness articulate through reforms in the symbolic power of the Asian race concept, it bears clarifying that, just as the racialization of Asian/Americans is not epiphenomenal to anti-Black racism, neither is it merely epiphenomenal (although it is necessary) to white supremacy—the implications of which run in multiple directions and can only be determined historically. In cases of interarticulations between Asian and white racial forms, correlated changes in both the symbolic and material power of Asianness within racial capitalism also function, in the final instance, to intensify systems of anti-Blackness. That is, in these contexts, self-assertions of Asiatic racial distinction within the matrix of preexisting ethnic ontologies can produce racial logics of anti-Blackness that are not necessarily defined by, even as they coalesce with, whiteness or the exigencies of U.S. empire. Instead, returning to what I have argued and attempted to demonstrate in part 1, competing imperialisms that come to a head at specific historical conjunctures of racial capitalist struggle are distinguishable at the same time that they are interlocked and codependent. As such, dominant reproductions of the Asian race concept can build on ideologies of Asian ethnoracial supremacy and anti-Blackness that are themselves not simply derivative of whiteness and can, indeed, even align with limited articulations of antiwhiteness. Moving toward a theorization of the latter, Helen Jun juxtaposes racialized ideologies of development in the postindustrial era effectively to desediment the discursive formation of "black-Korean conflict" hegemonic through the 1990s, clarifying a contradiction in which shifting racial logics apropos Asian/American mediate progressive visions of global capitalist hypermobility, correlated with the Pacific Rim as site and sign of global capitalist futurity; whereas intensified logics of anti-Blackness rationalize a new phase of urban enclosure disproportionately targeting working-class Black communities.[25] In this vein, much work remains to be seen and done to grapple with the planetary scope of contemporary East Asian capitalist development and the particular forms of racial distinction attendant on these world systems.[26]

In the historical gestalt of these dominant movements, cases of interarticulations between Asian and Black racial forms can, on the other hand, mobilize other epistemological formulations in order to instantiate a different mode of Asian/American racial ideological production, one that coalesces instead with what Woods refers to as the Blues ontology and exemplifies the latter's universalizing scope. Returning to the example of Nisei at the crossroads of racialized struggle, a closer reading of Lawson Fusao Inada's epistolary poem, excerpted from "Poems from Amache Camp," helps illustrate an example of such social dynamics:[27]

"Dear Lawson,
   2 Ys U R,
   2 Ys U B,
   I C U R
   2 Ys 4 Me!
           Your friend,
             Bobby"

Historically, and particularly in urban centers such as San Francisco and Los Angeles (for Inada specifically, the town of Fresno), Nisei youth lived in closer social proximity to African American youth than perhaps any other Japanese American generation due to the conditions of racial segregation through the 1940s and the racial alienation of World War II. In this context, the extent to which Nisei learned how to be "American" through African American perspectives or, conversely, through normative European American ones, significantly also shaped their camp experiences as well as their ontological frameworks that emerged in the wake. In Inada's case, in other works from *Legends from Camp* and beyond, he explicitly highlights his introduction to Blues music over the radio in Jerome, Arkansas, as a source of sustenance during his time in camp there as a youth. This broader context thus situates Inada's poem in his larger claims that African

American, more than European American, worldviews and culture mediated his own creative understanding of racialized humanity relative to the problems of U.S. empire and citizenship. Aesthetically, the influence of the Blues resounds in this poem's meter as well as in its paradoxical tone, the uplifting energy that stresses boundaries of captivity. In these regards, in his poetry, Inada has also reflected on the ways that Black music and English have shaped his relationship to language, under conditions in which "we were all criticized, continually corrected and ridiculed in school for the way we talked—for having accents, dialects, for misusing, abusing the language."[28] Thus the inventiveness of form—evinced in this letter-poem, for example, through its play with genre, vernacular, and deconstruction—instantiates uses of language that Inada and others, as represented by "Bobby," learned from both Japanese and African American intellectual traditions.

Notably, the generative interplay between the two ethnoracial forms, the historical and epistemological contents they mediate, does not negate the singularity of either one. For example, the influence of the Blues does not negate the influence of haiku, which is also prominent in the poem, present in its formal austerity as well as its evocation of kanji characters through Inada's play with letters. In the sociality thus channeled through aesthetic innovation, mixture and multiplicity define rather than violate formal integrity.[29] Viewed at a broader scale, these dynamics also animate Inada's lived striving to engage the global force of the Blues as an onto-epistemological fabric and the universalizing impact of the Black radical tradition: surrogating evolutions of his own ethnic ontology through which a nondominant Asian race concept can emerge, one that does not have to be a priori anti-Black. In this assertion, my aim is neither to analogize historical experiences of racism nor to feign resolution to fatal inequalities in dominant distributions of rights to life and killing vis-à-vis racialization, dominant productions and arrangements of racialized difference. Instead, I mean to draw attention to historical overdeterminations necessary to reproduce epistemologies of whiteness, Blackness, and the absolute principle of anti-Blackness in racial capitalist ontologies; the socialities forged in spaces of excess; and vital resources that may still exist in what remains after ephemeral moments of convergence have come to pass. Indeed, these resources may prove crucial when, as today's widening ideologies of supremacy and proliferating landscapes of terror indicate, fettered moments of convergence in our lives will only grow more frequent.

Faced now with the interceding role of aesthetics in giving historical shape to ontological struggle and racialized insecurities, we return, finally, to the place and logic of "the purloined letter," in which Barbara Johnson painstakingly theorizes, "The letter as signifier is thus not a thing or the absence of a thing, not a word or the absence of a word, not an organ or the absence of an organ, but a *knot* in the structure where words, things, and organs can neither be definably separated nor compatibly combined."[30] If, in this problem that Johnson presents, the letter acts as a signifier that can only be known in its effects, existing as a *difference* whose function is not wholly dependent on the knowledge or substance of its contents, then perhaps nowhere does this dilemma become more apparent than in the context of incarceration and, most immediately, in the incorporation of letters in practices of neutralizing human life and accelerating its end. To bring this chapter to its conclusion, then, I elaborate the latter in order to bring to the fore certain contradictory effects. On the one hand, studying the manipulation of letters as an act of torture underscores the breakdown of polarities between materiality and ideality and, furthermore, brings into focus the interlocking of micro- and macro-scales of punishment through dynamics of deprivation and excess. On the other hand, such violence—repression exercised precisely to destroy the essence of possibility that the letter as signifier *is*—itself arises as another of the letter's effects rather than its overturning. From this perspective, we may thus acknowledge, even if we cannot "know," the presence of its inner sociality that, like the letter itself, eludes containment and signifies an otherness for which there exists no accounting.

In fact, as I have attempted to illustrate in other contexts throughout parts 1 and 2, the obscurity of the life of paper relates paradoxically to the obvious rather than arcane significance of letter correspondence to hegemonic political and civic life. As such, long-standing normative logics of the letter's utility and efficacy appear to animate contemporary prisoner advocacy campaigns as well as to provide a frame for their political purpose. For example, in a 1976 anthology, *Through the Wall: Prison Correspondence,* the Los Angeles-based Communist activist Ethel Shapiro-Bertolini prefaces the national prison letter correspondence project in which she was involved:

> Almost overnight [the responses to our outreach] became staggering, overwhelming, and all-consuming. . . . We were snowed under by an unexpected

outpouring of deep emotions from a suffering and aching group of people who requested that their cries be heard through the wall. They all wanted to tell their stories. They all wanted the outside to hear them out in detail, objectively.[31]

Shapiro-Bertolini's ideological framework thus relies on notions of the letter's transparency, a seemingly natural and unmediated process of the letter's signification in which both emotional and empirical information also exists as "objectively" knowable. Such assumptions, in turn, ground her perspective that the anthology, as a political project, allows prisoners to be known and thus functions to expose truth.

Beyond such assertions of documentary objectivity, however, and perhaps much more fascinating, a subtle metadiscourse develops within the collection regarding the process of correspondence itself. In this regard, the imprisoned correspondents' writing about writing can offer a different frame to engage the work that the anthology performs, as the discourse articulates the dilemma of the letter as "knot" where the very essence of human communication comes together and falls apart simultaneously. For example, as Lee Brown writes about his conditions of writing from Vacaville State Prison in California, around 1974, "To speak of getting comfortable is ineffable e.g. have you ever tried writing on a book placed across your knees when the book is smaller than the paper itself?"[32] In another letter, Miguel Nevarez, writing on 28 June 1974 from solitary confinement at Leavenworth Penitentiary in Kansas, contextualizes his situation:[33]

> However, I must remind you that I am living under very primitive conditions sometimes I am without paper and pencil for days on end. I am constantly moved from cell to cell and have no idea when I'll be released to population. If our correspondence is somehow disrupted it is because of the above reasons or reasons which I can't possibly go into right now. There is no consistency or direction contained in the unlawful actions of my keepers.

These excerpts insinuate the letter's indefinable relationship to empiricism in at least two ways. First, the letter as such constitutes rather than merely describes the circumstances of political and existential crisis, as the correspondence mediates an experience of subjection that the letter's contents both reveal and cannot possibly reveal. Second, expressions of physical and sensory deprivation that cohere around the letter also indicate an indeterminate connection between the materiality of the letter and human embodiment, discernible in these passages through the effects of discipline and punishment. In these ways, the discourse that takes place through letter correspondence *about* letter correspondence does not document so much as instantiate struggles to survive living in prison, which imprisoned correspondents both objectively recount and confront the impossibility of objectively recounting—a contradiction that becomes part of the torture.

In this latter sense, allusions in the metadiscourse to physical abuse and material withholding are inextricable from psychological torture, violence exercised through the letter in attempts to arrest and break down cognitive capacities. In one instance, Eddie L. Taylor writes to Shapiro-Bertolini on 5 August 1974, from an unspecified location:[34]

I have a letter I sent to you returned to me twice now for a so-called institutional rule violation, (I'm only supposed to put two sheets of paper in an envelope) which is seldom enforced unless prison authorities wish to harass a prisoner for some reason. I may have to start sending you my story in manila envelopes (about 20 sheets at a time) because I cannot afford the cost in envelopes (we are limited in the number of envelopes we can purchase) at only two sheets per envelope; I have other people I correspond with.

In Taylor's Foucauldian example of micro-disciplining vis-à-vis institutional protocols of letter correspondence, the rules, although articulated in terms of material austerity, function less as a form of economic regulation than of psychological conditioning, as grounds for harassment or its threat that inures prisoners to the indignities of powerlessness. The hyper-vulnerabilities in this regard can heighten the dangers of correspondence beyond sustainability. For example, imprisoned in 1973 for participation in the Black liberation movement and a "twentieth-century escaped slave" since 1979,[35] Assata Shakur contextualizes her disengagement from letter writing while incarcerated:

I was receiving a lot of mail. . . . I wasn't able to answer all of those letters because the prison permitted us to write only two letters a week, subject to inspection and censorship by the prison authorities. It was hard for me to write anyway. I was also very paranoid about letters. I could not bear the thought of the police, FBI, guards, whoever, reading my letters and getting daily insight on how i was feeling and thinking. But i would like to offer my sincerest apology to those who were kind enough to write me over the years and who received no answer.[36]

Notably, in the examples presented by Taylor and Shakur, physical and mental disciplining at the micro-scale oscillates in function between training docile subjects and punishing those who refuse to be neutralized. This fluidity, seen through the effects of the letter itself—or, in Shakur's case, preemption of its effects through the letter's deferral—epitomizes the ultimately interlocked processes of creating and destroying racialized subjects under regimes of whiteness. That is, institutional reproduction rests on prisoners' subjectivization through the training of self-discipline that, as Taylor points out, effects a normalized system in which rules need only be "seldom enforced." Conversely, the examples demonstrate how routines of letter correspondence transition from creating consensual subjects to breaking recalcitrant ones in cases of resistance or failure to comply. Elaborating the subtleties in these dynamics of positive and negative force, contemporary abolitionist writer and activist, Stormy Ogden, member of the Kashia Pomo tribe, speaks about her experience at California Rehabilitation Center in Norco from 1981 to 1986:

> For any prisoner letters from the outside are very important and in many ways their only lifeline. I noticed that during the holidays and especially on Mother's Day, the women were more anxious to receive mail, but it was also a time when a few of the guards, male and female, were more likely to play "head games" [by withholding mail] with any of the women that might "buck" the rules.[37]

Ogden's characterization of the letter as signifier of an "only lifeline" shows how, in turn, the manipulation of mail by prison officials serves as a contradictory method of social control—permitting access to the lifeline of the letter as a reward for good behavior, on the one hand, or, on the other, depriving access at strategic moments as a mundane form of psychological torture, coercing submission to captivity.

In a different case evidencing further applications of this technique of punishment, Viet Mike Ngo, imprisoned at San Quentin in 2002, writes about the retaliation he faced as a result of his organizing for prison education and racial desegregation of prison housing.

The Hearing Officer who adjudicated the [administrative charges filed against me] dismissed all counts except one: corresponding with a volunteer, a non-serious offense. He found me guilty despite stating in his deposition that such correspondence appears to be allowed by prison regulations.

Prison officials informed me that the four month-long investigation, six months of solitary confinement, and five transfers was due to a non-serious, suspect, prison write-up for writing letters.[38]

In Ngo's instance, prison administrators exploited the indeterminate status of the letter as signifier to affect criminalization that, in turn, retroactively justified physical and psychological torture that they had already inflicted. Such retaliatory tactics, in fact, came into clearer view in 2011, when Todd Ashker, Arturo Castellanos, Sitawa N. Jamaa (R.N. Dewberry), George Franco, Antonio Guillen, Lewis Powell, Paul Redd, Alfred Sandoval, Danny Troxell, James Williamson, Ronnie Yandell, "and all other similarly situated prisoners" in Pelican Bay State Prison's Security Housing Unit (SHU), or long-term maximum-security solitary confinement, initiated hunger strikes that spread across the state as well as other parts of the country.[39] The Prisoner Hunger Strike Solidarity online blog, hosted by a coalition of organizations and individuals to "amplify the voices of CA prisoners on hunger strike," creates a channel to facilitate social support for strike participants; encouraging letter correspondence toward this end, site administrators qualify mail communications with the precaution:

> Please be mindful that the CDCR [California Department of Corrections and Rehabilitation] is policing mail & rejecting mail with reference to "hunger strikes." The CDCR is also using mail referring [to] the strike as retaliation, giving prisoners 128 write-ups if they have mail regarding the strike, which can result in denied parole, job loss, possible SHU placement (if the prisoner is not already in the SHU), and more.[40]

The Prisoner Hunger Strike Solidarity blog, in the final analysis, calls attention to a core contradiction of deprivation and excess that resonates at multiple levels. At a general level, the blog itself manifests expanded technological capacities that, alongside the letter, enable communities to establish or maintain social connection across carceral space. The production of this extended cyberspace, however, ultimately cannot supersede the limits of regulation and dispossession; rather, it must reproduce those limits even as it generates new avenues for communication that exceed existing walls. The CDCR's partnership with Facebook, in order to "actively monitor[] Facebook for accounts administered by inmates or on behalf of an inmate,"[41] marks another example of this universalizing scope of the PIC. In this vein, then, at the specific level of letter correspondence, this Solidarity blog posting foregrounds the letter's dialogical form as an added means through which people outside of prison become subject to and/or implicated in law enforcement as punishment. The letter, in this sense, again signals how the activity of torture exceeds the purview of prison administration and embeds itself in the productive habits of society as a whole: that is, dominant renderings of the letter situate imprisoned people's families, friends, and advocates as either participants or liabilities, their communications as collateral, in government's and prison administrators' exercise of violence. Indeed, the letter thus exists as a "knot" where the interconnectedness of carceral space, often perceived and experienced in discrete compartments, both articulates and disarticulates; where individualized punishment simultaneously devastates communal bodies.

Through this lens, the letter hence mediates the social diffusion or reproduction of punishment, taking place through processes of racialized as well as sexualized and gendered differentiation and subjection. Referring again to her time in Norco, California, Ogden recounts one such instance in the context of communal life forged within the prison itself:

> While I was in prison I was writing a Mono man that was in Soledad at the time. His older brother was part of the American Indian Movement, and as time went by, we started to write more and more about AIM and the different things that they did and what they did for the Indian community. One of the male "white" guards on the third watch began reading my mail more closely and making remarks about my "boyfriend" being one of those "AIMster Gangsters" and how we have got to stop living in Teepees and realize that the old days are gone. . . . I was the chairperson of the [American Indian] spiritual group there and we had an office space where we would meet once a week. Not too long after the guard started making remarks to me about AIM, they began to search the office on a regular schedule after we had our weekly meeting, with the excuse that they were looking for anything that might be "gang related." The guards would also go through our lockers or search our beds, look through our bead work or sacred material.[42]

In this case, prison guards' intrusions on letter correspondence anchor a web of violations that, in sum, reproduce conditions of genocide through a structure of racial-sexual violence. Fixating on the letter to effect the isolation and routine humiliation of Ogden herself in explicitly racialized, gendered, and sexualized terms, this atomized punishment unfolds as the disassembly of collective life: attacks on the relationships embedded in the letter as well as those taking place within the prison; sieges on indigenous women's individual and group relations creative of their autonomy, space, knowledge, health, healing, and spiritual practice.

In one final example, the letter materializes the normally concealed connection between disparate resolutions of carceral space and evidences the interlocking of differently gendered forms of violence. Ronnie K. Irwin, a member of the Detroit Black Panther Party at the time, writes to Shapiro-Bertolini from an unspecified location on 8 September 1972:[43]

> I am still receiving repercussions from my involvement in the Party. Recently the F.B.I. searched my son's mother's house (also an ex-Party member) and took nothing but all the letters I have written to her since I was first arrested in April 1971. This illegal seizure was meant to be a revengeful blow against me for not answering their questions when they came up here last spring.

In this instance, pretensions surrounding Irwin's letters again justify practices of intimidation and retaliatory violence that move from Irwin himself to his family, exceeding the boundaries of the prison and infiltrating those of their home. Theorizing from the standpoint of Irwin's son and son's mother, the implications for women and children in this context are at least twofold: they must contend not only with hyper-exposure to the specific forms of gendered and patriarchal violence visited on their own lives but also with their intermediary positioning in the forms of brutality differently visited on Irwin by FBI and prison officials.[44] These ordinary forms of systematic social dismantling thus index the adaptability rather than fixity of disciplinary limits as well as the diffuse and manifold reach of punishment. In this sense, prisons ultimately harness the power of the letter as signifier of connectivity to globalize terror in and through the mundane practices of our daily lives.

If studying these processes, in conclusion, has provided some insight into the reproduction of a white world, then perhaps it has also helped lay bare the challenges of substantiating the life of paper—overwhelmed or buried, as this life is, by tedious as well as spectacular applications of genocidal force. Indeed, in turning to the letter as a "breach," as Primo Levi calls it—a small gap in a tightly closed universe through which "hope could pass"[45]—even its effects in these ontological dimensions cannot strip the letter of certain vestiges of violence. When former political prisoner Ida P. McCray reflects, for example, "Pain is having to say too often in a letter, 'I love you,' and not being able to be there to comfort when [your children] need you,"[46] even the positive signification of the letter as lifeline reproduces an effect of pain.

Yet, articulated at the threshold of love and its undoing, this pain confirms, for better and for worse, that alienation cannot be understood outside of the sociality on which the processes of genocide fixate. In this sense, the letter as signifier of *love,* perhaps the knot of all knots, is both autonomous and inextricable from the worlds from which it came and to which it may travel. It is this dense paradox of the letter (or of Blackness, for that matter) which, unleashing a mystery beyond discipline or punishment, produces the effect of torture without being derivative of it. Instead, the acts of torture archived in this chapter, hailed by the letter rather than hailing it, attest to the life of paper in the forms of visceral response that the existence and potential of the letter provoke. The endeavor remains or returns, at last: to attempt analytically to distinguish rather than mistake the reactive violence that the letter triggers from the insurgent violence, the breaking through of social life, that it mediates.

SIX

Uses of the Profane

I AM, IN FACT, TALKING about an open secret—announced worldwide, for instance, on the front page of the *New York Times* on 8 January 2011: "The Handwritten Letter, an Art All but Lost, Thrives in Prison." In that story, the journalist Jeremy W. Peters observes, "Prisoners send handwritten letters not out of any romantic attachment to the old-fashioned craft of letter writing but out of necessity. Many prisons do not allow inmates access to computers. . . . In California, for example, prisoners are not permitted e-mail contact."[1] In other words, in this digital age of intricate virtual realities and social media networks, handwritten letters remain today as relevant as they ever were precisely because of the deadening conditions of deprivation and punishment elaborated in the previous chapter. Yet, under these circumstances, imprisoned communities' ongoing innovations in epistolarity, widely viewed as "an art all but lost"—as discarded, ineffectual, or obsolete as their artists—confound notions of Western civilization as a natural, predetermined destiny of technological advance that universally defines or absorbs all social movement. In this context, we may thus better understand letter correspondence as part of other legacies, underrecognized or taken for granted if only due to their imbrication in the very foundations of modernity, wherein oppressed communities have constantly generated new conditions of possibility for living by repurposing "old" or ostensibly obsolete technologies and engaging them to meet their own needs and priorities.[2] From this perspective, letters in this era of mass incarceration evince sustained connection to ways of life that have unfolded appositionally with Eurocentric forms of sociality, manifesting different epistemologies of time, space, information, and technology, other articulations of human becoming under duress.

In this light, this chapter focuses on the life of paper as it preserves conditions for communal life through the contemplation, embodiment, and practice of new forms of historical being since the mid-twentieth century. Beginning with consideration of imprisoned letter correspondence as a process of study, I situate epistolary activity as ontological meditation that takes place within extreme states of austerity and aloneness. Thus framing letters within Black radical traditions of preserving the sacred through the profane, I further contextualize correspondence within the broader scope of late twentieth-century freedom struggles. Through this lens, I examine mediations of historical and ontological change through intellectual labor, beginning with insurgent knowledges that came into material coherence alongside global liberation movements identifying as their stakes life and death as such. Outlining a worldview deliberately represented in essentialist and racial terms of Black and white, I pay particular attention to epistemological irruptions emanating from imprisoned populations, the pressures they exert at the thresholds of human being, and the aesthetic significance of letters to mediate social movement. In the wake of these struggles, and in the midst of ongoing culture wars to make meaning out of formal equality and its implications, I argue that the life of paper remains a site of collective preservation that both coheres in and exceeds the letter itself. Returning, then, to the materiality of the letter as a meta- or para-ontological signifier, I interrogate epistolary effects as they surrogate a creative shelter through which to inhabit and practice a mode of social being. In this sense, the life of paper instantiates a vital deliverance, a means of laying claims and being delivered to one another through dynamics of difference, a process of human disclosure as the brutal tenderness of coming into form rather than the latter's rote reproduction: quotidian performances of the existentially fragile, if not practically tedious, art of collective becoming always already toward death as unfathomable mystery.

DOING TIME

Never before have I written so long a letter. I'm afraid it is much too long to take your precious time. I can assure you that it would have been much shorter if I had been writing from a comfortable desk, but what else can one do when he is alone in a narrow jail cell, other than write long letters, think long thoughts and pray long prayers?[3]

One of the most prominent texts in the classification of U.S. prison literature as a genre, Dr. Martin Luther King Jr.'s 1963 "Letter from a Birmingham Jail" draws to its conclusion with the above aside, seemingly marginal to the more formal arguments and rhetorical thrust of King's treatise. Yet, paralleling arguments made in chapter 5, perhaps nothing else in or about his letter more aptly communicates the difference King himself proxies than the metadiscourse of the letter itself: attention to the sign of emerging revelation that indexes the ultimate concerns of King's message and thus proves quintessential rather than peripheral to it. Addressed to eight Alabama clergymen whose own open letter, "A Call for Unity," denounced the nonviolent campaigns for which King was arrested, "Letter from Birmingham City Jail" first circulated in various mainstream news sources as well as political and theological journals. In this context, the performativity of the letter—King's invocation of the epistle's place in the symbolic universe of Christianity and the explicit framing of his letter within this representational grid—ultimately makes apparent what Clyde Woods calls "the presence of contending ontologies" in the historical contradictions of modernity and the planetary scope of Christian thought, interpretation, and practice, made manifest through the local and global revolutionary struggles that animate King's writing.[4]

King's reference to the epistle's place at the heart of Christian tradition—as crux of the Bible's form, content, and injunctions—begins at the letter's outset. Upon addressing the immediate circumstances of his writing, King situates the letter and his presence in Birmingham as the evolution of journeys made by "prophets of the eighth century B.C." He turns his focus next to the apostle Paul, whose own missives, canonized in the Bible, must inspire the faithful "to carry the gospel of freedom beyond my own hometown." Thus couched in this context, allusion to the letter as signifier plays an integral role in King's rhetorical strategies to challenge both secular liberalism and religious conservatism, the twinned arms of white supremacy, in at least two ways. First, the metadiscursive framing of his letter provides the means through which he can disarticulate the colonial implications of Paul's mission and thereby disarm white hermeneutics of biblical discourse that sanctify conquest. This maneuver creates a pivotal space for King's evocation of an originary dilemma in prophetic tradition, wherein faith requires commitment to a disavowed world that seems not to *be* except in the epistle as signifier, a reminder of the divine. Second, this perspective thus establishes boundaries for the reception of the letter's message, in which King enjoins Christians to "recapture the sacrificial spirit of the early church." In this regard, King's epistemological stance imagines sacrifice not as a relation of genocide in support of "ideas and principles of popular opinion" but rather as living legacy of those who endured dispossession and criminalization in their commitment to a view of the gospel as "a thermostat that transformed the mores of society."[5]

If introductory allusions to the letter as divine signifier thus precipitate King's indictment of U.S. Southern power structures and, moreover, invest in his text prophetic authority, then King's closing remarks likewise seal the message. That is, the concluding metadiscourse of the letter again stands to auto-authenticate claims made in the missive itself. On the one hand, the awareness King brings to material conditions distinguishes his letter from the one by Southern clergy to which he is responding. As the conjuring of King's stark paraliterary surroundings heightens the sense of luxury inversely enjoyed by his adversaries, the tone of humility harnesses an irony that articulates the contradiction of King's sacrifice and the wealth of those whom he addresses. In this sense, these final observations made in the letter about the letter instantiate one of King's core claims, that Southern leaders must face God's judgment in the specificities of their own abundance. Perhaps more significantly, the contrasts in material wealth and political power ultimately correlate with the difference suggested between the abomination of "A Call to Unity" and the genealogy of divine inspiration from which King's epistle emerges.

On another level, King's closing aside also makes explicit that letter writing constitutes rather than merely describes the deepest experience of what it means to "do time." The significance of this point must be understood through the historical lens of the long Civil Rights Movement and, more specifically, its emergence following the international ratification and recognition of the United Nations Universal Declaration of Human Rights (1948) and the Geneva Conventions (1949). In this context, the massive numbers of people incarcerated, like King, for their participation in tactics ranging from civil disobedience to armed self-defense blurred the discursive and lived distinction between the status of "political prisoner," as defined in international human rights law, and U.S. "social" prisoners arrested for violations of civil or criminal law.[6] From this perspective, the activity of doing time in prison cannot be disentangled from the socialization of liberation movements themselves, their effects both to unravel the law as such and to generate spaces of unanticipated convergence.[7] In this carceral situation, then, where the very conditions of possibility for the existence of law meets the law's decoherence, the constitutive activity of letter writing can rearticulate a space and time from which a different kind of social order emerges.

Thus returning to King's concluding aside, the implications that may emerge are at least twofold. First, at an intensive scale, the activity of letter writing comes into view as a modality through which conditions of coercion become the backdrop for ascetic practice that tears into an inner opening. Problematics of this transformation are foregrounded in another metadiscourse of the letter presented by Terry Bradford, writing to Ethel Shapiro-Bertolini from a California prison on 17 June 1974:[8]

> Correspondence is one of the basic ways of keeping a society in sight and alleviating some of the pressures present in our every day life. It is a welcome change to have something to look forward to besides two meals a day and a sandwich, exercise every three days, showers once a week and a change of clothes whenever they have them. Just getting up in the morning looking at the shotgun across the tier doesn't make me feel good in the least. . . . All I have to do is get frustrated and give a guard a bloody nose and they can send me to the gas chamber. With nothing to keep my mind off the way I'm being treated, because of my being classified as a so-called black militant, I have one foot there already. This is existentialism.

In this passage, Bradford's meditation on "existentialism" identifies aggravated degrees and conditions of violence different from those insinuated in King's letter and moment of writing; perhaps correlatively, the intensity of Bradford's evocations of the simultaneously psychological, affective, and corporeal effects of letter correspondence also somewhat exceeds King's reflections. Nevertheless, both discourses position correspondence as a knot where circumstances of incarceration pose an ontological impasse, and the letter both realizes the despair of captivity and surrogates means of coming to other social terms. In this sense, whether it is the interconnectedness of King's long letters, long thoughts, and long prayers or Bradford's way of generating social vision and relief, correspondence in both formulations mediates a process of preservation: for King, of restoring within his isolation a sense of the sacred; for Bradford, with one foot in the gas chamber, of keeping another foot somewhere else. Finally, in the contemplative practice occasioned by the letter, exertions to grapple with the truth of suffering, to transform the brutal limits of austerity and dispossession into the thresholds of a deeper world, ultimately mark the place where figures of the criminal, scholar, and clergy—in and through the vital intercession of the epistolary—become indistinguishable from one other. From this perspective, the letter as signifier, consistent with emancipatory prophetic traditions, hence threatens the existing social order by problematizing or overturning dominant ontological assumptions of authority and, by extension, of who will inherit the earth.

Second, then, consideration of King's letter and the metadiscourse that frames it brings into clearer focus the more extensive deployment of the open letter throughout this period of struggle and the epistolary's integral role in the latter as *movement*. As Michael Hames-Garcia and others have argued in this regard, we must understand contemporary political writings from prison within literary traditions of enslaved and colonized peoples—in forms such as the slave narrative and the *testimonio*—that are defined by their organic roles in social movements and that subvert conventions of the Christian conversion narrative "to propose new models for conceptualizing freedom."[9] Thus situated within such historical legacies and formal features, the open letter comes into view as a means through which communities targeted for mass incarceration during this particular period of insurgency could mitigate the contradictions of repression. That is, deliberate interarticulations of public display and intimate engagement instantiated by the open letter distinctively maneuvered through contradictory effects of torture that, for their own part, manifested in forced isolation and social erasure, on the one hand, and in hyper-exposure related to the stripping of all privacy, on the other. In this context, the intervention of the open letter thus created an avenue through which social movements could work *through* the comprehensive regimenting of constraint and, within that, to express themselves in and as an open secret or conspiracy.

Open letters published in the Black Panther Party newspaper, for example, harnessed the performativity of the letter in dynamic ways to play with normative logics of public and private relationships in the context of incarceration and, in some contrast to the overtly religious framework and implications of King's epistle, to refashion the ontological fabric of collectivity in secular terms. On the one hand, pieces such as "A Letter from the Youth" (figure 30), published on 15 March 1970, illustrate the mobilization of the open letter to reimagine political community, ethics, and futurity through the perhaps hyperbolic performance of fictive kinship: emphasizing intimate

A Letter From The Youth

Dear Black Panthers,

   I think it isn't right for you to be in jail. Well, you and I know there are bad people in the world, and the cops and the judge are the same. You didn't think for one minute I believed all this hogwash did you? About bombing Macy's etc. I'm giving 10¢ and I'll contribute more too. They'll keep you in jail for life over my dead body. I'll raise over $10,000 someday, somehow but don't you worry I'll do it.

Elizabeth Watts
8 1/2 yrs. old

P.S.   I'll be a Panther when I grow up. Please write me.

FIGURE 30. "A Letter from the Youth," *The Black Panther,* 15 March 1970; from the Black Panther Party Collection, Southern California Library.

solidarity, intergenerational continuity, and shared visions of justice sustained across the divides of carceral space. In particular, this performative display of the education of feminized youth in defense of political prisoners plays with a tradition of Black female intellectual and moral leadership to achieve the uplift of "the race."[10] Visually, the simulation of personal prison correspondence—represented, for example, by the piece's mimetic epistolary layout and appended photograph—also neutralizes the stigma of criminalization by normalizing the signs of ostracism and adopting a shared aesthetic that blurs everyday distinctions between prison's inside and outside.

   On the other hand, "Open Letter to the People from the Brothers of Soledad North" (figure 31), published on 21 August 1971 and signed by "Political Prisoners and Prisoners of War of Correctional Training Facility North-Facility," differently harnesses the contradictory character of the epistolary to effect social connection and change. Most immediately, the

OPEN LETTER TO THE PEOPLE
FROM THE BROTHERS AT SOLEDAD NORTH

We, the brothers of Soledad-North, have again fallen victims to an insidious plot purposely designed to abort all efforts in securing meaningful dialogue with concerned Black people. The imposed restrictions at hand are only the latest in a series of continuous denials that have virtually placed us in a state rendering us incommunicado. We have run the gamut attempting to contact student groups, civic organizations, entertainment groups, etc., but in each case our initiative has been systematically and arbitrarily repelled.

To bridge this gap, we purpose that you, the people, demand your rights as conscious citizens and taxpayers, to inspect these twentieth century dungeons.

We do not expect any immediate results to flower, once a joint move is made to the California Department of Corrections. We know our advantage lies in a protracted survey, which will produce conclusive evidence. Evidence   enough to render a verdict of guilty upon all its perpetuators in any court of law, or a People's Tribunal. By coordinating our efforts, we on the inside can point out all the heavy stones and you on the outside can respond by turning them over for the purpose of investigation. Be prepared for incredulous findings, for after all the pebbles have been exposed, the faces under the big rocks will be those of California's Aristocracy.

We were prepared to submit to you the complete hierarchy of North-Facility's working staff. Along with this, we intend to depict the covert racism and the overt racist practices entrenched within its hiring and every day functioning policies. To illustrate a point, there are fifteen Academic Teaching positions on North-Facility's payroll. Of the fifteen here, there is not one Black incumbent. There are twelve Vocational Instructors. Only one is Black. It is not our intention to relegate or question capacity, but few, if any, parolees pursue employment in the field of shoe repair. There are fifteen Administrative positions; they are as follows: Deputy Superintendent, Associate Superintendent, In-Service Training Officer, two Program Administrators, two Correctional Counselors II, and eight Correctional Counselors I, and not one is

Black. There are fifteen secretarial and one stenographer's positions. And again not one is Black.

We could go on and on, but the truth is that we need your help to rebuff this rabid, pathological practice that emanates from the California Department of Corrections.

In the wake of all this, there are still other dehumanizing practices that are carried on under the guise of REHABILITATION. The now infamous "O"-Wing is but one case in point.

The protagonistic aristocracy vivaciously assures the public that these demonic dungeons are the manifested quarters of convicts not able to adjust to the population and rehabilitation offered them. So these twentieth century dungeons are supposedly maintained to readjust the convict to the normal synthesis of Society and the Department of Corrections and their supporters. In fact, the atrocities suffered by the convicts are too numerous to extensively voice, but here we'll present some of the sadistic, racist, dehumanizing tactics practiced by both the members of the Official Staff and other convicts of opposing ethnic groups.

First of all, the terms served in these dungeons range from five days to two years. There are many borthers who have not been, and will not be, allowed to enter the mainline population, not conotative to the supposedly physical threat they may pose, but rather due to the mental transition of awareness that would be influxed upon their brothers and the mainline population. This awareness would expose the Aristocracy. So, indubitably, you have Political Prisoners.

The food given the convicts is handled by racist perverts (convicts and staff members) who whimsically excrete urine, feces, and other would-be fatal anomalistic articles into the portions designated for the brothers.

Hygiene is deplorable. Showers and clothing changes are offered periodically. The variations of the periods without change is deemed solely by the persons; I'm sorry, mechanisms of the state known as CORRECTIONS OFFICERS. Don't let the papers fool you, the most liked officers are NOT assigned the hole. Mills was assigned to the hole.

Periodically supposed incidents, such as the one within the year when the three brothers were murdered. Black men are assaulted, and murdered at will, by these racist, sadistic, psychotic guards. Needless to say, of the other murders having been perpetrated and sagaciously promulgated to the people under the guise of suicide, heart attack, etc., little has been said because little is known. The recent military tactics insurged upon the North-Facility population are comparable to the "Strategic Hamlets" in Viet Nam. To note this action: 122 convicts were transferred from N.F. (46 Black, 37 Mexican-American, 38 White). Twenty of the Blacks transferred are currently in the "Adjustment Center" ("O" Wing and "X" Wing) compared to 18 Mexican-Americans and 7 Caucasians.

This was done under the pretense of "Institutional Convenience." Several of these Black men are held on trumped-up charges of conspiracy. They have been illegally interrogated, apprehended, and if you sit by, illegally convicted and systematically killed.

On the date that the Correctional Officer (Shull) died, the imprisoned populace was locked up and released after a period of two days with no Black men being sent to the A.C., but one week later a disturbance occurs in which no Blacks participated and 46 Black men were transferred. These men were, in fact, no threat to the security of this institution. Knowing the treatment received in the A.C., these men must readjust themselves to a new program, new rules, procedures, relationships with other inmates, not to mention the dispondent situation in which it places the men and their families. Think of the problem these men must have stabilizing themselves for release.

For us to give you, the people, a clear analysis of the situations we're subjected to, we must go directly to the roots perpetuating not only the aforementioned diabolical crimes against us, but also to you, the people.

Political Prisoners and Prisoners of War of
CORRECTIONAL TRAINING FACILITY
NORTH-FACILITY

FIGURE 31. "Open Letter to the People from the Brothers at Soledad North," *The Black Panther*, 21 August 1971; from the Black Panther Party Collection, Southern California Library.

piece relies on the public nature of the form to render visible the otherwise unseen forces of repression "that have virtually placed us in a state rendering us incommunicado." Inversely, the piece also relies on the letter's interpersonal qualities to marshal support from the letter's addressed audience, "conscious citizens and taxpayers" specifically and "the people" generally, who are prompted to initiate formal investigation of the racist practices exercised by the California Department of Corrections and to demand accountability. In these ways, such deployments of the open letter blend the formal expression of political grievance with the rhetorical appeal of familiarity. Shaped by these dynamics, this letter ends by emphasizing the dialogical relation, providing the means through which to both specify and unsettle the distinctions between "not only the aforementioned diabolical crimes against us, but also [against] you, the people," and, ultimately, to rearticulate matters of prison practice as matters of both intimate and public concern.

In the ritual repetition of such formal elements as those featured in the letter from the Brothers of Soledad North, in fact, the open letter served as a normative template for political manifestos during this time that made apparent the public nature and stakes of prison uprisings and connected the latter to struggles, aspirations, and people around the world. In this sense, just as King's open letter and its metadiscourse channel through the referential universe of Christianity to subvert or rearrange dominant logics within it, the open letter as political manifesto operates analogously through the referential universe of another foundation of modern civilization: that is, the displacement of Christian values into the onto-epistemological assumptions of liberal democratic tradition and the letter as consummate signifier of rights, rationality, and manhood or personhood. For instance, written amidst prisoner strikes and rebellions happening from California to New York,[11] in the wake of the imprisoned revolutionary George Jackson's assassination at San Quentin State Prison, which I will turn to shortly, the 1971 Attica Manifesto—signed by the "Attica Liberation Faction" and including the names Donald Noble, Peter Butler, Frank Lott, Carl Jones, and Herbert Blyden X—begins:[12]

We, the imprisoned men of Attica Prison, seek an end to the injustice suffered by all prisoners, regardless of race, creed, or color.

The preparation and content of this document has been constructed under the unified efforts of all races and social segments of this prison.

> ... Due to the conditional fact that Attica Prison is one of the most classic institutions of authoritative inhumanity upon men, the following manifesto of demands [is] being submitted:
> "Man's right to knowledge and free use thereof".

By way of repetition, the first two lines of this preamble refer back to the 1970 "Folsom Prisoners Manifesto of Demands and Anti-Oppression Platform," which itself ends with a metadiscourse of the manifesto as an "insist[ence] upon our human rights to the wisdom of awareness."[13] In each of these iterations, stylistic allusions both to the Declaration of Independence and to the U.S. Constitution formalize the manifesto's own performance of revolutionary democracy and mediate its effects. The opening lines, for example, mimetically identify the process of writing as constitutive of the very unfolding of democratic practice and its socialization to resignify historically the universal entitlements of man as well as the capacity for self-government. Moreover, emphasis on the concept of knowledge as the cornerstone of claims to humanity and to rights, as well as on the pursuit of knowledge as actualized by the letter or manifesto itself, works through intertwined Eurocentric ideals of manhood, rationality, and governmentality in order to overturn them. That is, rather than justifying or concealing racist genocide, this composition of knowing subjects operates rhetorically to disorder lines of exclusion, forging pathways to assert a new form of humanity precisely within the carceral limits of racialized dehumanization, gendered violence, and punishment that—bifurcating mind and body—manifests, on the one hand, as hyper-fixation on bodily regulation and, on the other, as denial or repression of consciousness. In these ways, the correspondence itself, its insistence on study, and its attention to problems of epistemology at the metalevel deliberately engage the representational structure of liberal democracy as a means of changing the course of historical being by creating new forms of knowledge or, perhaps in some cases, new ways of knowing what we already know. Thus disorienting the political limits of Western civilization and its freedoms, ultimately, the irony of the moniker "Attica" stands out in its suggestion of the ancient Athenian polis and the restoration of its highest ideals of common good by those who could only be understood by analogy as its enslaved rather than citizen class.[14]

Given prohibitions on personal contact at an intimate scale and civic access at a popular one, the deliberate turn to the open letter could hence create shared intellectual space for the socialization of insurgent worldviews and the refunctioning of knowledge production as a means of social reproduction. This renewal of creative possibility is particularly noteworthy in the context of ruptures in modern racial epistemology realized by social movements during this period—transformative rearticulations of racial logic as a means of subjectivizing and suturing global struggles to abolish capitalist white supremacy and the latter's reproductive imperatives of war, killing, exploitation, and impoverishment. Situated in this political violence and upheaval, the life of paper as site of individual and collective self-making facilitates precisely the cultural labor to produce a distinctive racial or para-racial form: a human identity emerging from the vexed space between historical struggles and their representation. In this sense, at the height of this insurrectionary period, the resonance of the letter as signifier and of aesthetic experiments with its self-referentiality provided distinctive means to effect openings in the contemplation, enunciation, and embodiment of different ways of being alive.

For example, these effects manifest explicitly in Fr. Daniel J. Berrigan's elaboration of the problem of whiteness in his "Letter to the Weathermen,"[15] initiated as a voice recording from "underground" in 1970 and published in the *Village Voice* in 1971 following his capture for burning draft cards in Catonsville, Maryland. In this open letter, Berrigan addresses fellow anti-imperialist activists in the Weather Underground Organization (WUO), formed in 1969 by Euro-American youth who experimented with targeted acts of violence in support of the Black Panther Party and other groups under intense police and FBI fire during this time. In fact, Berrigan qualifies this exchange by explaining his own tactics of resistance in a separate interview: "I never tried to hurt a person. I tried to do something symbolic with pieces of paper."[16] Thus attuned to the precarious interchanges between people and paper, paper's knotted mediations of violence as well as becoming, Berrigan begins "Letter to the Weathermen" precisely by focusing awareness on the sociality constituted by and through media itself:

Dear Brothers and Sisters,

Let me express a deep sense of gratitude that the chance has come to speak to you across the underground. It's a great moment; I rejoice in the fact that we can start a dialogue that I hope will continue through the smoke signals, all with a view to enlarging our circle. Indeed the times demand not that we narrow our method of communication but that we enlarge it, if anything new or better is to emerge. (I'm talking out of a set of rough notes; my idea is that I would discuss these ideas with you and possibly publish them later, by common agreement.). . . .

The threat is a very simple one; we are making connections, religious and moral connections, connections with prisoners and Cubans and Vietnamese. . . . We are guilty of making connections, we urge others to explore new ways of getting connected, of getting married, of educating children, of sharing goods and skills, of being religious, of being human, of resisting. . . . And I am guilty of making connections with you.

Harnessing the mixture and indeterminacy inherent in the letter form itself, the ambiguities of its orality and dialogical structure,[17] Berrigan's metadiscourse of the correspondence enacts precisely the "enlarging of our circle" demanded by the times. Breaking normative boundaries of and between audience, authorship, composition, and reception to produce through the aesthetic an open-ended relationship, this connectivity channels through text deliberately referring back to itself as provisional and in unceasing process, part of a signifying chain in active motion and whose meanings must come to life historically. Under these terms, compelling readers to confront the inseparability of the method of communication, the act of communication, and the anticipatory "new or better" way of living for which the missive serves as sign, the letter hence encircles the public realm from a social geography yet unseen in order to call attention to its own existence as life potential seeking greater articulation. In this sense, the letter self-consciously marks as well as performs the very exploration of "new ways of getting connected[,] . . . of being human"; indeed, enunciating or announcing itself as such, this metadiscourse of the communication itself becomes as important as the meditation on racialized humanity detailed in the body of the letter, bringing the letter's contents to life vis-à-vis the contouring of contingencies inherent in its form of appearance. This frame hence situates the materiality of the connection and the significance of its moment of recognition and reception as an event, one in which the letter itself moves from its objectivity to historical subjectivization.

If this metadiscourse thus interrupts rituals of dominant literary training and thereby the reproduction of citizen-subjects such training facilitates, "Letter to the Weathermen" also stages an intimate dialogue that likewise disarticulates the fantasy of omnipotence inherent in whiteness as onto-epistemology and, furthermore, problematizes the ideological displacement of its violence onto Others. For example, Berrigan addresses WUO:

> Your [rebellion] is a choice. . . . I must say, I have very little fear, from firsthand experience, of the violence of the Vietcong or Panthers (I hesitate to use the word violence), for their acts come from the proximate threat of extinction, from being invariably put on the line of self-defense. But the same cannot be said of us and our history. We stand outside the culture of these others, no matter what admiration or fraternity we feel with them; we are unlike them, we have other demons to battle.

In this formulation, through the open letter and its socialization—its capacity to place outside readers in a scandalizing position as simultaneously participants and voyeurs in the exchange—Berrigan and WUO present the problem of how to inhabit or transform whiteness from the standpoint of those for whom racist violence is their subjective inheritance and material power. Narrativizing how this particular dilemma of racialized being manifests in and as political action, Berrigan initiates this dialogical space not publicly to condemn WUO (especially given their ultimate convergence on the tactical choice of violence against property) but rather precisely to draw out the inextricability of the exercise of violence from whiteness as a racial form and its implications for shared projects of human connection. The letter thus serves as an aperture to examine whiteness as both historically constituted and ontologically consequential, further enjoining those with a privileged relation to whiteness to struggle with and through relations of difference, power, and their articulations in the lived specificities as well as generalizable ideals of decisive movement. In this sense, "we" are reminded, on the one hand, that the forms of appearance of violence itself cannot be considered outside of their distinct contexts of racism and, on the other, that denaturalizing whiteness as arbiter of claims to universal entitlement remains a project of life-and-death proportions whose contradictions cannot be ignored without compromising futurity itself. In the final instance, then, in the revolutionary affirmation occasioned by the letter, in "the very substance of our task of trying to keep connections, or to create new ones," the materialization of the letter itself chisels through whiteness, understood as the "normal conditions" of violence, and provides means to reproduce a different mode of existence through the letter's opening.

Therefore concluding with an insistence that "we are not killers, as America would stigmatize us, and indeed *as America perversely longs for us to be* [original emphasis]. We are something far different. . . . We struggle to embody [a new vision of things] day after day, to make it a reality among those we live with, so that people are literally disarmed by knowing us," Berrigan uses the letter to assert a contending (para)racial form that takes as its cues for enunciation precedents formulated through Blackness and also discernible in coeval articulations of the struggle to reembody. James Baldwin's "Open Letter to My Sister, Angela Davis," for instance, dated 19 November 1970 and originally published in the *New York Review of Books* on 7 January 1971, again mobilizes the contradictions of the open letter form, the intimate mode of address staged in a public venue, to situate the FBI's political persecution of Davis within an interpretive apparatus that brings into stark relief the long arc and real-time mass irruption of an insurgent Black sociality, its stakes and the world and worldviews constituted through it.[18] Baldwin's "Open Letter" ends thus:

The enormous revolution in Black consciousness which has occurred in your generation, my dear sister, means the beginning or the end of America. Some of us, white and Black, know how great a price has already been paid to bring into existence a new consciousness, a new people, an unprecedented nation. If we know, and do nothing, we are worse than the murderers hired in our name.

If we know, then we must fight for your life as though it were our own—which it is—and render impassible with our bodies the corridor to the gas chamber. For, if they take you in the morning, they will be coming for us that night.

Contextualized by a critique of racial capitalism, in which "we know that the fruits of this system have been ignorance, despair, and death," the conclusion of this missive crystallizes the historical and ontological stakes of racial epistemology and connects these stakes with embodied action in real time. With a view of racial capitalism—and thereby of whiteness—as the genocidal fantasy of mastery over life through human sacrifice, "Black consciousness" in this framework mediates the ongoing existence of a communalism wherein both those with a privileged relation to Blackness and those who can attest to its historical becoming must assume responsibility for the greater ontological preservation. In this sense, again instantiating the revolutionary assertion of racial identities as they mark and are marked by systematic killing, the letter realizes the knot where relations between mind, body, and collective being, cleaved in and by struggles through whiteness and white supremacy, remain in fatal danger and yet cannot be dismantled or fully disclaimed. Baldwin hence delivers the letter into history in order to affect the course of a moment in which what "we know" through the conduit of Black consciousness comes up against the precarity of living possibilities, their beginning or their end, that have not yet been determined.

Indeed, in the context of (para)racial forms generated through Black Power as episteme and the letter as medium, and pivotal to both the Attica uprising and the political trial of Angela Davis, perhaps no one's epistles in abolitionist imagination draw more attention to the letter as sign of a deliverance, or to the question of what it might mean to be sent and delivered to one another through the letter, than those of "Soledad Brother" George Jackson. In concert with other global liberation movements of his era, Jackson's prolific intellectual and organizing efforts to abolish racism from within the prison placed him under heinous conditions of solitary confinement and presaged his murder at San Quentin in August 1971.[19] In the wake of his assassination, Jackson's legacy continues to endure through his written works—namely, the widely circulated *Soledad Brother: The Prison Letters of George Jackson,* originally released in 1970, and the less popular political treatise, *Blood in My Eye,* published posthumously in 1972. Read alongside each other, at least two understated aspects of creative process come to the fore. First, discernible interchanges between epistolary contents in *Soledad Brother* and the theories formalized in *Blood in My Eye* illustrate the inextricability of the book form from ephemeral acts of study, debate, and articulation afforded in letter correspondence and its more improvised unfolding of thought: the process of the latter ultimately as revelatory as what emerges in the final instance as product.

Second, then, somewhat deviating from conventional hermeneutics surrounding (neo-) slave or captivity narratives that revolve around masculine heroism, Black male flights from feminized bondage to freedom, and the achievement of individual autonomy,[20] the dialogical condition of letter correspondence highlights the intrinsically communal process of human becoming and, in the case of *Soledad Brother,* restores greater focus on the interlocution of others; in particular, Jackson's parents, Georgia and Lester Jackson, emerge in their formative roles in Jackson's political thought, vision, and selfhood despite, or because of, their different positions. In this regard, the terrible beauty of these relationships, folded into the pages of their letters, is remarkable: contextualized by the state's comprehensive mediation of familial bonds and the systematic dehumanization facing George Jackson that induced in him a need to "rid myself of all sentiment and remove all possibility of love," as he wrote to his mother in June 1964. Under such constraints, the ongoing genocidal rupture of African American natal community, the letters in *Soledad Brother* thus attest to the heart of intimate struggles to constitute "a new consciousness, a new people" through the act of correspondence and its dialogical staking of a *claim*—claims of love and of belonging to one another, maintaining a social fabric that the dominant carceral geography exists to destroy.

From this perspective, as Nicole Fleetwood has argued of carceral family photographs, the personal letters only later made public in *Soledad Brother,* distinguishable from the open letter form, mark the intimate performance of love under duress and the socialization of emotional labor not necessarily captured by what appears as political. The claims made in and through this kind of process, moreover, reshape the limits of subjectivity and social being by stretching the boundaries of labors of love beyond the prescribed norms and physical enforcement of domesticity and its racial, gendered, and sexual ideological imperatives.[21] As such, the letter's distinct reproductive qualities—for instance, what Fleetwood points out as the opportunity words afford, unlike the photograph, "to process and to react" to the violent contradiction of connection and alienation laid bare by the sign—necessarily also unsettle carceral dynamics of space and time in the creation of a different world order. In *Soledad Brother,* for example, in an attempt to reconfigure relations of past and present, of presence and absence, of knowing and unknowing through the letter, George Jackson writes to Joan of the Soledad Defense Committee on "Real Date, 2 days A.D.," or 9 August 1970, two days after the murder of his younger brother, Jonathan Jackson:[22]

> Go over all the letters I've ever sent you, any reference to Georgia
> being less than a perfect revolutionary's mama must be removed. Do
> it now! I want no possibility of anyone misunderstanding her as I did.

In this literal amending of history as well as of organizing logics of space-time and subjects, George Jackson near the end of his life strives through the life of paper to return, as Hortense Spillers theorizes, to "the heritage of the mother that the African-American male must regain as an aspect of his own personhood."[23] Understood less as a nostalgic recuperation of wounded kinship than as George Jackson's decisive avowal of his own "being maternal,"[24] this request may ultimately signal the transformation less of Georgia Jackson than of George Jackson himself in his identification with her.

The simultaneous incompleteness of this maternal restoration, however—the impossibility, for example, of revising the archive without reinscribing the erasure of its vital contradictions—also presents the problem of *desire* as social movement that cannot be contained even by the boundaries of its own frame of reference. That is, even as George Jackson longs to correct the historical record, to bring it into greater conformity with revolutionary ideals of perfection as an act of mourning his brother's murder, it may be precisely their letters' lack of teleological sense, despite Jackson's own attempt to recover it, that itself animates the Black revolution: realizations of love beyond condition and intramural to the difference rather than reconciliation of conflicting generational worldviews at the letter's crossroad. This love thus calls attention to the limits of teleologies presented by aspirations of either respectability or revolution, as they are articulated in the Jackson family letters, and to the historical materialization of kinship in excess even of what is prescribed by the constraints of our own imaginations. Instead, wrought through the communal labor of coming to terms or of striving to come to terms with one another, it may be in the release of rather than the attachment to social perfectibility or knowing that, in the final instance, allows for the impossible—the reclamation of life after death, as well as the reclamation of life *before* it. Hence, in this view of the life of paper and its shift from formulaic narrative to living testament, letters enact the mundane and daily effort to figure out how to *exist,* neither according to any narrative telos nor even to an intellectual call to create new kinds of narrative forms, but precisely in the very act of grappling with the problems of being and social reproduction as such, the search for a way forward at the impasse of *not knowing*. In the final analysis, then, George Jackson's wishes were indeed fulfilled through his mother, not in changes to the epistolary record, but rather by changes that the epistolary itself fashioned, George and Georgia Jackson's voices interwoven with each other in such statements made by Georgia Jackson in the wake of his assassination:

> You see, that's the whole story of America. They take their violence and turn it back around on somebody else. . . . So if I were running the country, in America, I wouldn't open my mouth about violence—as many people as they've murdered in Vietnam in the past ten years and they're gonna talk about violence? As many Black people as get killed every day in this country and nobody knows or cares—and you tell me about violence? How they wiped out a whole nation of Indians and then you say something to me about violence—I don't wanna hear it!²⁵

In his own explanation of their unlikely turn to "so-called radicals for support," Lester Jackson's November 1971 *Ebony* magazine article, "A Dialogue with My Soledad Son," further relies on a theorization of correspondence for a language through which he can grieve both of his murdered sons. On the one hand, reinforced with visual cues such as the one presented in figure 32, the letter operates in the article to signify a knot where intimate and public mourning come together and form new ways to engage revolutionary Black politics in honor of George Jackson. Contextualized with a caption that begins, "Condolences continue to pour in through the mail. Many of the letters come from distant parts of the nation where sales of George's *Soledad Brother* skyrocketed in the weeks that followed the tragedy," the editorial framing of the image itself brings our awareness to the visual impact of the epistolary outpour as it represents the magnitude of public condolence, recognition, and regard for George Jackson's life.

Yet, alongside this interpretation—in which social meaning resides in acts of sending and the letter as commodity, in such volume, denotes a show of community—the multiplicity of subjects in this image troubles the seeming decidability of the letter's signification as it facilitates a politics of mourning. Namely, building on Fleetwood's contemplation of carceral ephemera as "haptic objects of love and belonging," the portrait of Lester Jackson *holding* the letters gestures to the significance of touch as it actualizes an affective experience and, in Fleetwood's argument, articulates the emotional labor needed to maintain intimate connections between imprisoned people and their loved ones.²⁶ The apposition, then, between the public epistolary display and the intimacy of

FIGURE 32. (Robert) Lester Jackson, from "A Dialogue with My Soledad Son," *Ebony*, November 1971, 80.

Lester Jackson's grieving accentuates a tension between political and infra- or parapolitical activity—their juxtaposition and continuum—breathing life into the letter as commodity as well as its reproduction in the image and, in turn, affecting their signification in dynamic rather than self-evident ways.

These tensions, for instance, provide grounds to appreciate the epistolary act of *receiving* without which acts of sending alone cannot constitute a commons. Moreover, lingering in this realm of negation, while the preexisting hermeneutic for the image privileges public recognition and esteem for George Jackson as the primary mode through which to celebrate him, deliberation of the contingencies of representability underscores the generative condition of the unknown or the unknowable—questions emanating from the ultimate impenetrability of relations of presence and absence surrounding Lester Jackson's image, George Jackson's spector within the image, and the letter as it brings both into focus. In this sense, it is the incognizable contradiction of the seeming transparency of the haptic experience and the opacity of its socially reproductive effects that qualifies the letter's signification and its mediation of layered or striated acts of loving, as both are visually augmented in figure 32. Such contradictions thus forge openings to intuit the letter's arbitration of a lifeworld that is neither directly correspondent with the discrete identities of senders or receivers nor limited to concrete acts and practices of sending and receiving. Instead, the life of paper manifests a sociality or its possibility precisely in its ceaseless oscillation between decidability and undecidability—love as connection both created by and beyond our "knowing," restoring the significance of the realm of absence as a condition of possibility for making sense of presence and, in that dialectic, providing a means to fathom or engage a process of mourning at the interstices of the seen and unseen, asserted and surrendered.

On the other hand, then, embedded in this ontological uncertainty, "A Dialogue with My Soledad Son" also routes through the letter as signifier in order to articulate a process of social reproduction. That is, Lester Jackson explicitly works through references to the epistolary in order to express Black male vulnerability and elaborate the labor of parental caregiving: a life of paper disclosed both in the context of his reflections on familial bonding before George Jackson's murder and in the article's instantiation of the emotional struggle to bury one's children in the aftermath. Of his own presence in *Soledad Brother,* for instance, Lester Jackson writes, "Realizing that George had developed intellectually . . . I'd plant a seed at the conclusion of each visit and see if it would grow in his newly expanded mind. Slowly I'd notice these seeds taking root, in letters written on both sides of the paper which he was permitted to send from the prison each week."[27] Similar to Fleetwood's analysis of the relation between prison photographs and reproductive labor, the letter in Lester Jackson's formulation likewise indexes the intimate and deliberate activity of maintaining the "roots" of kinship, mundane activity that simultaneously carries the historical weight of "being caught up in a narrative that is bigger than the self."[28] In this sense, Lester Jackson's titular positioning of *Soledad Brother* as a dialogue, alongside his paternal assertion of "planting seeds," grounds through a theorization of the letter his reclamation of the individual life, as well as an inhabitation of the collective life, stolen from him.

In this latter regard, it is also the letter as signifier that catalyzes the article's transition to narrativizing and grappling with the loss of George Jackson, as Lester Jackson writes, "While my son and I had our ideological differences, we had a spiritual coming together that last day August 9. . . . For days we waited for a word from our son. Our mail during the time was the usual array of bills, circulars and second-class junk. But no letters from George. Which was very unusual."[29] In this valuation of the life of paper, Lester Jackson distinguishes between the letter as capitalist commodity and the letter as sign of his son, a distinction that communicates or contains within it the very stakes of life and death. Under these terms, the letter's essential mediation of the production both of ideological differences and of spiritual comings-together highlights its role in building the connections definitive of human survival and transformation as such. Greater appreciation of the life of paper as a process of social reproduction can thus reorient our perspectives on political activity to centralize Safiya Bukhari's characterization of "the first revolution, that internal revolution," in which "picking up the gun was/is the easy part. The difficult part is the day-to-day[,] . . . [t]he hard, painstaking work of changing ourselves into new beings, of loving ourselves and our people, and working with them daily to create a new reality."[30] From this standpoint, the letter is but a sign of the commitment to, and the practice of, this preservation of communal life in the face of terror—which, as Lester Jackson also concludes in his tribute to his Soledad son, remains an abiding legacy and the condition of possibility for the wealth that remains in and as *people.*

In retrospect, then, such interventions of the letter may indicate that, while lasting gains remain to be seen politically or economically, radical movements of this period realized the unthinkable by way of cultural work generative of new productive and reproductive social relations, rupturing dominant ways of life as we know it through a comprehensive reconfiguration of human being. Through this lens—while now confronted with the political defeat or humiliation of past ideological experiments, social organizations, and material or policy gains; the seeming ephemerality of social movements; thwarted radical or revolutionary desires; the terror and bloodshed of counterinsurgency—mindfulness of the life of paper can nevertheless enrich our perspectives on communal sustainability even when circumstances seem to suggest that conditions for the latter have been effectively neutralized. In fact, in ensuing culture wars to narrativize mid- and late twentieth-century freedom struggles, to make meaning of them and embed these meanings in civic life and collective memory, appropriations of "ethnic" life writing and storytelling have shaped dominant movements to control the implications of formal equality and to reconstruct the ideological boundaries mediating racism. As contemporary debates on this problem have already suggested—for instance, in well-developed critiques of hegemonic multiculturalism[31]—formal resemblance to aesthetics shared by the life of paper betrays ontological difference. That is, uses of self- and community narrative by counterinsurgent ethnoracial elites have produced ideologies of both feminism and civil rights that valorize individual merit, exceptionalism, and equal rights or access to (rather than abolition of) the privileges of racial capitalism and its sin qua non of white supremacy.[32] Such appropriations thus hijack insurgent racial epistemologies from the liberation era to recast social crisis in the language of reified character and behavioral distinction, representable in binary terms of human achievement and degeneracy. These current wars of position thereby refashion dominant logics of "race" itself, culminating past hegemonic paradigms of religious, biological, and cultural difference in the present-day salience of color- and gender-blind concepts of proper citizenship and criminality that have justified the expansion of prisons and other killing zones in retrofitted global apartheid regimes.[33]

Yet, in ongoing struggles over the means of social reproduction and, as Richa Nagar and the Sangtin Writers assert, the uses of literacy "to constitute ourselves as political actors in institutions and processes both near and far,"[34] the letter as signifier continues to mediate a preservation of living possibility, particularly in the evolution of competing epistemologies of race as a category of existence and in ideological productions of what insurrectionists in the 1993 Lucasville (Southern Ohio Correctional Facility) uprising themselves—including Namir Abdul Mateen, Jason Robb, Siddique Abdullah Hasan, George Skatzes, and Keith Lamar—have identified as a "convict race."[35] In his latest collection of essays, *Writing on the Wall*,[36] for example, the journalist and political prisoner Mumia Abu-Jamal maintains the vital heritage of the Black radical tradition as it is reproduced in resistance to, or in excess rather than the institutionalization of, law and order. Engaging this work, Carolina Saldaña offers a hermeneutic to interpret Mumia's perspectives that again routes through the epistolary—enduring allusions to the letter as material horizon where history is touched by the unfathomable, sign of promise to those at once condemned and delivered in today's imperial twilight:

> The title of the book brings to mind the traditional gospel song, "Handwriting on the Wall," based on the bible story told in the Book of Daniel about letters written by a mysterious hand on a wall during a great feast given by the King of Babylon. "Somebody read it. Tell me what it says," goes the song. "Go get Daniel, somebody said." When the prophet and former prisoner Daniel was brought in to interpret the handwriting, he told King Belshazzar that his days were numbered and that his kingdom had come to an end. The prophecy was fulfilled that very night.[37]

"THERE IS NO SUCH PERSON"

That the prophecy has been fulfilled only in allegory may not so much demonstrate the letter's consequent meaninglessness as return us to the existential problem ingrained in the letter's unceasing indeterminacies: its constant repetition of prophecy itself in "the absolute uniqueness" and interminable dialectic of "the experience of the promise (the future) and the injunction of memory (the past)" that the letter occasions.[38] Jacques Derrida's meditations in *Archive Fever,* then, questions of how we are to think of the archive as a "there"—"this *taking place* or of this *having a place* of the *arkhē?*"[39]—resonate distinctively in the context of considering the life of paper as a contradictory kind of creative shelter through which to inhabit fractures in the present, in the carceral folds where dominant space-time simultaneously yokes and comes undone. Speaking precisely to this living dilemma in his piece, "Speaking the Impossible: Navigating through Silence to Voice,"[40] Yusef Toussaint Omowale constructs a metadiscourse through which to make sense of his own epistolary archive, interrogating the letter's role in generating a sense of social and historical presence in the brutal denouement of twentieth-century freedom struggles, the preemergence or return, the revival, of another coming promise, and the at times gut-wrenching inextricability of one from the other as they manifest in and as the problem of his own becoming.

Omowale's work begins by contextualizing his relationship to literacy and learning in his parents' involvement in the liberation movements of the late 1960s and the terror of subsequent counterinsurgency campaigns, the former bestowing on him a rich cultural and intellectual inheritance and the latter driving his father into exile in 1972 and eventually to imprisonment at Leavenworth State Penitentiary in 1983.[41] As intimate experiences of political violence and alienation thus structured his coming-of-age through the final decades of the twentieth century, Omowale characterizes the letter as a place "where I encountered my father," a realm of activity in which "we laughed, played ball, talked politics, and sometimes just sat together as I read behind the closed door of my room." In sum, he writes, "Letters allowed us to love."[42] On the one hand, then, in his theorization of the letter as "pathways to connections," letter correspondence with his father as well as with other fictive kin facilitates the production or preservation of relationships that, in turn, condition or animate broader terrains of Omowale's political engagement and intellectual development. Furthermore, in this formulation, the sociality of the letter also fosters rather than supplants the cultivation of a unique sense of self, as "letters created for me a sacred space that reaffirmed my pain, and enabled me to maintain a connection to my humanity. . . . [W]riting was the way I could fully experience my father and acknowledge the silences I carried within."[43] From this perspective, the letter as site of ontological articulation grounds the creation of social as much as of inner life, the dialectical production of communal and interior pathways, building circuitries through which to navigate as well as to metabolize the daily workings of oppression as they play out through the micro-scales of reproductive struggle.

On the other hand, however, Omowale's elaboration of the life of paper, to the overwhelming extent that the latter transpires in realms of absence, illustrates precisely Barbara Johnson's observation of "the limits of spatial logic as it relates to [the letter's] intelligibility."[44] That is, Omowale problematizes the structuring force of silence that, while inextricable from either the vitality of the letter specifically or his family's survival strategies more generally, nevertheless poses its own incoherencies that destabilize the very notion of shelter. In this regard, while Omowale positions the letter as signifier within a framework of affirmation—as sign that restores a sense of presence by acknowledging the silences within, even if the letter's contents do not or cannot speak them—such acknowledgment in its negative contradictions also risks a kind of auto-destruction, wherein to recognize silence or inhabit its break, in a context of "surveillance and incarceration [in which] there is much that cannot even be whispered," is further "to tempt drowning in a flood of collective histories of exploitation and oppression."[45] This existential dilemma, the undoing of order precisely in the striving to meet its need, likewise manifests in and as the limits of the metadiscourse of the letter itself to provide a hermeneutic. Namely, Omowale and, to a lesser extent, Lester Jackson as well in "A Dialogue With My Soledad Son" insert entire reproductions of correspondence in their texts, but they do not or cannot interpret the letters' contents or discursively articulate the material with the rest of their pieces as a whole. These discernible caesuras, impressions of a fundamental refusal or inability to incorporate or account for meaning despite the otherwise self-evident effort to do so, thus bring us to the outermost or deepest reaches of accessibility while also indicating the existence of a beyond that, in the letters' formal interruptions of structure, presents itself unambiguously and yet, in the letters' ultimate indecipherability, cannot be breached by any positive logic in the final analysis.

This life of paper therefore hinges on a stripping down or desedimentation of transparency, its futurity nestled in what is known but cannot be thought and its past full of memories of places and times that never were—such as where Omowale and his father "just sat together" and when they "played ball"—except that it can simultaneously be true that all of it *was*. There is something about this reproductive process, then, the liminality and at times volatility of this becoming in the self-consciousness of dynamics of presence and absence, positivity and negativity, through which a different mode of subjectivization emerges: brutal in the tenderness of each and every attempt or performance of the letter to open a way of being. In one of his letters, dated September 1990, for instance, Omowale writes to his father, "I will write Ida soon. I hesitate because I feel that my reply must be something special—something worthy of her letter/card."[46] This hesitation, another example of the generative force of negativity in the effects of the letter's reception as well as assertion, seems to harbor in it a wrestling with the essence of deliverance in all of its risk, the letter's affirmation and enunciation of subjectivity and of connection without an end and with effects that cannot be known or controlled—a fragility that is hence tethered to possibility as much as to anxiety. In this sense, as Johnson argues, the letter in its undecidability, the terrifying uncertainties of the interdependence of self and other, the production of otherness within the self, and the absolute difference inherent in Otherness as such, is "in a way the materialization of my death,"[47] a letting go of our own coherence in order to be sent.

Through this lens, Omowale's life of paper, in all of its self-consciousness as a response that, indeed, "must be something special," is also nothing other than the social reproduction of *double* consciousness in the very process of its emergence or breaking through, the multiplying of difference as the irruption of what Nahum Chandler might call a "paraontological" elegance.[48] The historical experience of this doubleness, situated in Omowale's broader narrative of how the life of paper has shaped and been shaped by his relationship to poetry and to becoming in and through language, manifests most immediately in both the distinction and the correlation Omowale makes between this universe of meaning, on the one hand, and its bearing on his inhabitation of white space-time and the latter's mediation through dominant literary culture, on the other. Naming this problem, he writes:

> Being held accountable, in my early years, to curriculum that did not create space for the realities of my existence caused me to bleed at my desk, hindering me from even considering academic participation. . . . Schooling pushed me further and further inside myself; and as it did, silence became less of an oasis and more of an abyss; less of a choice of resistance and more of a dysfunctional manifestation of oppression; limiting my future choices and opportunities.[49]

In this articulation of crisis, Omowale draws attention to a redoubling of the threat posed by the avowal of silence that, as I have attempted to crystallize, absolutely conditions the life of paper at the same time that it troubles the tendency toward any fixed order or its necessity. In the context of his embodied negation of and within racial capitalist institutions, then, Omowale identifies how his decisive claims to difference, alienated from the thresholds of creative shelter, can thereby induce a thrust into another kind of prison bound by violence and loss. Thus setting up a view of schooling as "a contradictory site of violence and liberatory transformation," a disciplinary regime from which he could nevertheless purloin tools for his own creativity, Omowale's piece approaches its end by testifying to the relentless vulnerability of moving through history at this brink.

In this light, the pressures that the life of paper exerts on dominant carceral geographies and institutions, as manifested in and through the full scope of Omowale's narrative, attest to the life of paper as enunciative of struggles to survive the burdens magnetized by Black life in order to realize the profound gifts—a struggle that marks not only a different kind of humanity, but, in all its multiplicities, a dense problematization of the very essence of what it means, what it entails, *to be.* The letter, therefore, in the signification of this problem posed by or as Blackness, does not promise any reconciliation or recovery from the ontological condition of natal alienation in the final analysis; instead, what life created in the striving or in the absence of fulfilled desire is different and other than what we have the capacity in the making to "know." The life of paper, in this sense, ultimately exemplifies the sanctity of a vital mystery and an improvisational performance of a way of being that opens out to, and is opened out by, this fathomlessness, as Omowale concludes by pronouncing his undertaking to "begin to speak the impossible to myself and others within a context of love," facing the terrible beauty of the possibilities of "freedom."

Indeed, such an undertaking returns us now, yet again and at last, to this first and final point on the effects of the letter: as much as the life of paper involves the production of letters, it is also the letter that produces *us* and, in doing so, nurtures the materialization of all our politics, literatures, histories, and places in the world as such. The implications of this contradiction are as awesome as they can be cruel in their mediation of battles we face over racial form today. For example, in the dilemma of parole letters, generic epistolary representations of the transformation from criminal to citizen—tropes that emphasize an inmate's remorse, preparation, and eagerness to be productive to U.S. society—thereby reproduce the onto-epistemological tenets of white supremacy and the grip of its total realities.[50] On the one hand, as in other cases discussed in parts 1 and 2, apparent conscriptions into dominant narratives of human rehabilitation or redemption demand a hermeneutics that can discern the difference and relations between "official" and "hidden" transcripts in order to ground such narratives in the specificities of their production.[51] Nevertheless, on the other hand, much work remains for us to do in contemplating how progressive ideologies and tactics of decarceration that work through discourses of proper citizenship necessarily consent to dominant ascriptions of criminality. As I have argued, uncritical acceptance of these terms in our radically changing ideological terrain functions precisely to reproduce the infrastructures of racialized apartheid and the historical conditions of possibility for genocide. From this perspective, if it is true that a rearticulation of hegemonic racial form is occurring through intensified discursive productions of citizenship and criminality, then the historical task remains: to keep exposing the social violence embedded in dominant constructions of the "citizen" and to prevent, rather than appropriate, its displacement in the "criminal." This continues to be a significant challenge for abolitionists today, as in the past, to the extent that dominant ideologies of guilt and innocence, deserving and undeserving, and abstracted constructions of "violent" and "nonviolent" offenders continue to serve unquestioningly as the basis of claims for greater justice.

In contrast, in her "Letter for the Parole of Jalil Muntaqim,"[52] Safiya Bukhari, former member of the New York chapter of the Black Panther Party, former political prisoner, and community organizer before her death in 2003, attends to the vitality of the Black radical tradition and reasserts its refusal or negation of dominant reproductions of human being, as she writes to the New York State parole board on 5 May 2002:[53]

I write this letter in support of Anthony Jalil Bottom's application for release on parole. I've procrastinated this long in hopes that God would guide my hand and give me exactly the right thing to say that would make a difference. Thus far, I have received no such guidance and time is running short, therefore I can only write what I know about Jalil and what I know to be his intentions should he be released on parole. . . . I don't know the one dimensional Anthony Bottom #77-A-4823. There is no such person. Jalil is a complex person. He's a human being, moved by his feelings, beliefs, and what he perceives to be the right thing to do.

In her indeterminate search for "the right thing to say," Bukhari's letter, situated in a lifetime of shared struggle alongside Muntaqim to transform the terms of humanity, attests to an irreducible "complex human being" whose formulation poses an essential challenge to dominant logics of personhood. Her letter thus enacts an undying commitment to the creative dilemma of collective being: the question of how to articulate human identity under the guidance of a paraontological force that supersedes the apparent omnipotence of civic life as social death and, moreover, of how to allow our selves to be articulated through that mystery even when we have no other choice but to create our own signs.

While the seemingly extraordinary materials in this chapter may appear anomalous to the vast majority of more mundane correspondences that go on daily among the Imprisoned, the selections here, just as the human life they enact, communicate the *essence* of a collective struggle that extends beyond individual cases or, as this chapter has argued, even their literary contents. Many letters written among criminalized communities throughout the carceral diaspora must press against the density of physical force and ideological machinations mediating their existence. As such, the resurgent humanity alive in the life of paper escapes from what Hortense Spillers calls "signifying property *plus*," that is, "markers so loaded with mythical prepossession that there is no easy way for the agents buried beneath them to come clean." The life of paper, then, reproduced in multiplicitous ways by people who "must strip down through layers of attenuated meanings, made an excess in time" in order to speak a truer word concerning themselves,[54] comes to terms with demands to reinvent a simultaneously "old" and "new" kind of yet indeterminate, emergent form of human being or being human. Such quotidian striving for new ways of historically preserving a oneness through difference, contextualized by perilous rearticulations of racial form in the "new Jim Crow" and exemplified in an understated way by the life of paper as a movement of human existence, constitutes a labor on which, as I have hoped to show or make urgent, our future indeed depends.

Epilogue

So I write. I write to say what I know and to find out what I don't. I write for love, the love of the young and old; for the energy that is me. I want people to love me and writing is my funnel to their mouths. I write for history. I write for my ancestors whose history is lost in a grave site; whose stories are only heard by worms. I write for the future: for the next generation so they'll know who I was. The I who lived and killed and died. I write so my nephew will know me in a way I don't know my uncles; the dead from war, the ones dead from life. I want to carry him on my words, teach him to fly with verbs, soothe him with nouns; sounds from my mind, through my pen, to his heart. I want him to know the real me.

And I write for me; for the visions calling me when I lay on my bunk and look at pictures of a past life. These visions are voices, these voices are words forgotten by man, except from me. I carry their burden. I am their savior—my nephew, my ancestors, their worms.

VIET MIKE NGO, "The Real Me"

MANY YEARS AND MANY many PAGES LATER, I think back now on the letters Viet Mike Ngo and I wrote during the latter part of his twenty-five years in California prisons, beginning with when I learned about him through abolitionist circles in my last year as an undergraduate and a few months after that when we met and worked together in the San Quentin College program—he as a "student" and I as a volunteer. Those were the months immediately preceding and following 11 September 2001, after which dominant blocs in the United States could call anything "terrorism" with some popular credibility and the ideological takedown of "radicalism" simultaneously resurfaced the premodern foundations of race thinking and, by equating religiously articulated supremacist extremism with left-wing political legacies, disgraced ongoing movements for social justice. Throughout that year, Ngo and I talked a lot about George Jackson, who was his role model at the time, and about thinkers like Angela Davis and Assata Shakur, who were mine. We went back and forth about details of our day-to-day work and lives, streaked with thoughts on big-picture issues like the possibilities and limits of pacifist resistance and principled violence, war and ideology, radical disembodiment, and, of course, what intimacy and love mean in all this chaos. Our writings intellectualized daydreams that we communicated through the eroticism of shared political desires: a romanticized vision, on my own part, that I know was sincere and also know is not the same as saying it was innocent. For my past indulgence in the notion that innocence exists, has any place or bearing, in the inferno of racial differentiation and violence, we paid a price—he more than I, to any extent that it is possible or necessary to think of these things in terms of quantity.

Those were the years that Ngo's work as a writer, political educator, and prison lawyer had finally started gaining traction, as alluded to in this book and documented by himself and others elsewhere.[1] He played a prominent role in the San Quentin education program's "student movement" for Ethnic Studies, which was generating a stir, and several of his suits against the California Department of Corrections (CDC) had cleared administrative hurdles to come into greater visibility and raise their stakes—suits addressing issues such as racial segregation, institutional retaliation, religious freedom, freedom of speech, sexual harassment, and inmate grievance procedures. At the peak of this momentum, San Quentin officials, given cause by other volunteers in the education program, conducted a cell search and seized allegedly illicit correspondence that subsequently justified Ngo's removal to solitary confinement. My letters to him established the basis for fabricated charges of "trafficking contraband," "circumventing procedures for information/materials going out," and something they called "over-familiarity," which the letters apparently evidenced and which was the only manufactured offense that stuck. A week later, prison administrators sent two other organizers of the push for Ethnic Studies, Rico Remeidio and Eddy Zheng, to the hole for potential association in a potential conspiracy.[2] Soon, state officials revoked Remeidio's parole date and transferred him to a higher security prison. Zheng remained in solitary confinement at San Quentin while his own chances for parole were crushed, and Ngo got lost in a series of transfers to psych wards and solitary confinement units across the state.

What those letters had the capacity to catalyze, how they were talked about—fueling stories of everything from my alleged victimhood to violent conspiracy to sexualized exploits to our differently gendered pathologies—the variety of effects the letters produced in that decisive intersection of narrative invention and material reality . . . Creating this book has allowed me to make something different of those purloined letters and the problems they posed. Through this work, I have attempted to distinguish and to clarify the difference between how letters mediate racism and reproduce as much as consume life through that base violence, on the one hand; and on the other, what letter correspondence actually means to the people involved in its activity, the struggles they claim and whose existence they hope to represent, what they understand themselves to be doing and, for that matter, the consciousness through which people understand or want themselves to *be* at all. This book has allowed me to name and situate a living dilemma in whole wide worlds of social meaning, history, struggle, and change, and although limited here to only a few distinct articulations of historical crisis, I have hoped to honor the countless communities of people who toil to transform suffering into something usable, and even beautiful: labors of love for which the letter is but one sign.

By the time we met, Ngo had long already assumed that he would die in prison, and many of his writings and interviews during that period hence express the inner life and survival of someone struggling through the most visceral awareness that every detail of every day is killing him. His piece, "The Real Me," thus begins by problematizing the "real" and pointing out the irony of the very concept of a "me" in this context, as he writes, "In a dimly lit classroom, I sit alone at an oaken table. . . . I want my insides to be like the oaken table—real." So he writes, and he qualifies why he writes, and to and for whom he writes: a drafting of human identity whose articulation necessitates the reformulation of all of existence as such, the composition of a "real me" exemplifying the ways that fatal constraints on the space of political enactment magnify the significance of subjective assertion and heighten the correlation of personhood to historical transformation.[3] In this sense, just as imagination maintains connections to the material forces conditioning it, so do acts that reimagine personhood become essential to altering material conditions, what Stuart Hall has called a process of "imaginary political re-identification, re-territorialization and re-identification," without which a counterpolitics cannot be constructed.[4] Ngo's desire to write another sociality into existence, then, speaks to the imaginative aspect of human being,

driven by cultivated vision of something palpable deep underneath the surface of existing material world order. In this visionary labor, our past does not
exist as recoverable and reified fact but as part of the poetics of our becoming
that must be narrativized, "always retold, rediscovered, reinvented."[5] Ngo's
multitemporal retellings in these regards, his life of paper generating an
(inter)subjectivity that connects George Jackson in Soledad with ancestors
in Vietnam, progeny with past, earth with ether, marks the repetition of a
promise—the evolution of an ontological fabric and the paraontological
mystery of its revelation within which human activity to manifest this matrix
creates our own saviors.

What a complex or poetic twist of fate, the ability now to contemplate the
difference between how we were talking about "struggle" those years back
and where things are at today. In 2005, Rico Remeidio won his release after
serving more than twenty-four years in prison. After many years of building
a robust public campaign for his own release, Eddy Zheng was also paroled
in 2005 after twenty-one years of incarceration. Zheng was immediately
transferred into Immigration and Customs Enforcement custody in Yuba
County, California, through February 2007, under order of deportation
authorized by the Antiterrorism and Effective Death Penalty Act and the
Illegal Immigration Reform and Immigrant Responsibility Act of 1996,
the 2001 Patriot Act, and restructurings of immigrant policing under the
Department of Homeland Security since 2003.[6] In April 2015, Zheng was
granted a full pardon by California governor Jerry Brown, and in December
2015, Zheng also won his long legal battle against deportation to China. Both
Remeidio and Zheng reside in the San Francisco Bay Area where they have
transitioned into new phases of their lives, finding their ways in this terrain
and resuming work in local politics, prison abolitionist organizing, and non-
profit work in youth advocacy and violence prevention.

After serving time for a quarter of a century, Viet Mike Ngo was himself
released to his family in Alameda, California, in April 2011 and, like other
members of his cohort, confronts the changes and continuities between requisites of survival on one side of the apartheid wall and another. In the days
of severest constraint and his deepest engagements with necropolitics, it read
to me that Ngo found his agency in the fullest and most sober attempts to
subjectivize through the facts of his dying. What must animate this dimension of "transition," in which the lived conditions of struggle have moved
with relative immediacy from the extremities of negativity to the problems
of positivity: from his self-identified role as a "grave digger"[7] to questions of

what remains or comes next, how to live with or through the day-to-day decisions and boundaries of the civilian world after a lifetime of seeing it from "the grave"? The struggle, perhaps for Mike specifically, but also as a problematic more generally, seems now to be not only a matter of the art of dying well, as "Lady Lazarus" Sylvia Plath put it (and whose own destiny, indeed, from an entirely different position, says something about the outcomes of domesticated whiteness), but also of how to address the question or dilemma of what it means to "make it," what it means to make it "out," what it means to make it out still *alive*?

As I review video footage of Rico Remeidio's participation in the San Francisco Reentry Summit, convened in 2006 by a collaboration of local and state government offices under the San Francisco Safe Communities and Reentry Council,[8] I watch and listen to him as he gracefully moves his way through one of the corollary struggles of "the struggle": how to speak for himself, from the position of one who has been asked, and in perhaps different ways also feels compelled, to represent or be representative of more than one. The panel moderator introduces Remeidio as an example of someone who has "successfully reentered society" and prompts him to comment on the question, "Looking back on your experiences as a parolee, what would have made your transition easier? And if you could sort of design your ideal reentry plan, what would it be?" Upon greeting his audience with humble expressions of thanks, Remeidio begins by shifting the frame of reference for such questions from normative limits of individual experience and exceptionalism to a context of systematic distress, as he slowly opens his response, "I been in a system where rehabilitation was, uh, practiced and changed into a punishment, and I think the system has a long ways to bring the rehabilitation back." By thus refusing to distinguish between positive ideologies of rehabilitation and negative applications of punishment, not allowing himself or us to forget their mutual constitution and routinized interarticulation as he lived them, Remeidio also subtly overturns the logic of "success" and its casting of failure, the structure of desire through which dominant parties understand "reentry" and, in these senses, the very notion or foundations of "society" as such. From this perspective, Remeidio's ensuing comments focus at a practical level on the need for quality transitional housing and support and for public investment to make these resources available to the majority of formerly incarcerated people who currently cannot access them. In his own case, his confirmation of the benefits of "a place where I can, you know, stay for a while and, and make a slow transition into society," approaches the problem of "reentry" most essentially as one of adjusting to changes in the dimensionality of space and time—a view that does not operate within the racial logics or enduring telos of "transition" as movements from savage to civilized, criminal to citizen.

In Remeidio's closing remarks, he returns to the CDC as problem rather than adjudicator for rehabilitation and, under these conditions, proposes that "people out here in the community need to actually go inside. . . . If we are really serious about helping prisoners and promote uh, safety, public safety, we need to get involved. We need to get involved. That's all I have to say." Contextualized by his own experience, Remeidio argues that endeavors to "bring love into the prisons" can disrupt the animosities fomented and mutually felt between "the community" and those who are incarcerated or positioned as "rejects of society." Again, we must understand Remeidio's intervention within the broader scope of his vision that draws distinctions between institutionalized modes of sociality and the quality or framework of involvement he intends. In this light, Remeidio's provocations to persist across the divides require that we also maintain dynamics of social recognition and relations that, even if they must unfold within them, do not abide by the systems that structure every aspect of our lives and exist to control our social reproduction. The challenge, then, becomes (or the "revolution" remains) how to manifest the totality of our involvements—simultaneously navigating the brutality of one set of historical boundaries, naturalized and seemingly fixed, while cognizant of other horizons that, by condition, we can realize only in their tender states of emergence and, furthermore, which cannot come into being through individual agency alone but only in the fortitude of our relationships, in or despite all the violence they sustain.

Finally, the life of paper comes back into focus again, from its contradictory obscurity to its self-evidence as a poetics of becoming. How easy it is to stop noticing this vitality, whose form of appearance is not as readily available as beauty the way we may consider art, or as readily available as power the way we may consider politics. Nevertheless, as I have attempted to show throughout this book, the gestalts of the letter and people's everyday investments in it have helped give rise to everything that modern sensibilities now know as literature as well as politics—as history, geography, theology, or humankind, for that matter. Moreover, in case after case, the life of paper has renewed foundations for the preservation of social bonds conducive to our own creativity, to our own senses of being alive and of growing into a shared existence—the evolution of lifeworlds that, even as they press against the chaos of their material condition, are not contingent on the terror and the killing that surrounds them. Instead, providing means for communities to develop autonomously from within the limits circumscribing the terms of mass violence and war, the life of paper as process of social reproduction thus resonates as an enduring part of interconnected struggles to deepen our involvements at other scales of historical articulation, as an ongoing source and resource for the disclosure of this ultimate concern.

In the final analysis, then, one last effect of the letter uncovers itself through the realization of how truly magnificent "The Real Me" is, each and all people, like Ngo, who toil every day in tedious and seemingly unremarkable ways to make it through the moment alive, without sacrificing our selves or each other—the search for consciousness, love, histories, and visions—even as everything in this world of domination induces auto-destruction. In this sense, the existence of the letter testifies to struggles to regenerate "life after death"[9] in our very present wherein just as the burdens haunting Ngo's hunger to write remain, so do the terms of this world's "salvation": hinged on the breathtaking perseverance of so many communities and so many people who labor day after day at the margins of an other reality, at scales beyond what Western civilization can bear. Concentrated on this immense undertaking, I have sought to clarify how the life of paper, making its way across murderous landscapes and from its realms of negativity or in its negative contours, helps give shape to ideological, epistemological, and ontological grounds for the opening out of a way of being that honors, or that is turned toward, the mystery of both death and life to come.

ACKNOWLEDGMENTS

Every name here, of course, signifies its own volume of stories. I extend my regrets to the many people who have moved me in ways that remain outside the margins of recollection here. Any texture and beauty contained in these pages are a result of our shared gifts.

Ruthie Gilmore's singular interventions, over many years and of practically every variety, created entries for me back into my own imagination—acts of genius, love, and leadership that involved nothing less than giving me the most profound gift, a qualitative experience of freedom. Jack Halberstam, with extraordinary generosity and by brilliance of example, gave me the courage to do things my way without apology. Robin Kelley taught me over and over again how to see, not just as a scholar, but as an artist. David Lloyd patiently allowed me to do "figure eights" around theory until I made myself dizzy and then always set me back on course. This committee actually believed me when I said I could do this and saw my deepest potential through all the times I lacked faith. I am forever grateful. A few other guides have influenced my path with parallel gravity. Fred Moten, more than anyone, took time and care always to show me the poetics of each thing. Clyde Woods, given over to the Blues, helped me understand power and taught me not to block the gifts. Grace Hong read not one but two complete drafts of the manuscript and helped me edit with the conceptual and practical insights of an interlocutor sent by her divine namesake. Nahum Chandler, too, meticulously poured through a draft of the book and took most seriously its thinking and "writerly-ness" with a respect for craft and calling I have found precious. So blessed, all shortcomings of this book are only my own.

Deepest thanks to Niels Hooper, Bradley Depew, Kate Warne, Sheila Berg, Cynthia Landeen, and the rest of the team at UC Press; to Jodi Kim,

George Lipsitz, and Dylan Rodríguez as well for their most gracious reader's comments that articulated my highest hopes for this book. Colleen Lye availed her insights and support at crucial moments. I benefited, too, from the early support of Thomas Lay, Richard Morrison, and the late Helen Tartar. Along the way, I have enjoyed the privileges of institutional support from the College of Arts and Sciences and Center for Law, History, and Culture at the University of Southern California; the Chinese Historical Society of Southern California (CHSSC); the Southern California Library; the Asian American Studies Center, Bunche Center for Afro-American Studies, and Institute of American Cultures at the University of California, Los Angeles; and the Center for the Study of Women in Society, College of Arts and Sciences, and Oregon Humanities Center at the University of Oregon. My additional thanks to Louis Fiset at the University of Washington, Bill Greene at the National Archives and Records Administration—Pacific Region, and Eugene Moy at CHSSC for their assistance with archival research.

I am humbled and honored by those who have trusted me with their stories and enabled me to share them in this work, particularly Satsuki Ina, Bessie Masuda, Stormy Ogden, Yusef Omowale, Rico Remeidio, Toru Saito, and Eddy Zheng. For Viet Mike Ngo, I can now only reserve a special silence in recognition of the lessons and profound gifts of his friendship that have influenced the course of my destiny.

Each of my life cycles at UCLA introduced me to people who have helped facilitate my growth as a scholar: early support came from Robert Hill, Kirstie McClure, the late Don Nakanishi, Daniel Solórzano and the many of us he mentored in our Critical Race Studies Research Apprenticeship Course, Mary Thomas, and the Department of Chicana/o Studies; at the Bunche Center for African American Studies, Lisbeth Gant-Britton, Jan Freeman, Darnell Hunt, Mark Sawyer, and Alex Tucker; at the Asian American Studies Center, Sarah Chong, Marjorie Lee, Betty Leung, Meg Thornton, Melany de la Cruz-Viesca, and David Yoo, with special thanks to Mary Uyematsu Kao and John Kao who treated me as a daughter. I thank, too, students in my first classes as instructor of record, "Culture, Media, and Los Angeles" and "'Afro-Asian' Politics in US History and Culture," as well as TA Melody Frierson; Sarah Haley, Mauricio Magaña, and Thu-huong Nguyen-vo further enriched my time as a postdoctoral fellow. During another fellowship period at Stanford University, I benefited especially from the generosity and interventions of Allison Hobbes, Shelley Fisher-Fishkin, Ban Wang, and Kevin Kim.

Some of my fondest memories will always remain bound to the years I spent as a doctoral student at the University of Southern California, with encouragement and help from department staff Sandra Jones, Jujuana Preston, Kitty Lai, and Sonia Rodriguez; faculty Macarena Gomez-Barris, Sarah Gualtieri, Edwin Hill, Jane Iwamura, Kara Keeling, Dorinne Kondo, Viet Nguyen, Laura Pulido, David Roman, Leland Saito, George Sánchez, and Francille Wilson; fellow beginning sojourners Brandon Best, Thang Dao, Anjali Nath, Anthony Rodríguez, Orlando Serrano, and Margarita Smith; a brilliant community created by friends, including Wendy Cheng, Michelle Commander, Araceli Esparza, Laura Fugikawa, Jesus Hernández, Imani Johnson, Deb Najjar, Mark Padoongpatt, Mica Smith, Anton Smith, and Yushi Yamazaki; swans Todd Honma and Jake Peters; and the cherished sisterhoods of Genevieve Carpio, Perla Guerrero, Gretel Vera-Rosas, Tasneem Siddiqui, and Terrion Williamson.

The abundance I have enjoyed at the University of Oregon has allowed me to finish this book. Donella Alston, Julie Anderson, Melissa Bowers, Josh Buetow, Robin Knudson, Beth Magee, Marilyn Reid, and David Yorgesen offered generous logistical help. Colleagues in English graciously welcomed and supported me, with special thanks to Kirby Brown, Karen Ford, Lisa Gilman, Sangita Gopal, Priscilla Ovalle, Paul Peppis, Mark Quigley, Alison Lau Stephens, Avinnash Tawari, Courtney Thorsson, David Vázquez, Sarah Wald, and Mary Wood, alongside the catalyzing energies of David Li, George Rowe, Danielle Seid, and Betsy Wheeler who served on the search that gave me a job. The community extended by my treasured colleagues in Ethnic Studies—Charise Cheney, Michael Hames-Garcia, Brian Klopetek, Ernesto Martínez, Alaí Reyes-Santos, Laura Pulido, and the better parts of our trifecta, Lynn Fujiwara and Lani Teves—was exactly the lifeline I needed to find my way. Dan Martinez-HoSang, carrying over from ASE a feeling of home, took time and care to look out for me and teach me the ropes at a new place. The Center for the Study of Women in Society's Women of Color cohort, directed by Michelle McKinley and Sangita Gopal, has also made my will and work much stronger here. The friendships of Diedrick Brackens, Loren Kajikawa, Angela Joya, Geoff Kennedy, Norma Martinez-HoSang, Steve Morozumi, Jennifer O'Neal, Kathleen Rubio, and Mika Tanner have brightened the rainy days.

How far back can one go as a scholar? I remain grateful for the early educational influences of Susana Ackerman, Matt Barmore, John DeBenedetti, Peter Divine, John Harrington, Eugene Ide, Jim McGarry, Charles C.

Murphy, Steven Nejasmich, Kathy Purcell, Michael Shaughnessy, and Paul Totah. As an undergraduate, I was transformed by the mentorship of Joy James and Daniel Kim and friendships, lasting even if constrained by time and distance, with Liz Appel, Kohei Ishihara, Dina Lopez, Ariana Mangual, Cyriac Matthew, Amit Sarin, Sam Seidel, Sushma Sheth, Sarath Suong, Audrey Tendell, and Craig Zheng. Youthful time spent with Elizabeth Alsop, David Coolidge, Shane DeSilva, Jiminie Ha, Jack Ohly, Tony Plunkett, Nicholas Reville, Andrei Scheinkman, Michael Bell-Smith, and Elyse Steinberg encouraged my creativity at a most formative time in my life.

A number of people during the intervening years humbled me with their leadership, talents, and protection, including Charles Carbone, Craig Gilmore, Roseli Ilano, Michelle LeTourneau, Stephen Liebb, Monica Waiyi Ly, Albert Mai, Claude Marks, Tung and Mylan Ngo, Dylan Rodríguez, Jared Sexton, Setsu Shigamatsu, Shelley Smith, Watani Stiner, and old friends at the East Bay Asian Youth Center—Adriana Betti, Mario Campbell, Wardell Myles, and especially Peter Kim. So dear to my heart since our childhood days, Liz Lee was the very first to suggest, during one of our sessions at Royal Grounds on Fillmore following a run through the Presidio (when the city still felt like our City), that I could write about letters. Adamu Chan has engaged the life of paper with the truest vulnerability and severity. Leggers Martin Bernard, Martin Diekhoff, Howard Gest, the late and greatest Patti Kahn (Renato and Paulita always with us at the finish line), Egzine Richardson, and Kathryn Tyus (Rhys and Ailey, too, if pie or pancakes were involved) truly taught me how to go the distance. I would have lost my way, too, without Dr. Marie Moore. Raquel Chavez and Michele Welsing took care of me like a sister; Yusef Omowale held so much with me and has his own place here.

Returning to the people who know the child me: the love, wisdom, and prayers of Rev. Dr. Trinity Ordona, Desiree Thompson, Kim Alvarenga, Linnette Peralta-Haynes, and Oziah sustained me through hard years. My Goo-Ma and Goo-Zhueng, the Li family (Dai Beau Gow and Beau So, Chiquita Sharon, and Jason), and the Li family (Sai Beau Gow and Beau So, Roxane, Gavin, and Shawn) helped raise me and gave me peace and shelter all the times I so desperately needed it. The Tsui, Mui, and Koong families have been a part of ours since forever. My seester Selene, Eric, Raiden, and Blaze; Wilman (forever my kid brother), Jennifer, Calypso, and the little one coming; and my parents, Martin Honto and Magdalen Kimwai Luk, have seen me through each and every growing pain, loved me even when I don't give them enough to love, and always welcome back the seemingly wayward daughter. At the risk of sounding too Chinese (Willay, this is the closest you're getting to *The Joy Luk Club*), our mom is the first person I want to make proud and our dad my first, last, and best teacher.

NOTES

INTRODUCTION

1. H. T. Loomis, *Practical Letter Writing* (Cleveland, OH: Practical Text Book Company, 1897), 3.

2. David Barton and Nigel Hall, eds., *Letter Writing as a Social Practice* (Amsterdam: John Benjamins, 2000); Asa Briggs and Peter Burke, *A Social History of the Media: From Gutenberg to the Internet* (Cambridge: Polity Press, 2005); Elizabeth Heckendorn Cook, *Epistolary Bodies: Gender and Genre in the Eighteenth-Century Republic of Letters* (Stanford, CA: Stanford University Press, 1996); Rebecca Earle, *Epistolary Selves: Letters and Letter-Writers, 1600–1945* (Brooksfield, VT: Ashgate, 1999).

3. Benedict Anderson, *Imagined Communities: Reflections on the Origin and Spread of Nationalism,* rev. ed. (New York: Verso, 2006 [1983]); William Merrill Decker, *Epistolary Practices: Letter Writing in America before Telecommunications* (Chapel Hill: University of North Carolina Press, 1998); William J. Gilmore, *Reading Becomes a Necessity of Life: Material and Cultural Life in Rural New England, 1780–1835* (Knoxville: University of Tennessee Press, 1992); Amanda Gilroy and W. M. Verhoeven, *Epistolary Histories: Letters, Fiction, Culture* (Charlottesville: University of Virginia Press, 2000); Richard Hoggart, *The Uses of Literacy: Aspects of Working-Class Life* (New York: Penguin Books, 2009 [1957]).

4. Richard D. Brown, *Knowledge Is Power* (Oxford: Oxford University Press, 1989); Richard R. John, *Spreading the News: The American Postal System from Franklin to Morse* (Cambridge, MA: Harvard University Press, 1995); Richard Thomas Stillson, *Spreading the Word: A History of Information in the California Gold Rush* (Lincoln: University of Nebraska Press, 2006).

5. Ying-wan Cheng, *Postal Communication in China and Its Modernization, 1860–1896* (Cambridge, MA: Harvard University Press, 1970), 2.

6. Vladimir Lenin, "The State and Revolution" (1871), accessed 11 January 2016, https://www.marxists.org/archive/lenin/works/1917/staterev/ch03.htm#s3.

7. Antonio Gramsci, *Letters from Prison, Volume 2,* ed. Frank Rosengarten, trans. Raymond Rosenthal (New York: Columbia University Press, 1994), 58; see

also Barbara Harlow, *Barred: Women, Writing, and Political Detention* (Middletown, CT: Wesleyan University Press, 1992), xvii.

8. Leopoldina Fortunati, *The Arcane of Reproduction: Housework, Prostitution, Labor and Capital,* trans. H. Creek (New York: Autonomedia, 1995 [1981]).

9. Jacques Lacan, "The Youth of Gide, or the Letter and Desire," in *Ecrits: The First Complete Edition in English,* trans. Bruce Fink (New York: Norton, 2007 [1958]), 623; original emphasis.

10. Ibid., 625.

11. Perhaps his most evoked work on this topic is Jacques Derrida, *The Post Card: From Socrates to Freud and Beyond* (Chicago: University of Chicago Press, 1987); for further problematization of the methods and stakes of deconstruction vis-à-vis a more precise analytic of "desedimentation," see also Nahum Dimitri Chandler, *X—The Problem of the Negro as a Problem for Thought* (New York: Fordham University Press, 2013), 185–88, note 2.

12. See, e.g., Anne L. Bower, *Epistolary Responses: The Letter in 20th-Century American Fiction and Criticism* (Tuscaloosa: University Alabama Press, 1997); Joe Bray, *The Epistolary Novel: Representations of Consciousness* (New York: Routledge, 2003); Linda S. Kauffman, *Special Delivery: Epistolary Modes in Modern Fiction* (Chicago: University of Chicago Press, 1992); Sunka Simon, *Mail-Orders: The Fiction of Letters in Postmodern Culture* (New York: State University of New York Press, 2002); Liz Stanley, "The Epistolarium: On Theorizing Letters and Correspondences," *Auto/Biography* 12 (2004): 201–35.

13. Earle, *Epistolary Selves,* 8.

14. See, e.g., Michel Foucault, *The History of Sexuality, Vol. 1: An Introduction,* trans. Robert Hurley (New York: Vintage, 1990); Michel Foucault, *The Archaeology of Knowledge: And the Discourse on Language,* trans. A.M. Sheridan Smith (New York: Pantheon Books, 1972); Lisa Lowe, *Immigrant Acts: On Asian American Cultural Politics* (Durham, NC: Duke University Press, 1996); Edward W. Said, *Culture and Imperialism* (New York: Random House, 1993); Raymond Williams, *Marxism and Literature* (Oxford: Oxford University Press, 1978).

15. W. E. B. DuBois, *The Souls of Black Folk: Essays and Sketches* (Chicago: A. C. McClurg & Co., 1903).

16. For fuller elaboration of the problematic, see, in particular, Nahum Dimitri Chandler, "Of Exorbitance: The Problem of the Negro as a Problem for Thought," *Criticism* 50, no. 3 (2008): 345–410.

17. While scholarship on the "prison industrial complex" in the emerging field of Critical Prison Studies is too prolific to recount, early and influential examples include Mumia Abu-Jamal, *Live from Death Row* (Boston, MA: Addison-Wesley, 1995); Angela Y. Davis, *Are Prisons Obsolete?* (New York: Seven Stories Press, 2003); Mike Davis, *City of Quartz: Excavating the Future in Los Angeles* (New York: Vintage, 1990); Ruth Wilson Gilmore, "Fatal Couplings of Power and Difference: Notes on Racism and Geography," *Professional Geographer* 54, no. 1 (2002): 15–24; Joy James, ed., *The New Abolitionists: (Neo)Slave Narratives and Contemporary*

Prison Writings (Albany: State University of New York Press, 2005); Joy James, ed., *Imprisoned Intellectuals: America's Political Prisoners Write on Life, Liberation, and Rebellion* (Lanham, MD: Rowman & Littlefield, 2003); Joy James, ed., *States of Confinement: Policing, Detention, and Prisons* (New York: Palgrave Macmillan, 2002); Joy James, *Resisting State Violence: Radicalicism, Gender, and Race in U.S. Culture* (Minneapolis: University of Minnesota Press, 1996); Christian Parenti, *Lockdown America* (New York: Verso Books, 1999); Dylan Rodríguez, *Forced Passages: Imprisoned Radical Intellectuals and the U.S. Prison Regime* (Minneapolis: University of Minnesota Press, 2006); Clyde Woods, *Development Arrested: Race, Power, and the Blues in the Mississippi Delta* (New York: Verso Books, 1998).

Most recently, leading abolitionists have problematized the term *mass incarceration* itself, contextualized in its appropriation by the "Establishment Left" to mystify the foundations of white supremacy and reinforce the reproduction of white citizen-subjects in current movements for prison reform (see, e.g., Dylan Rodríguez and Casey Goonan, "Policing and the Violence of White Being: An Interview with Dylan Rodríguez," *Black Scholar*, 12 September 2016, http://www.theblackscholar.org/policing-violence-white-interview-dylan-rodriguez/). I continue to use the term *mass incarceration* throughout this book for the way it signifies and builds on a discursive formation that has unfolded within ongoing historical contingencies and as part of ongoing historical struggles. The specificities of my argument ultimately lend historicity to the term's present emergence in public discourse and the varied ideological perspectives offered through its use therein, from a provisional intellectual genealogical perspective.

18. Lowe, *Immigrant Acts; The Intimacies of Four Continents*. Durham, NC: Duke University Press, 2015.

19. Ruth Wilson Gilmore, "Race, Prisons and War: Scenes from the History of US Violence," *Socialist Register 2009: Violence Today* 45 (2009): 73–87; Gilmore, "Fatal Couplings of Power and Difference."

20. Ruth Wilson Gilmore, *Golden Gulag: Prisons, Surplus, Crisis, and Opposition in Globalizing California* (Berkeley: University of California Press, 2007); Kelly Lytle Hernández, "Hobos in Heaven: Race, Incarceration, and the Rise of Los Angeles, 1880–1910," *Pacific Historical Review* 83, no. 3 (August 2014): 410–47; Kelly Lytle Hernández, "Amnesty or Abolition? Felons, Illegals, and the Case for a New Abolition Movement," *Boom: A Journal of California* 1, no. 4 (2011): 54–68; Clyde Woods, *Black California Dreamin': The Crises of California's African-American Communities* (Santa Barbara: UCSB Center for Black Studies Research, 2012), http://escholarship.org/uc/item/63g6128j.

21. Adam McKeown, *Melancholy Order: Asian Migration and the Globalization of Borders* (New York: Columbia University Press, 2008).

22. I thank Chon Noriega and the audience at the 2013 UCLA Institute of American Cultures Fall Forum for bringing this research to my attention. See Jane Catherine Berlo, *Plains Indian Drawings 1865–1935* (New York: Harry N. Abrams, 1996); Colin Gordon Calloway, *Ledger Narratives: The Plains Indian Drawings of*

the Lansburgh Collection at Dartmouth College (Norman: University of Oklahoma Press, 2012); "Plains Indian Ledger Art Project," accessed 8 November 2016, https://plainsledgerart.org/ledgers/index/1/.

23. Ruth Wilson Gilmore, "Race and Globalization," in *Geographies of Global Change: Remapping the World,* ed. R. J. Johnston, Peter J. Taylor, and Michael Watts (Malden, MA: Blackwell, 2002), 261.

24. Among other earlier interventions, see also Barbara Jean Fields, "Slavery, Race and Ideology in the United States of America," *New Left Review* 181 (June 1990): 95–118; Stuart Hall, "Gramsci's Relevance for the Study of Race and Ethnicity," *Journal of Communication Inquiry* 10, no. 2 (1 June 1986): 5–27; Stuart Hall, "Race, Articulation and Societies Structured in Dominance," in *Sociological Theories: Race and Colonialism* (Paris: UNESCO, 1980), 305–45.

25. Carl Takei, "From Mass Incarceration to Mass Control, and Back Again: How Bipartisan Criminal Justice Reform May Lead to a For-Profit Nightmare," SSRN Scholarly Paper (Social Science Research Network, Rochester, NY, 3 March 2016), http://papers.ssrn.com/abstract=2741932.

26. Stefano Harney and Fred Moten, "Michael Brown," *Boundary 2* 42, no. 4 (1 November 2015): 81–87.

27. Katherine McKittrick, *Demonic Grounds: Black Women and the Cartographies of Struggle* (Minneapolis: University of Minnesota Press, 2006), 130–31.

28. Clyde Woods, "Life after Death," *Professional Geographer* 54, no. 1 (2002): 64.

29. The body of theorization here is too rich to cite fully. Of the most influential for this study are Chandler, *X—The Problem of the Negro as a Problem for Thought;* W. E. B. DuBois, *Black Reconstruction in America 1860–1880* (New York: Simon and Schuster, 1935); Gilmore, "Fatal Couplings of Power and Difference"; C. L. R. James, *The Black Jacobins: Toussaint L'Ouverture and the San Domingo Revolution* (New York: Vintage Books, 1963); C. L. R. James, "Black Studies and the Contemporary Student" (1969), in *At the Rendezvous of Victory: Selected Writings* (London: Allison & Busby, 1984), 389–404; Robin D. G. Kelley, *Freedom Dreams: The Black Radical Imagination* (Boston: Beacon Press, 2003); Robin D. G. Kelley, *Race Rebels: Culture, Politics, and the Black Working Class* (New York: Free Press, 1996); Fred Moten, "The Case of Blackness," *Criticism* 50, no. 2 (3 July 2008): 177–218; Fred Moten, *In the Break: The Aesthetics of the Black Radical Tradition* (Minneapolis: University of Minnesota Press, 2003); Cedric J. Robinson, *Black Marxism: The Making of the Black Radical Tradition* (Chapel Hill: University of North Carolina Press, 2000 [1983]); Woods, *Development Arrested;* Sylvia Wynter, "No Humans Involved: An Open Letter to My Colleagues," *Forum N.H.I.: Knowledge for the 21st Century* 1, no. 1 (1994): 42–73; see also as examples, Brent Hayes Edwards, *The Practice of Diaspora: Literature, Translation, and the Rise of Black Internationalism* (Cambridge, MA: Harvard University Press, 2009); Edouard Glissant, *Poetics of Relation,* trans. Betsy Wing (Ann Arbor: University of Michigan Press, 1997); Avery F. Gordon, *Ghostly Matters: Haunting and the Sociological Imagination* (Minneapolis: University of Minnesota Press, 1997); Saidiya V. Hartman, *Scenes of Subjection: Terror, Slavery, and Self-Making in Nineteenth-Century America* (New York: Oxford University Press,

1997); Kara Keeling, *The Witch's Flight: The Cinematic, the Black Femme, and the Image of Common Sense* (Durham, NC: Duke University Press, 2007); Colleen Lye, "The Afro-Asian Analogy," *PMLA* 123, no. 5 (1 October 2008): 1732–36; Nikhil Pal Singh, *Black Is a Country: Race and the Unfinished Struggle for Democracy* (Cambridge, MA: Harvard University Press, 2004); Alexander G. Weheliye, *Phonographies: Grooves in Sonic Afro-Modernity* (Durham, NC: Duke University Press, 2005).

30. Michel Foucault, *Ethics: Subjectivity and Truth (Essential Works of Foucault, 1954–1984, Vol. 1)*, ed. Paul Rabinow (New York: New Press, 1998), 207, 209.

31. Sylvia Wynter, "Ethno or Socio Poetics," *Alcheringa/Boston University* 2, no. 2 (1976): 78–81; here and elsewhere in quotations from Wynter, capitalization follows the original.

32. Ibid., 85; see also Stefano Harney and Fred Moten, *The Undercommons: Fugitive Planning & Black Study* (New York: Autonomedia, 2013); Robin D. G. Kelley, "A Poetics of Anticolonialism," *Monthly Review* 51, no. 6 (1999), http://monthlyreview .org/1999/11/01/a-poetics-of-anticolonialism/; Katherine McKittrick, ed., *Sylvia Wynter: On Being Human as Praxis* (Durham, NC: Duke University Press, 2015); Cherrie Moraga and Gloria Anzaldúa, eds., *This Bridge Called My Back: Writings by Radical Women of Color*, 2nd ed. (New York: Kitchen Table / Women of Color Press, 1984); Robinson, *Black Marxism*.

33. Wynter, "Ethno or Socio Poetics," 89.

34. Yunte Huang, "Angel Island and the Poetics of Error," in *Poetry and Cultural Studies: A Reader*, ed. Maria Damon and Ira Livingston (Champaign: University of Illinois Press, 2009), 305; see also Yunte Huang, *Transpacific Imaginations: History, Literature, Counterpoetics* (Cambridge, MA: Harvard University Press, 2008).

35. Huang, "Angel Island and the Poetics of Error," 304.

36. Wynter, "Ethno or Socio Poetics," 89.

37. Moten, *In the Break*, 254.

38. Lowe, *Immigrant Acts;* Said, *Culture and Imperialism*, 71–79.

39. Colleen Lye, "Racial Form," *Representations* 104, no. 1 (1 November 2008): 92–101; Colleen Lye, *America's Asia: Racial Form and American Literature, 1893–1945* (Princeton, NJ: Princeton University Press, 2005). Related to these problems, other work in Asian American Studies examines how disparate, historically overlapping processes of racialization have created embodied yet incoherent racial identities. See, e.g., Kandice Chuh, *Imagine Otherwise: On Asian Americanist Critique* (Durham, NC: Duke University Press, 2003); Hyun Yi Kang, *Compositional Subjects: Enfiguring Asian/American Women* (Durham, NC: Duke University Press, 2002); Daniel Y. Kim, *Writing Manhood in Black and Yellow: Ralph Ellison, Frank Chin, and the Literary Politics of Identity* (Stanford, CA: Stanford University Press, 2005); Jodi Kim, *Ends of Empire: Asian American Critique and the Cold War* (Minneapolis: University of Minnesota Press, 2010); Lye, "The Afro-Asian Analogy."

40. For elaboration of these problems of historical method, see David A. Gerber, "Epistolary Ethics: Personal Correspondence and the Culture of Emigration in the Nineteenth Century," *Journal of American Ethnic History* 19, no. 4 (1 July 2000):

3–23; David A. Gerber, "The Immigrant Letter between Positivism and Populism: The Uses of Immigrant Personal Correspondence in Twentieth-Century American Scholarship," *Journal of American Ethnic History* 16, no. 4 (1 July 1997): 3–34.

41. Aurora Levins Morales, *Medicine Stories: History, Culture and the Politics of Integrity* (Cambridge, MA: South End Press, 1999), 40.

42. Regarding the latter, visit Freedom Archives, accessed 4 February 2016, http://freedomarchives.org/; Southern California Library, accessed 4 February 2016, http://www.socallib.org/.

43. The broader literatures problematizing historiography and the archive are vast. Among those most influential for this project are Walter Benjamin, *Illuminations,* trans. Harry Zohn (New York: Schocken Books, 2007 [1936]); Jacques Derrida, *Archive Fever: A Freudian Impression* (Chicago: University of Chicago Press, 1998); Foucault, *The Archaeology of Knowledge;* Jacquelyn Dowd Hall, "The Long Civil Rights Movement and the Political Uses of the Past," *Journal of American History* 91, no. 4 (1 March 2005): 1233–63; Achille Mbembe, "On the Power of the False," trans. Judith Inggs, *Public Culture* 14, no. 3 (2002): 629–41; Ann Laura Stoler, *Along the Archival Grain: Epistemic Anxieties and Colonial Common Sense* (Princeton, NJ: Princeton University Press, 2010).

44. Megan Sweeney, *Reading Is My Window: Books and the Art of Reading in Women's Prisons* (Chapel Hill: University of North Carolina Press, 2010).

45. Among the vast literatures in these areas, influential examples are Kamau Brathwaite, *History of the Voice: The Development of Nation Language in Anglophone Caribbean Poetry* (London: New Beacon Books, 1984); Glissant, *Poetics of Relation;* Gordon, *Ghostly Matters;* Moraga and Anzaldúa, *This Bridge Called My Back;* José Esteban Muñoz, "Ephemera as Evidence: Introductory Notes to Queer Acts," *Women & Performance: A Journal of Feminist Theory* 8, no. 2 (1 January 1996): 5–16; John Yau, *Radiant Silhouette: New & Selected Work, 1974–1988* (Santa Rosa, CA: Black Sparrow Press, 1989).

46. For examples, see Daphne Brooks, *Bodies in Dissent: Spectacular Performances of Race and Freedom, 1850–1910* (Durham, NC: Duke University Press, 2006); Wendy Hui Kyong Chun, "The Enduring Ephemeral, or the Future Is a Memory," *Critical Inquiry* 35, no. 1 (2008): 148–71; Ann Cvetkovich, *An Archive of Feelings: Trauma, Sexuality, and Lesbian Public Cultures* (Durham, NC: Duke University Press, 2003); David L. Eng, *Racial Castration: Managing Masculinity in Asian America* (Durham, NC: Duke University Press, 2001); Carla Freccero, *Queer/Early/Modern* (Durham, NC: Duke University Press, 2005); Judith Halberstam, *In a Queer Time and Place: Transgender Bodies, Subcultural Lives* (New York: New York University Press, 2005); Grace Kyungwon Hong, *Death beyond Disavowal: The Impossible Politics of Difference* (Minneapolis: University of Minnesota Press, 2015); Alondra Nelson, Thuy Linh N. Tu, and Alicia Headlam Hines, eds., *Technicolor: Race, Technology, and Everyday Life* (New York: New York University Press, 2001); Joseph R. Roach, *Cities of the Dead: Circum-Atlantic Performance* (New York: Columbia University Press, 1996); Stephanie Nohelani Teves, "Tradition and Performance," in *Native Studies Keywords,* ed. Stephanie Nohelani

Teves, Andrea Smith, and Michelle Raheja (Tucson: University of Arizona Press, 2015); Weheliye, *Phonographies.*

47. Edwards, *The Practice of Diaspora;* Lewis Hyde, *The Gift: Creativity and the Artist in the Modern World* (New York: Vintage Books, 1983).

48. Dean Spade, *Normal Life: Administrative Violence, Critical Trans Politics, and the Limits of Law* (Boston, MA: South End Press, 2011).

49. See also M. Jacqui Alexander, *Pedagogies of Crossing: Meditations on Feminism, Sexual Politics, Memory, and the Sacred* (Durham, NC: Duke University Press, 2006); Cathy J. Cohen, "Punks, Bulldaggers, and Welfare Queens: The Radical Potential of Queer Politics?," *GLQ: A Journal of Lesbian and Gay Studies* 3, no. 4 (1997): 437–65; Mariarosa Dalla Costa and Selma James, *The Power of Women and the Subversion of the Community* (London: Falling Wall Press, 1972); Angela Y. Davis, *Women, Race, & Class* (New York: Vintage Books, 1981); Roderick A. Ferguson, *Aberrations in Black: Toward a Queer of Color Critique* (Minneapolis: University of Minnesota Press, 2004); Hall, "Race, Articulation and Societies Structured in Dominance."

50. Assata Shakur, *Assata: An Autobiography* (Chicago: Lawrence Hill Books, 1987).

PART ONE

1. Erika Lee, *At America's Gates: Chinese Immigration during the Exclusion Era, 1882–1943* (Chapel Hill: University of North Carolina Press, 2003).

2. See Madeline Hsu, *Dreaming of Gold, Dreaming of Home: Transnationalism and Migration Between the United States and South China, 1882–1943* (Stanford, CA: Stanford University Press, 2000); Estelle T. Lau, *Paper Families: Identity, Immigration Administration, and Chinese Exclusion* (Durham, NC: Duke University Press, 2007); Lee, *At America's Gates;* Haiming Liu, *The Transnational History of a Chinese Family: Immigrant Letters, Family Business, and Reverse Migration* (New Brunswick, NJ: Rutgers University Press, 2005); Eithne Luibheid, *Entry Denied: Controlling Sexuality at the Border* (Minneapolis: University of Minnesota Press, 2002); Mae M. Ngai, *Impossible Subjects: Illegal Aliens and the Making of Modern America* (Princeton, NJ: Princeton University Press, 2005).

3. See Ruth Wilson Gilmore, "Forgotten Places and the Seeds of Grassroots Planning," in *Engaging Contradictions: Theory, Politics, and Methods of Activist Scholarship,* ed. Charles R. Hale (Berkeley: University of California Press, 2008), 31–61.

4. Lisa Lowe, *Immigrant Acts: On Asian American Cultural Politics* (Durham, NC: Duke University Press, 1996); see also Roderick A. Ferguson, *Aberrations in Black: Toward a Queer of Color Critique* (Minneapolis: University of Minnesota Press, 2004); Grace Kyungwon Hong, *The Ruptures of American Capital: Women of Color Feminism and the Culture of Immigrant Labor* (Minneapolis: University of Minnesota Press, 2006).

1. Bruce A. Elleman, *Modern Chinese Warfare, 1795–1989* (New York: Routledge, 2001); Chi-Ming Hou, "Some Reflections on the Economic History of Modern China (1840–1949)," *Journal of Economic History* 23, no. 4 (1963): 595–605; Bowei Lu, Guoping Wang, and Caishi Dong, *The Revolution of 1911: Turning Point in Modern Chinese History* (Beijing: Foreign Languages Press, 1991); Edward J.M. Rhoads, *China's Republican Revolution: The Case of Kwangtung, 1895–1913* (Cambridge, MA: Harvard University Press, 1975); Ranbir Vohra, *China's Path to Modernization: A Historical Review from 1800 to the Present* (Englewood Cliffs, NJ: Prentice Hall, 1987); Peter Worthing, *A Military History of Modern China: From the Manchu Conquest to Tian'anmen Square* (Westport, CT: Praeger, 2007); Yongming Zhou, *Historicizing Online Politics: Telegraphy, the Internet, and Political Participation in China* (Stanford, CA: Stanford University Press, 2006), 40–41, 47–49.

2. Janet Lee Scott, *For Gods, Ghosts and Ancestors: The Chinese Tradition of Paper Offerings* (Kowloon: Hong Kong University Press, 2007), 6.

3. Roderick Cave, *Chinese Paper Offerings* (New York: Oxford University Press, 1998), 1; Dard Hunter, *Chinese Ceremonial Paper: A Monograph Relating to the Fabrication of Paper and Tin Foil and the Use of Paper in Chinese Rites and Religious Ceremonies* (Chillicothe, OH: Mountain House Press, 1937); Scott, *For Gods, Ghosts and Ancestors,* 21.

4. Floyd Alonzo McClure, *Chinese Handmade Paper,* ed. Elaine Koretsky (Newtown, PA: Bird & Bull Press, 1986 [1928]); Jixing Pan, "The Origin of Papermaking in the Light of Scientific Research on Recent Archeological Discoveries," in *Chinese Studies: Papers Presented at a Colloquium at the School of Oriental and African Studies, University of London, 24–26 August 1987,* ed. Francis Wood (London: British Library, 1988), 176–80.

5. Jacob Eyferth, "Craft Knowledge at the Interface of Written and Oral Cultures," *East Asian Science, Technology and Society: An International Journal* 4, no. 2 (2010): 210; Jacob Eyferth, "Socialist Deskilling: The Struggle over Skills in a Rural Craft Industry, 1949–1965," in *How China Works: Perspectives on the Twentieth-Century Industrial Workplace,* ed. Jacob Eyferth (New York: Routledge, 2006), 42.

6. Christopher A. Reed, *Gutenberg in Shanghai: Chinese Print Capitalism, 1876–1937* (Vancouver: University of British Columbia Press, 2005); Zhou, *Historicizing Online Politics,* 40.

7. Quoted in Ying-wan Cheng, *Postal Communication in China and Its Modernization, 1860–1896* (Cambridge, MA: Harvard University Press, 1970), vii.

8. Reed, *Gutenberg in Shanghai,* 17.

9. Territory in Shanghai was ceded along with Hong Kong in the 1842 Treaty of Nanjing that declared the end of the first British Opium War. The SMC's Constitution consisted of Land Regulations drafted by the land renters themselves, its governing body elected from among the foreign ratepayers and its franchise extended according to tax paid. In addition to excluding Chinese from membership, the SMC did not pay taxes to the Chinese government. It identified its main tasks as the

administration of SMC police/paramilitary forces, public works, and public health. See Charles W. Dougan, *The Shanghai Postal System* (State College, PA: American Philatelic Society, 1981); J. H. Haan, "Origin and Development of the Political System in the Shanghai International Settlement," *Journal of the Hong Kong Branch of the Royal Asiatic Society* 22 (1982): 31–64; Chi-Ming Hou, "Some Reflections on the Economic History of Modern China (1840–1949)," *Journal of Economic History* 23, no. 4 (1963): 595–605; Rhoads, *China's Republican Revolution*.

10. Reed, *Gutenberg in Shanghai*, 15–17.

11. Cheng, *Postal Communication in China and Its Modernization, 1860–1896*; Dougan, *The Shanghai Postal System*; Shi Fan, ed., *The Stamps of China 1878–1981* (Beijing: Foreign Languages Press, 1983).

12. James W. Carey, *Communication as Culture: Essays on Media and Society* (Boston, MA: Psychology Press, 1989), 223–24; Richard Menke, *Telegraphic Realism: Victorian Fiction and Other Information Systems* (Stanford, CA: Stanford University Press, 2007). Carey notes that the need to create coherent U.S. railroad schedules established Standard Time in 1883, setting the precedent for the worldwide hegemony of fixed time for transportation and communication.

13. Erik Baark, *Lightning Wires: The Telegraph and China's Technological Modernization, 1860–1890* (Westport, CT: Greenwood Press, 1997), 71, 80–81; Lu, Wang, and Dong, *The Revolution of 1911*, 119; Zhou, *Historicizing Online Politics*, 14.

14. Cheng, *Postal Communication in China and Its Modernization, 1860–1896*; Dougan, *The Shanghai Postal System*. Prior to the implementation of the new postal system, colonial mail circulated through the semiautonomous British Hong Kong Post Office, opened in 1841, as well as "guest posts" opened by the United States, Japan, France, Germany, Italy, and Russia in occupied territories.

15. Joseph Edkins, *The Religious Condition of the Chinese: With Observations on the Prospects of Christian Conversion Amongst That People* (London: Routledge, Warnes, & Routledge, 1859), 1–2.

16. Thomas Francis Carter, *The Invention of Printing in China and Its Spread Westward* (New York: Columbia University Press, 1925), ix.

17. Ibid., 238; Ts'ai Lun (Wade-Giles Romanization system; Cai Lun in Pinyin) is credited as having invented paper in the Yuanxing period of the Eastern Han dynasty, or ca. 105 C.E., and became popularly known as the god of papermakers after his story was first recorded by the Chinese historian Fan Ye (397–445). The contemporary archaeologist Pan Jixing points out that "plant fiber paper made of hemp datable before Christ has been excavated five times in various places in China in 1933, 1957, 1973, 1978, and 1979." Pan thus concludes, "Paper was invented in the Western Han dynasty, in the second to the first century BC. Its inventor, therefore, was not Cai Lun, but craftsmen whose names are unknown.... Papermaking, like other ancient techniques, could not have been invented accidentally by a single person, but must have gone through a historical evolution. Our experience of making paper has taught us that an individual could not perfect processes of papermaking, which is a collaborative labor.... There is no basis for further perpetuating the theory that Cai Lun invented paper." See Pan, "The Origin of Papermaking," 177–78, 180.

18. During this period in China, at the nascent nation-state scale, numerous historical blocs both indigenous and foreign to the territory continually battled for political control, all of whom struggled for and none of whom won the hegemony. While myriad movements led to an unstable Chinese Republican government in 1911 and helped give birth to a unified modern Chinese national identity, it was dominant without being hegemonic, working through ideologies of a modern bourgeois revolution that could not ultimately reconcile the material and social conditions of the 90 percent of the population who were rural peasants. From 1911 until the start of a lawless warlord period in 1916, imperialist Chinese blocs, under former Qing military commander and new president of the republic, Yuan Shikai, reconsolidated and dominated in government positions to negotiate Westernized restructuring and alliance with colonial powers in the name of the Chinese nation-state. See Elleman, *Modern Chinese Warfare, 1795–1989;* Ranajit Guha, *Dominance without Hegemony: History and Power in Colonial India* (Cambridge, MA: Harvard University Press, 1997); Hou, "Some Reflections on the Economic History of Modern China (1840–1949)"; Lu, Wang, and Dong, *The Revolution of 1911;* Vohra, *China's Path to Modernization;* Worthing, *A Military History of Modern China.*

19. The categories I will rely on to construct this analysis, namely, the "Imperialist Chinese" and "Nationalist Party" blocs, mark more of a general attempt to organize and clarify a density of information rather than an assertion of these categories as fixed or even adequate; in fact, Reed argues that there is no historical consensus about this period. I do not name explicitly a Chinese "capitalist" or "bourgeoisie" historical bloc, as is more common in Marxian analyses of capitalist development, because of what I can discern of the basic differences between Chinese and European capitalisms. As the dynamics of late Qing restructuring set the conditions for how Chinese national capitalism would take root and grow, the specificities of the preexisting imperial, social, and epistemological order, as well as the parasitism of Western capitalism, created circumstances in which Chinese national capitalism was never imagined as a "free market" the same way other systems were. Instead, beginning with Self-Strengthening policies of the 1860s, those in the position and with the will to develop a form of Chinese capitalism were bound to, when they were not identical with, reformers in Qing government. Upsurges and declines thereafter of a small number of fully privately run Chinese capitalist enterprises were not viable due to the challenges of securing sustainable operating capital. Moreover, the uneven trajectory of industrial reorganization beginning at this time did not follow any teleology; rather, premodern and modern forms of industry continued to mature in apposition rather than necessarily in competition with one another. In these senses, a conceivable Chinese bourgeoisie or aspiring capitalist contingent does not seem to define its own social body during this period, so much as these actors weres scattered and constantly moving between other preestablished or more coherent historical blocs, each increasingly articulated through competing (proto)nationalist discourses and all vying for emergent-state power, with different ideas for how Chinese national capitalism should be designed and grow and particularly in relation to threats posed by Western capitalist forces.

The emergent Nationalist Party bloc overlapped with what I have labeled the Imperialist Chinese bloc in significant ways. In 1905, Sun Yatsen consolidated various disparate anti-Qing revolutionary groups into the Teng Meng Hui (Alliance Society), which he hoped to unite under the platform of the Three People's Principles: nationalism (unity among all people as Chinese); democracy (overthrowing the existing imperial order and establishing China as a modern nation-state); and people's livelihood (equalizing land rights through a combination of capitalist and socialist laws and practices). The strength of the first and second principles, derived mostly from their articulation with essentialist anti-Manchu fervor, unified vast segments of the population. However, resistance to the third principle, in the struggle to define what Chinese capitalism would be, led to divided and inconsistent loyalties among members, with many people regularly switching their allegiances between blocs during and following the revolutionary period. While Sun Yatsen himself remained steadfastly devoted to the Three People's Principles, others within the ranks of the Ten Meng Hui espoused different party lines. These primarily refer to a "One People's Principle," i.e., nationalism based on anti-Manchu sentiment and Han purity; and the "Two People's Principles," nationalism and commitment to a republican constitution organizing China as a nation-state. Teng Meng Hui reconsolidated as the Goumindang (KMT, Chinese Nationalist Party) after Yuan Shikai took the republican presidency in 1912 and ruled nonetheless as self-appointed emperor. My cursory research leads me to assume that the two blocs, Nationalist and Imperialist, eventually moved toward consolidation as one under the KMT led by Chiang Kai-shek, rising to dominance in 1928 and defeated by the Communist bloc in 1949. See Elleman, *Modern Chinese Warfare, 1795–1989;* Eyferth, "Craft Knowledge at the Interface of Written and Oral Cultures"; Hou, "Some Reflections on the Economic History of Modern China (1840–1949)"; Lu, Wang, and Dong, *The Revolution of 1911;* Vohra, *China's Path to Modernization;* Worthing, *A Military History of Modern China.*

20. Reed, *Gutenberg in Shanghai,* 12–13.

21. Ibid., 300; in 2008, China's national intelligentsia revised "the four great inventions" in light of the colonial influence of its first discursive iteration. The new references are papermaking and printing (considered as one invention), bronze, silk, and porcelain. See "Do We Need to Redefine the Top Four Inventions?," *Beijing Review,* 28 August 2008, http://www.bjreview.com.cn/special/txt/2008–08/26 /content_146777.htm.

22. I offer here a slight revision, based on a different way of thinking about essentialism and ontological totality, of the formulation presented in Wendy Cheng, "Strategic Orientalism: Racial Capitalism and the Problem of 'Asianness,'" *African Identities* 11, no. 2 (2013): 148–58.

23. Benedict Anderson, *Imagined Communities: Reflections on the Origin and Spread of Nationalism,* rev. ed. (New York: Verso, 2006 [1983]).

24. Adam McKeown, *Chinese Migrant Networks and Cultural Change: Peru, Chicago, and Hawaii 1900–1936* (Chicago: University of Chicago Press, 2001), 119.

25. Scott, *For Gods, Ghosts and Ancestors,* 216.

26. Lu, Wang, and Dong, *The Revolution of 1911;* Reed, *Gutenberg in Shanghai,* 220–21, 270–79.

27. Rhoads, *China's Republican Revolution,* 148, 154. According to Rhoads, the independent Canton Merchants' Self-Government Society represented the most active local movement in Guangdong at the turn of the century. Self-Government Society activists were removed from Canton's official chamber of commerce, instead aligning with merchants organized as the independent Canton Seventy-Two Guilds. These organizations contended with the Qing-sanctioned Association for the Study of Self-Government. Responding to demands for more regional and local political autonomy, Qing reforms at the time included the creation of provincial assemblies that were ultimately accountable to the central government yet had some independent ability to decide how to adapt general mandates to local conditions. Under these terms, the traditional government-scholar elite and the emergent merchant class also organized to win positions on the Provincial Assembly in Guangdong, formalized in 1909.

28. Ibid., 15–17, 127.

29. McKeown, *Chinese Migrant Networks and Cultural Change,* 66.

30. Lau, *Paper Families,* 61–62; McKeown, *Chinese Migrant Networks and Cultural Change,* 66–70; Ronald Takaki, *Strangers from a Different Shore: A History of Asian Americans* (New York: Penguin, 1989), 22–24.

31. Oscar O. Winther, "Promoting the American West in England, 1865–1890," *Journal of Economic History* 16, no. 4 (1956): 507–8.

32. Rhoads, *China's Republican Revolution,* 27. These newspapers were the *China Mail* (founded in 1845), the *Daily Press* (1857), and the *Telegraph* (1881).

33. Lau, *Paper Families,* 61–63; Takaki, *Strangers from a Different Shore,* 22–24; see also Kil Young Zo, *Chinese Emigration into the United States, 1850–1880* (New York: Arno Press, 1971).

34. See Rodolfo Acuña, *Occupied America: A History of Chicanos* (New York: Harper & Row, 1988); Tomás Almaguer, *Racial Fault Lines: The Historical Origins of White Supremacy in California* (Berkeley: University of California Press, 1994); Martha Menchaca, *Recovering History, Constructing Race: The Indian, Black, and White Roots of Mexican Americans* (Austin: University of Texas Press, 2001).

35. Ruth Wilson Gilmore, *Golden Gulag: Prisons, Surplus, Crisis, and Opposition in Globalizing California* (Berkeley: University of California Press, 2007).

36. Almaguer, *Racial Fault Lines,* 13–14, 32–41; W. E. B. DuBois, *Black Reconstruction in America 1860–1880* (New York: Simon and Schuster, 1935), 28; Reginald Horsman, *Race and Manifest Destiny: The Origins of American Racial Anglo-Saxonism* (Cambridge, MA: Harvard University Press, 1981); Alexander Saxton, *The Indispensable Enemy: Labor and the Anti-Chinese Movement in California* (Berkeley: University of California Press, 1971).

37. See William Deverell, *Whitewashed Adobe: The Rise of Los Angeles and the Remaking of Its Mexican Past* (Berkeley: University of California Press, 2005); Greg Hise, "Border City: Race and Social Distance in Los Angeles," *American Quarterly* 56, no. 3 (2004): 545–58; Saxton, *The Indispensable Enemy,* 21–37; Mark Wild, *Street*

Meeting: Multiethnic Neighborhoods in Early Twentieth-Century Los Angeles (Berkeley: University of California Press, 2005).

38. See Daniel R. Headrick, *The Tools of Empire: Technology and European Imperialism in the Nineteenth Century* (Oxford: Oxford University Press, 1981); Clyde Woods, *Development Arrested: Race, Power, and the Blues in the Mississippi Delta* (New York: Verso Books, 1998), 60.

39. Frank H. Spearman, "The First Transcontinental Railroad," *Harper's Monthly Magazine* 109 (November 1904): 715–16.

40. David Howard Bain, *Empire Express: Building the First Transcontinental Railroad* (New York: Penguin Books, 2000); Richard D. Brown, *Knowledge Is Power* (Oxford: Oxford University Press, 1989); Carey, *Communication as Culture;* William Deverell, *Railroad Crossing: Californians and the Railroad, 1850–1910* (Berkeley: University of California Press, 1996); Richard R. John, *Spreading the News: The American Postal System from Franklin to Morse* (Cambridge, MA: Harvard University Press, 1995); Richard Thomas Stillson, *Spreading the Word: A History of Information in the California Gold Rush* (Lincoln: University of Nebraska Press, 2006); Richard White, *Railroaded: The Transcontinentals and the Making of Modern America* (New York: Norton, 2011).

41. See Douglas Flamming, *Bound for Freedom: Black Los Angeles in Jim Crow America* (Berkeley: University of California, 2006); Helen Heran Jun, *Race for Citizenship: Black Orientalism and Asian Uplift from Pre-Emancipation to Neoliberal America* (New York: New York University Press, 2011); Laura Pulido, *Black, Brown, Yellow, and Left: Radical Activism in Los Angeles* (Berkeley: University of California, 2005); George J. Sanchez, "Face the Nation: Race, Immigration, and the Rise of Nativism in Late Twentieth Century America," *International Migration Review* 31, no. 4 (1 December 1997): 1009–30.

42. DuBois, *Black Reconstruction;* Eric Foner, *Reconstruction: America's Unfinished Revolution, 1863–1877* (New York: Harper & Row, 1988); Woods, *Development Arrested.*

43. Quoted in James W. Loewen, *The Mississippi Chinese: Between Black and White* (Long Grove, IL: Waveland Press, 1971), 22.

44. DuBois, *Black Reconstruction,* 670.

45. Douglas S. Massey and Nancy A. Denton, *American Apartheid: Segregation and the Making of the Underclass* (Cambridge, MA: Harvard University Press, 1993); Bobby M. Wilson, *America's Johannesburg: Industrialization and Racial Transformation in Birmingham* (New York: Rowman & Littlefield, 2000).

46. In Woods, *Development Arrested,* 100–101.

47. Fred Moten, "The Case of Blackness," *Criticism* 50, no. 2 (3 July 2008): 177–218; Fred Moten, "Black Op," *PMLA* 123, no. 5 (2008): 1743–47; Clyde Woods, "Necropolitics Blues" (paper presented at the Critical Ethnic Studies Conference, Riverside, CA, 2010); Woods, *Development Arrested,* 100–101; cf. Orlando Patterson, *Slavery and Social Death: A Comparative Study* (Cambridge, MA: Harvard University Press, 1982).

48. Loewen, *The Mississippi Chinese,* 21–26.

49. Almaguer, *Racial Fault Lines,* 46–74; Matthew Frye Jacobson, *Whiteness of a Different Color: European Immigrants and the Alchemy of Race* (Cambridge, MA: Harvard University Press, 1999); Pulido, *Black, Brown, Yellow, and Left.*

50. Ping Chiu, *Chinese Labor in California, 1850–1880: An Economic Study* (Madison: State Historical Society of Wisconsin for the Dept. of History, University of Winconsin, 1967); DuBois, *Black Reconstruction;* Barbara Jean Fields, "Slavery, Race and Ideology in the United States of America," *New Left Review* 181 (June 1990): 95–118; Foner, *Reconstruction;* Lowe, *Immigrant Acts;* Elizabeth Sutherland Martínez, *De Colores Means All of Us: Latina Views for a Multi-Colored Century* (Boston, MA: South End Press, 1998); Takaki, *Strangers from a Different Shore.*

51. Jun, *Race for Citizenship;* Colleen Lye, *America's Asia: Racial Form and American Literature, 1893–1945* (Princeton, NJ: Princeton University Press, 2005).

52. Lee, *At America's Gates;* Lowe, *Immigrant Acts;* Jean Pfaelzer, *Driven Out: The Forgotten War against Chinese Americans* (Berkeley: University of California Press, 2008); Saxton, *The Indispensable Enemy;* Takaki, *Strangers from a Different Shore.*

53. Mark V. Cushman, "Uncertain Frontiers: Asian Immigration and U.S. Citizenship in the Age of Expansion" (PhD diss., Johns Hopkins University, 1999), 6–7, 90–91, 148–53.

54. See Alice Childress, "A Candle in Gale Wind," in *Black Women Writers (1950–1980),* ed. Mari Evans (Garden City, NY: Anchor Books, 1984), 111–16; Frederick Douglass, *Narrative of the Life of Frederick Douglass* (New York: Dover Publications, 1995 [1845]); W. E. B. DuBois, *The Souls of Black Folk: Essays and Sketches* (Chicago: A. C. McClurg & Co., 1903); Evelyn Nakano Glenn, *Unequal Freedom: How Race and Gender Shaped American Citizenship and Labor* (Cambridge, MA: Harvard University Press, 2002).

55. DuBois, *Black Reconstruction;* Foner, *Reconstruction.*

56. Andrea Smith, *Conquest: Sexual Violence and American Indian Genocide* (Boston, MA: South End Press, 2005), 35–36.

57. Luana Ross, *Inventing the Savage: The Social Construction of Native American Criminality* (Austin: University of Texas Press, 1998), 17–18; Woods, *Development Arrested.*

58. Mae M. Ngai, *Impossible Subjects: Illegal Aliens and the Making of Modern America* (Princeton, NJ: Princeton University Press, 2005), 19.

59. H. Mark Lai, Genny Lim, and Judy Yung, *Island: Poetry and History of Chinese Immigrants on Angel Island 1910–1940* (Seattle: University of Washington Press, 1991); Takaki, *Strangers from a Different Shore.*

60. Adam McKeown, *Melancholy Order: Asian Migration and the Globalization of Borders* (New York: Columbia University Press, 2008).

61. Daniel Chu and Samuel Chu, *Passage to the Golden Gate: A History of the Chinese in America to 1910* (New York: Doubleday, 1967); Hsu, *Dreaming of Gold, Dreaming of Home;* H. Mark Lai, *Becoming Chinese American: A History of Communities and Institutions* (Walnut Creek, CA: Rowman Altamira, 2004).

62. Rhoads, *China's Republican Revolution,* 149; see also Baark, *Lightning Wires.* Chinese entrepreneurs could not raise the start-up capital to establish the ultimately failed Guangdong-Guangxi Mail Steamship Company until 1907.

63. Cushman, "Uncertain Frontiers," 157–58.

64. Robert Barde, "The Scandalous Ship Mongolia," *Steamboat Bill,* no. 250 (2004): 112–18; Lai, Lim, and Yung, *Island;* Lee, *At America's Gates.*

65. Ruth Wilson Gilmore, "Race, Prisons and War: Scenes from the History of US Violence," *Socialist Register 2009: Violence Today* 45 (2009): 82.

66. See Kelly Lytle Hernández, *Migra! A History of the U.S. Border Patrol* (Berkeley: University of California, 2010).

67. Luibheid, *Entry Denied;* Adam McKeown, "The Ritualization of Regulation: The Enforcement of Chinese Exclusion in the United States and China," *American Historical Review* 108, no. 2 (2003): 377–403; Natalia Molina, *Fit to Be Citizens? Public Health and Race in Los Angeles, 1879–1939* (Berkeley: University of California Press, 2006); Anna Pegler-Gordon, "Chinese Exclusion, Photography, and the Development of U.S. Immigration Policy," *American Quarterly* 58, no. 1 (2006): 51–77; Nayan Shah, *Contagious Divides: Epidemics and Race in San Francisco's Chinatown* (Berkeley: University of California Press, 2001).

68. Lai, Lim, and Yung, *Island,* 100. Original footnote for "Yingtai Island" reads: "An island in the Nan Hai (Southern Lake), west of the Forbidden City in Peking. Emperor Guangxu (1875–1908) was imprisoned here by the Empress Dowager Cixi in 1898 after a coup d'etat to halt his reform programs."

CHAPTER TWO

1. Chi-Ming Hou, "Some Reflections on the Economic History of Modern China (1840–1949)," *Journal of Economic History* 23, no. 4 (1963): 598.

2. Charles W. Dougan, *The Shanghai Postal System* (State College, PA: American Philatelic Society, 1981), 6.

3. Quoted in Ying-wan Cheng, *Postal Communication in China and Its Modernization, 1860–1896* (Cambridge, MA: Harvard University Press, 1970), vii.

4. Ibid., 45–46.

5. Ruth Wilson Gilmore, "Forgotten Places and the Seeds of Grassroots Planning," in *Engaging Contradictions: Theory, Politics, and Methods of Activist Scholarship,* ed. Charles R. Hale (Berkeley: University of California Press, 2008), 31–61; Roderick A. Ferguson, *Aberrations in Black: Toward a Queer of Color Critique* (Minneapolis: University of Minnesota Press, 2004); Judith Halberstam, *In a Queer Time and Place: Transgender Bodies, Subcultural Lives* (New York: New York University Press, 2005); Grace Kyungwon Hong, *The Ruptures of American Capital: Women of Color Feminism and the Culture of Immigrant Labor* (Minneapolis: University of Minnesota Press, 2006); Lisa Lowe and David Lloyd, *The Politics of Culture in the Shadow of Capital* (Durham, NC: Duke University Press, 1997); Alondra Nelson, Thuy Linh N. Tu, and Alicia Headlam Hines, eds., *Technicolor: Race,*

Technology, and Everyday Life (New York: New York University Press, 2001); Clyde Woods, *Development Arrested: Race, Power, and the Blues in the Mississippi Delta* (New York: Verso Books, 1998).

6. Adam McKeown, *Chinese Migrant Networks and Cultural Change: Peru, Chicago, and Hawaii 1900–1936* (Chicago: University of Chicago Press, 2001), 66–69.

7. H. Mark Lai, *Becoming Chinese American: A History of Communities and Institutions* (Walnut Creek, CA: Rowman Altamira, 2004), 23–25.

8. See Adam McKeown, "The Ritualization of Regulation: The Enforcement of Chinese Exclusion in the United States and China," *American Historical Review* 108, no. 2 (2003): 377–403.

9. Erika Lee, *At America's Gates: Chinese Immigration during the Exclusion Era, 1882–1943* (Chapel Hill: University of North Carolina Press, 2003).

10. Estelle T. Lau, *Paper Families: Identity, Immigration Administration, and Chinese Exclusion* (Durham, NC: Duke University Press, 2007), 77–113, 148; McKeown, "The Ritualization of Regulation."

11. Many thanks to Grace Hong for helping me articulate this argument.

12. Lisa Lowe, *Immigrant Acts: On Asian American Cultural Politics* (Durham, NC: Duke University Press, 1996), 125.

13. See Joe Bray, *The Epistolary Novel: Representations of Consciousness* (New York: Routledge, 2003); Anne L. Bower, *Epistolary Responses: The Letter in 20th-Century American Fiction and Criticism* (Tuscaloosa: University of Alabama Press, 1997); Terry Castle, *Clarissa's Ciphers: Meaning and Disruption in Richardson's "Clarissa"* (Ithaca, NY: Cornell University Press, 1982); Elizabeth Heckendorn Cook, *Epistolary Bodies: Gender and Genre in the Eighteenth-Century Republic of Letters* (Stanford, CA: Stanford University Press, 1996); Rebecca Earle, *Epistolary Selves: Letters and Letter-Writers, 1600–1945* (Brooksfield, VT: Ashgate, 1999); Amanda Gilroy and W. M. Verhoeven, *Epistolary Histories: Letters, Fiction, Culture* (Charlottesville: University of Virginia Press, 2000).

14. For more examples, see also Lau, *Paper Families,* 55–57.

15. Edward C. Tolman, "Cognitive Maps in Rats and Men," *Psychological Review* 55, no. 4 (1948): 189–208; cf. Fredric Jameson, "Postmodernism, or The Cultural Logic of Late Capitalism," *New Left Review* I, no. 146 (August 1984): 53–92.

16. Eithne Luibheid, *Entry Denied: Controlling Sexuality at the Border* (Minneapolis: University of Minnesota Press, 2002), 49.

17. Lau, *Paper Families,* 131–32.

18. Haiming Liu, *The Transnational History of a Chinese Family: Immigrant Letters, Family Business, and Reverse Migration* (New Brunswick, NJ: Rutgers University Press, 2005), 21. In this work, Liu compiles, translates, and analyzes the Chang family archive of letters spanning three generations. The archive is now housed at the Chinese Historical Society of Southern California, which also generously supported and assisted in my research for this chapter.

19. Quoted in Liu, *The Transnational History of a Chinese Family,* 97–98.

20. Robert Yeok-Yin Eng, *Economic Imperialism in China: Silk Production & Exports, 1861–1932* (Berkeley: Institute of East Asian Studies, University of California, 1986); Philip C. Huang, *The Peasant Family and Rural Development in the Yangzi Delta, 1350–1988* (Stanford, CA: Stanford University Press, 1990); Min-hsiung Shih, *The Silk Industry in Ch'ing China,* trans. E-Tu Zen Sun (Ann Arbor: Center for Chinese Studies, University of Michigan Press, 1976), 30–54; Alvin Y. So, *The South China Silk District: Local Historical Transformation and World System Theory* (New York: State University of New York Press, 1986).

21. See Janice Stockard, *Daughters of the Canton Delta: Marriage Patterns and Economic Strategies in South China, 1860–1930* (Stanford, CA: Stanford University Press, 1992).

22. David A. Gerber, "Epistolary Ethics: Personal Correspondence and the Culture of Emigration in the Nineteenth Century," *Journal of American Ethnic History* 19, no. 4 (1 July 2000): 3–23; David A. Gerber, "The Immigrant Letter between Positivism and Populism: The Uses of Immigrant Personal Correspondence in Twentieth-Century American Scholarship," *Journal of American Ethnic History* 16, no. 4 (1 July 1997): 3–34.

23. H. Mark Lai, Genny Lim, and Judy Yung, *Island: Poetry and History of Chinese Immigrants on Angel Island 1910–1940* (Seattle: University of Washington Press, 1991), 14–19. According to Lai, Lim, and Yung, by 1922, Assistant Secretary of Labor Edward J. Henning and Commissioner General of Immigration W. W. Husband themselves declared the island facilities filthy and unfit for human habitation. Nevertheless, Angel Island continued in operation until fire destroyed its administration building in 1940.

24. David L. Eng, *Racial Castration: Managing Masculinity in Asian America* (Durham, NC: Duke University Press, 2001); Nayan Shah, *Contagious Divides: Epidemics and Race in San Francisco's Chinatown* (Berkeley: University of California Press, 2001).

25. Lai, Lim, and Yung, *Island.*

26. Shah, *Contagious Divides;* cf. Carolina Bank Muñoz, *Transnational Tortillas: Race, Gender, and Shop-Floor Politics in Mexico and the United States* (Ithaca, NY: Cornell University Press, 2008).

27. See Tung Pok Chin, *Paper Son: One Man's Story* (Philadephia, PA: Temple University Press, 2000).

28. Yu-Fang Cho, *Uncoupling American Empire: Cultural Politics of Deviance and Unequal Difference, 1890–1910* (Albany: State University of New York Press, 2015); Leopoldina Fortunati, *The Arcane of Reproduction: Housework, Prostitution, Labor and Capital,* trans. H. Creek (New York: Autonomedia, 1995 [1981]).

29. Luibheid, *Entry Denied;* Natalia Molina, *Fit to Be Citizens? Public Health and Race in Los Angeles, 1879–1939* (Berkeley: University of California Press, 2006); Shah, *Contagious Divides;* see also George J. Sanchez, *Becoming Mexican American: Ethnicity, Culture, and Identity in Chicano Los Angeles, 1900–1945* (New York: Oxford University Press, 1995); Alexandra Minna Stern, *Eugenic Nation: Faults and*

Frontiers of Better Breeding in Modern America (Berkeley: University of California Press, 2005). This perspective is distinct from but not entirely incompatible with the narratives presented by Chinese women petitioning for legal entry as upper-class wives and mothers, who differentiated their respectability from concubines and prostitutes.

30. "Letter Log: Correspondence from Customs Surveyor to Various, Nov 20, 1887 to Nov 18, 1889," NARA–Pacific Region, San Francisco (unprocessed).

31. See Anna Pegler-Gordon, "Chinese Exclusion, Photography, and the Development of U.S. Immigration Policy," *American Quarterly* 58, no. 1 (2006): 51–77.

32. See Tan Chung, "The Harmony of Civilization and Prosperity for All: Selected Papers of Beijing Forum (2004–2008): Where from the 'Secret of Expression' of Chinese Civilization?," *Procedia—Social and Behavioral Sciences* 2, no. 5 (1 January 2010): 7100.

33. Colleen Lye, *America's Asia: Racial Form and American Literature, 1893–1945* (Princeton, NJ: Princeton University Press, 2005), 7.

34. Cf. Clyde Woods, "Life after Death," *Professional Geographer* 54, no. 1 (2002): 66.

35. Lai, Lim, and Yung, *Island,* 16–17; L. Ling-chi Wang, "Politics of the Repeal of the Chinese Exclusion Laws," in *The Repeal and Its Legacy: Proceedings of the Conference on the 50th Anniversary of the Repeal of the Exclusion Acts* (San Francisco: Chinese Historical Society of America, 1994), 78.

36. Houston A. Baker Jr. and Patricia Redmond, *Afro-American Literary Study in the 1990s* (Chicago: University of Chicago Press, 1989); V. P. Franklin, *Living Our Stories, Telling Our Truths: Autobiography and the Making of the African-American Intellectual Tradition* (New York: Scribner, 1995); Henry Louis Gates, *The Signifying Monkey: A Theory of African-American Literary Criticism* (New York: Oxford University Press, 1989); Madelyn Jablon, *Black Metafiction: Self-Consciousness in African American Literature* (Iowa City: University of Iowa Press, 1999); Gayl Jones, *Liberating Voices: Oral Tradition in African American Literature* (Cambridge, MA: Harvard University Press, 1991); John Edgar Wideman, "Why Mumia Matters to the Nation and World" (Educators for Mumia Abu-Jamal, 9 June 2005), http://www.emajonline.com/2005/06/why-mumia-matters-to-the-nation-and-world-by-john-edgar-wideman/.

37. Chin, *Paper Son,* 25.

38. Janet Lee Scott, *For Gods, Ghosts and Ancestors: The Chinese Tradition of Paper Offerings* (Kowloon: Hong Kong University Press, 2007), 20.

39. Hortense J. Spillers, *Black, White, and in Color: Essays on American Literature and Culture* (Chicago: University of Chicago Press, 2003), 117; see also Toni Morrison, *Sula* (New York: Vintage International, 1973).

40. Chin, *Paper Son;* Peter Kwong, *Forbidden Workers: Illegal Chinese Immigrants and American Labor* (New York: New Press, 1997); Lai, *Becoming Chinese American.*

41. Shah, *Contagious Divides.*

42. Scott, *For Gods, Ghosts and Ancestors,* 20.

PART TWO

1. Miné Okubo, *Citizen 13660*, repr. ed. (Seattle: University of Washington Press, 1983 [1946]).

2. Adam McKeown, *Melancholy Order: Asian Migration and the Globalization of Borders* (New York: Columbia University Press, 2008).

3. Ruth Wilson Gilmore, "Fatal Couplings of Power and Difference: Notes on Racism and Geography," *Professional Geographer* 54, no. 1 (2002): 15–24; Stuart Hall, "Race, Culture, and Communications: Looking Backward and Forward at Cultural Studies," *Rethinking Marxism* 5, no. 1 (1 March 1992): 10–18.

4. McKeown, *Melancholy Order;* E. P. Thompson, *The Making of the English Working Class* (New York: Vintage Books, 1966); Clyde Woods, *Development Arrested: Race, Power, and the Blues in the Mississippi Delta* (New York: Verso Books, 1998); Randall Williams, *The Divided World: Human Rights and Its Violence* (Minneapolis: University of Minnesota Press, 2010).

5. McKeown, *Melancholy Order,* 201–2.

6. McKeown, *Melancholy Order;* Mae M. Ngai, *Impossible Subjects: Illegal Aliens and the Making of Modern America* (Princeton, NJ: Princeton University Press, 2005).

7. Saburo Ienaga, *The Pacific War: 1931–1945* (New York: Pantheon Books, 1979); Walter LaFeber, *The Clash: U.S.-Japanese Relations throughout History* (New York: Norton, 1998); McKeown, *Melancholy Order;* Ronald Takaki, *Strangers from a Different Shore: A History of Asian Americans* (New York: Penguin, 1989).

8. Nellie Wong, *Dreams in Harrison Railroad Park* (Berkeley: Kelsey Street Press, 1977).

9. In Ronald Takaki, *Double Victory: A Multicultural History of America in World War II* (Boston, MA: Back Bay Books, 2001), 119.

10. Iris Chang, *The Rape of Nanking: The Forgotten Holocaust of World War II* (New York: Penguin Books, 1998); cf. Takashi Fujitani, *Race for Empire: Koreans as Japanese and Japanese as Americans during World War II* (Berkeley: University of California Press, 2011).

11. Quoted in Takaki, *Double Victory,* 120.

12. Fred Moten, "Black Op," *PMLA* 123, no. 5 (2008): 1743–47; Michel Foucault, *The History of Sexuality, Volume 1: An Introduction,* trans. Robert Hurley (New York: Vintage Books, 1990).

CHAPTER THREE

1. The term *Japanese American* as used in this chapter refers to people of Japanese ancestry living in the United States; it is not intended to name a self-asserted political identity or denote citizenship status. I also use the term *Nikkei,* following from common scholarly and social usage, to refer generally to people of Japanese ancestry or the Japanese diaspora.

2. Brian Masaru Hayashi, *Democratizing the Enemy: The Japanese American Internment* (Princeton, NJ: Princeton University Press, 2004).

3. See Nahum Dimitri Chandler, *X—The Problem of the Negro as a Problem for Thought* (New York: Fordham University Press, 2013), 1.

4. George J. Sanchez, "Disposable People, Expendable Neighborhoods," in *A Companion to Los Angeles,* ed. William Deverell and Greg Hise (Hoboken, NJ: Wiley-Blackwell, 2010), 129–46.

5. Bob Kumamoto, "The Search for Spies: American Counterintelligence and the Japanese American Community 1931–1942," *Amerasia Journal* 6, no. 2 (1 October 1979): 45–75; cf. Lane R. Hirabayashi and James A. Hirabayashi, "A Reconsideration of the United States Military's Role in the Violation of Japanese-American Citizenship Rights," in *Ethnicity and War,* ed. Winston A. Van Horne and Thomas V. Tonnesen (Milwaukee: University of Wisconsin System, American Ethnic Studies Coordinating Committee/Urban Corridor Consortium, 1984), 87–110; Greg Robinson, *By Order of the President: FDR and the Internment of Japanese Americans* (Cambridge, MA: Harvard University Press, 2001); Michi Weglyn, *Years of Infamy: The Untold Story of America's Concentration Camps* (New York: Morrow Quill Paperbacks, 1976).

6. Kumamoto, "The Search for Spies," 56; emphasis in original ONI document.

7. Gary Okihiro, *Cane Fires: The Anti-Japanese Movement in Hawaii, 1865–1945* (Philadephia, PA: Temple University Press, 1991); Robinson, *By Order of the President.*

8. Louis Fiset, "Return to Sender: U.S. Censorship of Enemy Alien Mail in World War II," *National Archives and Records Administration Prologue Magazine,* Spring 2001, http://www.archives.gov/publications/prologue/2001/spring/mail-censorship-in-world-war-two-1.html; Louis Fiset, *Imprisoned Apart: The World War II Correspondence of an Issei Couple* (Seattle: University of Washington Press, 1998).

9. Roger Daniels, *Prisoners without Trial: Japanese Americans in World War II* (New York: Hill and Wang, 1993).

10. Kumamoto, "The Search for Spies."

11. Ibid.; George Lipsitz, *Possessive Investment in Whiteness* (Philadelphia, PA: Temple University Press, 1998), 185–211.

12. The secret Munson Report, commissioned by FDR and written by Special Representative of the State Department Curtis B. Munson in November 1941, contains "four divisions of Japanese to be considered"—Issei, Nisei, Kibei, and Sansei—followed by subjective definitions. For clips of the report, see Michi Weglyn, *Years of Infamy,* 42.

13. See May M. Ngai, *Impossible Subjects: Illegal Aliens and the Making of Modern America* (Princeton, NJ: Princeton University Press, 2005; Robinson, *By Order of the President;* Ronald Takaki, *Strangers from a Different Shore: A History of Asian Americans* (New York: Penguin, 1989).

14. Fiset, *Imprisoned Apart;* Kumamoto, "The Search for Spies."

15. Fiset, "Return to Sender"; Fiset, *Imprisoned Apart*.

16. Fiset, "Return to Sender," 1–3; Ngai, *Impossible Subjects*, 175–76.

17. Fiset, *Imprisoned Apart*, 31; Hayashi, *Democratizing the Enemy*, 86.

18. Emery Clay III, Stephen Hosapple, and Satsuki Ina, *From a Silk Cocoon*, DVD (Hesono O Productions and Center for Asian American Media, 2006); Daniels, *Prisoners without Trial;* Roger Daniels, "Relocation, Redress, and the Report: A Historical Appraisal," in *Japanese Americans: From Relocation to Redress,* ed. Roger Daniels, Sandra C. Taylor, and Harry H. L. Kitano (Salt Lake City: University of Utah Press, 1986), 6; Donna K. Nagata, *Legacy of Injustice: Exploring the Cross-Generational Impact of the Japanese American Internment* (New York: Plenum Press, 1993), xiii.

19. Kumamoto, "The Search for Spies," 71.

20. Toru Saito, Interview with author, Berkeley, CA, 28 March 2010. Saito was born in 1937 and raised in Richmond, California. He and family were imprisoned in Topaz, Utah, and returned to Richmond after the war. As an adult, Saito worked as a group counselor at the Alameda County Probation Department Juvenile Hall; he also served as a correctional officer at the Marin County Adult Jail Honor Farm and at Napa County Jail. Saito is an author, musician, and singer. He and Bessie Masuda have been married since 1997.

21. Shirley Castelnuovo, *Soldiers of Conscience: Japanese American Military Resisters in World War II* (Westport, CT: Praeger, 2008); Daniels, *Prisoners without Trial;* Lawson Fusao Inada, ed., *Only What We Could Carry: The Japanese American Internment Experience* (Berkeley, CA: Heyday, 2000); Robinson, *By Order of the President*.

22. Daniels, *Prisoners without Trial*, 46–47; Violet Kazue De Cristoforo, *May Sky: There Is Always Tomorrow: An Anthology of Japanese American Concentration Camp Kaiko Haiku* (Los Angeles, CA: Sun and Moon Press, 1997); Marita Sturken, "The Absent Images of Memory: Remembering and Reenacting the Japanese Internment," *Positions* 5, no. 3 (Winter 1997): 687–707.

23. There are countless dimensions to the question of what purposes EO 9066 served and many other important directions or perspectives that scholars have taken to pursue it. Artist, historian, and camp survivor Michi Weglyn made an incisive early argument that U.S. prison camps were part of a globally designed American racism that positioned diasporic Japanese as expendable civilians (hostages) whom, if necessary, the United States could manipulate as collateral or barter as concessions in international prisoner of war exchanges. See Weglyn, *Years of Infamy,* 56; cf. Hayashi, *Democratizing the Enemy,* 5–6; Robinson, *By Order of the President,* 66–67. As extreme as this may seem, the extradition of fourteen-year-old Nisei Marion Kanemoto in exchange for American POWs in Japan provides evidence for such a claim. See Stephen Hosapple and Satsuki Ina, *Children of the Camps,* DVD (Center for Asian American Media, 1999). Conversely, Nisei students who were studying abroad in Japan when the United States entered World War II were not allowed to return. As in the case of Mary Kimoto, they were both witness to and victims of bombings and air raids perpetrated by the U.S. military on "foreign" soil,

while censorship of international mail also prevented them from knowing the status of their families in camps. See Mary Kimoto Tomita, *Dear Miye: Letters Home from Japan, 1939–1946* (Stanford, CA: Stanford University Press, 1997).

24. See, e.g., Karen Leong and Myla Vicente Carpio, eds., "Carceral States," *Amerasia Journal* 42, no. 1 (2016); Colleen Lye, *America's Asia: Racial Form and American Literature, 1893–1945* (Princeton, NJ: Princeton University Press, 2005); Valerie J. Matsumoto, *Farming the Home Place: A Japanese Community in California, 1919–1982* (Ithaca, NY: Cornell University Press, 1993); Gary Okihiro and David Drummond, "The Concentration Camps and Japanese Economic Losses in California Agriculture, 1900–1942," in Daniels, Taylor, and Kitano, *Japanese Americans,* 168–75.

25. Hannah Arendt, *The Origins of Totalitarianism* (New York: Harcourt, Brace and Co., 1951), 440; Bill Nasson, *The South African Boer War 1899–1902* (New York: Oxford University Press, 1999), 192, 218–24; Thomas Pakenham, *The Boer War* (New York: Random House, 1979), 248–50.

26. Nasson, *The South African Boer War 1899–1902,* 267; Sylvia R. Lazos Vargas, "History, Legal Scholarship, and LatCrit Theory: The Case of Racial Transformations circa the Spanish American War, 1896–1900," *Denver University Law Review* 78, no. 4 (2001): 924.

27. Paul Kramer, *The Blood of Government* (Chapel Hill: University of North Carolina Press, 2006), 153; see also Richard E. Welch, "American Atrocities in the Philippines: The Indictment and the Response," *Pacific Historical Review* 43, no. 2 (May 1974): 245.

28. Kramer, *The Blood of Government,* 131, 152–53.

29. E. San Juan, "We Charge Genocide: A Brief History of US in the Philippines," *Politicalaffairs.net: Marxist Thought Online,* 2005, http://politicalaffairs .net/we-charge-genocide-a-brief-history-of-us-in-the-philippines/. According to San Juan, his figure "doesn't include the thousands of Moros [Muslims in the Philippines] killed in the first two decades of U.S. colonial domination."

30. Paul Gilroy, *Against Race: Imagining Political Culture beyond the Color Line* (Cambridge, MA: Harvard University Press, 2000); Achille Mbembe, "Necropolitics," *Public Culture* 15, no. 1 (21 December 2003): 11–40.

31. In Studs Terkel, *"The Good War": An Oral History of World War Two* (New York: Pantheon Books, 1984), 200–201; cf. Gerald F. Linderman, *The World within War: America's Combat Experience in World War II* (Cambridge, MA: Harvard University Press, 1999), 143–87.

32. While outside the scope of this chapter, the perspective offered here could be elaborated to analyze Nikkei concentration camps instituted in other Allied nation-states or territories throughout the Americas, the majority organized by the U.S. State Department. Other countries participating in Nikkei reconcentration included Canada, Australia, Peru, Bolivia, Colombia, Costa Rica, the Dominican Republic, Ecuador, El Salvador, Guatemala, Haiti, Honduras, Mexico, Nicaragua, Panama, Peru, and Venezuela. See Weglyn, *Years of Infamy,* 59; Robinson, *By Order of the President.*

33. Campbell Craig and Sergey Radchenko, *The Atomic Bomb and the Origins of the Cold War* (New Haven, CT: Yale University Press, 2008); Stefan Kuhl, *The Nazi Connection: Eugenics, American Racism, and German National Socialism* (New York: Oxford University Press, 1994); Robert Jay Lifton and Greg Mitchell, *Hiroshima in America: Fifty Years of Denial* (New York: Putnam's Sons, 1995); Linderman, *The World within War*; Steven Okazaki, *White Light / Black Rain*, DVD (Farallon Films, 2007); Alexandra Minna Stern, *Eugenic Nation: Faults and Frontiers of Better Breeding in Modern America* (Berkeley: University of California Press, 2005); Ronald Takaki, *Double Victory: A Multicultural History of America in World War II* (Boston, MA: Back Bay Books, 2001); Lisa Yoneyama, *Hiroshima Traces: Time Space, and Dialectics of Memory* (Berkeley: University of California Press, 1999), 9–13.

34. Roger Daniels, *The Decision to Relocate the Japanese Americans* (Philadephia, PA: J. B. Lippincott Co., 1975); Louis Fiset, *Camp Harmony: Seattle's Japanese Americans and the Puyallup Assembly Center* (Champaign: University of Illinois Press, 2009), 48, 55–56; Heather C. Lindquist, *Children of Manzanar* (Berkeley, CA: Heyday, 2012), 1, 134.

35. See Barbara Jean Fields, "Slavery, Race and Ideology in the United States of America," *New Left Review* 181 (June 1990): 95–118.

36. Weglyn, *Years of Infamy,* 35, 284.

37. Lynne Horiuchi, "Dislocations: The Built Environments of Japanese American Internment," in *Guilt by Association: Essays on Japanese Settlement, Internment, and Relocation in the Rocky Mountain West,* ed. Mike Mackey (Casper, WY: Western History Publications, 2001), 265.

38. Daisuke Kitagawa, *Issei and Nisei: The Internment Years* (New York: Seabury Press, 1967), 75; see also Lindquist, *Children of Manzanar,* 134.

39. Fiset, *Camp Harmony,* 5, 61–62; Lindquist, *Children of Manzanar,* 4.

40. Horiuchi, "Dislocations," 256, 259.

41. Fiset, *Camp Harmony,* 73–78, 83, 106.

42. Authur A. Hansen and David A. Hacker, "The Manzanar Riot: An Ethnic Perspective," *Amerasia Journal* 2, no. 2 (1 October 1974): 118; Lindquist, *Children of Manzanar,* 4; Ngai, *Impossible Subjects.*

43. Cf. Lye, *America's Asia.*

44. See Ruth Wilson Gilmore, "Race and Globalization," in *Geographies of Global Change: Remapping the World,* ed. R. J. Johnston, Peter J. Taylor, and Michael Watts (Malden, MA: Blackwell, 2002), 261–74; Robin D. G. Kelley, *Hammer and Hoe: Alabama Communists during the Great Depression* (Chapel Hill: University of North Carolina Press, 1990); Woods, *Development Arrested.*

45. Fiset, "Return to Sender"; see also Nasson, *The South African Boer War 1899–1902.*

46. Fiset, "Return to Sender"; George H. Roeder, *The Censored War: American Visual Experience during World War Two* (New Haven, CT: Yale University Press, 1993), 8. FDR issued EO 8985 under the First War Powers Act, which granted the president broad powers in time of war. Immediately preceding EO 8985, on

8 December 1941, the secretary of war formally initiated censorship of telephone and telegraph wires crossing international borders. On presidential authority, the postal censorship program began on 11 December, set up by FBI director J. Edgar Hoover and implemented by the War Department.

47. Roeder, *The Censored War*, 2, 9.

48. Fiset, "Return to Sender," 4–5.

49. Fiset, *Imprisoned Apart*, 102–3.

50. Fiset, "Return to Sender," 5–6; Hayashi, *Democratizing the Enemy*, 83–85; Weglyn, *Years of Infamy*, 62–63; "NJAHS Military Intelligence Service Oral History Project," National Japanese American Historical Society, accessed February 17, 2016, https://www.njahs.org/military-intelligence-service-oral-history-project/. In this contradictory context, while the Japanese language was initially outlawed as a preventive measure against espionage, it was also elevated in priority as a tool for U.S. spying and military operations. According to the National Japanese American Historical Society, the War Department's first Japanese-language school opened on 1 November 1941 with an inaugural class of four Nisei instructors and 60 students, 58 Nisei and 2 whites. By 1946, the language program had grown to 160 instructors, 3,000 students, and more than 125 classrooms.

51. Fiset, *Imprisoned Apart*, 102–3.

52. Louis Fiset, "Censored! U.S. Censors and Internment Camp Mail in World War II," in Mackey, *Guilt by Association*, 90.

53. Roeder, *The Censored War*, 8.

54. Fiset, *Camp Harmony*, 146–48, 167.

55. Fiset, "Return to Sender," 4.

56. Walter Benjamin, *Illuminations*, trans. Harry Zohn (New York: Schocken Books, 2007 [1936]); Antonio Gramsci, *Selections from the Prison Notebooks of Antonio Gramsci*, trans. Quintin Hoare and Geoffrey Nowell-Smith (New York: International Publishers, 1971); Max Horkheimer and Theodor W. Adorno, "The Culture Industry: Enlightenment as Mass Deception," in *Dialectic of Enlightenment*, trans. Edmund Jephcott (Stanford, CA: Stanford University Press, 2002 [1944]), 35–62.

57. Emily Roxworthy, *The Spectacle of Japanese American Trauma: Racial Performativity and World War II* (Honolulu: University of Hawaii Press, 2008).

58. Joanne Oppenheim, *Dear Miss Breed: True Stories of the Japanese American Incarceration during World War II and a Librarian Who Made a Difference* (New York: Scholastic Books, 2006), 127.

59. Oppenheim, *Dear Miss Breed*. The Clara Breed Collection is housed at the Japanese American National Museum in Los Angeles; see http://www.janm.org/collections/clara-breed-collection/?page=2&nf=1.

60. Sanchez, "Disposable People, Expendable Neighborhoods"; see also Hansen and Hacker, "The Manzanar Riot: An Ethnic Perspective"; Gary Y. Okihiro, "Religion and Resistance in America's Concentration Camps," *Phylon* 45, no. 3 (1984): 220–33.

61. Natalia Molina, *Fit to Be Citizens? Public Health and Race in Los Angeles, 1879–1939* (Berkeley: University of California Press, 2006); Nayan Shah, *Contagious*

Divides: Epidemics and Race in San Francisco's Chinatown (Berkeley: University of California Press, 2001); Stern, *Eugenic Nation*.

62. Okihiro, "Religion and Resistance in America's Concentration Camps," 222; see also Jane Elizabeth Dusselier, *Artifacts of Loss: Crafting Survival in Japanese American Concentration Camps* (New Brunswick, NJ: Rutgers University Press, 2008).

63. Lye, *America's Asia*.

64. Cf. Edward W. Said, *Culture and Imperialism* (New York: Random House, 1993).

65. Bessie Masuda, Interview with author, Berkeley, CA, 28 March 2010.

66. Cf. Mimi Thi Nguyen, *The Gift of Freedom: War, Debt, and Other Refugee Passages* (Durham, NC: Duke University Press, 2012); Thu-huong Nguyen-vo, *The Ironies of Freedom: Sex, Culture, and Neoliberal Governance in Vietnam* (Seattle: University of Washington Press, 2009).

67. Oppenheim, *Dear Miss Breed*, 94–95.

68. Zada Taylor, "War Children on the Pacific: A Symposium Article," *Library Journal* 67 (15 June 1942): 558.

69. Clara Breed, "Americans with the Wrong Ancestors," *Horn Book Magazine* 19 (1943): 120.

70. Oppenheim, *Dear Miss Breed*, 224.

71. Taylor, "War Children on the Pacific," 558.

72. Hansen and Hacker, "The Manzanar Riot: An Ethnic Perspective," 118; Kitagawa, *Issei and Nisei: The Internment Years;* S. Frank Miyamoto, "Resentment, Distrust, and Insecurity at Tule Lake," in *Views from Within: The Japanese American Evacuation and Resettlement Study*, ed. Yuji Ichioka (Los Angeles: Asian American Studies Center, University of California at Los Angeles, 1989), 127–40.

73. Castelnuovo, *Soldiers of Conscience,* 12–17; "NJAHS Military Intelligence Service Oral History Project."

74. Densho, "Sites of Shame," accessed February 17, 2016, http://www.densho .org/sitesofshame/facilities.xml; Hansen and Hacker, "The Manzanar Riot: An Ethnic Perspective."

75. Tule Lake Committee, *Second Kinenhi: Reflections on Tule Lake* (San Francisco: Tule Lake Committee and John R. and Reiko Ross, 2000), 16; Weglyn, *Years of Infamy,* 122–28.

76. Chizu Omori, "The Loyalty Questionnaire," in Mackey, *Guilt by Association,* 277–86.

77. Castelnuovo, *Soldiers of Conscience;* Densho, "Sites of Shame"; Clay, Hosapple, and Ina, *From a Silk Cocoon;* Masuda, Interview with author, Berkeley, CA; Ngai, *Impossible Subjects;* Weglyn, *Years of Infamy.*

78. Omori, "The Loyalty Questionnaire."

79. Ichioka, *Views from Within;* Edward Spicer, "The Use of Social Scientists by the War Relocation Authority," *Human Organization* 5, no. 2 (1 April 1946): 16–36; Orin Starn, "Engineering Internment: Anthropologists and the War Relocation Authority," *American Ethnologist* 13, no. 4 (1 November 1986): 700–720; Peter T.

Suzuki, "Anthropologists in the Wartime Camps for Japanese Americans: A Documentary Study," *Dialectical Anthropology* 6, no. 1 (1 August 1981): 23–60.

80. Chandler, *X—The Problem of the Negro as a Problem for Thought;* Stephen Jay Gould, *The Mismeasure of Man* (New York: Norton, 1981); Sandra Harding, *The "Racial" Economy of Science: Toward a Democratic Future* (Bloomington: Indiana University Press, 1993).

81. Susan Koshy, "Morphing Race into Ethnicity: Asian Americans and Critical Transformations of Whiteness," *Boundary 2* 28, no. 1 (2001): 153–94; see also Matthew Frye Jacobson, *Whiteness of a Different Color: European Immigrants and the Alchemy of Race* (Cambridge, MA: Harvard University Press, 1999); Claire Jean Kim, "The Racial Triangulation of Asian Americans," *Politics & Society* 27, no. 1 (1 March 1999): 105–38; Lye, *America's Asia;* Stern, *Eugenic Nation.*

82. Daniel Y. Kim, "Once More, with Feeling: Cold War Masculinity and the Sentiment of Patriotism in John Okada's No-No Boy," *Criticism* 47, no. 1 (2005): 65–83; Gary Y. Okihiro, "Japanese Resistance in America's Concentration Camps: A Re-Evaluation," *Amerasia Journal* 2, no. 1 (1 October 1973): 20–34.

83. Cf. Ruth Wilson Gilmore, "What Is to Be Done?," *American Quarterly* 63, no. 2 (2011): 245–65.

84. Castelnuovo, *Soldiers of Conscience,* 17; Daniels, *Prisoners without Trial,* 69.

85. Fiset, "Return to Sender," 15; Tule Lake Committee, *Second Kinenhi: Reflections on Tule Lake;* Weglyn, *Years of Infamy,* 157–59. According to the community-based organization, the Tule Lake Committee, this entailed the construction of an eight-foot double "man-proof" fence around the camp perimeter and an increase of Military Police to a full battalion. Raymond R. Best assumed the administrative lead at Tule Lake, appointed for his experience setting up the WRA penal colonies or "citizen isolation" camps in Moab and Leupp.

86. Barbara Takei and Judy Tachibana, *Tule Lake Revisited: A Brief History and Guide to the Tule Lake Internment Camp Site* (Sacramento, CA: T&T Press, 2001), 30.

87. Tule Lake Committee, *Second Kinenhi: Reflections on Tule Lake,* 17.

88. Daniels, *Prisoners without Trial,* 57.

89. Fiset, *Imprisoned Apart,* 155.

90. Quoted in Hosapple and Ina, *Children of the Camps.*

91. Saito, Interview with author, Berkeley, CA.

CHAPTER FOUR

1. Jacques Derrida, *The Post Card: From Socrates to Freud and Beyond* (Chicago: University of Chicago Press, 1987), 48; see also Elizabeth Cook, *Epistolary Bodies: Gender and Genre in the Eighteenth-Century Republic of Letters* (Stanford, CA: Stanford University Press, 1996), 23; William Merrill Decker, *Epistolary Practices: Letter Writing in America before Telecommunications* (Chapel Hill: University of North Carolina Press, 1998), 16.

2. Terry Eagleton, *The Rape of Clarissa: Writing, Sexuality, and Class Struggle in Samuel Richardson* (Minneapolis: University of Minnesota Press, 1982), 51–52.

3. Carolyn Steedman, *Dust: The Archive and Cultural History* (New Brunswick, NJ: Rutgers University Press, 2002), 75.

4. Eagleton, *The Rape of Clarissa*, 54.

5. Louis Fiset, *Imprisoned Apart: The World War II Correspondence of an Issei Couple* (Seattle: University of Washington Press, 1998), 243. The University of Washington Library Special Collections currently houses the Iwao Matsushita Papers from which Fiset's volume is drawn.

6. Quoted in Fiset, *Imprisoned Apart*, 219.

7. Lawson Fusao Inada, ed., *Only What We Could Carry: The Japanese American Internment Experience* (Berkeley, CA: Heyday, 2000), 82–83.

8. Bessie Masuda, Interview with author, Berkeley, CA, 28 March 2010.

9. As recently as 16 April 2015, the lede for a front page story in the *Los Angeles Times* begins: "Nancy Oda's parents had an expression whenever she brought up her family's imprisonment behind barbed wire during World War II. "They said *'shikata ga nai—'* it can't be helped," recalls Oda. But Oda, who was born in a relocation camp at Tule Lake near the California-Oregon border, won't tolerate passivity anymore." See Catherine Saillant, "Japanese Americans' Protests Halt Auction of Internment Camp Items," *Los Angeles Times,* 16 April 2015, http://www.latimes.com/local/california/la-me-auction-internment-artifacts-20150417-story.html.

10. Quoted in Fiset, *Imprisoned Apart, 165.*

11. Ibid., 168.

12. See Judith Halberstam, *Female Masculinity* (Durham, NC: Duke University Press, 1998).

13. External forces as well as internal communal dynamics exacerbated conditions of gendered alienation. For example, Hanaye writes to Iwao on 21 July 1943, "Mr. Moringaga, who lives in Block 2, is a very considerate person, opening my windows, etc. for me. Unfortunately I can't invite him to dinner to repay his kindness because single women in this camp have to be careful about rumors being spread about them." Such comments indicate further constraints due to intracommunity ascriptions of gendered and sexual deviance that reinforced forms of isolation and segregation imposed by the prison camp and its administrators. See Fiset, *Imprisoned Apart,* 250.

14. Ibid., 107.

15. Quoted in Fiset, *Imprisoned Apart,* 168.

16. Ibid., 149.

17. Ibid., 231.

18. Ibid., 239.

19. Cf. Fred Moten, "Black Op," *PMLA* 123, no. 5 (2008): 1743–47; Fred Moten, *In the Break: The Aesthetics of the Black Radical Tradition* (Minneapolis: University of Minnesota Press, 2003).

20. Quoted in Fiset, *Imprisoned Apart,* 234.

21. Ibid., 240.

22. Cf. David Lloyd, "Representation's Coup," *Interventions* 16, no. 1 (2 January 2014): 1–29.

23. Fred Moten and Stefano Harney, "The University and the Undercommons SEVEN THESES," *Social Text* 22, no. 2 79 (20 June 2004): 101–15.

24. In Judy Barrett Litoff and David Clay Smith, *Since You Went Away: World War II Letters from American Women on the Home Front* (New York: Oxford University Press, 1991), 216. My gratitude to Mary Uyematsu Kao for introducing me to her aunt's letters in this anthology.

25. Louis Fiset, *Detained, Interned, Incarcerated: U.S. Enemy Noncombatant Mail in WWII* (Chicago: Collectors Club of Chicago, 2010), 32.

26. Masuda, Interview with author, Berkeley, CA. Bessie Masuda was born in Stockton in 1929 and raised in Lodi. As a teenager after the camps, she was separated from her family again, leaving school to earn income as a domestic worker in San Francisco so that she could send money home to her family. The archive of letters in this chapter came back to the Masuda family after Bessie Masuda's sister paged their father's FBI dossier from the National Archives in Washington, DC.

27. Cf. Hortense J. Spillers, *Black, White, and in Color: Essays on American Literature and Culture* (Chicago: University of Chicago Press, 2003), 203. It remains unclear whether more than one family, perhaps in attached pages or enclosures not included in the Masuda archive, signed this petition or sent identical petitions separately. In any case, the argument here regarding multivalent collectivity and metonymy would still apply.

28. Karen Jackson Ford, "The Lives of Haiku Poetry: Self, Selflessness, and Solidarity in Concentration Camp Haiku," in *Cary Nelson and the Struggle for the University,* ed. Michael Rothberg and Peter K. Garrett (New York: State University of New York Press, 2009), 60–61.

29. Karen Jackson Ford, "Marking Time in Native America: Haiku, Elegy, Survival," *American Literature* 81, no. 2 (1 June 2009): 333–59.

30. Violet Kazue de Cristoforo, *May Sky: There Is Always Tomorrow: An Anthology of Japanese American Concentration Camp Kaiko Haiku* (Los Angeles, CA: Sun and Moon Press, 1997), 23–25, 42–43 According to Kazue de Cristoforo, members of the Delta Ginshu Haiku Kai (Stockton) and the Valley Ginsha Haiku Kai (Fresno) met once a month and negotiated rules of reading, debate, and voting to develop collectively the kaiko form. As the United States prepared to declare war against Japan, the Central Valley poets destroyed most of their collections, anticipating that their work would likely become a political liability.

31. Ibid., 23.

32. Ford, "The Lives of Haiku Poetry," 62.

33. Kazue de Cristoforo, *May Sky,* 16. Perhaps partly to fulfill this injunction, formally structured haiku kai reproduced themselves inside internment and civilian prison camps, such as the reorganization of several Fresno poets as the Denson Valley Ginsha in Jerome, AR (61). Because poetry was often written in secret, it often spoke more freely about feelings and conditions than other censored materials being

produced (Keiho Soga et al., *Poets behind Barbed Wire: Tanka Poems,* ed. and trans. Jiro Nakano and Kay Nakano [Honolulu, HI: Bamboo Ridge Press, 1983], 5).

34. Ford, "The Lives of Haiku Poetry," 67.

35. Daisuke Kitagawa, *Issei and Nisei: The Internment Years* (New York: Seabury Press, 1967), 35. Reverend Kitagawa was born and raised in Japan and emigrated to the United States in 1937 to attend seminary. He was ministering in Washington state when the United States initiated Nikkei removal.

36. Kazue de Cristoforo, *May Sky,* 44. According to Kazue de Cristoforo, former member of the Valley Ginsha, Ozawa was transferred to the Gila Indian Reservation Sanatorium in 1942 after contracting tuberculosis at the Fresno Assembly Center. She notes, "In spite of this unforeseen development, he still managed to correspond with members of both the Valley Ginsha and Delta Ginsha, wherever they were, to give them advice and to critique their work" (44).

37. See also Fiset, *Imprisoned Apart,* 128.

38. Kazue de Cristoforo, *May Sky,* 10.

39. Cf. Akira Mizuta Lippit, *Atomic Light (Shadow Optics)* (Minneapolis: University of Minnesota Press, 2005); María Josefina Saldaña-Portillo, *The Revolutionary Imagination in the Americas and the Age of Development* (Durham, NC: Duke University Press, 2003).

40. Soga et al., *Poets behind Barbed Wire,* 5.

41. Vanessa Gould, *Between the Folds,* DVD (PBS Independent Lens, 2010).

42. Jane Elizabeth Dusselier, *Artifacts of Loss: Crafting Survival in Japanese American Concentration Camps* (New Brunswick, NJ: Rutgers University Press, 2008), 43, 99–103, 131–34.

43. As the website of the UC Berkeley Bancroft Library's JERS Digital Archive states, "The Japanese American Evacuation and Resettlement Study (JERS) was a research project initiated in 1942 at the University of California, Berkeley. It aimed to document and examine the mass internment of Japanese Americans by embedding Nisei social science students recruited from the Berkeley campus into selected internment sites. The Study also documented the resettlement phase in the city of Chicago. The collection is comprised of daily journals, field reports, life histories, and secondary research materials collected and compiled by the research staff. There is also extensive correspondence between staff, evacuees, and others. These records were deposited in the University Library in August 1948 by sociologist and Director of JERS, Dorothy Swaine Thomas." Yuji Ichioka's edited volume, *Views from Within,* also seeks to provide a documentary account of JERS and reassesses its significance, including perspectives from original Nisei JERS recruits, S. Frank Miyamoto and James Sakoda. See "The Japanese American Evacuation and Resettlement: A Digital Archive—The Bancroft Library—University of California, Berkeley," accessed 20 February 2016, http://vm136.lib.berkeley.edu/BANC/collections/jais/abouttheproject.html; Yuji Ichioka, ed., *Views from Within: The Japanese American Evacuation and Resettlement Study* (Los Angeles: Resource Development and Publications, Asian American Studies Center, University of California at Los Angeles, 1989); see

also "Japanese American Evacuation and Resettlement Records," BANC MSS 67/14 c, folder B12.50 (2/2), UC Berkeley Bancroft Library, accessed 20 February 2016, http://www.oac.cdlib.org/ark:/28722/bk0013c8x33/?brand=oac4.

44. From Electric Shadows/ITVS Media online interactive archive, "Face to Face: Stories from the Aftermath of Infamy, Marion Kanemoto," accessed 20 February 2016, http://archive.itvs.org/facetoface/stories/marion.html (emphasis added); also see interview with Marion Kanemoto, "Elk Grove Unified School District's Time of Remembrance (Online Archive)," accessed 20 February 2016, http://www.egusd.net/tor/flash_video/interviews/m_kanemoto/clip2/mkanemoto2.html.

45. Quoted in Heather C. Lindquist, *Children of Manzanar* (Berkeley, CA: Heyday, 2012), 29.

46. Quoted in Ibid., 69.

47. Lawson Fusao Inada, *Legends from Camp: Poems* (Minneapolis, MN: Coffee House Press, 1992), 26.

48. Bessie Masuda, Interview with Center for Arkansas History and Culture, University of Arkansas, Little Rock, accessed February 19, 2016, https://www.youtube.com/watch?v = Z31iLSt7YYE. See also http://ualr.edu/cahc/. Critically, Masuda's stance on schooling in Rohwer does not mark an innate or universal refusal of education, rationality, or individual achievement, since she notes in another interview (with author, 28 March 2010) that before reconcentration, "I did well in grammar school. I *loved* school, and I *loved* to study, and I *loved* to be the first to do anything, you know? (laughs)." Rather, Masuda's antagonism marks a historically specific response to particular terms and conditions that would change again upon reuniting with her father at family segregation camp at Crystal City, TX. In the latter situation, Masuda's academic performance again shifted as she excelled in Japanese language school, rising five grade levels in two years. While racial and nationalist distinctions embedded in linguistic identity (cf. Gary Y. Okihiro, "Religion and Resistance in America's Concentration Camps," *Phylon* 45, no. 3 [1984]: 220–33) may appear to be a primary explanation for Masuda's trajectory, in her remarks, Masuda expresses parallel enthusiasm both for English-language learning before the war and for Japanese-language learning after family reunification. This parity suggests that the most salient factor may not be in the form of language but the extent to which the learning process itself could coexist with and/or negate Masuda's preferential option for selfhood rooted in collective experience.

49. Cf. Wendy Hui Kyong Chun, "The Enduring Ephemeral, or the Future Is a Memory," *Critical Inquiry* 35, no. 1 (2008): 148–71.

50. Louis Fiset, "Return to Sender: U.S. Censorship of Enemy Alien Mail in World War II," *National Archives and Records Administration Prologue Magazine,* Spring 2001, 16, http://www.archives.gov/publications/prologue/2001/spring/mail-censorship-in-world-war-two-1.html.

51. Efforts to deport "enemy aliens" to Japan included the passage of Public Law 405, or the Renunciation Act, signed by Congress on 1 July 1944. This measure pressured Nikkei dissidents to renounce their U.S. citizenship and repatriate

"voluntarily"—a strategic option for those seeking ways to keep their families together in the event that the United States would ultimately deport Issei internees to Japan involuntarily. See Emery Clay III, Stephen Hosapple, and Satsuki Ina, *From a Silk Cocoon,* DVD (Hesono O Productions and Center for Asian American Media, 2006); Tule Lake Committee, *Second Kinenhi: Reflections on Tule Lake* (San Francisco: Tule Lake Committee and John R. and Reiko Ross, 2000).

52. Quoted in Clay, Hosapple, and Ina, *From a Silk Cocoon.*

53. Satsuki Ina, Interview with author, Sacramento, CA, 31 March 2010.

54. In Clay, Hosapple, and Ina, *From a Silk Cocoon.*

55. Ina, Interview with author, Sacramento, CA.

56. Ibid.

57. Japanese Cultural & Community Center of Northern California, *From Our Side of the Fence: Growing Up in America's Concentration Camps,* ed. Brian Komei Dempster (San Francisco: Kearny Street Workshop, 2001), xxii.

58. Cedric J. Robinson, "Manichaeism and Multiculturalism," in *Mapping Multiculturalism,* ed. Avery F. Gordon and Christopher Newfield (Minneapolis: University of Minnesota Press, 1996), 122.

PART THREE

1. Walter Benjamin, *Illuminations,* trans. Harry Zohn (New York: Schocken Books, 2007 [1936]), 91.

2. Alice Yang, "Redress Movement," in *Densho Encyclopedia* (Densho Encyclopedia, June 2014), http://encyclopedia.densho.org/Redress%20movement/.

3. Ruth Wilson Gilmore, *Golden Gulag: Prisons, Surplus, Crisis, and Opposition in Globalizing California* (Berkeley: University of California Press, 2007); Kelly Lytle Hernández, "Hobos in Heaven: Race, Incarceration, and the Rise of Los Angeles, 1880–1910," *Pacific Historical Review* 83, no. 3 (August 2014): 410–47.

4. Laurence B. De Graaf, Kevin Mulroy, and Quintard Taylor, *Seeking El Dorado: African Americans in California* (Seattle: University of Washington Press, 2013); Douglas Flamming, *Bound for Freedom: Black Los Angeles in Jim Crow America* (Berkeley: University of California, 2006); Regina Freer, "L.A. Race Woman: Charlotta Bass and the Complexities of Black Political Development in Los Angeles," *American Quarterly* 56, no. 3 (2004): 607–32; Josh Sides, *L.A. City Limits: African American Los Angeles from the Great Depression to the Present* (Berkeley: University of California Press, 2004); Quintard Taylor, *In Search of the Racial Frontier: African Americans in the American West 1528–1990* (New York: Norton, 1999).

5. Taylor, *In Search of the Racial Frontier,* 253–54.

6. Eric Avila, *Popular Culture in the Age of White Flight: Fear and Fantasy in Suburban Los Angeles* (Berkeley: University of California Press, 2004); Mike Davis, *City of Quartz: Excavating the Future in Los Angeles* (New York: Vintage, 1990);

Gilmore, *Golden Gulag;* Greg Hise, "Border City: Race and Social Distance in Los Angeles," *American Quarterly* 56, no. 3 (2004): 545–58; Laura Pulido, *Black, Brown, Yellow, and Left: Radical Activism in Los Angeles* (Berkeley: University of California, 2005); Sides, *L.A. City Limits;* Mark Wild, *Street Meeting: Multiethnic Neighborhoods in Early Twentieth-Century Los Angeles* (Berkeley: University of California Press, 2005).

7. Richard O. Moore, *Take This Hammer (the Director's Cut),* Online (San Francisco Bay Area Television Archive, 2013), https://diva.sfsu.edu/collections/sfbatv/bundles/216518.

8. Committee on African American Parity, "The Unfinished Agenda: The Economic Status of African Americans in San Francisco, 1964–1990" (Human Rights Commission of San Francisco, 1993), 5–10.

9. Alex Cherian, *The Making of "Take This Hammer,"* Online (San Francisco Bay Area Television Archive, 2012), https://diva.sfsu.edu/collections/sfbatv/bundles/210522.

10. Davis, *City of Quartz;* Gilmore, *Golden Gulag;* Gerald Horne, *Fire This Time: The Watts Uprising and the 1960s* (Charlottesville: University of Virginia Press, 1995); Pulido, *Black, Brown, Yellow, and Left;* Sides, *L.A. City Limits.*

11. Horne, *Fire This Time,* 16, 64.

12. Ibid., 64.

13. Davis, *City of Quartz;* Horne, *Fire This Time,* 146–47, 165–67.

14. Cathleen Decker, "Watts Riots Shifted State to the Right, But New Demographics Pushed It Left," *Los Angeles Times,* 5 August 2015, http://www.latimes.com/local/politics/la-me-pol-watts-politics-20150806-story.html#page=1.

15. See, e.g., Patricia Hill Collins, *Black Feminist Thought: Knowledge, Consciousness, and the Politics of Empowerment* (New York: Routledge, 2000); Helen Heran Jun, *Race for Citizenship: Black Orientalism and Asian Uplift from Pre-Emancipation to Neoliberal America* (New York: New York University Press, 2011); Mari Matsuda, "We Will Not Be Used," *UCLA Asian American Pacific Islands Law Journal* 1 (1993): 79–84; Glenn K. Omatsu, "The 'Four Prisons' and the Movements of Liberation," *Amerasia Journal* 15, no. 1 (1989): xv–xxx; Vijay Prashad, *The Karma of Brown Folk,* (Minneapolis: University of Minnesota Press, 2001); Hortense J. Spillers, *Black, White, and in Color: Essays on American Literature and Culture* (Chicago: University of Chicago Press, 2003).

16. Susan Koshy, "Morphing Race into Ethnicity: Asian Americans and Critical Transformations of Whiteness," *Boundary 2* 28, no. 1 (2001): 153–94.

17. See, e.g., Lisa Marie Cacho, *Social Death: Racialized Rightlessness and the Criminalization of the Unprotected* (New York: New York University Press, 2012); Grace Kyungwon Hong, *The Ruptures of American Capital: Women of Color Feminism and the Culture of Immigrant Labor* (Minneapolis: University of Minnesota Press, 2006); Jun, *Race for Citizenship;* Chandan Reddy, *Freedom with Violence: Race, Sexuality, and the US State* (Durham, NC: Duke University Press, 2011); Randall Williams, *The Divided World: Human Rights and Its Violence* (Minneapolis: University of Minnesota Press, 2010).

CHAPTER FIVE

1. See, e.g., Dipesh Chakrabarty, *Provincializing Europe: Postcolonial Thought and Historical Difference* (Princeton, NJ: Princeton University Press, 2000); Jacquelyn Dowd Hall, "The Long Civil Rights Movement and the Political Uses of the Past," *Journal of American History* 91, no. 4 (1 March 2005): 1233–63; Robin D. G. Kelley, *Hammer and Hoe: Alabama Communists during the Great Depression* (Chapel Hill: University of North Carolina Press, 1990); Peter Linebaugh and Marcus Rediker, *The Many-Headed Hydra: Sailors, Slaves, Commoners, and the Hidden History of the Revolutionary Atlantic* (New York: Beacon Press, 2000); E. P. Thompson, *The Making of the English Working Class* (New York: Vintage, 1966); Howard Zinn, *A People's History of the United States: 1492–Present*, 20th anniversary ed. (New York: HarperCollins, 2003). For a critique specifically of the "activist bildungsroman," see also Eric Tang, "How the Refugees Stopped the Bronx from Burning," *Race & Class* 54, no. 4 (1 April 2013): 48–66.

2. Cf. Barbara Jean Fields, "Slavery, Race and Ideology in the United States of America," *New Left Review* 181 (June 1990): 95–118.

3. "Race, Prisons and War: Scenes from the History of US Violence," *Socialist Register 2009: Violence Today* 45 (2009): 73–87; "Forgotten Places and the Seeds of Grassroots Planning," in *Engaging Contradictions: Theory, Politics, and Methods of Activist Scholarship*, ed. Charles R. Hale (Berkeley: University of California Press, 2008), 31–61; *Golden Gulag: Prisons, Surplus, Crisis, and Opposition in Globalizing California* (Berkeley: University of California Press, 2007); "Fatal Couplings of Power and Difference: Notes on Racism and Geography," *Professional Geographer* 54, no. 1 (2002): 15–24.

4. Mike Davis, *City of Quartz: Excavating the Future in Los Angeles* (New York: Vintage Books, 1990).

5. Christian Parenti, *Lockdown America* (New York: Verso Books, 1999).

6. Roderick A. Ferguson, *Aberrations in Black: Toward a Queer of Color Critique* (Minneapolis: University of Minnesota Press, 2004); Grace Kyungwon Hong, "Existentially Surplus: Women of Color Feminism and the New Crises of Capitalism," *GLQ: A Journal of Lesbian and Gay Studies* 18, no. 1 (2012): 87–106; Lisa Lowe, *Immigrant Acts: On Asian American Cultural Politics* (Durham, NC: Duke University Press, 1996); Lisa Lowe and David Lloyd, *The Politics of Culture in the Shadow of Capital* (Durham, NC: Duke University Press, 1997).

7. James Kilgore, "Confronting Prison Slave Labor Camps and Other Myths," *Social Justice* Online (28 August 2013), http://www.socialjusticejournal.org/?p=235.

8. James A. Manos, "From Commodity Fetishism to Prison Fetishism: Slavery, Convict-Leasing, and the Ideological Productions of Incarceration," in *Death and Other Penalties: Philosophy in a Time of Mass Incarceration*, ed. Geoffrey Adelsberg, Lisa Guenther, and Scott Zeman (New York: Fordham University Press, 2015), 54.

9. Ibid., 58.

10. Zora Neale Hurston, "How It Feels to Be Colored Me," *World Tomorrow* 11 (May 1928): 215–16.

11. Manos, "From Commodity Fetishism to Prison Fetishism," 54.

12. Cf. George J. Sanchez, "Face the Nation: Race, Immigration, and the Rise of Nativism in Late Twentieth Century America," *International Migration Review* 31, no. 4 (1 December 1997): 1009–30.

13. Cf. Jared Sexton, "People-of-Color-Blindness Notes on the Afterlife of Slavery," *Social Text* 28, no. 2 103 (20 June 2010): 31–56.

14. Colleen Lye, "The Afro-Asian Analogy," *PMLA* 123, no. 5 (1 October 2008): 1732–36; and "Racial Form," *Representations* 104, no. 1 (1 November 2008): 92–101.

15. Kenneth W. Warren, *What Was African American Literature?* (Cambridge, MA: Harvard University, 2012).

16. Michelle Alexander, *The New Jim Crow: Mass Incarceration in the Age of Colorblindness* (New York: New Press, 2010).

17. See, e.g., Nahum Dimitri Chandler, *X—The Problem of the Negro as a Problem for Thought* (New York: Fordham University Press, 2013); Brent Hayes Edwards, *The Practice of Diaspora: Literature, Translation, and the Rise of Black Internationalism* (Cambridge, MA: Harvard University Press, 2009); Stefano Harney and Fred Moten, *The Undercommons: Fugitive Planning & Black Study* (New York: Automedia, 2013). Robin D. G. Kelley, *Freedom Dreams: The Black Radical Imagination* (Boston, MA: Beacon Press, 2003); Cedric J. Robinson, *Black Marxism: The Making of the Black Radical Tradition* (Chapel Hill: University of North Carolina Press, 2000); Sylvia Wynter, "Ethno or Socio Poetics," *Alcheringa/Boston University* 2, no. 2 (1976): 78–94.

18. See Katherine McKittrick and Clyde Woods, eds., *Black Geographies and the Politics of Place* (Cambridge, MA: South End Press, 2007); Clyde Woods, *Development Arrested: Race, Power, and the Blues in The Mississippi Delta* (New York: Verso Books, 1998).

19. Clyde Woods, "Katrina's World: Blues, Bourbon, and the Return to the Source," *American Quarterly* 61, no. 3 (2009): 429.

20. For further analysis of the effects of this model to reproduce anti-Blackness in more recent times, see Tiffany Willoughby-Herard, "More Expendable than Slaves? Racial Justice and the After-Life of Slavery," *Politics, Groups, and Identities* 2, no. 3 (3 July 2014): 506–21.

21. Katherine McKittrick, ed., *Sylvia Wynter: On Being Human as Praxis* (Durham, NC: Duke University Press, 2015).

22. See, e.g., Victor Bascara, *Model-Minority Imperialism* (Minneapolis: University of Minnesota Press, 2006); Yu-Fang Cho, *Uncoupling American Empire: Cultural Politics of Deviance and Unequal Difference, 1890–1910* (Albany: State University of New York Press, 2015); Grace Kyungwon Hong, *The Ruptures of American Capital: Women of Color Feminism and the Culture of Immigrant Labor* (Minneapolis: University of Minnesota, 2006); Moon-Ho Jung, *Coolies and Cane: Race, Labor, and Sugar in the Age of Emancipation* (Baltimore, MD: Johns Hopkins University Press, 2006); Jodi Kim, *Ends of Empire: Asian American Critique and the Cold War* (Minneapolis: University of Minnesota Press, 2010); Lisa Lowe, *The Intimacies of Four Continents* (Durham, NC: Duke University Press, 2015); Glenn K. Omatsu, "The 'Four Prisons' and the Movements of Liberation," *Amerasia Journal* 15, no. 1

(1989): xv–xxx; Vijay Prashad, *Everybody Was Kung Fu Fighting: Afro-Asian Connections and the Myth of Cultural Purity* (Boston, MA: Beacon Press, 2002); Chandan Reddy, *Freedom with Violence: Race, Sexuality, and the US State* (Durham, NC: Duke University Press, 2011); Edlie Wong, *Racial Reconstruction: Black Inclusion, Chinese Exclusion, and the Fictions of Citizenship* (New York: New York University Press, 2015); Lisa Yun, *The Coolie Speaks: Chinese Indentured Laborers and African Slaves in Cuba* (Philadephia, PA: Temple University Press, 2008).

23. Lye, "The Afro-Asian Analogy."

24. Christine Hong, "Illustrating the Postwar Peace: Miné Okubo, the 'Citizen-Subject' of Japan, and *Fortune* Magazine," *American Quarterly* 67, no. 1 (2015): 105–40.

25. Helen Heran Jun, *Race for Citizenship: Black Orientalism and Asian Uplift from Pre-Emancipation to Neoliberal America* (New York: New York University Press, 2011).

26. See H. L. T. Quan, *Growth against Democracy: Savage Developmentalism in the Modern World* (Lanham, MD: Lexington Books, 2012).

27. Lawson Fusao Inada, *Legends from Camp: Poems* (Minneapolis, MN: Coffee House Press, 1992), 26.

28. Ibid., 57.

29. Cf. Laura Harris, "What Happened to the Motley Crew? C. L. R. James, Hélio Oiticica, and the Aesthetic Sociality of Blackness," *Social Text* 30, no. 3 112 (21 September 2012): 49–75.

30. Barbara Johnson, "The Frame of Reference: Poe, Lacan, Derrida," *Yale French Studies,* no. 55–56 (1 January 1977): 498; original emphasis.

31. Ethel Shapiro-Bertolini and Andrew Richter, eds., *Through the Wall: Prison Correspondence* (Culver City, CA: Peace Press, 1976), vii–viii.

32. Ibid., 26.

33. Ibid., 310.

34. Ibid., 115.

35. Assata Shakur, "I Am a 20th Century Escaped Slave," *www.counterpunch .org,* December 30, 2014, http://www.counterpunch.org/2014/12/30/an-open-letter-to-the-media/.

36. Assata Shakur, *Assata: An Autobiography* (Chicago: Lawrence Hill Books, 1987), 49.

37. Stormy Ogden, "The Use of Letters as Social Control," 26 July 2010 (email correspondence with the author).

38. Ngo, in Eddy Zheng, ed., *Other: An Asian & Pacific Islander Prisoners' Anthology* (Hayward, CA: Asian Prisoner Support Committee, 2007), 75; see also Joy James, ed., *The New Abolitionists: (Neo)Slave Narratives and Contemporary Prison Writings* (Albany: State University of New York Press, 2005), 249–58; Dylan Rodríguez, *Forced Passages: Imprisoned Radical Intellectuals and the U.S. Prison Regime* (Minneapolis: University of Minnesota Press, 2006), 92–104.

39. The Pelican Bay hunger strikers' original five demands are as follows: end group punishment and administrative abuse; abolish "debriefing" (coercive infor-

mation gathering) policy and modify active/inactive gang status criteria; comply with official recommendations regarding end to long-term solitary confinement; provide adequate and nutritious food; and provide programming and privileges for indefinite SHU status inmates. See Pelican Bay Hunger Strikers, "Prisoners' Demands," *Prisoner Hunger Strike Solidarity,* 3 April 2011, https://prisonerhungerstrikesolidarity.wordpress.com/the-prisoners-demands-2/.

40. Prisoner Hunger Strike Solidarity, "Take Action," *Prisoner Hunger Strike Solidarity,* accessed 25 September 2015, https://prisonerhungerstrikesolidarity.wordpress.com/take-action-2/.

41. California Department of Corrections and Rehabilitation, "CDCR Will Report Prohibited Inmate Accounts to Facebook," *CDCR Today,* 8 August 2011, http://cdcrtoday.blogspot.com/2011/08/cdcr-and-facebook-security-will.html.

42. Ogden, "The Use of Letters as Social Control" (email correspondence with the author).

43. Shapiro-Bertolini and Richter, *Through the Wall: Prison Correspondence,* 8.

44. Cf. Angela Y. Davis, "Reflections on the Black Woman's Role in the Community of Slaves," *Massachusetts Review* 13, no. 1–2 (1972): 81–100; Barbara Harlow, *Barred: Women, Writing, and Political Detention* (Middletown, CT: Wesleyan University Press, 1992); Joy James, *Shadowboxing: Representations of Black Feminist Politics* (New York: St. Martin's Press, 1999).

45. Primo Levi, *If This Is a Man* (New York: Abacus Books, 1987), 54.

46. Christine Schoefer, "Cry Out: Women Behind Bars," *Yes! Magazine,* 30 September 2000, http://www.yesmagazine.org/issues/is-it-time-to-close-the-prisons/cry-out-women-behind-bars.

CHAPTER SIX

1. Jeremy W. Peters, "The Handwritten Letter, an Art All but Lost, Thrives in Prison," *New York Times,* 8 January 2011, B4.

2. Alondra Nelson, Thuy Linh N. Tu, and Alicia Headlam Hines, eds., *Technicolor: Race, Technology, and Everyday Life* (New York: New York University Press, 2001), 8; see also Ann Cvetkovich, *An Archive of Feelings: Trauma, Sexuality, and Lesbian Public Cultures* (Durham, NC: Duke University Press, 2003); Judith Halberstam, *In a Queer Time and Place: Transgender Bodies, Subcultural Lives* (New York: New York University Press, 2005); Kara Keeling, *The Witch's Flight: The Cinematic, the Black Femme, and the Image of Common Sense* (Durham, NC: Duke University Press, 2007); Alexander G. Weheliye, *Phonographies: Grooves in Sonic Afro-Modernity* (Durham, NC: Duke University Press, 2005).

3. Quoted in Joy James, ed., *Imprisoned Intellectuals: America's Political Prisoners Write on Life, Liberation, and Rebellion* (Lanham, MD: Rowman & Littlefield, 2003), 46.

4. Clyde Woods, "Life after Death," *Professional Geographer* 54, no. 1 (2002): 62–66.

5. Quoted in James, *Imprisoned Intellectuals*, 34–35, 43–44.

6. See Safiya Bukhari, *The War Before: The True Life Story of Becoming a Black Panther, Keeping the Faith in Prison, and Fighting for Those Left Behind* (New York: Feminist Press at CUNY, 2010). Bukhari argues that the name and definition of "political prisoner" matter as a human rights issue, since the U.S. government continues to deny that U.S. political prisoners exist and thus does not recognize the latter's rights under international law. U.S. human rights attorney Ronald L. Kuby offers this definition: "The definition [of a political prisoner] is someone whose actions [which contextualize and provoke incarceration] were taken in furtherance of the principles articulated in the United Nations Universal Declaration of Human Rights. That document speaks specifically of liberation movements; it speaks of equality among races and religions. So any individual who engages in a racist act— for example, a white supremacist who wants to reinstitute slavery or someone who wants to impose his religion on anyone—is excluded from that definition" (quoted on 222–23).

Started in 1998, the Jericho Movement to free political prisoners and POWs in the United States is specific about who falls under the category "political prisoner." Bukhari explains, "Jericho is designed to raise the issues of these political cases. From the very beginning they were political [because imprisonment is tied to active involvement in collectively organized social justice movements]. Once we push those through and get the US government to acknowledge and the world to recognize the fact that these people are political prisoners, then we can open the door and bring other people through. Then we can bring in those cases of those people who became political in prison" (210–11).

7. Cf. Christina Heatherton, "University of Radicalism: Ricardo Flores Magón and Leavenworth Penitentiary," *American Quarterly* 66, no. 3 (2014): 557–81.

8. Ethel Shapiro-Bertolini and Andrew Richter, eds., *Through the Wall: Prison Correspondence* (Culver City, CA: Peace Press, 1976), 225–26.

9. Michael Roy Hames-Garcia, *Fugitive Thought: Prison Movements, Race, and the Meaning of Justice* (Minneapolis: University of Minnesota Press, 2004), 102, 115; see also Mumia Abu-Jamal, *Live from Death Row* (Boston, MA: Addison-Wesley, 1995); Barbara Harlow, *Barred: Women, Writing, and Political Detention* (Middletown, CT: Wesleyan University Press, 1992); Barbara Harlow, *Resistance Literature* (London: Methuen, 1987); James, *Imprisoned Intellectuals*; Joy James, *Shadowboxing: Representations of Black Feminist Politics* (New York: St. Martin's Press, 1999); Dylan Rodríguez, *Forced Passages: Imprisoned Radical Intellectuals and the U.S. Prison Regime* (Minneapolis: University of Minnesota Press, 2006); John Edgar Wideman, "Why Mumia Matters to the Nation and World" (Educators for Mumia Abu-Jamal, 9 June 2005), http://www.emajonline.com/2005/06/why-mumia-matters-to-the-nation-and-world-by-john-edgar-wideman/.

10. Cf. Anna Julia Cooper, *A Voice from the South* (Xenia, OH: Aldine Printing House, 1892); Ida B. Wells, *Southern Horrors and Other Writings; The Anti-Lynching Campaign of Ida B. Wells, 1892–1900*, ed. Jacqueline Jones Royster, 1st ed. (Boston, MA: Bedford/St. Martin's, 1996).

11. See Dan Berger, *Captive Nation: Black Prison Organizing in the Civil Rights Era* (Chapel Hill: University of North Carolina Press, 2014); Lee Bernstein, *America Is the Prison: Arts and Politics in Prison in the 1970s* (Chapel Hill: University of North Carolina Press, 2010); Jamie Bissonette et al., *When the Prisoners Ran Walpole: A True Story in the Movement for Prison Abolition* (Boston, MA: South End Press, 2008); Louis J. Massiah, Thomas Ott, and Terry Kay Rockefeller, *Eyes on the Prize: A Nation of Law? (1968–1971)*, DVD (Blackside Media, 1990).

12. "The Attica Liberation Faction Manifesto of Demands and Anti-Depression Platform," in *The New Abolitionists: (Neo)Slave Narratives and Contemporary Prison Writings*, ed. Joy James (Albany: State University of New York Press, 2005), 303.

13. Angela Y. Davis et al., *If They Come in the Morning: Voices of Resistance* (New Rochelle, NY: Third Press, 1971), 63.

14. Cf. Joy James, *Seeking the Beloved Community: A Feminist Race Reader* (Albany: State University of New York Press, 2013).

15. Reprinted in James, *Imprisoned Intellectuals*, 242–47. Daniel Berrigan (1921–2016), ordained in the Society of Jesus in 1952, was exiled to South America by church officials in 1965 for comments made in support of acts protesting the U.S. war in Vietnam. After returning to the United States, Daniel and his younger brother, Philip Berrigan, served several federal sentences for acts of political resistance, most notably, for burning draft cards as members of the Catonsville Nine in 1969 and for hammering nuclear warheads and pouring their blood on government documents as part of the Plowshares Eight witness in 1980. For further background on Berrigan as well as the Weather Underground Organization, see James, *Imprisoned Intellectuals*, 239–41.

16. Daniel Berrigan and Robert Coles, *The Geography of Faith: Conversations between Daniel Berrigan, When Underground, and Robert Coles* (Boston, MA: Beacon Press, 1971), 62.

17. Besides Jacques Derrida, *The Post Card: From Socrates to Freud and Beyond* (Chicago: University of Chicago Press, 1987), renewed attention to the epistolary includes Elizabeth Cook, *Epistolary Bodies: Gender and Genre in the Eighteenth-Century Republic of Letters* (Stanford, CA: Stanford University Press, 1996); William Merrill Decker, *Epistolary Practices: Letter Writing in America before Telecommunications* (Chapel Hill: University of North Carolina Press, 1998); Rebecca Earle, *Epistolary Selves: Letters and Letter-Writers, 1600–1945* (Brooksfield, VT: Ashgate, 1999); Amanda Gilroy and W. M. Verhoeven, *Epistolary Histories: Letters, Fiction, Culture* (Charlottesville: University of Virginia Press, 2000); Linda S. Kauffman, *Special Delivery: Epistolary Modes in Modern Fiction* (Chicago: University of Chicago Press, 1992). For extended critique of "The Purloined Letter" discourses and arguments regarding the indeterminacy of the letter, see Lindon Barrett, *Blackness and Value: Seeing Double* (New York: Cambridge University Press, 1999), 185–213.

18. In 1970, following her removal from teaching philosophy at the University of California, Los Angeles, for her activism and membership in the Communist Party, Davis was placed on the FBI's Ten Most Wanted list. Police and FBI pursued

her on false charges connected to the attempt made by Jonathan Jackson, seventeen-year-old brother of George Jackson, to negotiate his brother's release and free James McClain, Ruchell Magee, and William Christmas from prison during their appearance at the Marin County Courthouse in California on 7 August 1970. Law enforcement officials killed Jonathan Jackson, McClain, Christmas, and hostage Judge Harold Haley during the armed confrontation. The guns in Jonathan Jackson's possession were registered under Angela Davis's name, as Jonathan Jackson and Davis worked closely together as members of the Soledad Brothers Defense Committee (see note 19) and Jonathan Jackson served as Davis's bodyguard during a period in which she was receiving regular death threats. The "Free Angela Davis" campaign gained international prominence during her sixteen months of incarceration and won her acquittal on all charges in 1972. See James, *Imprisoned Intellectuals,* 62–63; "Open Letter to My Sister Angela Davis" is also reprinted in Davis et al., *If They Come in the Morning,* 13–18.

19. On 21 August 1971, George Jackson was murdered at San Quentin State Prison during an uprising in the Adjustment Center, in a series of events that remain unclear. George Lester Jackson was born in Chicago in 1941 and raised in Los Angeles after 1956. Between 1958 and 1960, he was in and out of youth correctional facilities and jail for minor allegations; in 1960, he confessed to participating in a gas station robbery in exchange for a light sentence of one year to life, which became life imprisonment. While incarcerated, he studied radical political philosophy from solitary confinement and joined the Black Panther Party for Self-Defense, for which he served as field marshal. Prison administrators transferred him to Soledad Prison in 1969 for his political organizing activities, including cofounding the self-defense group the Black Guerilla Family. In 1970, attorney Faye Stender formed the Soledad Brothers Defense Committee after George Jackson, Fleeta Drumgo, and John Cluchette were indicted for allegedly killing a prison guard, one month after guards had shot and killed at least three inmates, including Jackson's mentor, in the exercise yard. After the death of his brother, Jonathan Jackson, during the attempted takeover of the Marin County Courthouse in 1970, and following his transfer back to San Quentin, George Jackson was shot from the back by guards during an armed escape attempt. See Freedom Archives, *Prisons on Fire: George Jackson, Attica, and Black Liberation,* CD (AK Press, San Francisco, 2002); James, *Imprisoned Intellectuals,* 85–86.

20. See Joy James, "Black Revolutionary Icons and 'Neoslave' Narratives," *Social Identities* 5, no. 2 (1999): 135–59.

21. Nicole R. Fleetwood, "Posing in Prison: Family Photographs, Emotional Labor, and Carceral Intimacy," *Public Culture* 27, no. 3 77 (1 September 2015): 487–511.

22. George Jackson, *Soledad Brother: The Prison Letters of George Jackson,* new ed. (Chicago: Chicago Review Press, 1994 [1970]), 329.

23. Hortense J. Spillers, *Black, White, and in Color: Essays on American Literature and Culture* (Chicago: University of Chicago Press, 2003), 228; see also Fred Moten, *In the Break: The Aesthetics of the Black Radical Tradition* (Minneapolis: University of Minnesota Press, 2003), 15.

24. Moten, *In the Break,* 13–18.

25. Anonymous, "Work Print" film, *George Jackson/San Quentin* (San Francisco: Freedom Archives), accessed 29 October 2015, http://www.freedomarchives.org /George%20Jackson.html.

26. Fleetwood, "Posing in Prison," 490.

27. Lester Jackson, "A Dialogue with My Soledad Son," *Ebony,* November 1971, 76.

28. Fleetwood, "Posing in Prison," 508.

29. Jackson, "A Dialogue," 78.

30. Bukhari, *The War Before,* 13.

31. David Theo Goldberg, ed., *Multiculturalism: A Critical Reader* (Cambridge, MA: Wiley-Blackwell, 1995); Avery F. Gordon and Christopher Newfield, eds., *Mapping Multiculturalism* (Minneapolis: University of Minnesota Press, 1996).

32. Cf. Victor Bascara, *Model-Minority Imperialism* (Minneapolis: University of Minnesota Press, 2006); Lisa Marie Cacho, *Social Death: Racialized Rightlessness and the Criminalization of the Unprotected* (New York: New York University Press, 2012); Hames-Garcia, *Fugitive Thought;* Grace Kyungwon Hong, "Existentially Surplus: Women of Color Feminism and the New Crises of Capitalism," *GLQ: A Journal of Lesbian and Gay Studies* 18, no. 1 (2012): 87–106; Susan Koshy, "Morphing Race into Ethnicity: Asian Americans and Critical Transformations of Whiteness," *Boundary 2* 28, no. 1 (2001): 153–94; Jodi Malemed, *Represent and Destroy* (Minneapolis: University of Minnesota Press, 2011); Toni Morrison, "'Rootedness: The Ancestor as Foundation,'" in *Black Women Writers (1950–1980): A Critical Evaluation,* ed. Mari Evans (New York: Doubleday, 1984), 339–45; Glenn K. Omatsu, "The 'Four Prisons' and the Movements of Liberation," *Amerasia Journal* 15, no. 1 (1989): xv–xxx; Sylvia Wynter, "No Humans Involved: An Open Letter to My Colleagues," *Forum N.H.I.: Knowledge for the 21st Century* 1, no. 1 (1994): 42–73.

33. As this book goes into production, this remains a competing, if not hegemonic, political tendency in the United States despite domination by a ruling party that has revived racial ideologies based on religious, biological, and cultural fundamentalisms.

34. Richa Nagar and Sangtin Writers, *Playing with Fire: Feminist Thought and Activism through Seven Lives in India* (Minneapolis: University of Minnesota Press, 2006), 154.

35. Staughton Lynd, *Lucasville: The Untold Story of a Prison Uprising* (Philadelphia: Temple University Press, 2004); cf. Ruth Wilson Gilmore, *Golden Gulag: Prisons, Surplus, Crisis, and Opposition in Globalizing California* (Berkeley: University of California Press, 2007); James, *The New Abolitionists.*

36. Mumia Abu-Jamal, *Writing on the Wall: Selected Prison Writings of Mumia Abu-Jamal* (San Francisco: City Lights, 2014).

37. Carolina Saldaña, "Mumia Abu-Jamal's Eighth Book: *Writing on the Wall* (Review)," *Countercurrents,* 5 September 2015, http://www.countercurrents.org /saldana050915.htm.

38. Jacques Derrida, *Archive Fever: A Freudian Impression* (Chicago: University of Chicago Press, 1998), 76.

39. Ibid., 1.

40. Yusef Toussaint Omowale, "Speaking the Impossible: Navigating through Silence to Voice," in *Cultural Studies in Education,* ed. Antonia Darder (Claremont, CA: Claremont Graduate University School of Educational Studies, 1998), 90–105.

41. Joseph Omowale, former member of the Black Panther Party and active in the U.S. Black liberation movement at the time of his fugitivity, hijacked a plane to Cuba in 1972 amidst escalating violence and assassinations by the FBI Counter-Intelligence Program (COINTELPRO). His exile began the same year Yusef Toussaint Omowale was born and extended for over a decade. Joseph Omowale eventually returned to the United States and was apprehended by the FBI in 1983; he was released from Leavenworth State Penitentiary in 1990. See Omowale, "Speaking the Impossible," 92–93; Andy Rosenblatt and Michael H. Cottman, "Miami Hijacking Suspect Arrested," *Miami Herald,* 5 December 1983, http://www.latinamericanstudies.org/hijackers/suspect-arrested.htm.

42. Omowale, "Speaking the Impossible," 92.

43. Ibid., 96.

44. Barbara Johnson, "The Frame of Reference: Poe, Lacan, Derrida," *Yale French Studies,* no. 55–56 (1 January 1977): 481.

45. Omowale, "Speaking the Impossible," 96.

46. Ibid., 97.

47. Johnson, "The Frame of Reference," 503.

48. Nahum Dimitri Chandler, *X—The Problem of the Negro as a Problem for Thought* (New York: Fordham University Press, 2013); see also Fred Moten, "The Case of Blackness," *Criticism* 50, no. 2 (3 July 2008): 177–218.

49. Omowale, "Speaking the Impossible," 104.

50. Cf. James, "Black Revolutionary Icons and 'Neoslave' Narratives," 137–38. Generically, the Law Dictionary provides the following guidelines: "Parole letters are letters written either by an incarcerated person or by his or her supporters. Intelligently written parole letters attesting to the offender's character, reformation and plans to improve his or her life will be read by the parole panel and may make the difference between release and denial." See "How to Write a Parole Letter," *Law Dictionary,* accessed 18 November 2015, http://thelawdictionary.org/article/how-to-write-a-parole-letter/.

51. James C. Scott, *Domination and the Arts of Resistance: Hidden Transcripts* (New Haven, CT: Yale University Press, 1990).

52. Bukhari, *The War Before,* 202–3.

53. Jalil Muntaqim began organizing as a youth in San Francisco with the National Association for the Advancement of Colored People (NAACP) and joined the Black Panther Party at the age of eighteen after the assassination of Martin Luther King Jr. Along with fellow Black Panther/Black Liberation Army members Albert "Nuh" Washington and Herman Bell, Muntaqim was targeted by COINTELPRO for his political activities and incarcerated in 1971 on contested charges of killing two NYPD officers. Muntaqim and Bell remain incarcerated in New York; Washington died of liver cancer at New York's Coxsackie Correctional

Facility in April 2000. In 2009, Muntaqim and Bell were the only two of the "San Francisco 8" who were *not* exonerated in the 2007 reopening of a case in which the state attempted to retry the 1971 killing of a San Francisco police officer. The original ordeal, lasting from 1971 to 1975, peaked in 1973 with the arrest of three members of the Black Panthers/Black Liberation Army, John Bowman, Ruben Scott, and Harold Taylor, in New Orleans, Louisiana, and ended in dropped charges due to proof of the use of torture by New Orleans police to extract false confessions and false testimony. In July 2011, Muntaqim and Bell pleaded no contest/guilty to reduced charges with no additional prison sentence. Muntaqim continues to organize, educate, and write about issues of social justice, incarceration, and human rights. See James, *Imprisoned Intellectuals*, 104–6; Bukhari, *The War Before*, 33, 167; Freedom Archives, "Free the SF8—Committee for the Defense of Human Rights," accessed 19 November 2015, http://freethesf8.org/.

54. Spillers, *Black, White, and in Color*, 203.

EPILOGUE

1. For Viet Mike Ngo's account of events, see "Lesson Learned in Prison College," in *Other: An Asian & Pacific Islander Prisoners' Anthology,* ed. Eddy Zheng (Hayward, CA: Asian Prisoner Support Committee, 2007), 73–75; Dylan Rodríguez and Viet Mike Ngo, "Ethnic Studies in the Age of the Prison-Industrial Complex: Reflections on 'Freedom' and Capture, Praxis, and Immobilization," in *Pedagogies of the Global: Knowledge in the Human Interest,* ed. Arif Dirlik (Boulder, CO: Paradigm Publishers, 2006), 113–31. See also Ngo's "You Have to Be Intimate with Your Despair," in *The New Abolitionists: (Neo)Slave Narratives and Contemporary Prison Writings,* ed. Joy James (Albany: State University of New York Press, 2005), 249–50; Dylan Rodríguez, *Forced Passages: Imprisoned Radical Intellectuals and the U.S. Prison Regime* (Minneapolis: University of Minnesota Press, 2006), 75–112; William C. Collins, "Prisoner Access to the Courts," in *Prison and Jail Administration: Practice and Theory,* ed. Peter M. Carlson (Burlington, MA: Jones & Bartlett, 2013), 508.

2. Rico Remeidio, German Yambao, and Eddy Zheng, "Other: Voices of Asian Prisoners" (paper presented at the Critical Resistance Conference, Oakland, CA, 28 September 2008), http://www.asianprisonersupport.com/videos/; Eddy Zheng, "EddyZheng.com," accessed 6 December 2015, http://eddyzheng.com/.

3. Allen Feldman, *Formations of Violence: The Narrative of the Body and Political Terror in Northern Ireland* (Chicago: University of Chicago Press, 1991), 10.

4. Stuart Hall, "Old and New Identities, Old and New Ethnicities," in *Culture, Globalization and the World-System: Contemporary Conditions for the Representation of Identity,* ed. Anthony D. King (Minneapolis: University of Minnesota Press, 1997), 52–53.

5. Ibid., 57–58.

6. Contemporary interarticulations of mass incarceration, immigration, U.S. policy, and the "War on Terror" remain an urgent site for further research and

advocacy. Specific to Asian American communities, see Lynn Fujiwara, *Mothers without Citizenship: Asian Immigrant Families and the Consequences of Welfare Reform* (Minneapolis: University of Minnesota Press, 2008); Sunaina Maira, "Radical Deportation: Alien Tales from Lodi and San Francisco," in *The Deportation Regime: Sovereignty, Space, and the Freedom of Movement,* ed. Nicholas De Genova and Nathalie Peutz (Durham NC: Duke University Press, 2010), 295–328; Nicole Newnham and David Grabias, *Sentenced Home* (Independent Television Service, 2006), http://www.pbs.org/independentlens/sentencedhome/film.html. For more information on Zheng's case, see also *Breathin': The Eddy Zheng Story,* a forthcoming documentary film by Ben Wang, http://www.eddyzhengstory.com/.

7. Viet Mike Ngo, "Grave Digger," *Amerasia Journal* 29, no. 1 (2003): 179.

8. Rico Remeidio, "Making Rehabilitation Work: Creating Opportunities for Formerly Incarcerated Individuals" (paper presented at the San Francisco Reentry Summit, San Francisco, 27 September 2006), https://www.youtube.com/watch?v=1ufUaV9Hqpo. See also Megan Corcoran, "San Francisco Seeks Reentry for Returning California Prisoners," *Beyond Chron,* 27 September 2006, http://www.beyondchron.org/san-francisco-seeks-reentry-for-returning-california-prisoners/.

9. Clyde Woods, "Life after Death," *Professional Geographer* 54, no. 1 (2002): 62–66.

BIBLIOGRAPHY

Abu-Jamal, Mumia. *Live from Death Row.* Boston, MA: Addison-Wesley, 1995.
———. *Writing on the Wall: Selected Prison Writings of Mumia Abu-Jamal.* San Francisco: City Lights, 2014.
Acuña, Rodolfo. *Occupied America: A History of Chicanos.* New York: Harper & Row, 1988.
Alexander, M. Jacqui. *Pedagogies of Crossing: Meditations on Feminism, Sexual Politics, Memory, and the Sacred.* Durham, NC: Duke University Press, 2006.
Alexander, Michelle. *The New Jim Crow: Mass Incarceration in the Age of Colorblindness.* New York: New Press, 2010.
Almaguer, Tomás. *Racial Fault Lines: The Historical Origins of White Supremacy in California.* Berkeley: University of California Press, 1994.
Anderson, Benedict. *Imagined Communities: Reflections on the Origin and Spread of Nationalism.* Rev. ed. New York: Verso, 2006 [1983].
Anonymous. "Work Print." *George Jackson / San Quentin.* San Francisco: Freedom Archives. Accessed 29 October 2015. http://www.freedomarchives.org /George%20Jackson.html.
Arendt, Hannah. *The Origins of Totalitarianism.* New York: Harcourt, Brace and Co., 1951.
Avila, Eric. *Popular Culture in the Age of White Flight: Fear and Fantasy in Suburban Los Angeles.* Berkeley: University of California Press, 2004.
Baark, Erik. *Lightning Wires: The Telegraph and China's Technological Modernization, 1860–1890.* Westport, CT: Greenwood Press, 1997.
Bain, David Howard. *Empire Express: Building the First Transcontinental Railroad.* New York: Penguin Books, 2000.
Baker, Houston A., Jr., and Patricia Redmond. *Afro-American Literary Study in the 1990s.* Chicago: University of Chicago Press, 1989.
Barde, Robert. "The Scandalous Ship Mongolia." *Steamboat Bill,* no. 250 (2004): 112–18.
Barrett, Lindon. *Blackness and Value: Seeing Double.* New York: Cambridge University Press, 1999.

Barton, David, and Nigel Hall, eds. *Letter Writing as a Social Practice.* Amsterdam: John Benjamins, 2000.

Bascara, Victor. *Model-Minority Imperialism.* Minneapolis: University of Minnesota Press, 2006.

Benjamin, Walter. *Illuminations.* Translated by Harry Zohn. New York: Schocken Books, 2007 [1936].

Berger, Dan. *Captive Nation: Black Prison Organizing in the Civil Rights Era.* Chapel Hill: University of North Carolina Press, 2014.

Berlo, Jane Catherine. *Plains Indian Drawings 1865–1935.* New York: Harry N. Abrams, 1996.

Bernstein, Lee. *America Is the Prison: Arts and Politics in Prison in the 1970s.* Chapel Hill: University of North Carolina Press, 2010.

Berrigan, Daniel, and Robert Coles. *The Geography of Faith: Conversations between Daniel Berrigan, When Underground, and Robert Coles.* Boston, MA: Beacon Press, 1971.

Bissonette, Jamie, Ralph Hamm, Robert Dellelo, and Edward Rodman. *When the Prisoners Ran Walpole: A True Story in the Movement for Prison Abolition.* Boston, MA: South End Press, 2008.

Bower, Anne L. *Epistolary Responses: The Letter in 20th-Century American Fiction and Criticism.* Tuscaloosa: University of Alabama Press, 1997.

Brathwaite, Kamau. *History of the Voice: The Development of Nation Language in Anglophone Caribbean Poetry.* London: New Beacon Books, 1984.

Bray, Joe. *The Epistolary Novel: Representations of Consciousness.* New York: Routledge, 2003.

Breed, Clara. "Americans with the Wrong Ancestors." *Horn Book Magazine* 19 (1943): 253–61.

Briggs, Asa, and Peter Burke. *A Social History of the Media: From Gutenberg to the Internet.* Cambridge: Polity Press, 2005.

Brooks, Daphne. *Bodies in Dissent: Spectacular Performances of Race and Freedom, 1850–1910.* Durham, NC: Duke University Press, 2006.

Brown, Richard D. *Knowledge Is Power.* Oxford: Oxford University Press, 1989.

Bukhari, Safiya. *The War Before: The True Life Story of Becoming a Black Panther, Keeping the Faith in Prison, and Fighting for Those Left Behind.* New York: Feminist Press at CUNY, 2010.

Cacho, Lisa Marie. *Social Death: Racialized Rightlessness and the Criminalization of the Unprotected.* New York: New York University Press, 2012.

California Department of Corrections and Rehabilitation. "CDCR Will Report Prohibited Inmate Accounts to Facebook." *CDCR Today,* 8 August 2011. http://cdcrtoday.blogspot.com/2011/08/cdcr-and-facebook-security-will.html.

Calloway, Colin Gordon. *Ledger Narratives: The Plains Indian Drawings of the Lansburgh Collection at Dartmouth College.* Norman: University of Oklahoma Press, 2012.

Carey, James W. *Communication as Culture: Essays on Media and Society.* Boston, MA: Psychology Press, 1989.

Carter, Thomas Francis. *The Invention of Printing in China and Its Spread Westward.* New York: Columbia University Press, 1925.

Castelnuovo, Shirley. *Soldiers of Conscience: Japanese American Military Resisters in World War II.* Westport, CT: Praeger, 2008.

Castle, Terry. *Clarissa's Ciphers: Meaning and Disruption in Richardson's "Clarissa."* Ithaca, NY: Cornell University Press, 1982.

Cave, Roderick. *Chinese Paper Offerings.* New York: Oxford University Press, 1998.

Chakrabarty, Dipesh. *Provincializing Europe: Postcolonial Thought and Historical Difference.* Princeton, NJ: Princeton University Press, 2000.

Chandler, Nahum Dimitri. "Of Exorbitance: The Problem of the Negro as a Problem for Thought." *Criticism* 50, no. 3 (2008): 345–410.

———. *X—The Problem of the Negro as a Problem for Thought.* New York: Fordham University Press, 2013.

Chang, Iris. *The Rape of Nanking: The Forgotten Holocaust of World War II.* New York: Penguin Books, 1998.

Cheng, Wendy. "Strategic Orientalism: Racial Capitalism and the Problem of 'Asianness.'" *African Identities* 11, no. 2 (2013): 148–58.

Cheng, Ying-wan. *Postal Communication in China and Its Modernization, 1860–1896.* Cambridge, MA: Harvard University Press, 1970.

Cherian, Alex. *The Making of Take This Hammer.* Online. San Francisco Bay Area Television Archive, 2012. https://diva.sfsu.edu/collections/sfbatv/bundles/210522.

Childress, Alice. "A Candle in Gale Wind." In *Black Women Writers (1950–1980),* edited by Mari Evans, 111–16. Garden City, NY: Anchor Books, 1984.

Chin, Tung Pok. *Paper Son: One Man's Story.* Philadephia, PA: Temple University Press, 2000.

Chiu, Ping. *Chinese Labor in California, 1850–1880: An Economic Study.* Madison: State Historical Society of Wisconsin for the Dept. of History, University of Wincinsin, 1967.

Cho, Yu-Fang. *Uncoupling American Empire: Cultural Politics of Deviance and Unequal Difference, 1890–1910.* Albany: State University of New York Press, 2015.

Chu, Daniel, and Samuel Chu. *Passage to the Golden Gate: A History of the Chinese in America to 1910.* New York: Doubleday, 1967.

Chuh, Kandice. *Imagine Otherwise: On Asian Americanist Critique.* Durham, NC: Duke University Press, 2003.

Chun, Wendy Hui Kyong. "The Enduring Ephemeral, or the Future Is a Memory." *Critical Inquiry* 35, no. 1 (2008): 148–71.

Chung, Tan. "The Harmony of Civilization and Prosperity for All: Selected Papers of Beijing Forum (2004–2008): Where from the 'Secret of Expression' of Chinese Civilization?" *Procedia—Social and Behavioral Sciences* 2, no. 5 (1 January 2010): 7098–7119.

Clay III, Emery, Stephen Hosapple, and Satsuki Ina. *From a Silk Cacoon.* DVD. Hesono O Productions and Center for Asian American Media, 2006.

Cohen, Cathy J. "Punks, Bulldaggers, and Welfare Queens: The Radical Potential of Queer Politics?" *GLQ: A Journal of Lesbian and Gay Studies* 3, no. 4 (1997): 437–65.

Collins, Patricia Hill. *Black Feminist Thought: Knowledge, Consciousness, and the Politics of Empowerment.* New York: Routledge, 2000.

Collins, William C. "Prisoner Access to the Courts." In *Prison and Jail Administration: Practice and Theory,* edited by Peter M. Carlson, 508. Burlington, MA: Jones & Bartlett Publishers, 2013.

Committee on African American Parity. "The Unfinished Agenda: The Economic Status of African Americans in San Francisco, 1964–1990." Human Rights Commission of San Francisco, 1993.

Cook, Elizabeth Heckendorn. *Epistolary Bodies: Gender and Genre in the Eighteenth-Century Republic of Letters.* Stanford, CA: Stanford University Press, 1996.

Cooper, Anna Julia. *A Voice from the South.* Xenia, OH: Aldine Printing House, 1892.

Corcoran, Megan. "San Francisco Seeks Reentry for Returning California Prisoners." *Beyond Chron,* 27 September 2006. http://www.beyondchron.org/san-francisco-seeks-reentry-for-returning-california-prisoners/.

Craig, Campbell, and Sergey Radchenko. *The Atomic Bomb and the Origins of the Cold War.* New Haven, CT: Yale University Press, 2008.

Cushman, Mark V. "Uncertain Frontiers: Asian Immigration and U.S. Citizenship in the Age of Expansion." PhD diss., Johns Hopkins University, 1999.

Cvetkovich, Ann. *An Archive of Feelings: Trauma, Sexuality, and Lesbian Public Cultures.* Durham, NC: Duke University Press, 2003.

Dalla Costa, Mariarosa, and Selma James. *The Power of Women and the Subversion of the Community.* London: Falling Wall Press, 1972.

Daniels, Roger. *Prisoners without Trial: Japanese Americans in World War II.* New York: Hill and Wang, 1993.

———. "Relocation, Redress, and the Report: A Historical Appraisal." In *Japanese Americans: From Relocation to Redress,* edited by Roger Daniels, Sandra C. Taylor, and Harry H. L. Kitano, 3–9. Salt Lake City: University of Utah Press, 1986.

———. *The Decision to Relocate the Japanese Americans.* Philadephia, PA: J.B. Lippincott Co., 1975.

Davis, Angela Y. *Are Prisons Obsolete?* New York: Seven Stories Press, 2003.

———. "Reflections on the Black Woman's Role in the Community of Slaves." *Massachusetts Review* 13, no. 1–2 (1972): 81–100.

———. *Women, Race, & Class.* New York: Vintage Books, 1981.

Davis, Angela Y., Ruchell Magee, Soledad Brothers, and Other Political Prisoners. *If They Come in the Morning: Voices of Resistance.* New Rochelle, NY: Third Press, 1971.

Davis, Mike. *City of Quartz: Excavating the Future in Los Angeles.* New York: Vintage Books, 1990.

De Graaf, Laurence B., Kevin Mulroy, and Quintard Taylor. *Seeking El Dorado: African Americans in California.* Seattle: University of Washington Press, 2013.

Decker, Cathleen. "Watts Riots Shifted State to the Right, but New Demographics Pushed It Left." *Los Angeles Times,* 5 August 2015. http://www.latimes.com/local/politics/la-me-pol-watts-politics-20150806-story.html#page=1.

Decker, William Merrill. *Epistolary Practices: Letter Writing in America before Telecommunications.* Chapel Hill: University of North Carolina Press, 1998.

Densho. "Sites of Shame." Accessed 17 February 2016. http://www.densho.org/sitesofshame/facilities.xml.

Derrida, Jacques. *Archive Fever: A Freudian Impression.* Chicago: University of Chicago Press, 1998.

———. *The Post Card: From Socrates to Freud and Beyond.* Chicago: University of Chicago Press, 1987.

Deverell, William. *Railroad Crossing: Californians and the Railroad, 1850–1910.* Berkeley: University of California Press, 1996.

———. *Whitewashed Adobe: The Rise of Los Angeles and the Remaking of Its Mexican Past.* Berkeley: University of California Press, 2005.

"Do We Need to Redefine the Top Four Inventions?" *Beijing Review,* 28 August 2008. http://www.bjreview.com.cn/special/txt/2008–08/26/content_146777.htm.

Dougan, Charles W. *The Shanghai Postal System.* State College, PA: American Philatelic Society, 1981.

Douglass, Frederick. *Narrative of the Life of Frederick Douglass.* New York: Dover Publications, 1995 [1845].

DuBois, W. E. B. *Black Reconstruction in America 1860–1880.* New York: Simon and Schuster, 1935.

———. *The Souls of Black Folk: Essays and Sketches.* Chicago: A. C. McClurg & Co., 1903.

Dusselier, Jane Elizabeth. *Artifacts of Loss: Crafting Survival in Japanese American Concentration Camps.* New Brunswick, NJ: Rutgers University Press, 2008.

Eagleton, Terry. *The Rape of Clarissa: Writing, Sexuality, and Class Struggle in Samuel Richardson.* Minneapolis: University of Minnesota Press, 1982.

Earle, Rebecca. *Epistolary Selves: Letters and Letter-Writers, 1600–1945.* Brooksfield, VT: Ashgate, 1999.

Edkins, Joseph. *The Religious Condition of the Chinese: With Observations on the Prospects of Christian Conversion Amongst That People.* London: Routledge, Warnes, & Routledge, 1859.

Edwards, Brent Hayes. *The Practice of Diaspora: Literature, Translation, and the Rise of Black Internationalism.* Cambridge, MA: Harvard University Press, 2009.

"Elk Grove Unified School District's Time of Remembrance (Online Archive)." Accessed 20 February 2016. http://www.egusd.net/tor/flash_video/interviews/m_kanemoto/clip2/mkanemoto2.html.

Elleman, Bruce A. *Modern Chinese Warfare, 1795–1989.* New York: Routledge, 2001.

Eng, David L. *Racial Castration: Managing Masculinity in Asian America.* Durham, NC: Duke University Press, 2001.

Eng, Robert Yeok-Yin. *Economic Imperialism in China: Silk Production & Exports, 1861–1932.* Berkeley: Institute of East Asian Studies, University of California, 1986.

Eyferth, Jacob. "Craft Knowledge at the Interface of Written and Oral Cultures." *East Asian Science, Technology and Society: An International Journal* 4, no. 2 (2010): 185–205.

———. "Socialist Deskilling: The Struggle over Skills in a Rural Craft Industry, 1949–1965." In *How China Works: Perspectives on the Twentieth-Century Industrial Workplace,* edited by Jacob Eyferth, 41–58. New York: Routledge, 2006.

"Face to Face: Stories from the Aftermath of Infamy, Marion Kanemoto." Accessed 20 February 2016. http://archive.itvs.org/facetoface/stories/marion.html.

Fan, Shi, ed. *The Stamps of China 1878–1981.* Beijing: Foreign Languages Press, 1983.

Feldman, Allen. *Formations of Violence: The Narrative of the Body and Political Terror in Northern Ireland.* Chicago: University of Chicago Press, 1991.

Ferguson, Roderick A. *Aberrations in Black: Toward a Queer of Color Critique.* Minneapolis: University of Minnesota Press, 2004.

Fields, Barbara Jean. "Slavery, Race and Ideology in the United States of America." *New Left Review* 181 (June 1990): 95–118.

Fiset, Louis. *Camp Harmony: Seattle's Japanese Americans and the Puyallup Assembly Center.* Champaign: University of Illinois Press, 2009.

———. "Censored! U.S. Censors and Internment Camp Mail in World War II." In *Guilt by Association: Essays on Japanese Settlement, Internment, and Relocation in the Rocky Mountain West,* edited by Mike Mackey, 69–100. Casper, WY: Western History Publications, 2001.

———. *Detained, Interned, Incarcerated: U.S. Enemy Noncombatant Mail in WWII.* Chicago: Collectors Club of Chicago, 2010.

———. *Imprisoned Apart: The World War II Correspondence of an Issei Couple.* Seattle: University of Washington Press, 1998.

———. "Return to Sender: U.S. Censorship of Enemy Alien Mail in World War II." *National Archives and Records Administration Prologue Magazine,* Spring 2001. http://www.archives.gov/publications/prologue/2001/spring/mail-censorship-in-world-war-two-1.html.

Flamming, Douglas. *Bound for Freedom: Black Los Angeles in Jim Crow America.* Berkeley: University of California, 2006.

Fleetwood, Nicole R. "Posing in Prison: Family Photographs, Emotional Labor, and Carceral Intimacy." *Public Culture* 27, no. 3 (1 September 2015): 487–511.

Foner, Eric. *Reconstruction: America's Unfinished Revolution, 1863–1877.* New York: Harper & Row, 1988.

Ford, Karen Jackson. "Marking Time in Native America: Haiku, Elegy, Survival." *American Literature* 81, no. 2 (1 June 2009): 333–59.

———. "The Lives of Haiku Poetry: Self, Selflessness, and Solidarity in Concentration Camp Haiku." In *Cary Nelson and the Struggle for the University,* edited by Michael Rothberg and Peter K. Garrett, 59–74. New York: State University of New York Press, 2009.

Fortunati, Leopoldina. *The Arcane of Reproduction: Housework, Prostitution, Labor and Capital.* Translated by H. Creek. New York: Autonomedia, 1995 [1981].

Foucault, Michel. *The Archaeology of Knowledge: And the Discourse on Language.* Translated by A. M. Sheridan Smith. New York: Pantheon Books, 1972.

———. *Ethics: Subjectivity and Truth (Essential Works of Foucault, 1954–1984, Vol. 1).* Edited by Paul Rabinow. New York: New Press, 1998.

———. *The History of Sexuality, Vol. 1: An Introduction.* Translated by Robert Hurley. New York: Vintage Books, 1990.

Franklin, V. P. *Living Our Stories, Telling Our Truths: Autobiography and the Making of the African-American Intellectual Tradition.* New York: Scribner's, 1995.

Freccero, Carla. *Queer/Early/Modern.* Durham, NC: Duke University Press, 2005.

Freedom Archives. "Free the SF8—Committee for the Defense of Human Rights." Accessed 19 November 2015. http://freethesf8.org/.

———. *Prisons on Fire: George Jackson, Attica, and Black Liberation.* CD. San Francisco: AK Press, 2002.

Freer, Regina. "L.A. Race Woman: Charlotta Bass and the Complexities of Black Political Development in Los Angeles." *American Quarterly* 56, no. 3 (2004): 607–32.

Fujitani, Takashi. *Race for Empire: Koreans as Japanese and Japanese as Americans during World War II.* Berkeley: University of California Press, 2011.

Fujiwara, Lynn. *Mothers without Citizenship: Asian Immigrant Families and the Consequences of Welfare Reform.* Minneapolis: University of Minnesota Press, 2008.

Gates, Henry Louis. *The Signifying Monkey: A Theory of African-American Literary Criticism.* New York: Oxford University Press, 1989.

Gerber, David A. "Epistolary Ethics: Personal Correspondence and the Culture of Emigration in the Nineteenth Century." *Journal of American Ethnic History* 19, no. 4 (1 July 2000): 3–23.

———. "The Immigrant Letter between Positivism and Populism: The Uses of Immigrant Personal Correspondence in Twentieth-Century American Scholarship." *Journal of American Ethnic History* 16, no. 4 (1 July 1997): 3–34.

Gilmore, Ruth Wilson. "Fatal Couplings of Power and Difference: Notes on Racism and Geography." *Professional Geographer* 54, no. 1 (2002): 15–24.

———. "Forgotten Places and the Seeds of Grassroots Planning." In *Engaging Contradictions: Theory, Politics, and Methods of Activist Scholarship,* edited by Charles R. Hale, 31–61. Berkeley: University of California Press, 2008.

———. *Golden Gulag: Prisons, Surplus, Crisis, and Opposition in Globalizing California.* Berkeley: University of California Press, 2007.

———. "Race and Globalization." In *Geographies of Global Change: Remapping the World,* edited by R. J. Johnston, Peter J. Taylor, and Michael Watts, 261–74. Malden, MA: Blackwell, 2002.

———. "Race, Prisons and War: Scenes from the History of US Violence." *Socialist Register 2009: Violence Today* 45 (2009): 73–87.

————. "What Is to Be Done?" *American Quarterly* 63, no. 2 (2011): 245–65.

Gilmore, William J. *Reading Becomes a Necessity of Life: Material and Cultural Life in Rural New England, 1780–1835.* Knoxville: University of Tennessee Press, 1992.

Gilroy, Amanda, and W. M. Verhoeven. *Epistolary Histories: Letters, Fiction, Culture.* Charlottesville: University of Virginia Press, 2000.

Gilroy, Paul. *Against Race: Imagining Political Culture beyond the Color Line.* Cambridge, MA: Harvard University Press, 2000.

Glenn, Evelyn Nakano. *Unequal Freedom: How Race and Gender Shaped American Citizenship and Labor.* Cambridge, MA: Harvard University Press, 2002.

Glissant, Edouard. *Poetics of Relation.* Translated by Betsy Wing. Ann Arbor: University of Michigan Press, 1997.

Goldberg, David Theo, ed. *Multiculturalism: A Critical Reader.* Cambridge, MA: Wiley-Blackwell, 1995.

Gordon, Avery F. *Ghostly Matters: Haunting and the Sociological Imagination.* Minneapolis: University of Minnesota Press, 1997.

Gordon, Avery F., and Christopher Newfield, eds. *Mapping Multiculturalism.* Minneapolis: University of Minnesota Press, 1996.

Gould, Stephen Jay. *The Mismeasure of Man.* New York: Norton, 1981.

Gould, Vanessa. *Between the Folds.* DVD. PBS Independent Lens, 2010.

Gramsci, Antonio. *Letters from Prison, Volume 2.* Edited by Frank Rosengarten. Translated by Raymond Rosenthal. New York: Columbia University Press, 1994.

————. *Selections from the Prison Notebooks of Antonio Gramsci.* Translated by Quintin Hoare and Geoffrey Nowell-Smith. New York: International Publishers, 1971.

Guha, Ranajit. *Dominance without Hegemony: History and Power in Colonial India.* Cambridge, MA: Harvard University Press, 1997.

Haan, J. H. "Origin and Development of the Political System in the Shanghai International Settlement." *Journal of the Hong Kong Branch of the Royal Asiatic Society* 22 (1982): 31–64.

Halberstam, Judith. *Female Masculinity.* Durham, NC: Duke University Press, 1998.

————. *In a Queer Time and Place: Transgender Bodies, Subcultural Lives.* New York: New York University Press, 2005.

Hall, Jacquelyn Dowd. "The Long Civil Rights Movement and the Political Uses of the Past." *Journal of American History* 91, no. 4 (1 March 2005): 1233–63.

Hall, Stuart. "Gramsci's Relevance for the Study of Race and Ethnicity." *Journal of Communication Inquiry* 10, no. 2 (1 June 1986): 5–27.

————. "Old and New Identities, Old and New Ethnicities." In *Culture, Globalization and the World-System: Contemporary Conditions for the Representation of Identity,* edited by Anthony D. King, 41–68. Minneapolis: University of Minnesota Press, 1997.

————. "Race, Articulation and Societies Structured in Dominance." In *Sociological Theories: Race and Colonialism,* 305–45. Paris: UNESCO, 1980.

————. "Race, Culture, and Communications: Looking Backward and Forward at Cultural Studies." *Rethinking Marxism* 5, no. 1 (1 March 1992): 10–18.

Hames-Garcia, Michael Roy. *Fugitive Thought: Prison Movements, Race, and the Meaning of Justice*. Minneapolis: University of Minnesota Press, 2004.

Hansen, Arthur A., and David A. Hacker. "The Manzanar Riot: An Ethnic Perspective." *Amerasia Journal* 2, no. 2 (1 October 1974): 112–57.

Harding, Sandra. *The "Racial" Economy of Science: Toward a Democratic Future*. Bloomington: Indiana University Press, 1993.

Harlow, Barbara. *Barred: Women, Writing, and Political Detention*. Middletown, CT: Wesleyan University Press, 1992.

——. *Resistance Literature*. London: Methuen, 1987.

Harney, Stefano, and Fred Moten. "Michael Brown." *Boundary 2* 42, no. 4 (1 November 2015): 81–87.

——. *The Undercommons: Fugitive Planning & Black Study*. New York: Autonomedia, 2013.

Harris, Laura. "What Happened to the Motley Crew?: C. L. R. James, Hélio Oiticica, and the Aesthetic Sociality of Blackness." *Social Text* 30, no. 3 112 (21 September 2012): 49–75.

Hartman, Saidiya V. *Scenes of Subjection: Terror, Slavery, and Self-Making in Nineteenth-Century America*. New York: Oxford University Press, 1997.

Hayashi, Brian Masaru. *Democratizing the Enemy: The Japanese American Internment*. Princeton, NJ: Princeton University Press, 2004.

Headrick, Daniel R. *The Tools of Empire: Technology and European Imperialism in the Nineteenth Century*. Oxford: Oxford University Press, 1981.

Heatherton, Christina. "University of Radicalism: Ricardo Flores Magón and Leavenworth Penitentiary." *American Quarterly* 66, no. 3 (2014): 557–81.

Hernández, Kelly Lytle. "Amnesty or Abolition? Felons, Illegals, and the Case for a New Abolition Movement." *Boom: A Journal of California* 1, no. 4 (2011): 54–68.

——. "Hobos in Heaven: Race, Incarceration, and the Rise of Los Angeles, 1880–1910." *Pacific Historical Review* 83, no. 3 (August 2014): 410–47.

——. *Migra! A History of the U.S. Border Patrol*. Berkeley: University of California, 2010.

Hirabayashi, Lane R., and James A. Hirabayashi. "A Reconsideration of the United States Military's Role in the Violation of Japanese-American Citizenship Rights." In *Ethnicity and War*, edited by Winston A. Van Horne and Thomas V. Tonnesen, 87–110. Milwaukee: University of Wisconsin System, American Ethnic Studies Coordinating Committee / Urban Corridor Consortium, 1984.

Hise, Greg. "Border City: Race and Social Distance in Los Angeles." *American Quarterly* 56, no. 3 (2004): 545–58.

Hoggart, Richard. *The Uses of Literacy: Aspects of Working-Class Life*. New York: Penguin Books, 2009 [1957].

Hong, Christine. "Illustrating the Postwar Peace: Miné Okubo, the 'Citizen-Subject' of Japan, and *Fortune* Magazine." *American Quarterly* 67, no. 1 (2015): 105–40.

Hong, Grace Kyungwon. *Death beyond Disavowal: The Impossible Politics of Difference*. Minneapolis: University of Minnesota Press, 2015.

———. "Existentially Surplus: Women of Color Feminism and the New Crises of Capitalism." *GLQ: A Journal of Lesbian and Gay Studies* 18, no. 1 (2012): 87–106.

———. *The Ruptures of American Capital: Women of Color Feminism and the Culture of Immigrant Labor.* Minneapolis: University of Minnesota Press, 2006.

Horiuchi, Lynne. "Dislocations: The Built Environments of Japanese American Internment." In *Guilt by Association: Essays on Japanese Settlement, Internment, and Relocation in the Rocky Mountain West,* edited by Mike Mackey, 255–76. Casper, WY: Western History Publications, 2001.

Horkheimer, Max, and Theodor W. Adorno. "The Culture Industry: Enlightenment as Mass Deception." In *Dialectic of Enlightenment,* translated by Edmund Jephcott, 35–62. Stanford, CA: Stanford University Press, 2002 [1944].

Horne, Gerald. *Fire This Time: The Watts Uprising and the 1960s.* Charlottesville: University of Virginia Press, 1995.

Horsman, Reginald. *Race and Manifest Destiny: The Origins of American Racial Anglo-Saxonism.* Cambridge, MA: Harvard University Press, 1981.

Hosapple, Stephen, and Satsuki Ina. *Children of the Camps.* DVD. Center for Asian American Media, 1999.

Hou, Chi-Ming. "Some Reflections on the Economic History of Modern China (1840–1949)." *Journal of Economic History* 23, no. 4 (1963): 595–605.

"How to Write a Parole Letter." *The Law Dictionary.* Accessed 18 November 2015. http://thelawdictionary.org/article/how-to-write-a-parole-letter/.

Hsu, Madeline. *Dreaming of Gold, Dreaming of Home: Transnationalism and Migration between the United States and South China, 1882–1943.* Stanford, CA: Stanford University Press, 2000.

Huang, Philip C. *The Peasant Family and Rural Development in the Yangzi Delta, 1350–1988.* Stanford, CA: Stanford University Press, 1990.

Huang, Yunte. "Angel Island and the Poetics of Error." In *Poetry and Cultural Studies: A Reader,* edited by Maria Damon and Ira Livingston, 301–9. Champaign: University of Illinois Press, 2009.

———. *Transpacific Imaginations: History, Literature, Counterpoetics.* Cambridge, MA: Harvard University Press, 2008.

Hunter, Dard. *Chinese Ceremonial Paper: A Monograph Relating to the Fabrication of Paper and Tin Foil and the Use of Paper in Chinese Rites and Religious Ceremonies.* Chillicothe, OH: Mountain House Press, 1937.

Hurston, Zora Neale. "How It Feels to Be Colored Me." *World Tomorrow* 11 (May 1928): 215–16.

Hyde, Lewis. *The Gift: Creativity and the Artist in the Modern World.* New York: Vintage Books, 1983.

Ichioka, Yuji, ed. *Views from Within: The Japanese American Evacuation and Resettlement Study.* Los Angeles: Resource Development and Publications, Asian American Studies Center, University of California at Los Angeles, 1989.

Ienaga, Saburo. *The Pacific War: 1931–1945.* New York: Pantheon Books, 1979.

Inada, Lawson Fusao. *Drawing the Line.* Minneapolis, MN: Coffee House Press, 1997.

————. *Legends from Camp: Poems.* Minneapolis, MN: Coffee House Press, 1992.

————, ed. *Only What We Could Carry: The Japanese American Internment Experience.* Berkeley, CA: Heyday, 2000.

Jablon, Madelyn. *Black Metafiction: Self-Consciousness in African American Literature.* Iowa City: University of Iowa Press, 1999.

Jackson, George. *Soledad Brother: The Prison Letters of George Jackson.* New ed. Chicago: Chicago Review Press, 1994 [1970].

Jackson, Lester. "A Dialogue with My Soledad Son." *Ebony,* November 1971.

Jacobson, Matthew Frye. *Whiteness of a Different Color: European Immigrants and the Alchemy of Race.* Cambridge, MA: Harvard University Press, 1999.

James, C. L. R. *The Black Jacobins: Toussaint L'Ouverture and the San Domingo Revolution.* New York: Vintage Books, 1963.

————. "Black Studies and the Contemporary Student." In *At the Rendezvous of Victory: Selected Writings,* 389–404. London: Allison & Busby, 1984.

James, Joy. "Black Revolutionary Icons and 'Neoslave' Narratives." *Social Identities* 5, no. 2 (1999): 135–59.

————, ed. *Imprisoned Intellectuals: America's Political Prisoners Write on Life, Liberation, and Rebellion.* Lanham, MD: Rowman & Littlefield, 2003.

————. *Resisting State Violence: Radicalicism, Gender, and Race in U.S. Culture.* Minneapolis: University of Minnesota Press, 1996.

————. *Seeking the Beloved Community: A Feminist Race Reader.* Albany: State University of New York Press, 2013.

————. *Shadowboxing: Representations of Black Feminist Politics.* New York: St. Martin's Press, 1999.

————, ed. *States of Confinement: Policing, Detention, and Prisons.* New York: Palgrave Macmillan, 2002.

————, ed. *The New Abolitionists: (Neo)Slave Narratives and Contemporary Prison Writings.* Albany: State University of New York Press, 2005.

Jameson, Fredric. "Postmodernism, or The Cultural Logic of Late Capitalism." *New Left Review* 1, no. 146 (August 1984): 53–92.

"The Japanese American Evacuation and Resettlement: A Digital Archive—The Bancroft Library—University of California, Berkeley." Accessed 20 February 2016. http://vm136.lib.berkeley.edu/BANC/collections/jais/abouttheproject.html.

"Japanese American Evacuation and Resettlement Records." BANC MSS 67/14 c, folder B12.50 (2/2). UC Berkeley, Bancroft Library. Accessed 20 February 2016. http://www.oac.cdlib.org/ark:/28722/bk0013c8x33/?brand=oac4.

Japanese Cultural & Community Center of Northern California. *From Our Side of the Fence: Growing Up in America's Concentration Camps.* Edited by Brian Komei Dempster. San Francisco: Kearny Street Workshop, 2001.

John, Richard R. *Spreading the News: The American Postal System from Franklin to Morse.* Cambridge, MA: Harvard University Press, 1995.

Johnson, Barbara. "The Frame of Reference: Poe, Lacan, Derrida." *Yale French Studies,* no. 55–56 (1 January 1977): 457–505.

Jones, Gayl. *Liberating Voices: Oral Tradition in African American Literature.* Cambridge, MA: Harvard University Press, 1991.

Jun, Helen Heran. *Race for Citizenship: Black Orientalism and Asian Uplift from Pre-Emancipation to Neoliberal America.* New York: New York University Press, 2011.

Jung, Moon-Ho. *Coolies and Cane: Race, Labor, and Sugar in the Age of Emancipation.* Baltimore, MD: Johns Hopkins University Press, 2006.

Kang, Hyun Yi. *Compositional Subjects: Enfiguring Asian / American Women.* Durham, NC: Duke University Press, 2002.

Kauffman, Linda S. *Special Delivery: Epistolary Modes in Modern Fiction.* Chicago: University of Chicago Press, 1992.

Kazue de Cristoforo, Violet. *May Sky: There Is Always Tomorrow: An Anthology of Japanese American Concentration Camp Kaiko Haiku.* Los Angeles, CA: Sun and Moon Press, 1997.

Keeling, Kara. *The Witch's Flight: The Cinematic, the Black Femme, and the Image of Common Sense.* Durham, NC: Duke University Press, 2007.

Kelley, Robin D. G. *Freedom Dreams: The Black Radical Imagination.* Boston: Beacon Press, 2003.

———. *Hammer and Hoe: Alabama Communists During the Great Depression.* Chapel Hill: University of North Carolina Press, 1990.

———. "A Poetics of Anticolonialism." *Monthly Review* 51, no. 6 (1999). http://monthlyreview.org/1999/11/01/a-poetics-of-anticolonialism/.

———. *Race Rebels: Culture, Politics, and the Black Working Class.* New York: Free Press, 1996.

Kilgore, James. "Confronting Prison Slave Labor Camps and Other Myths." *Social Justice* Online (28 August 2013). http://www.socialjusticejournal.org/?p=235.

Kim, Claire Jean. "The Racial Triangulation of Asian Americans." *Politics & Society* 27, no. 1 (1 March 1999): 105–38.

Kim, Daniel Y. "Once More, with Feeling: Cold War Masculinity and the Sentiment of Patriotism in John Okada's 'No-No Boy.'" *Criticism* 47, no. 1 (2005): 65–83.

———. *Writing Manhood in Black and Yellow: Ralph Ellison, Frank Chin, and the Literary Politics of Identity.* Stanford, CA: Stanford University Press, 2005.

Kim, Jodi. *Ends of Empire: Asian American Critique and the Cold War.* Minneapolis: University of Minnesota Press, 2010.

Kitagawa, Daisuke. *Issei and Nisei: The Internment Years.* New York: Seabury Press, 1967.

Koshy, Susan. "Morphing Race into Ethnicity: Asian Americans and Critical Transformations of Whiteness." *Boundary 2* 28, no. 1 (2001): 153–94.

Kramer, Paul. *The Blood of Government.* Chapel Hill: University of North Carolina Press, 2006.

Kuhl, Stefan. *The Nazi Connection: Eugenics, American Racism, and German National Socialism.* New York: Oxford University Press, 1994.

Kumamoto, Bob. "The Search for Spies: American Counterintelligence and the Japanese American Community 1931–1942." *Amerasia Journal* 6, no. 2 (1 October 1979): 45–75.

Kwong, Peter. *Forbidden Workers: Illegal Chinese Immigrants and American Labor.* New York: New Press, 1997.

Lacan, Jacques. "The Youth of Gide, or the Letter and Desire." In *Ecrits: The First Complete Edition in English.* Translated by Bruce Fink. New York: Norton, 2007 [1958].

LaFeber, Walter. *The Clash: U.S.-Japanese Relations throughout History.* New York: Norton, 1998.

Lai, H. Mark. *Becoming Chinese American: A History of Communities and Institutions.* Walnut Creek, CA: Rowman Altamira, 2004.

Lai, H. Mark, Genny Lim, and Judy Yung. *Island: Poetry and History of Chinese Immigrants on Angel Island 1910–1940.* Seattle: University of Washington Press, 1991.

Lau, Estelle T. *Paper Families: Identity, Immigration Administration, and Chinese Exclusion.* Durham, NC: Duke University Press, 2007.

Lazos Vargas, Sylvia R. "History, Legal Scholarship, and LatCrit Theory: The Case of Racial Transformations circa the Spanish American War, 1896–1900." *Denver University Law Review* 78, no. 4 (2001): 921–63.

Lee, Erika. *At America's Gates: Chinese Immigration during the Exclusion Era, 1882–1943.* Chapel Hill: University of North Carolina Press, 2003.

Lenin, Vladimir. "The State and Revolution" (1871). https://www.marxists.org /archive/lenin/works/1917/staterev/ch03.htm#s3.

Leong, Karen, and Myla Vicente Carpio, eds. "Carceral States." *Amerasia Journal* 42, no. 1 (2016).

"Letter Log: Correspondence from Customs Surveyor to Various, Nov 20, 1887 to Nov 18, 1889." National Archives and Records Administration–Pacific Region (unprocessed).

Levi, Primo. *If This Is a Man.* New York: Abacus Books, 1987.

Lifton, Robert Jay, and Greg Mitchell. *Hiroshima in America: Fifty Years of Denial.* New York: Putnam's Sons, 1995.

Linderman, Gerald F. *The World within War: America's Combat Experience in World War II.* Cambridge, MA: Harvard University Press, 1999.

Lindquist, Heather C. *Children of Manzanar.* Berkeley, CA: Heyday, 2012.

Linebaugh, Peter, and Marcus Rediker. *The Many-Headed Hydra: Sailors, Slaves, Commoners, and the Hidden History of the Revolutionary Atlantic.* New York: Beacon Press, 2000.

Lippit, Akira Mizuta. *Atomic Light (Shadow Optics).* Minneapolis: University of Minnesota Press, 2005.

Lipsitz, George. *Possessive Investment in Whiteness.* Philadelphia, PA: Temple University Press, 1998.

Litoff, Judy Barrett, and David Clay Smith. *Since You Went Away: World War II Letters from American Women on the Home Front.* New York: Oxford University Press, 1991.

Liu, Haiming. *The Transnational History of a Chinese Family: Immigrant Letters, Family Business, and Reverse Migration.* New Brunswick, NJ: Rutgers University Press, 2005.

Lloyd, David. "Representation's Coup." *Interventions* 16, no. 1 (2 January 2014): 1–29.

Loewen, James W. *The Mississippi Chinese: Between Black and White.* Long Grove, IL: Waveland Press, 1971.

Loomis, H. T. *Practical Letter Writing.* Cleveland, OH: Practical Text Book Company, 1897.

Lowe, Lisa. *Immigrant Acts: On Asian American Cultural Politics.* Durham, NC: Duke University Press, 1996.

———. *The Intimacies of Four Continents.* Durham, NC: Duke University Press, 2015.

Lowe, Lisa, and David Lloyd. *The Politics of Culture in the Shadow of Capital.* Durham, NC: Duke University Press, 1997.

Lu, Bowei, Guoping Wang, and Caishi Dong. *The Revolution of 1911: Turning Point in Modern Chinese History.* Beijing: Foreign Languages Press, 1991.

Luibheid, Eithne. *Entry Denied: Controlling Sexuality at the Border.* Minneapolis: University of Minnesota Press, 2002.

Lye, Colleen. "The Afro-Asian Analogy." *PMLA* 123, no. 5 (1 October 2008): 1732–36.

———. *America's Asia: Racial Form and American Literature, 1893–1945.* Princeton, NJ: Princeton University Press, 2005.

———. "Racial Form." *Representations* 104, no. 1 (1 November 2008): 92–101.

Lynd, Staughton. *Lucasville: The Untold Story of a Prison Uprising.* Philadelphia, PA: Temple University Press, 2004.

Maira, Sunaina. "Radical Deportation: Alien Tales from Lodi and San Francisco." In *The Deportation Regime: Sovereignty, Space, and the Freedom of Movement,* edited by Nicholas De Genova and Nathalie Peutz, 295–328. Durham NC: Duke University Press, 2010.

Malemed, Jodi. *Represent and Destroy.* Minneapolis: University of Minnesota Press, 2011.

Manos, James A. "From Commodity Fetishism to Prison Fetishism: Slavery, Convict-Leasing, and the Ideological Productions of Incarceration." In *Death and Other Penalties: Philosophy in a Time of Mass Incarceration,* edited by Geoffrey Adelsberg, Lisa Guenther, and Scott Zeman, 43–59. New York: Fordham University Press, 2015.

Martínez, Elizabeth Sutherland. *De Colores Means All of Us: Latina Views for a Multi-Colored Century.* Boston, MA: South End Press, 1998.

Massey, Douglas S., and Nancy A. Denton. *American Apartheid: Segregation and the Making of the Underclass.* Cambridge, MA: Harvard University Press, 1993.

Massiah, Louis J., Thomas Ott, and Terry Kay Rockefeller. *Eyes on the Prize: A Nation of Law? (1968–1971).* DVD. Blackside Media, 1990.

Masuda, Bessie. Interview with Center for Arkansas History and Culture, University of Arkansas, Little Rock. Accessed 19 February 2016. https://www.youtube.com/watch?v = Z31iLSt7YYE.

Matsuda, Mari. "We Will Not Be Used." *UCLA Asian American Pacific Islands Law Journal* 1 (1993): 79–84.

Matsumoto, Valerie J. *Farming the Home Place: A Japanese Community in California, 1919–1982.* Ithaca, NY: Cornell University Press, 1993.

Mbembe, Achille. "Necropolitics." *Public Culture* 15, no. 1 (21 December 2003): 11–40.

———. "On the Power of the False." Translated by Judith Inggs. *Public Culture* 14, no. 3 (2002): 629–41.

McClure, Floyd Alonzo. *Chinese Handmade Paper.* Edited by Elaine Koretsky. Newtown, PA: Bird & Bull Press, 1986.

McKeown, Adam. *Chinese Migrant Networks and Cultural Change: Peru, Chicago, and Hawaii 1900–1936.* Chicago: University of Chicago Press, 2001.

———. *Melancholy Order: Asian Migration and the Globalization of Borders.* New York: Columbia University Press, 2008.

———. "The Ritualization of Regulation: The Enforcement of Chinese Exclusion in the United States and China." *American Historical Review* 108, no. 2 (2003): 377–403.

McKittrick, Katherine. *Demonic Grounds: Black Women and the Cartographies of Struggle.* Minneapolis: University of Minnesota Press, 2006.

———, ed. *Sylvia Wynter: On Being Human as Praxis.* Durham, NC: Duke University Press, 2015.

McKittrick, Katherine, and Clyde Woods, eds. *Black Geographies and the Politics of Place.* Cambridge, MA: South End Press, 2007.

Menchaca, Martha. *Recovering History, Constructing Race: The Indian, Black, and White Roots of Mexican Americans.* Austin: University of Texas Press, 2001.

Menke, Richard. *Telegraphic Realism: Victorian Fiction and Other Information Systems.* Stanford, CA: Stanford University Press, 2007.

Mitsui, James Masao. *From a Three-Cornered World.* Seattle: University of Washington Press, 1997.

Miyamoto, S. Frank. "Resentment, Distrust, and Insecurity at Tule Lake." In *Views from Within: The Japanese American Evacuation and Resettlement Study,* edited by Yuji Ichioka, 127–40. Los Angeles: Asian American Studies Center, University of California at Los Angeles, 1989.

Molina, Natalia. *Fit to Be Citizens? Public Health and Race in Los Angeles, 1879–1939.* Berkeley: University of California Press, 2006.

Moore, Richard O. *Take This Hammer (the Director's Cut).* Online. San Francisco Bay Area Television Archive, 2013. https://diva.sfsu.edu/collections/sfbatv/bundles/216518.

Moraga, Cherríe, and Gloria Anzaldúa, eds. *This Bridge Called My Back: Writings by Radical Women of Color.* 2nd ed. New York: Kitchen Table / Women of Color Press, 1984.

Morales, Aurora Levins. *Medicine Stories: History, Culture and the Politics of Integrity.* Cambridge, MA: South End Press, 1999.

Morrison, Toni. "Rootedness: The Ancestor as Foundation." In *Black Women Writers (1950–1980): A Critical Evaluation,* edited by Mari Evans, 339–45. New York: Doubleday, 1984.

———. *Sula.* New York: Vintage International, 1973.

Moten, Fred. "Black Op." *PMLA* 123, no. 5 (2008): 1743–47.

———. "The Case of Blackness." *Criticism* 50, no. 2 (3 July 2008): 177–218.

———. *In the Break: The Aesthetics of the Black Radical Tradition.* Minneapolis: University of Minnesota Press, 2003.

Moten, Fred, and Stefano Harney. "The University and the Undercommons SEVEN THESES." *Social Text* 22, no. 2 79 (20 June 2004): 101–15.

Muñoz, Carolina Bank. *Transnational Tortillas: Race, Gender, and Shop-Floor Politics in Mexico and the United States.* Ithaca, NY: Cornell University Press, 2008.

Muñoz, José Esteban. "Ephemera as Evidence: Introductory Notes to Queer Acts." *Women & Performance: A Journal of Feminist Theory* 8, no. 2 (1 January 1996): 5–16.

Nagar, Richa, and Sangtin Writers. *Playing with Fire: Feminist Thought and Activism through Seven Lives in India.* Minneapolis: University of Minnesota Press, 2006.

Nagata, Donna K. *Legacy of Injustice: Exploring the Cross-Generational Impact of the Japanese American Internment.* New York: Plenium Press, 1993.

Nasson, Bill. *The South African Boer War 1899–1902.* New York: Oxford University Press, 1999.

Nelson, Alondra, Thuy Linh N. Tu, and Alicia Headlam Hines, eds. *Technicolor: Race, Technology, and Everyday Life.* New York: New York University Press, 2001.

Newnham, Nicole, and David Grabias. *Sentenced Home.* Independent Television Service, 2006. http://www.pbs.org/independentlens/sentencedhome/film.html.

Ngai, Mae M. *Impossible Subjects: Illegal Aliens and the Making of Modern America.* Princeton, NJ: Princeton University Press, 2005.

Ngo, Viet Mike. "Grave Digger." *Amerasia Journal* 29, no. 1 (2003): 179.

———."Lesson Learned in Prison College." In *Other: An Asian & Pacific Islander Prisoners' Anthology,* ed. Eddy Zheng (Hayward, CA: Asian Prisoner Support Committee, 2007), 73–75.

———. "The Real Me." In *Other: An Asian & Pacific Islander Prisoners' Anthology,* ed. Eddy Zheng, 116–17. Hayward, CA: Asian Prisoner Support Committee, 2007.

Nguyen, Mimi Thi. *The Gift of Freedom: War, Debt, and Other Refugee Passages.* Durham, NC: Duke University Press, 2012.

Nguyen-vo, Thu-huong. *The Ironies of Freedom: Sex, Culture, and Neoliberal Governance in Vietnam.* Seattle: University of Washington Press, 2009.

"NJAHS Military Intelligence Service Oral History Project." National Japanese American Historical Society. Accessed 17 February 2016. https://www.njahs.org /military-intelligence-service-oral-history-project/.

Ogden, Stormy. "The Use of Letters as Social Control," e-mail correspondence with author, 26 July 2010.

Okazaki, Steven. *White Light / Black Rain*. DVD. Farallon Films, 2007.

Okihiro, Gary. *Cane Fires: The Anti-Japanese Movement in Hawaii, 1865–1945*. Philadephia, PA: Temple University Press, 1991.

———. "Japanese Resistance in America's Concentration Camps: A Re-Evaluation." *Amerasia Journal* 2, no. 1 (1 October 1973): 20–34.

———. "Religion and Resistance in America's Concentration Camps." *Phylon* 45, no. 3 (1984): 220–33.

Okihiro, Gary, and David Drummond. "The Concentration Camps and Japanese Economic Losses in California Agriculture, 1900–1942." In *Japanese Americans: From Relocation to Redress*, edited by Roger Daniels, Sandra C. Taylor, and Harry H. L. Kitano, 168–75. Salt Lake City: University of Utah Press, 1986.

Okubo, Miné. *Citizen 13660*. Reprint. Seattle: University of Washington Press, 1983 [1946].

Omatsu, Glenn K. "The 'Four Prisons' and the Movements of Liberation." *Amerasia Journal* 15, no. 1 (1989): xv–xxx.

Omori, Chizu. "The Loyalty Questionnaire." In *Guilt by Association: Essays on Japanese Settlement, Internment, and Relocation in the Rocky Mountain West*, edited by Mike Mackey, 277–86. Casper, WY: Western History Publications, 2001.

Omowale, Yusef Toussaint. "Speaking the Impossible: Navigating through Silence to Voice." In *Cultural Studies in Education*, edited by Antonia Darder, 90–105. Claremont, CA: Claremont Graduate University School of Educational Studies, 1998.

Oppenheim, Joanne. *Dear Miss Breed: True Stories of the Japanese American Incarceration during World War II and a Librarian Who Made a Difference*. New York: Scholastic Books, 2006.

Pakenham, Thomas. *The Boer War*. New York: Random House, 1979.

Pan, Jixing. "The Origin of Papermaking in the Light of Scientific Research on Recent Archeological Discoveries." In *Chinese Studies: Papers Presented at a Colloquium at the School of Oriental and African Studies, University of London, 24–26 August 1987*, edited by Francis Wood, 176–80. London: British Library, 1988.

Parenti, Christian. *Lockdown America*. New York: Verso Books, 1999.

Patterson, Orlando. *Slavery and Social Death: A Comparative Study*. Cambridge, MA: Harvard University Press, 1982.

Pegler-Gordon, Anna. "Chinese Exclusion, Photography, and the Development of U.S. Immigration Policy." *American Quarterly* 58, no. 1 (2006): 51–77.

Prisoner Hunger Strike Solidarity. "Prisoners' Demands." Accessed 3 April 2011. https://prisonerhungerstrikesolidarity.wordpress.com/the-prisoners-demands-2/.

———. "Take Action." Accessed 25 September 2015. https://prisonerhungerstrike solidarity.wordpress.com/take-action-2/.

Peters, Jeremy W. "The Handwritten Letter, an Art All but Lost, Thrives in Prison." *New York Times*, 8 January 2011.

Pfaelzer, Jean. *Driven Out: The Forgotten War against Chinese Americans*. Berkeley: University of California Press, 2008.

"Plains Indian Ledger Art Project." Accessed 8 November 2016. https://plainsledgerart
.org/ledgers/index/1/.

Prashad, Vijay. *Everybody Was Kung Fu Fighting: Afro-Asian Connections and the
Myth of Cultural Purity.* Boston, MA: Beacon Press, 2002.

———. *The Karma of Brown Folk.* Minneapolis: University of Minnesota Press,
2001.

Pulido, Laura. *Black, Brown, Yellow, and Left: Radical Activism in Los Angeles.*
Berkeley: University of California Press, 2005.

Quan, H. L. T. *Growth against Democracy: Savage Developmentalism in the Modern
World.* Lanham, MD: Lexington Books, 2012.

Reddy, Chandan. *Freedom with Violence: Race, Sexuality, and the US State.* Durham, NC: Duke University Press, 2011.

Reed, Christopher A. *Gutenberg in Shanghai: Chinese Print Capitalism, 1876–1937.*
Vancouver: University of British Columbia Press, 2005.

Remeidio, Rico. "Making Rehabilitation Work: Creating Opportunities for Formerly Incarcerated Individuals." Paper presented at the San Francisco Reentry
Summit, 2006, San Francisco, 27 September 2006. https://www.youtube.com
/watch?v=1ufUaV9Hqp0.

Remeidio, Rico, German Yambao, and Eddy Zheng. "Other: Voices of Asian Prisoners." Paper presented at the Critical Resistance Conference, Oakland, CA, 28
September 2008. http://www.asianprisonersupport.com/videos/.

Rhoads, Edward J. M. *China's Republican Revolution: The Case of Kwangtung,
1895–1913.* Cambridge, MA: Harvard University Press, 1975.

Roach, Joseph R. *Cities of the Dead: Circum-Atlantic Performance.* New York:
Columbia University Press, 1996.

Robinson, Cedric J. *Black Marxism: The Making of the Black Radical Tradition.*
Chapel Hill: University of North Carolina Press, 2000.

———. "Manichaeism and Multiculturalism." In *Mapping Multiculturalism,*
edited by Avery F. Gordon and Christopher Newfield, 116–26. Minneapolis:
University of Minnesota Press, 1996.

Robinson, Greg. *By Order of the President: FDR and the Internment of Japanese
Americans.* Cambridge, MA: Harvard University Press, 2001.

Rodríguez, Dylan. *Forced Passages: Imprisoned Radical Intellectuals and the U.S.
Prison Regime.* Minneapolis: University of Minnesota Press, 2006.

Rodríguez, Dylan, and Casey Goonan. "Policing and the Violence of White Being:
An Interview with Dylan Rodríguez." *Black Scholar,* 12 September 2016.
http://www.theblackscholar.org/policing-violence-white-interview-dylan-
rodriguez/.

Rodríguez, Dylan, and Viet Mike Ngo. "Ethnic Studies in the Age of the Prison-
Industrial Complex: Reflections on 'Freedom' and Capture, Praxis, and Immobilization." In *Pedagogies of the Global: Knowledge in the Human Interest,* edited
by Arif Dirlik, 113–131. Boulder, CO: Paradigm Publishers, 2006.

Roeder, George H. *The Censored War: American Visual Experience during World
War Two.* New Haven, CT: Yale University Press, 1993.

Rosenblatt, Andy, and Michael H. Cottman. "Miami Hijacking Suspect Arrested." *Miami Herald,* 5 December 1983. http://www.latinamericanstudies.org/hijackers /suspect-arrested.htm.

Ross, Luana. *Inventing the Savage: The Social Construction of Native American Criminality.* Austin: University of Texas Press, 1998.

Roxworthy, Emily. *The Spectacle of Japanese American Trauma: Racial Performativity and World War II.* Honolulu: University of Hawaii Press, 2008.

Said, Edward W. *Culture and Imperialism.* New York: Random House, 1993.

Saillant, Catherine. "Japanese Americans' Protests Halt Auction of Internment Camp Items." *Los Angeles Times,* 16 April 2015. http://www.latimes.com/local /california/la-me-auction-internment-artifacts-20150417-story.html.

Saldaña, Carolina. "Mumia Abu-Jamal's Eighth Book: Writing on the Wall (Review)." *Countercurrents,* 5 September 2015. http://www.countercurrents.org /saldana050915.htm.

Saldaña-Portillo, María Josefina. *The Revolutionary Imagination in the Americas and the Age of Development.* Durham, NC: Duke University Press, 2003.

San Juan, E. "We Charge Genocide: A Brief History of US in the Philippines." *Politicalaffairs.net: Marxist Thought Online,* 2005. http://politicalaffairs.net /we-charge-genocide-a-brief-history-of-us-in-the-philippines/.

Sanchez, George J. *Becoming Mexican American: Ethnicity, Culture, and Identity in Chicano Los Angeles, 1900–1945.* New York: Oxford University Press, 1995.

———. "Disposable People, Expendable Neighborhoods." In *A Companion to Los Angeles,* edited by William Deverell and Greg Hise, 129–46. Hoboken, NJ: Wiley-Blackwell, 2010.

———. "Face the Nation: Race, Immigration, and the Rise of Nativism in Late Twentieth Century America." *International Migration Review* 31, no. 4 (1 December 1997): 1009–30.

Saxton, Alexander. *The Indispensable Enemy: Labor and the Anti-Chinese Movement in California.* Berkeley: University of California Press, 1971.

Schoefer, Christine. "Cry Out: Women Behind Bars." *Yes! Magaine,* 30 September 2000. http://www.yesmagazine.org/issues/is-it-time-to-close-the-prisons/cry-out-women-behind-bars.

Scott, James C. *Domination and the Arts of Resistance: Hidden Transcripts.* New Haven, CT: Yale University Press, 1990.

Scott, Janet Lee. *For Gods, Ghosts and Ancestors: The Chinese Tradition of Paper Offerings.* Kowloon: Hong Kong University Press, 2007.

Sexton, Jared. "People-of-Color-Blindness Notes on the Afterlife of Slavery." *Social Text* 28, no. 2 103 (20 June 2010): 31–56.

Shah, Nayan. *Contagious Divides: Epidemics and Race in San Francisco's Chinatown.* Berkeley: University of California Press, 2001.

Shakur, Assata. *Assata: An Autobiography.* Chicago: Lawrence Hill Books, 1987.

———. "I Am a 20th Century Escaped Slave." 30 December 2014. http://www .counterpunch.org/2014/12/30/an-open-letter-to-the-media/.

Shapiro-Bertolini, Ethel, and Andrew Richter, eds. *Through the Wall: Prison Correspondence*. Culver City, CA: Peace Press, 1976.

Shih, Min-hsiung. *The Silk Industry in Ch'ing China*. Translated by E-Tu Zen Sun. Ann Arbor: Center for Chinese Studies, University of Michigan Press, 1976.

Sides, Josh. *L.A. City Limits: African American Los Angeles from the Great Depression to the Present*. Berkeley: University of California Press, 2004.

Simon, Sunka. *Mail-Orders: The Fiction of Letters in Postmodern Culture*. New York: State University of New York Press, 2002.

Singh, Nikhil Pal. *Black Is a Country: Race and the Unfinished Struggle for Democracy*. Cambridge, MA: Harvard University Press, 2004.

Smith, Andrea. *Conquest: Sexual Violence and American Indian Genocide*. Boston, MA: South End Press, 2005.

So, Alvin Y. *The South China Silk District: Local Historical Transformation and World System Theory*. New York: State University of New York Press, 1986.

Soga, Keiho, Taisanboku Mori, Sojin Tokiji Takei, and Muin Otokichi Ozaki. *Poets Behind Barbed Wire: Tanka Poems*. Edited and translated by Jiro Nakano and Kay Nakano. Honolulu, HI: Bamboo Ridge Press, 1983.

Spade, Dean. *Normal Life: Administrative Violence, Critical Trans Politics, and the Limits of Law*. Boston, MA: South End Press, 2011.

Spearman, Frank H. "The First Transcontinental Railroad." *Harper's Monthly Magazine* 109 (November 1904): 711–20.

Spicer, Edward. "The Use of Social Scientists by the War Relocation Authority." *Human Organization* 5, no. 2 (1 April 1946): 16–36.

Spillers, Hortense J. *Black, White, and in Color: Essays on American Literature and Culture*. Chicago: University of Chicago Press, 2003.

Stanley, Liz. "The Epistolarium: On Theorizing Letters and Correspondences." *Auto/Biography* 12 (2004): 201–35.

Starn, Orin. "Engineering Internment: Anthropologists and the War Relocation Authority." *American Ethnologist* 13, no. 4 (1 November 1986): 700–720.

Steedman, Carolyn. *Dust: The Archive and Cultural History*. New Brunswick, NJ: Rutgers University Press, 2002.

Stern, Alexandra Minna. *Eugenic Nation: Faults and Frontiers of Better Breeding in Modern America*. Berkeley: University of California Press, 2005.

Stillson, Richard Thomas. *Spreading the Word: A History of Information in the California Gold Rush*. Lincoln: University of Nebraska Press, 2006.

Stockard, Janice. *Daughters of the Canton Delta: Marriage Patterns and Economic Strategies in South China, 1860–1930*. Stanford, CA: Stanford University Press, 1992.

Stoler, Ann Laura. *Along the Archival Grain: Epistemic Anxieties and Colonial Common Sense*. Princeton, NJ: Princeton University Press, 2010.

Sturken, Marita. "The Absent Images of Memory: Remembering and Reenacting the Japanese Internment." *Positions* 5, no. 3 (Winter 1997): 687–707.

Suzuki, Peter T. "Anthropologists in the Wartime Camps for Japanese Americans: A Documentary Study." *Dialectical Anthropology* 6, no. 1 (1 August 1981): 23–60.

Sweeney, Megan. *Reading Is My Window: Books and the Art of Reading in Women's Prisons.* Chapel Hill: University of North Carolina Press, 2010.

Takaki, Ronald. *Double Victory: A Multicultural History of America in World War II.* Boston, MA: Back Bay Books, 2001.

———. *Strangers from a Different Shore: A History of Asian Americans.* New York: Penguin, 1989.

Takei, Barbara, and Judy Tachibana. *Tule Lake Revisited: A Brief History and Guide to the Tule Lake Internment Camp Site.* Sacramento, CA: T&T Press, 2001.

Takei, Carl. "From Mass Incarceration to Mass Control, and Back Again: How Bipartisan Criminal Justice Reform May Lead to a For-Profit Nightmare." SSRN Scholarly Paper. Social Science Research Network, Rochester, NY, 3 March 2016. http://papers.ssrn.com/abstract=2741932.

Tang, Eric. "How the Refugees Stopped the Bronx from Burning." *Race & Class* 54, no. 4 (1 April 2013): 48–66.

Taylor, Quintard. *In Search of the Racial Frontier: African Americans in the American West 1528–1990.* New York: Norton, 1999.

Taylor, Zada. "War Children on the Pacific: A Symposium Article." *Library Journal* 67 (15 June 1942): 558–62.

Terkel, Studs. *"The Good War": An Oral History of World War Two.* New York: Pantheon Books, 1984.

Teves, Stephanie Nohelani. "Tradition and Performance." In *Native Studies Keywords,* edited by Stephanie Nohelani Teves, Andrea Smith, and Michelle Raheja. Tucson: University of Arizona Press, 2015.

Thompson, E. P. *The Making of the English Working Class.* New York: Vintage Books, 1966.

Tolman, Edward C. "Cognitive Maps in Rats and Men." *Psychological Review* 55, no. 4 (1948): 189–208.

Tomita, Mary Kimoto. *Dear Miye: Letters Home from Japan, 1939–1946.* Stanford, CA: Stanford University Press, 1997.

Tule Lake Committee. *Second Kinenhi: Reflections on Tule Lake.* San Francisco: Tule Lake Committee and John R. and Reiko Ross, 2000.

Vohra, Ranbir. *China's Path to Modernization: A Historical Review from 1800 to the Present.* Englewood Cliffs, NJ: Prentice Hall, 1987.

Wang, L. Ling-chi. "Politics of the Repeal of the Chinese Exclusion Laws." In *The Repeal and Its Legacy: Proceedings of the Conference on the 50th Anniversary of the Repeal of the Exclusion Acts,* 66–80. San Francisco: Chinese Historical Society of America, 1994.

Warren, Kenneth W. *What Was African American Literature?* Cambridge, MA: Harvard University Press, 2012.

Weglyn, Michi. *Years of Infamy: The Untold Story of America's Concentration Camps.* New York: Morrow Quill Paperbacks, 1976.

Weheliye, Alexander G. *Phonographies: Grooves in Sonic Afro-Modernity.* Durham, NC: Duke University Press, 2005.

Welch, Richard E. "American Atrocities in the Philippines: The Indictment and the Response." *Pacific Historical Review* 43, no. 2 (May 1974): 233–53.

Wells, Ida B. *Southern Horrors and Other Writings; The Anti-Lynching Campaign of Ida B. Wells, 1892–1900.* Edited by Jacqueline Jones Royster. 1st ed. Boston, MA: Bedford / St. Martin's, 1996.

White, Richard. *Railroaded: The Transcontinentals and the Making of Modern America.* New York: Norton, 2011.

Wideman, John Edgar. "Why Mumia Matters to the Nation and World." Educators for Mumia Abu-Jamal, 9 June 2005. http://www.emajonline.com/2005/06/why-mumia-matters-to-the-nation-and-world-by-john-edgar-wideman/.

Wild, Mark. *Street Meeting: Multiethnic Neighborhoods in Early-Twentieth-Century Los Angeles.* Berkeley: University of California Press, 2005.

Williams, Randall. *The Divided World: Human Rights and Its Violence.* Minneapolis: University of Minnesota Press, 2010.

Williams, Raymond. *Marxism and Literature.* Oxford: Oxford University Press, 1978.

Willoughby-Herard, Tiffany. "More Expendable than Slaves? Racial Justice and the After-Life of Slavery." *Politics, Groups, and Identities* 2, no. 3 (3 July 2014): 506–21.

Wilson, Bobby M. *America's Johannesburg: Industrialization and Racial Transformation in Birmingham.* New York: Rowman & Littlefield, 2000.

Winther, Oscar O. "Promoting the American West in England, 1865–1890." *Journal of Economic History* 16, no. 4 (1956): 506–13.

Wong, Edlie. *Racial Reconstruction: Black Inclusion, Chinese Exclusion, and the Fictions of Citizenship.* New York: New York University Press, 2015.

Wong, Nellie. *Dreams in Harrison Railroad Park.* Berkeley, CA: Kelsey Street Press, 1977.

Woods, Clyde. *Black California Dreamin': The Crises of California's African-American Communities.* Santa Barbara: UCSB Center for Black Studies Research, 2012. http://escholarship.org/uc/item/63g6128j.

———. *Development Arrested: Race, Power, and the Blues in the Mississippi Delta.* New York: Verso Books, 1998.

———. "Katrina's World: Blues, Bourbon, and the Return to the Source." *American Quarterly* 61, no. 3 (2009): 427–53.

———. "Life after Death." *Professional Geographer* 54, no. 1 (2002): 62–66.

———. "Necropolitics Blues." Paper presented at the Critical Ethnic Studies Conference, Riverside, CA, 2010.

Worthing, Peter. *A Military History of Modern China: From the Manchu Conquest to Tian'anmen Square.* Westport, CT: Praeger, 2007.

Wynter, Sylvia. "Ethno or Socio Poetics." *Alcheringa / Boston University* 2, no. 2 (1976): 78–94.

———. "No Humans Involved: An Open Letter to My Colleagues." *Forum N.H.I.: Knowledge for the 21st Century* 1, no. 1 (1994): 42–73.

Yang, Alice. "Redress Movement." In *Densho Encyclopedia.* Densho Encyclopedia, June 2014. http://encyclopedia.densho.org/Redress%20movement/.

Yau, John. *Radiant Silhouette: New & Selected Work, 1974–1988*. Santa Rosa, CA: Black Sparrow Press, 1989.

Yoneyama, Lisa. *Hiroshima Traces: Time, Space, and Dialectics of Memory*. Berkeley: University of California Press, 1999.

Yun, Lisa. *The Coolie Speaks: Chinese Indentured Laborers and African Slaves in Cuba*. Philadephia, PA: Temple University Press, 2008.

Zheng, Eddy, ed. *Other: An Asian & Pacific Islander Prisoners' Anthology*. Hayward, CA: Asian Prisoner Support Committee, 2007.

Zhou, Yongming. *Historicizing Online Politics: Telegraphy, the Internet, and Political Participation in China*. Stanford, CA: Stanford University Press, 2006.

Zinn, Howard. *A People's History of the United States: 1492–Present*. Twentieth anniversary ed. New York: HarperCollins, 2003.

Zo, Kil Young. *Chinese Emigration into the United States, 1850–1880*. New York: Arno Press, 1971.

INDEX

Communist China, 41
concentration camps, 13, 100–102, 104–5,
    115
Cristoforo, Kazue de, 144–45
Cuba, 100–101
Cushman, Mark V., 46

Daniel, the biblical, 214
Daughters of the American Revolution, 82
Davis, Angela, 206–7, 222, 271n18
Davis, Mike, 172
Dear Miss Breed (Oppenheim), 109–13
Death Valley, CA, 115
Delta Ginsha Haiku Kai, 144
democracy: capitalism and, 46; detention
    and, 46; internment and, 103, 161; Nisei
    youth's belief in, 113, 140; racial, 48, 105,
    113, 121, 149; revolutionary, 202
Dempster, Brian Komei, 158–59
Densmore, John B., 25–27, 65
Densmore Investigation, 25–28, 58
Derrida, Jacques, 7, 120, 215
detained, the: civilizing mission for the, 82,
    110; enemy noncombatants, 98; gender
    segregation, 75; immigration interroga-
    tions, 59–62, 65–66; interrogation of
    the, 59–62, 65–66; introduction, 3–4;
    letters of, 73; Pacific Mail sheds hous-
    ing, 48; racialization of, 11–12, 29. *See
    also* migrants, Chinese
detention centers, immigrant: Angel
    Island, 11, 18, 25–29, 49–50, 73, 75, 82;
    INS, 99; private administration of, 12
Dewberry, R. N., 189
"A Dialogue with My Soledad Son"
    (Jackson), 210–12, 211*fig*, 216
difference, production of, 16
Dougan, C. W., 53
Drumgo, Fleeta, 272n19
DuBois, W. E. B., 8

Eagleton, Terry, 120–21
Earle, Rebecca, 8
Edkins, Joseph, 37–38
education of American Indians, 47
Eisenhower, Milton, 117
Employment Service, U.S., 104
enemy aliens: correspondence, censorship

of, 107; registration and internment, 99,
    103; status reversal, 122, 135–36, 139, 143
enemy noncombatants, 98–99
Ennis, Edward J., 140–42, 153*fig*, 154–55,
    156*fig*
epistles, 195–96
error, poetics of, 18
ethnic cleansing, 96, 105, 110
Ethnic Studies, 21–22, 179, 222
ethnopoetics, 17
eugenics movements, 110
Executive Order 8985, 106
Executive Order 9066, 96, 99–105, 108, 113,
    255n23
existence, aesthetics of, 16–19
existentialism, 197

Facebook, 189–190
Fairbank, John L., 35, 53
families: African American, 166–67;
    imagined genealogies of Chinese, 25–30,
    51–52, 58–62, 62–64*fig*, 65, 66–67*fig*,
    123; normative patriarchy of Chinese,
    69, 69–70*fig*, 71, 72*fig*, 73; same-sex, 73
Farm Security Administration, 104
FBI, 97–98, 99, 117, 191, 203
Federal Reserve Bank of San Francisco, 104
Federal Security Organization, 104
Fiset, Louis, 98, 104, 106, 122, 157
Fleetwood, Nicole, 208, 210, 212
"Folsom Prisoners Manifesto of Demands
    and Anti-Oppression Platform," 202
Ford, Ezell, 171
Ford, Karen Jackson, 143–44
Fort Lincoln detention center, 99, 157
Fort Missoula detention center, 99, 118,
    132, 148
Fort Stanton detention center, 99
Foucault, Michel, 16
"Four Great Inventions of Ancient China"
    (stamp), 24*fig*, 39
"The Four Great Inventions of Ancient
    China" (Zhong Guo si da fa ming), 40
Fourteenth Amendment, 46
Franco, George, 189
Free Soil Movement, 11, 29, 43, 44
free speech, 108
Friends of the Indians, 47

From a Silk Cocoon (Ina), 157
From a Three-Cornered World (mitsui), 120
From Our Side of the Fence (Dempster, ed.),
159

Garner, Eric, 171
genealogies, imagined: coaching letters, 26,
 51, 58–62, 62–64*fig*, 66–67*fig*, 123;
 paper families, 25–30, 51–52, 58, 61–65,
 78, 82–85
Geneva Convention, 106–7, 196
genocide: anti-Black, 176; carceral, 168–69,
 171–73, 176–181, 190, 202, 219; colonial,
 46, 49; imperialist, 101; of plantation
 slavery, 49; racialization organizing,
 116; WW II, 100–102, 104
Gentleman's Agreement, 91
geographies: Black, 15; carceral, 10, 19, 93,
 171–72
German resident aliens, 97–99
Gibson, Otis, 82
Gilmore, Ruth Wilson, 10, 11, 49, 171, 173
Gold Mountain firms, 58
Goumindang (KMT), 245n19
Gramsci, Antonio, 6–7
Grant, Oscar, 171
Gray, Freddie, 171
Great Britain, 100–101, 105
Great Migration, 163
Great Northern Telegraph Company, 37
Guangdong, China, 34–35, 40–42, 50, 65,
 68–69
guerrilla armies, 100–101
Guillen, Antonio, 189

haiku, 143–48, 157, 184
Haley, Harold, 272n18
Hall, Stuart, 223
Hames-Garcia, Michael, 198
Han Chinese, 34
handwriting: Chinese, 82; connections,
 forming through, 147–150; training the
 interned in, 148, 148*fig*
"Handwriting on the Wall" (song), 214
"The Handwritten Letter, an Art all but
 Lost, Thrives in Prison" (Peters), 193
Han dynasty, 36
Hart, Robert, 37, 53

Hasan, Siddique Abdullah, 214
Hatashita, Isohei, 123–24, 125
Hiroshima, 102
historians, 120–21
history, literature in shaping, 61
homosociality, 22–23
Hong, Christine, 181
Hoover, J. Edgar, 99, 103
Horiuchi, Lynne, 104
Horne, Gerald, 165
Hou, Chi-Ming, 52
Huang, Yunte, 18
human right, letter correspondence as a,
 107
Hunter's Point, 164–65
hupomnemata, 16
Hurston, Zora Neale, 176

I Chan postal system, 53
Illegal Immigration Reform and Immi-
 grant Responsibility Act, 224
immigrants, Chinese. *See* migrants,
 Chinese
Immigration Act of 1924, 92
Immigration and Naturalization Service
 (INS), 59–62, 65–66, 98–99, 106
immigration law: Chinese Exclusion Act,
 25, 46, 51, 82; Illegal Immigration
 Reform and Immigrant Responsibility
 Act, 224; Immigration Act of 1924, 92;
 Japanese Exclusion Act, 96; Johnson-
 Reed Immigration Act, 29, 96; Magnuson Act, 93; Page Act, 46, 48, 79, 82;
 reforming enforcement of, 25–29, 58
immigration policy, U.S.: Asian exclusion
 era, 25–28, 46–47, 51, 75, 82, 92–93;
 literacy tests, 47; quota systems, 92, 93
imperialism, 34, 90–93, 97, 101–2
Imperialist Chinese, 244n19
impersonality, aesthetic theory of, 144
imprisoned, the: commodification of,
 175–76; disfranchisement, 178; hunger
 strikes by, 189; introduction, 4, 161–68;
 labor force, 170, 173–74; letters to,
 reasons for lack of, 6–7; political prisoners, 196, 271n6; powerlessness, 187;
 punishment of, 187–190, 222; release
 and transition of, 224–26; social con-

trol, 188; social prisoners, 196; submission of, 188; torture of, 187–190, 198, 207; women, violence against, 190–91

imprisoned, letters of the: empiricism, relationship to, 186–87; handwritten, necessity of, 193; illegal seizures of, 191; inspection and censorship, 187–190; labors of love, 208–11; as literature, 194–95, 198; mediating preservation, 197–98; mitigating contradictions of repression, 198; open letters, use of, 198–99, 200*fig*, 201–7; (para)racial form, 206–7; pathways to connections, 215–17; political, 194–98; political manifestos, 201–3; seizure of, 222; writing about writing, 186–87; writing as contemplative practice, 194, 197–98

Imprisoned Apart (Fiset), 122

Ina, Itaru, 157

Ina, Kiyoshi, 157

Ina, Satsuki, 157–58

Ina, Shizuko Mitsui, 157

Inada, Lawson Fusao, 96, 123–24, 150, 183–84

incarceration, mass: capitalism and, 172–77; emergence of, research on, 169–170; history of, 11; introduction, 167–69; racialization of, 9–12; Resistant Strains depiction of, 162; socializing a common sense of, 105; structural foundations for, 49; term usage, 237n17. *See also* internment camps

Indochina, 92

Inoue, Megumi, 122

International Settlement of Shanghai, 29, 36, 43

interned, the: adaptation and resilience, 126; alienation of, 96, 98, 103, 110–12, 131–32, 135, 151, 261n13; compensation for, 162–63; deportation of, 265n51; economic dispossession, 105; enemy classification of, 117, 135–39; generational estrangement, 114; government authorities, confrontations with, 152–57; introduction, 4, 12, 89–95; isolation, feelings of, 106; loyalty of, 112–13, 135–143, 151–55; outsiders, dependence on, 135–39; processing of, 104–5; public

support, access to, 112–13; reconciliation, 109–13; release for fitness, 115–17; resistance, constraints on expressions of, 108, 114–15; self-assertion, performances of, 107–8, 112, 151–57; social life, 115–16, 147; torture and abuse of, 102, 107; vulnerabilities of, 122–24

interned, letters of the: on adaptation and resilience, 126, 128; censorship of, 106–9, 114, 122–25, 157–58; circumventing restrictions on, 157; comfort and assurance of, 129–130; communal imagination in, 134–35; a form of reproductive labor, 126, 128; handwritten, importance of, 148–150; as life-preserving activity, 125; multilayered nature of, 133–34; otherness articulated in, 131; personal boundaries, porosity of, 135; social cohesion through, 93; on stakes and effects of separations, 122–23, 128–130; transgressing constraints, 128–29; vulnerabilities exposed in, 122–23

interned, women: gendered segregation of, 126, 128, 261n13; manifestations of duress, 118–19, 128

interned Issei: alienation of, 110; deportation of, 265n51; ethnic cleansing project, 110; generational estrangement, 114; isolation of, 106; letters importance to, 130; loyal/disloyal sorting, 135; passivity of, 125; poetry/camp haiku, 144–48

interned Nisei youth: aesthetic disciplining of, 110–13; alienation of, 111–12; Americanization of, 109–14, 149–151, 183–84; epistolary training for, 110–13; faith in America, 113–14; generational estrangement, 114; hurt of historical trauma, 113–14; innocence and resilience of, 109; music sustaining, 183; social connections, 149–151

interned, separations of the: acceptance vs. consent for, 123, 125–26, 128; attempts to end, 139–143; criminal segregation centers, 117; gendered, 117, 126, 128, 261n13; generational, 117; Loyalty Questionnaire forcing, 117; stakes and effects of, 122–23, 128–130

Masuda, Susie, 140–42
Masuda, Taro George, 135–37, 138*fig*, 139, 154–55, 156*fig*
Mateen, Namir Abdul, 214
Matsushita, Hanaye, 118, 121–23, 125–133, 133*fig*, 145, 146*fig*
Matsushita, Iwao, 118, 121–22, 125–133, 133*fig*, 145, 146*fig*
Maurer, Katherine, 82
Maximum Security Democracy (Resistant Strains Collective), 161
McBride, Renisha, 171
McClain, James, 272n18
McCray, Ida P., 192
McKeon, Adam, 40, 57
McKeown, Adam, 10
McKinley, William, 100–101
Meiji period, 108
memory, 60–61
merchant-capitalist class, 55, 57–58
Mexican Americans, 45, 162
migrants, Chinese: becoming a new self, 59; disfranchisement, 47; imagined gene-alogies, 25–30, 51–52, 61–65, 78, 82–85; legal categories of, 51; life of paper for, 30–31; male, privileging of, 65, 73; migration services, payment for, 54–58; subordinating through exclusion, 46–47; techniques of control, 47; transportation of, 48; World War II and social positioning of, 92–93. *See also* detained, the; women, migrant Chinese
migrants, Japanese. *See* Issei
migration: Western, policing of, 91; west-ward, U.S., 44, 163–64
migration, Asian: factors stimulating, 42; from Japan, 91–93; international polic-ing of, 10
Military Stockade (WRA), 117
minchu, 53–55, 53*fig*
Ming dynasty, 36
Minidoka, ID, 118, 148
mitsui, james masao, 120
Moab, UT, 115
modernity: African American, 179–180; engineering imperialist space, 90; as a global project of scientific management and apartheid, 90; Others of, 17; poesis

in, 17–18; trans-Pacific perspective, 33–38
Montana widow, 128, 129
Moore, Richard O., 164
Morales, Aurora Levins, 21
Morrison, Toni, 85
Moten, Fred, 19
Moynihan, Daniel, 166–67
Muntaqim, Jalil, 219, 275n43
Muraoka, Raymond, 149–150
Murdock, Roger, 166

Nagar, Richa, 214
Nagasaki, 102
Nakano, Jiro, 147
Nakano, Kay, 147
National Coalition for Redress/Repara-tions (NCRR), 162–63
National Council for Japanese American Redress (NCJAR), 162
nationalism, 92
nativism, U.S., 167, 177
Naturalization Act of 1790, 93
"The Negro Family: A Case for National Action" (Moynihan), 166–67
Nevarez, Miguel, 186
New Culture Movement, 41
Ngo, Viet Mike, 188–89, 221–25, 227
Nikkei, term usage, 253n1. *See also* Japanese Americans
Nikkei redress movement, 162–63
Nisei youth, interned: aesthetic disciplin-ing of, 110–13; alienation, 111–12; Amer-icanization of, 109–14, 149–151, 183–84; epistolary training for, 110–13; faith in America, 113–14; generational estrange-ment, 114; hurt of historical trauma, 113–14; innocence and resilience of, 109; music sustaining, 183; social connec-tions, 149–151
Noble, Donald, 201
no-no boys, 117, 158
novel, 19, 61, 120

Obama (Barack) administration, 12, 173
Oda, Nancy, 261n9
Odum, Howard, 45
Office of Censorship (OOC), 106–7

What Was African American Literature?
(Warren), 177
white, legal recognition as, 45
whiteness: alienation of Chinese women
from, 81; Californian, 43; epistemology
of, 47; as form and practice of citizenship, 103; material power of, 182; Negro,
103
white supremacy, 11–12, 44–45, 79, 92, 108,
180–82, 195
"The Widely Lesser-Known Truth"
(Inada), 96
Williamson, James, 189
Winther, Oscar O., 42
women: African American, 199; racial-
sexual violence of the imprisoned,
190–91
women, migrant Chinese: creating paper
families, 78, 82–85; criminalization of,
48, 75, 77, 79; deportation of, 48; exclusion of, 46; literacy training, 82–85;
prostitution for debt payment, 77–78,
80; racial disciplining, 82; social activism surrounding, 78–79, 79*fig*, 81–82;
working-class, dangers faced by, 77–78,
80*fig*. *See also* migrants, Chinese

Wong, Nellie, 92–93
Woods, Clyde, 15, 44, 179, 183, 195
working-classes: Chinese, exclusion of, 46,
51; migrant Chinese women, 46, 77–78,
80*fig;* race-class structures, formation
of, 45–46
Work Progress Administration, 104
World War I, 92, 105
World War II, 92–93, 99, 102, 105–8
Writing on the Wall (Abu-Jamal), 214
Wynter, Sylvia, 17, 18

X, Herbert Blyden, 201

Yandell, Ronnie, 189
Yang, Alice, 162
Yangtze region, 69
Yi Zhan, 36
Youyi (postal system), 36
Yu (postal system), 36
Yuan Shikai, 245n19
Yung, Judy, 75

Zhao dynasty, 36
Zheng, Eddy, 222–23, 224
Zizhihui, 75